URBAN LAND ECONOMICS

Sixth Edition

Jack Harvey
B.Sc. (Econ.), Dip. Ed. (Oxford)
and
Ernie Jowsey
B.A. (Econ) M.A. PGCE

First edition (published as *The Economics of Real Property*) 1981
Reprinted 1985, 1986
Second edition (published as *Urban Land Economics*) 1987
Reprinted 1988, 1989, 1990
Third edition 1992
Reprinted 1993, 1994
Fourth edition 1996
Reprinted 1997, 1998
Fifth edition 2000
Reprinted 2001
Sixth edition 2004

Published by
PALGRAVE MACMILLAN
Houndmills, Basingstoke, Hampshire RG21 6XS and
175 Fifth Avenue, New York, N.Y. 10010
Companies and representative throughout the world

PALGRAVE MACMILLAN is the global academic imprint of
the Palgrave Macmillan division of St. Martin's Press, LLC and of
Palgrave Macmillan Ltd. Macmillan® is a registered trademark in
the United States, United Kingdom and other countries. Palgrave is a
registered trademark in the European Union and other countries.

ISBN 1–4039–00019

This book is printed on paper suitable for recycling and made from fully
managed and sustained forest sources.

A catalogue record for this book is available from the British Library.

10   9   8   7   6   5   4   3   2   1
13 12 11 10 09 08 07 06 05 04

Printed and bound in China

I am the basis of all wealth, the heritage of the wise, the thrifty and prudent.

I am the poor man's joy and comfort, the rich man's prize, the right hand of capital, the silent partner of many thousands of successful men.

I am the solace of the widow, the comfort of old age, the cornerstone of security against misfortune and want. I am handed down to children, through generations, as a thing of greatest worth.

I am the choicest fruit of toil. Credit respects me. Yet I am humble. I stand before every man, bidding him know me for what I am and possess me.

I grow and increase in value through countless days. Though I seem dormant, my worth increases, never failing, never ceasing, time is my aid and population heaps up my gain. Fire and the elements I defy, for they cannot destroy me.

My possessors learn to believe in me; invariably they become envied. While all things wither and decay, I survive. The centuries find me younger, increasing with strength.

The thriftless speak ill of me. The charlatans of finance attack me. I am trustworthy. I am sound. Unfailingly I triumph and detractors are disproved.

Minerals and oils come from me. I am producer of food, the basis for ships and factories, the foundation of banks.

Yet I am so common that thousands, unthinking and unknowingly, pass by me.

I am land.

Lou Scott, *What is Real Estate?*

Contents

PART I

WELFARE AND ECONOMIC EFFICIENCY

CHAPTER 1

Economic Efficiency through the Price System

After studying this chapter you will be able to:

- **Explain the concept of Pareto optimality**
- **Define and illustrate economic efficiency**
- **Show how the price system can bring about economic efficiency**

1.1 Welfare and economic efficiency

Maximising welfare

We can start with the proposition that society's aim is to maximise its welfare. Two factors which will influence welfare are: (a) the way society uses its limited resources; and (b) the distribution of income between members of society.

The first is the subject-matter of positive economics; it is possible to analyse it scientifically. Economic efficiency is achieved when society has secured the best allocation of its limited resources, in the sense that the maximum possible satisfaction is obtained.

The second, the distribution of income, does not lend itself to scientific analysis. The reason is that satisfaction, like love and pain, is personal to the individual and cannot be measured on any objective scale. Taking a small amount of income from the rich man and giving it to a poor man may increase welfare, since the former's loss may be little compared with the

3

latter's gain. But we can never be sure: since we cannot measure welfare cardinally, interpersonal comparisons are impossible. Thus, while distributional efficiency is necessary to maximise welfare, it cannot be dealt with scientifically, and decisions on income redistribution ultimately rest with the politician.

This book is concerned with economic efficiency, with particular reference to the allocation of land resources. This does not mean that we shall ignore the redistribution of income. Politicians carry out such redistribution in the field of real property, both directly through taxation, for example, income tax and inheritance tax, and indirectly by intervening in the free operation of the price system, for example, by rent control and subsidies to social housing. What the economist has to point out is how such redistributive measures may impinge on the efficient allocation of resources. The politician can then weigh the balance of advantage.

Pareto optimality

In discussing economic efficiency, therefore, the economist side-steps the distributional problem which may result from a reallocation of resources (see pp. 147–8). He does this by adopting the narrow Pareto-optimality condition: *welfare is maximised when no one can be made better off without somebody else being made worse off.* Thus any improvement in economic efficiency which involves nobody losing will represent an increase in welfare.

Efficiency in the use of resources is often called Pareto optimality or Pareto efficiency in honour of the Italian economist Vilfredo Pareto (1848–1923) who first introduced this concept.

For instance, in Figure 1.1 we start from the initial income position *X*, with *A*'s income equal to *OA* and *B*'s equal to *OB*. A movement to *Y* would represent an increase in welfare for both *A* and *B*; a movement to *Z* would increase *B*'s welfare without reducing *A*'s. Both *Y* and *Z* therefore represent

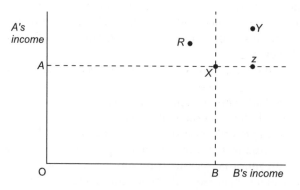

Figure 1.1 Pareto and non-Pareto improvements

Pareto improvements. It is impossible, however, to say whether position *R* represents an overall gain or loss, since *A*'s income has increased but *B*'s has fallen.

1.2 Conditions necessary for Pareto optimality

The weakness of the strict Pareto-optimality condition is that its application is restricted to only those cases where there are gainers but no losers resulting from the reallocation of resources. Even so, it does enable us to specify three conditions which must be fulfilled simultaneously for the efficient allocation of resources. First, no improvement can be achieved by an exchange of goods between persons, that is, there is *exchange efficiency*. Second, no increase in output can be obtained by producers substituting one factor for another, that is, there is *factor-combination efficiency*. Third, from the maximum overall output of goods which can be obtained from society's limited resources, that assortment is produced which gives society the greatest possible satisfaction, that is, there is *economic efficiency*. We shall examine each in turn.

We simplify this analysis by assuming: (a) resources consist of a limited quantity of land and capital; (b) two goods are produced, food and manufactured goods.

(1) Exchange efficiency

Figures 1.2(a) and 1.2(b) represent the 'indifference maps' of consumers *A* and *B* respectively. Each indifference curve shows combinations of food and manufactured goods which yield equivalent satisfaction, and the further the indifference curve is from the origin, the greater the satisfaction obtained, as shown by the unspecified units, 10, 15, and so on. Note that the indifference curve is convex to the origin. This denotes a diminishing marginal rate of substitution, an increasing amount of one good having to be given up in order to obtain an additional unit of another. It assumes that there is no 'conspicuous consumption' when people buy goods simply to impress others.

We can depict the preferences of *A* and *B* in an 'Edgeworth box' (see Figure 1.3). *B*'s indifference map is rotated 180°, so that the origin is O_B. The length of the vertical side of the box denotes the maximum food available to be exchanged, and the horizontal side the maximum amount of manufactured goods.

Suppose *A* and *B* commence with an initial distribution at *K*, where *A* has $O_A f$ food and $O_A m$ manufactured goods, and *B* has $O_B f$ food and $O_B m$ manufactured goods. *K* is not a Pareto-optimal situation. *A* could move

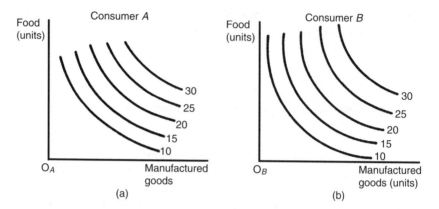

Figure 1.2 Indifference maps of consumers A *and* B

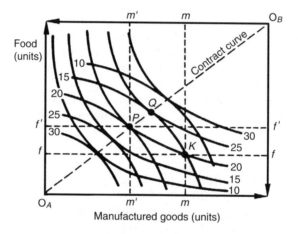

Figure 1.3 Efficiency in exchange

along his indifference curve substituting food for manufactured goods until he reached the point *P*, where, being on the same indifference curve 20, he would feel no worse off. On the other hand, this exchange increases *B*'s satisfaction, putting him on a higher indifference curve 20 (from 15) where he has O_Bf' food and O_Bm' manufactured goods.

Had *A* been the more skilful bargainer, position *Q* could have been reached, and here *A* would have been on curve 25 without *B* being worse off. In practice, they are likely to end up somewhere between *P* and *Q*. What is important to note, however, is that a Pareto-optimal position will be achieved only when the marginal rate of substitution between any two goods is the same for each consumer, as at *P* and *Q* where their indifference curves are tangential. Indeed, it is possible to find such a point for all combinations of food and manufactured goods. A line joining these points is known as a 'contract curve', and Pareto optimality will only hold provided that the division of available goods between consumers is on this curve.

(2) Factor-combination efficiency

We can use the same technique to specify an efficiency condition for combining factors of production. In Figures 1.4(a) and 1.4(b) we have isoquants showing how two factors, land and capital, can be combined to produce given quantities of food and manufactured goods respectively. Note that the isoquants are convex to the origin. This denotes a diminishing marginal rate of *technical* substitution between factors, an increasing amount of one factor being needed to compensate for the loss of a unit of the other factor if the same quantity of output is to be produced.

Again, these isoquant maps can be combined in an Edgeworth box by rotating the manufactured goods origin through 180° (see Figure 1.5). The length of the vertical side represents the amount of capital available, and the horizontal side the maximum amount of land.

Assume initially that production is at N, with O_Fl land and O_Fk capital used to produce 25 units of food, and O_Ml' land and O_Mk' capital used to produce 20 units of manufactured goods. N is not an efficient situation. By transferring land from food to manufactured-goods production and capital from manufactured-goods to food production, we can move to C (with a net gain of 15 units of manufactured goods), or to D (with a net gain of 10 units of food), or to an in-between position (showing some net gain of both manufactured goods and food).

Thus a Pareto-optimal position will be achieved only when the marginal rate of technical substitution between factors is the same in each use and for

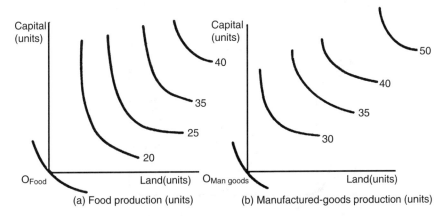

(a) Food production (units)   (b) Manufactured-goods production (units)

Figure 1.4 Combinations of land and capital to produce food and manufactured goods

all producers. As before, we can obtain a contract curve (the dashed line *AE* in Figure 1.5) joining all points for all combinations of land and capital where this condition holds. Pareto optimality requires that, according to the assortment of goods required, factors must be combined on the appropriate point on the contract curve, otherwise society can be better off by a reshuffling of resources.

(3) Economic efficiency

From Figure 1.5 we can derive the various combinations of food and manufactured goods which it is possible to obtain from the limited supply of land and capital. These outputs are achieved only if land and capital are combined efficiently: that is, each combination of land and capital must be found on the contract curve.

For the various points *A* to *E* on the contract curve, we obtain the following outputs:

	Food (units)	Manufactured goods (units)
A	0	50
B	20	40
C	25	35
D	35	20
E	40	0

Figure 1.6 graphs these outputs, smoothing them in the curve *AE*. This represents a production-possibility or transformation curve for this society. Any point within the production-possibility curve, for example *V*, is not a Pareto optimum because it is *technically* inefficient, as more of both goods can be obtained with the limited land and capital resources.

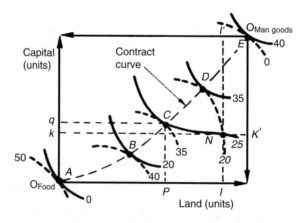

Figure 1.5 Efficiency in factor combination

But while *technical efficiency* is a necessary condition for Pareto optimality, it is not sufficient. *Economic efficiency* requires that the actual product-mix is the one which gives society maximum satisfaction.

We therefore have to relate the production-possibility curve to society's preferences.

Ignoring the conceptual difficulties involved, let I^1 and I^2 represent two indifference curves of society. While a product-mix D is on the production-possibility curve, it does not maximise society's welfare, since by producing more food and less manufactured goods a higher indifference curve I^2 can be attained at C, where the indifference curve and production-possibility curve just touch. We therefore have a third condition of Pareto optimality: consumers' marginal rate of substitution between products shown by the indifference curve must equal the marginal rate of transformation between products shown by the production-possibility curve.

1.3 Achieving the conditions of economic efficiency

Alternative methods

In our model, society maximises welfare when 25 units of food and 35 units of manufactured goods are produced. Thus in Figure 1.5 the optimum

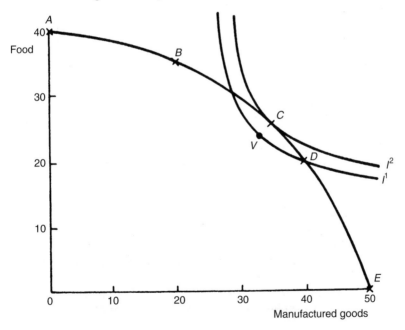

Figure 1.6　The production-possibility curve and society's preference for food and manufactured goods

allocation of resources is achieved when O_{Fp} land and O_{Fq} capital are used to grow food, and the remainder produce manufactured goods.

Broadly speaking, there are two methods by which the above resource allocation can be carried out: government fiat and the price system. While the former can overcome certain defects in the price system, for example the external effects (social benefits and social costs of private decisions could be 'internalised' (see pp. 186, 302)), it faces formidable difficulties. Not only does it have to assess people's preferences, but it has the gigantic administrative task of allocating resources in the optimum proportions to produce the goods and services preferred.

In contrast, the price system assumes that the individual is the sole judge of his welfare and that, both as a consumer and as a producer, he acts through markets to maximise that welfare. Economic efficiency is achieved through Adam Smith's 'invisible hand'. As we shall see, however, this will only apply when many rigorous conditions prevail. Nevertheless, since, in Britain's mixed economy, most decisions are taken through the price system, we shall concentrate on this.

Pareto optimality through the price system

Exchange efficiency is achieved by the consumer relating his preferences to market prices in order to maximise satisfaction from his limited resources.

In a perfect market a single price is established at which food and manufactured goods can be exchanged. In Figure 1.7 the distance of the line *FM* from the origin indicates the limit of consumer *A*'s resources, his budget line. The slope of this budget line reflects the relative prices of food and manufactured goods. Consumer *A* could spend all of his money on food and reach point *OF*, or all of his money on manufactured goods and reach point *OM*; or buy some combination of both goods on the budget line *FM*. Consumer *A* will maximise his welfare when the budget price line touches the highest possible indifference curve. Here the marginal rate of substitution of food for manufactured goods is equal to their relative prices.

But since there is a single market price at which food exchanges for manufactured goods, and consumer *B* adopts the same course, it follows that the marginal rate of substitution of food for manufactured goods is the same for each consumer. Thus the condition for exchange efficiency is satisfied.

Put in Marshallian terms, (after Alfred Marshall, 1842–1924) the equilibrium condition in spending on goods occurs when, for all consumers:

$$\frac{\text{Marginal utility of food}}{\text{Marginal utility of manufactured goods}} = \frac{\text{Price of food}}{\text{Price of manufactured goods}} \quad (1.1)$$

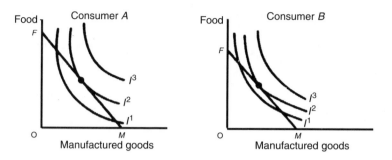

Figure 1.7 Consumer equilibrium

A similar argument can be applied to factor combinations – *technical efficiency*. Individual producers combine land and capital to obtain maximum output from a limited budget. Demand and supply in the factor market will establish a price at which land and capital are exchanged, the demand for each factor being dependent upon the price of the finished product. The food producer therefore employs those quantities of land and capital where the marginal rate of technical substitution equals their relative price. But since there is only one price at which land exchanges for capital, and since the manufactured-goods producer adopts the same profit-maximising course, it follows that the marginal rate of technical substitution of land for capital is the same in the production of both food and manufactured goods. Thus the condition for factor-combination efficiency is achieved.

Put in Marshallian terms, the equilibrium condition in combining factors occurs when, in all uses and for all producers:

$$\frac{\text{Marginal physical product of land}}{\substack{\text{Marginal physical product of} \\ \text{manufactured goods}}} = \frac{\text{Price of land}}{\substack{\text{Price of manufactured} \\ \text{goods}}} \qquad (1.2)$$

How *economic efficiency* is achieved through the price system is more easily explained by translating the production-possibility curve into Marshallian terms.

As we have seen, there is a single price in the market at which food is exchanged against manufactured goods. The production-possibility curve shows, for any combination, the rate at which food can be transformed into manufactured goods. This transformation rate can be referred to as the *opportunity cost*, which, in perfect competition, is reflected in marginal costs (given no external costs). Thus the rate of transformation at any point on the production-possibility curve equals:

$$\frac{\text{Marginal cost of food}}{\text{Marginal cost of manufactured goods}} \qquad (1.3)$$

However, in perfect competition, a farmer growing food will produce that output where the price of food (P_f) equals the marginal cost of a unit of food (MC_f). Similarly, the output of manufactured goods will be where the price of manufactured goods (P_m) equals the marginal cost of a unit of manufactured goods (MC_f).

Since we are dealing with equalities, we can divide the first equation by the second, giving:

$$\frac{P_f}{P_m} = \frac{MC_f}{MC_m} \tag{1.4}$$

That is, the relative price of food and manufactured goods is equal to the marginal rate of transformation between food and manufactured goods. But equilibrium for both consumers A and B is where the relative price of food and manufactured goods is equal to the marginal rate of substitution of manufactured goods for food. Thus the condition for economic efficiency is fulfilled.

In the simple Marshallian formulation, by combining (1.1) and (1.4), we have:

$$\frac{MU_f}{MU_m} = \frac{P_f}{P_m} = \frac{MC_f}{MC_m} \tag{1.5}$$

1.4 Conditions necessary for economic efficiency through the price system

The careful reader will have noticed that before commencing the above outline of the working of the price system no assumptions were made. This was done deliberately in order not to interrupt the flow of the main argument. Our analysis, however, implicitly assumed that certain conditions held, particularly all the strict requirements of perfect competition, the absence of 'spillover' benefits and costs (often referred to as 'externalities'), and the ability of the market mechanism to supply all goods and services provided society is able and willing to pay the necessary costs. We shall examine each in turn.

Perfect competition

For market prices to reflect both consumers' satisfaction and producers' costs, certain conditions must exist:

(1) A PERFECT MARKET

There must be a perfect market, so that any price differences are quickly eliminated. Consumers and producers must seek to maximise utility and profits respectively and, in doing so, be unhampered by legal and other constraints.

(2) PERFECT KNOWLEDGE

There must be perfect knowledge, in that consumers are aware of any price differences which temporarily exist in the market, and entrepreneurs of any super-normal profits being made by other firms, the costs of producing different outputs, production costs using different techniques, and so on. Moreover, there should be no costs of obtaining knowledge, no ostentatious buying and no 'brain-washing' advertising. Even such 'static' assumptions as these are impossible in real life. But the difficulties are magnified when allowance is made for dynamic conditions – something outside the simple price-mechanism model. Dynamic conditions, for instance, produce uncertainty as regards the size of future demand, the nature of competitors' plans and changes in government policy.

Where market facts are deficient, personal assessments have to be made. Since these are likely to be subject to degrees of inaccuracy, Adam Smith's 'invisible hand' which automatically brings about the desired adjustments in the economy only acts in practice through a process of trial and error.

Only if conditions (1) and (2) are fulfilled, will there be common prices throughout the market for each product or factor of production.

(3) $P = MR = MC$

Producers maximise profits by producing that output where marginal revenue equals marginal cost ($MR = MC$). But this will only represent economic efficiency if marginal revenue equals price ($MR = P$), since production must proceed to the point where the satisfaction which the consumer derives from an additional unit of the good equals the cost to society of producing that unit, that is $P = MC$.

However, price will only equal marginal revenue under conditions of perfect competition (see Figure 1.8(a)). Here the producer is a 'price-taker', accepting the market price as given. For this situation to occur there must be many producers each supplying so small a quantity to the market that no single producer can influence the market price. Furthermore, there must be freedom of entry into the industry. Similar conditions must apply in selling factors of production.

In contrast, where there is imperfect competition, marginal revenue is less than price. Suppose that a monopoly exists with cost and revenue conditions, as indicated in Figure 1.8(b). Basic theory of the firm suggests that it would produce an amount OM_1, at a price OP_1, whereas in a competitive market (in long-run equilibrium) OM would have been produced at a price of OP. The latter equates marginal cost with price which conforms

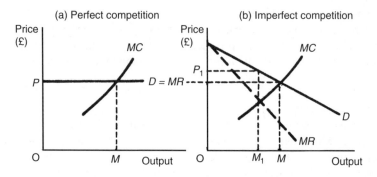

Figure 1.8 Equilibrium output under perfect competition and imperfect competition

to the wishes of consumers as expressed through the price mechanism. Under monopoly too little is produced at too high a price. The demand for factors of production in this particular activity is lower than it would be in the absence of monopoly, and so there is a distortion of factor prices – which has its repercussions on more competitive sectors of the economy. Thus monopolistic forms of organisation are suspect, though a final decision can only be made after possible advantages, for example, economies of scale, are taken into account.

(4) INCREASING COSTS
For perfect competition to exist, the MC curve must be rising to cut the horizontal demand curve from below (see Figure 1.8(a)). However, certain industries, chiefly those that have to produce on a large scale, have decreasing costs (a falling MC curve) at the relevant part of the demand curve. This means that, to obtain an equilibrium output, the MR curve would have to be downward-sloping in order to cut the MC curve (Figure 1.9). Thus at the equilibrium output (OM), price (OP) is greater than marginal cost (OC) and so the conditions of economic efficiency are not fulfilled.

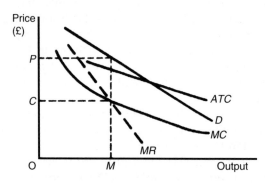

Figure 1.9 Equilibrium output under conditions of decreasing cost

(5) Perfect mobility of factors of production

The price system operates imperfectly if factors of production do not move in response to changes in relative prices. Transport costs and housing costs, for example, restrict mobility. Above all, any movement takes time, and this is particularly so with land resources, since buildings have a long life.

Immobility may also give rise to imperfect competition and super-normal profits, for example, allowing the owner of a site vital for a proposed development to exercise monopoly powers.

Externalities: spillover benefits and costs

In the market, private consumers and producers seek to maximise their own benefits and profits. However, this assumes that their decisions impose no indirect benefits or costs on others. In practice, this is often not so, especially in the use of land resources. For example, flowers in people's gardens give pleasure to passers-by or the design of a new house may destroy the architectural harmony of a whole street. In the decision-making process allowances should be made for such spillover benefits and costs.

Community goods and services

The pure price system implicitly assumes that all economic goods are capable of being priced in the market, but this is possible only if the enjoyment of a good or service can be confined to those people willing to pay for it. With some goods and services, such as defence, street-lighting, common land and National Trust open spaces, it is impossible or impractical to exclude non-payers, since anybody can be a 'free-rider'. Goods from which the community benefits, therefore, have to be provided collectively and financed, not by charging individuals as they use them, but by subscription (for example, the Royal Society for the Protection of Birds), by advertising and sponsorship (for example, commercial television) or, more usually, by taxation (for example, defence, street-lighting, common land). Indeed, as we shall see in Chapter 21, a Pareto improvement may be effected by providing collectively, rather than privately, goods where exclusion *is* possible.

Other weaknesses of the price system

It is necessary to mention briefly some other weaknesses of the price system.

First, the above is essentially a purely static theory. Economic decisions also span time, so that a choice has to be made between present and future benefits. For example, the decision to designate land as a National Park must involve consideration not only of the present community's preference, but also of the probable preferences of future generations. This involves accuracy in estimating such future benefits and costs, and is thus likely to conflict with our previous condition of perfect knowledge. Consideration of allocating resources over time, however, will be postponed to Chapter 11.

Second, the price system cannot guarantee full employment, while decisions are influenced by inflation expectations. With the first, government action is demanded politically; with the second, miscalculation can distort resource allocation.

Third, the price system only operates within the existing distribution of income. There are as many Pareto-optimal situations as there are possible distributions of income. But, as we have seen, redistribution of income is ultimately a political decision.

Using the price system

The above qualifications imply that the market economy is unlikely to be fully efficient in allocating resources. On the other hand, allocation by government fiat in a 'command economy' can present even greater problems. At least the market system does start with the advantage that economic decisions are based on prices which reflect, albeit somewhat imperfectly, consumers' preferences and relative costs.

This points to the compromise of a 'mixed economy'. This uses the price system as the basis for allocating resources, but, recognising its defects, relies on the government to provide, as far as possible, the conditions necessary for its efficient functioning.

Such is the approach of this book. Allocation of land resources is still mainly through the price mechanism of a market economy. We examine this system and analyse its efficiency in the light of economic principles and the institutional background. We then examine the rationale of government interference in the market, assessing the extent to which improvements are possible.

Summary

Society's welfare is influenced by economic efficiency and the distribution of income between members of the society. Economic efficiency is achieved when society has secured the best allocation of its limited resources. And economists adopt the very limited welfare criteria of Pareto-optimality: welfare is maximised when no one can be made better off without somebody else being made worse off.

Pareto-optimality requires

- exchange efficiency
- factor-combination or technical efficiency
- economic efficiency

The price system can achieve these types of efficiency if these conditions are met:

1. A perfect market
2. Perfect knowledge
3. Price = Marginal Revenue = Marginal Cost
4. Increasing costs
5. Perfect mobility of factors of production

So the free market and the price system can achieve economic efficiency if these conditions are met. There may be problems, however, with externalities, community goods and services, allocation of resources over time and the distribution of income. As a result, all economies are mixed economies, with allocation of most resources by the price mechanism, but with government intervention to try to correct the imperfections. Land and property resources are also allocated in this way.

Review questions

1. Illustrate with a diagram and with examples a Pareto improvement and a non-Pareto improvement.
2. Use a production possibility curve to illustrate the concept of economic efficiency.
3. What are the conditions necessary to achieve economic efficiency through the price system?
4. What reasons are there for economic efficiency not to be achieved in the world of property?
5. What are externalities? Give examples from the property sector.

Recommended Reading

J. Harvey, *Modern Economics*, 7th edn (London: Macmillan, 1998) chs 1, 5, 10 and 11.

R. G. Lipsey and K. A. Chrystal, *Principles of Economics*, 9th edn (Oxford: Oxford University Press, 1999) chs 3,7.

M. Parkin, M. Powell and K. Matthews *Economics*, 5th edn (Harlow: Addison Wesley Longman, 2003).

B. Walker (1981), *Welfare Economics and Urban Problems* (London: Hutchinson, 1981) chs 1–4.

PART II
REAL PROPERTY

CHAPTER 2

Characteristics of the Real Property Market

After studying this chapter you will be able to:

- **Explain how markets work**
- **Explain and give examples of property rights or interests**
- **Assess the efficiency of the real property market**

2.1 Is there a real property market?

What is a market?

Modern economies are often referred to as 'exchange economies'. Instead of people producing directly for their own wants, they specialise in production in order to increase total output. Thus both factors of production and final products are exchanged. Exchanges take place because both buyers and sellers benefit from them (see Figure 1.3).

To effect exchanges, buyers and sellers must be put in touch with one another. Any arrangement for doing this can be termed 'the market'. It can be formal, as with the Stock Exchange and the New Covent Garden Market, or informal, as with worldwide dealings in goods through the Internet or in foreign currencies through computer links.

In the market economy, exchanges take place on the basis of prices determined in the market by the interaction of demand and supply. Because the formation of price is central to the functions of the market, we can define a market as *any arrangement by which buyers and sellers are brought together to fix a price at which goods can be exchanged.*

Allocating land resources and real property through the price mechanism therefore poses three questions.

(1) In what sense is there a 'real property market'?
(2) How efficient is the market in indicating changes in demand and supply for the same kind of property by means of changes in a common price?
(3) How does the market function to bring demand and supply into equilibrium (a) in the short run; and (b) in the long run?

The first two questions will be answered in this chapter, the third in Chapter 3.

The meaning of 'the real property market'

'Real property' refers to a particular type of good – land, or resources embodied in land. The point is that neither is physically movable. This characteristic distinguishes it from labour and capital and from other goods.

Although land resources are not movable, property can be owned by some person or institution. Moreover, exchanges take place. Thus the real property market is simply the arrangement by which buyers and sellers of virgin land, agricultural estates, industrial buildings, offices, shops and houses are brought together to determine a price at which the particular property can be exchanged. Sometimes the market is formal (for example, auctions advertised nationally), sometimes informal (for example, introductions by estate agents, deals between principals). Indeed, it is not possible to distinguish the means by which people are informed from 'the market'. Much real property is advertised in journals (such as the *Estates Gazette*) and newspapers, all of which can therefore be said to be part of the market. In other words, 'the real property market' is an abstract term aggregating all transactions in real property throughout the country. Even so, it is possible to distinguish sub-markets for different types of property, for example, prime shop properties and for different geographical areas, such as City of London office blocks, houses in a given locality. Each fulfils, albeit perhaps imperfectly, the basic functions of a market.

Real property rights

At this point it is essential to emphasise that what the real property market actually deals in is 'property rights', often referred to as 'interests'. In this, however, it is no different from any other market. I may, for instance, go to Burton and purchase a suit. In this case the suit is handed over to me and I am given the exclusive right to wear it as long as I wish, and even to part with that right by selling it to somebody else. Alternatively, I could hire a suit from Moss Bros. Here my right to wear the suit would be restricted to a specified period and subject to conditions regarding damage, and so on. In the first case there is little formal definition of my right: the suit is simply handed over to me upon payment for it. On the other hand, when I hire a suit my restricted rights are more likely to be clearly defined in a written agreement which, by implication, also excludes Moss Bros from letting anybody else wear the suit during the specified period.

Similarly with real property – here it is not possible to hand over land and buildings in the same way as would be the case with movable goods. It is much more obvious, therefore, that it is 'rights' which are dealt in, especially as, accompanying the transaction, there is a written statement defining the exact rights which are being transferred. In short, the real property market deals in the rights relating to real property rather than in the land and buildings themselves.

With real property, too, the separation of rights is more usual than with personal property. The largest collection of rights which a person can hold in real property is 'fee simple absolute': that is, the unencumbered freehold. But all the rights inherent in the ownership of 'fee simple absolute' can be separated and transferred individually to other people. Thus a lease may be granted to a person to erect a building on a plot of land and to enjoy the rights to this building and land for a ninety-nine-year period on payment of a specified yearly sum to the lessor. Provided the terms of the lease are fulfilled, the lessor's rights are, for ninety-nine years, now restricted to the receipt of a freehold ground rent. The freehold has thus been divided into two interests: the leasehold and the freehold ground rent. In any given land resource different people may have many different rights – for example, a freehold ground rent, a head-lease, a sub-lease, a mortgage, a rent charge, and so on.

It is worth noting that the exact rights transferred can be finely adjusted according to the individual preferences of the seller or buyer, for example, by a restrictive covenant. Such a fine differentiation to meet the individual preferences of sellers and buyers is achieved automatically through the free-market mechanism and is reflected in prices.

Four aspects of real property rights need emphasis. First, within his rights the 'fee simple absolute' owner can possess, use, abuse and even destroy his real property. He can sell rights in such a way as to restrict their future use (for example, by covenant), or he can bequeath them to distant heirs. Even so, his rights are limited: (i) he can only use his property subject to other people's property rights (for example, easements may exist giving other persons 'ancient lights', or the right to take drains or pipe water across his freehold interest); (ii) he is subject to the legal restraints imposed by planning Acts, building regulations and similar legislation.

Second, an interest comes into existence simply because a bundle of certain rights is wanted. But no rights would be wanted unless their owner could exclude others from them. What, for example, would you give for fishing rights in a country where poaching was no offence and suffered no penalty? Thus the concept of *rights* is essentially a legal one: it presupposes that there is a sovereign power which will, if necessary, protect the rights vested in the owner. Moreover, being a legal concept, a right must be clearly defined. This implies limitations to the right. Thus a right is merely exclusive, not absolute or unlimited. In fact, different rights are really only differences in 'exclusiveness'.

Third, where rights are well defined and the costs of negotiating and enforcing contracts are small compared with the benefits of the transaction, an exchange system based on prices works smoothly. Economic theory tends to assume these conditions. At times, however, the failure to define rights unambiguously may lead to economic inefficiency. Thus it is generally felt that persons with low income should enjoy some form of housing subsidy. In practice, however, this right has not been made explicit. It has not been attached, as intended, to the persons, but to the occupation of a particular property, such as a rent-controlled flat (where the landlord virtually subsidises the tenant) or a council house. This right is not transferable to another property and, as a result, people occupying such accommodation are restricted in their mobility as compared with owner-occupiers.

Fourth, because real property is durable, the rights existing in real property have a long time-scale. Moreover, no problem of storing such rights exists, though there may be management costs. Real property rights, like stocks and shares, are therefore demanded as investment assets (see Chapter 5). Indeed, the real property market can now be regarded as a part of the wider investment asset market, its significance in this respect having increased in recent years.

2.2 The efficiency of the real property market

The nature of the real property market

Since a defective market mechanism will impair the efficiency with which resources are allocated through the price system, we have to ask: How efficient is the real property market in registering changes in demand and supply through their effect on price?

The efficiency of a market depends on both technical and economic characteristics.

(1) TECHNICAL CHARACTERISTICS
Physical conditions should ensure that price differences for the same commodity within the market are eliminated easily and quickly. This

comes about by buyers moving to the cheaper parts and sellers moving to the dearer. This requires that both buyers and sellers must have up-to-date knowledge of price differences and base their actions solely on price. Moreover, dealing costs should be small relative to the value of the transaction.

With the real property market, certain factors not only make it difficult to obtain up-to-date knowledge but lead to dealing costs being relatively high. As regards the first, knowledge tends to be obtained infrequently and is limited geographically. Most occupiers (as distinct from investors) move in response to changes in family circumstances, income or business conditions. Only rarely do they move for the sole purpose of making a gain from a price or rent difference. Moreover, with occupational interests, buyers tend to have a demand which is essentially local, either because their knowledge of the prospects of their business is confined to a particular district or because, as workers, they have to be within easy travelling distance of their place of work. On the other hand, for a holiday or retirement residence people in Britain may compare prices in Cornwall, Spain or the Bahamas. Here the cost and time involved in travelling to work no longer count.

Nor can paying for advice completely overcome this difficulty of lack of knowledge. Because of differences of location, size, construction and age, most units of real property have special characteristics, making 'grading', the most efficient form of description, difficult. Of course, some interests, such as freehold ground rents, can be described accurately. Others, such as houses, shops, offices or industrial premises, may have labels attached according to the physical characteristics of the structure (for example, high-rise or low-rise, in good repair or in need of modernisation, a large or small number of units) or by location (such as city centre or suburban, London or provincial). Indeed, it is possible to say fairly accurately what price a special location, such as Oxford Street, will fetch. Yet even within these 'grades' individual properties have their own characteristics. Their great heterogeneity means that a professional valuer cannot *fully* assess their respective merits. To some degree, therefore, his valuation is subjective. Thus, unlike transport costs, costs of obtaining knowledge are not absolutely certain, and a purchaser would normally go to the trouble of making a personal inspection and discussing with his adviser the weight to be given to special characteristics.

This does not, however, diminish the role played by valuers and agents in the property market. Indeed, where knowledge is difficult to obtain, their specialised functions assume an even greater importance for the smooth working of the market, since they provide information on the availability, type and price of properties, assist or conduct negotiations, arrange finance and insurance, and collaborate with conveyancers.

Furthermore, the professional adviser can suggest the most appropriate method of selling a property. Whereas *private treaty* allows flexibility in lotting and is cheaper, negotiations may drag on and even fail. In contrast, if

bidding exceeds the reserve price, *public auction* affords an immediate contract. Moreover auction is particularly suitable where a property is difficult
to value because of special characteristics, while competitive bidding may
push the price above that expected. On the other hand, careful lotting is
necessary, as renegotiation is difficult once particulars have been published,
and for the buyer there may be the costs of prior survey, legal advice and
financial arrangements.

Tender by sealed bid has advantages additional to those of auction. The
buyer can be selected on identity as well as price, while confidentiality may
be attractive. Above all, where a property has a unique quality – for example, for a developer marrying different sites – the price paid may include
consumer's surplus (the total value that buyers place on the property).
However, the risk is that some prospective buyers may be reluctant to 'bid'
blind so that the successful bid is below the price which could have been
achieved at auction.

The difficulty of obtaining knowledge necessitates payments for professional advice which, together with legal fees and stamp duty, add to the
expense of property transactions and cause them to take longer to complete
compared with those in stocks and shares. Even so, transaction costs are, in
principle, no different from the costs usually incurred in transporting goods
within the market. Thus they have the same effect as transport costs: if they
are high relative to the value of the commodity dealt in, they tend to separate
markets geographically, or at least, to reduce their sensitivity to small
changes in demand and supply.

In practice, therefore, 'the real property market' is an omnibus term
covering a number of separate markets. Moreover, whereas some markets
are quite distinct (such as urban housing and Scottish grouse moors), others
are closely related and overlapping (for example, houses and shops can be
sold for both occupation and investment). Some, where institutional investment demand dominates, are national (even international) in coverage
(for example, offices and prime shop property). Others, where demand is
local, tend to be divided geographically (such as owner-occupied houses
and seaside hotels). Moreover, even within these markets, differences in
rent persist, changes in demand not being fully effective until leases have
expired.

Nevertheless, all markets and sub-markets have this in common – the
commodity traded in is *real property rights*, even though such rights can take
a variety of forms.

(2) ECONOMIC CHARACTERISTICS
In addition to its physical features, we must examine the market's economic
characteristics, particularly as regards the extent to which competition prevails. We have to ask: Is there freedom of entry into the market? Does the
market consist of many buyers and sellers, each so small that no one can
exert monopsony or monopoly powers?

Generally speaking, there is freedom of entry into real property markets, resulting in many buyers and many sellers. But we must also recognise that certain conditions allow an owner to gain some monopolistic control. Such conditions are: (i) the geographical divisions of the market lead to imperfect competition between local markets; (ii) the imperfection of the capital market may prevent some would-be buyers from borrowing the large sums required for certain purchases, such as multi-storey office blocks; (iii) the spatial fixity of real property puts certain site-owners in a strong position relative to a buyer. Consider, for instance, a developer who has purchased every freehold interest except one for a given project. The owner of the outstanding site can exploit his monopoly power by demanding a price far in excess of that paid for the other sites, and so virtually secure all the developer's super-normal profit from the scheme.

Conclusions

Prices are the signals which indicate changes in the conditions of demand and supply. In their turn supply and demand adjust to these signals (see Chapter 3).

Where markets are defective, price signals work at less than full efficiency, and adjustments in supply and demand are sluggish. Relatively high costs of dealing, incurred either in obtaining knowledge or in the necessary legal procedures, restrict the extent to which a small price change can motivate adjustments to supply and demand. Furthermore, any limitation of the market localises demand and supply, making it easier for imperfect competition to exist.

Our examination of the real property market suggests how it might be improved. Any institution or government action which serves to make knowledge better or more readily available is likely to be beneficial. Under this heading we would include professional associations which prescribe standards of competence in valuers; universities and professional bodies which develop improved methods of valuation; estate agents who record property details in computer data banks; and newspapers and journals which advertise current prices. Similarly, if the prices paid in real property transactions were made public on the Land Registry (a government 'freedom of information' proposal), the additional knowledge could improve market efficiency.

Again, any move which reduces the legal costs of transfer can help the market to respond to small changes in price. Thus the government could encourage competition between solicitors, speed up and simplify procedures – possibly through the central Land Registry – and reduce stamp duties.

Where imperfect competition exists in the market, there is an even stronger case for government intervention. Economic analysis shows that, where a monopoly is set up mainly for marketing purposes, the economies of rationalisation tend to fade into the background. The same applies to real property firms, such as land speculators, who seek to secure monopoly selling powers. Thus in our earlier example of a property owner obstructing comprehensive development by demanding a price above the competitive one, the government can intervene by using its powers of compulsory purchase.

We must not overemphasise the barriers in the real property market. Better knowledge can result from the increasing mobility of people and funds, and from the more sophisticated methods of calculating values. And, by and large, prices do respond, albeit somewhat sluggishly, to changes in market conditions; *given sufficient time*, the necessary adjustments to supply and demand do take place. How these adjustments come about through the mechanism of the market will now be examined.

Summary

Markets are any arrangement by which buyers and sellers are brought together to fix a price at which goods can be exchanged. Real property involves land, agricultural estates, industrial buildings, offices, shops and houses which can be exchanged in formal and informal markets. There are many sub-markets and the 'real property market' is an abstract aggregate of these.

The real property market deals in 'property rights' or clearly defined legal interests. These rights can be separated, for example into the leasehold and freehold ground rent. If rights are clearly defined and the costs of negotiating and enforcing contracts are small relative to the overall transaction, the market, based on prices works efficiently.

The efficiency of real property markets is reduced by:

- imperfect knowledge (which creates a role for specialists such as valuers)
- imperfect competition (monopoly interests)
- relatively high costs of dealing

Nevertheless, prices of real property do respond – given sufficient time – to changes in market conditions of supply and demand.

Review questions

1. What is a market?
2. Is there a single real property market?
3. What is meant by 'fee simple absolute'?
4. Explain why property rights can be traded.
5. Suggest at least three ways in which the real property market can be made more efficient.

Recommended Reading

J. Harvey, *Modern Economics*, 7th edn (London: Macmillan, 1998) pp. 27–31.

J. E. Manser, *Economics: A Foundation Course for the Built Environment* (London, E&FN Spon, 1994).

CHAPTER 3

Functions of the Real Property Market

After studying this chapter you will be able to:
- Classify the main categories of property interests
- Explain and illustrate the functions of the real property market

3.1 Dealings in real property interests

Classification of interests

Although a fuller description of the characteristics of the various types of property interests will be given in Chapter 5, it is useful to indicate here the main categories

(1) *Freeholds* (FHs) involve the holder in the full financial risks of ownership, and if rents rise through inflation, a freehold interest provides a hedge against inflation.
(2) *Leaseholds* occur where a freeholder grants a lease for a number of years, during which time he parts with some of his equity interest in exchange for a premium and/or for a regular fixed money income. Thus leaseholds are equivalent to fixed money interest-bearing bonds, though they assume a greater equity interest as the lease nears its reversion date.
(3) *Freehold ground rents* (FGRs) are paid on long leases of undeveloped land. Certainty of payment means that FGRs are similar to an investment in gilt-edged securities.
(4) *Mortgages* are long-term money loans against the security of property. Since interest and capital repayment in money terms are fairly certain, mortgages can be regarded as almost equivalent to debentures and medium-term government bonds.

Who deals in real property interests?

Buyers and sellers of real property can be divided into occupiers and investors.

Occupiers demand property either for *use*, as a consumer good (such as a house, garage, mooring rights), or as a producer good (such as a shop, farm, office, factory). As a consumer good, property is wanted for the satisfaction it yields directly, and demand varies with tastes, income, and so on. As a producer good, the demand is derived from the contribution it makes to production, and thus depends upon its marginal revenue productivity. It should be noted that occupiers are found in both the private and public sectors. Thus government departments and defence forces require offices, land, warehouses, etc., but their transactions are supervised by a co-ordinating agency, Property Advisors to the Civil Estate (PACE) which superseded Property Holdings. (Chapters 4 and 18 will analyse the main factors affecting the occupation demand for different types of property.)

Investors regard property primarily as a *store of wealth*, an alternative to other types of investment asset. But, as we shall see in Chapter 5, investment demand cannot be completely separated from occupation demand. Not only is investment in real property possible because some occupiers prefer to rent rather than to buy their premises, but the amount of rent paid will affect the capital value of the interest.

In discussing the functions of the market we give examples from both occupation and investment dealings since they differ as regards the major considerations affecting demand and supply.

3.2 Functions of the real property market

In any market the price of a good reflects current conditions of demand and supply. But the market does more than *indicate*. Because buyers and sellers respond to these price signals, it also *motivates*. In short, the price system functions through the market.

Thus we can break down the functions of the real property market as follows.

(1) To ALLOCATE EXISTING REAL PROPERTY RESOURCES AND INTERESTS
Because land resources are scarce (that is, not unlimited in supply), they have to be allocated between the various uses and people wanting them. This is

achieved by arriving at the *equilibrium* market price – the price which equates
the resources (or interests) being offered for sale with what people wish to
buy. Thus the market reflects preferences and allocates available supply
accordingly. It is important to note, however, that analysis tends to assume
static conditions in a perfectly competitive market.

Let us illustrate this by looking at the market from the point of view of
investors. Different people prefer different types of interest. A retired
person, for instance, is likely to choose the high and certain income of an
FGR. On the other hand, an insurance company which emphasises its 'with-
profits' bonuses will emphasise the capital growth associated with an 'equity'
interest, and will thus prefer freeholds. We can illustrate by means of an
'Edgeworth-box' diagram (see Figure 3.1).

Assume a supply of FGRs equal to *OX* and of FHs equal to *OY*. The
indifference curves of the retired person are shown by the thinner lines; those
of the insurance company (rotated 180°) by the bolder lines. The shapes of
these indifference curves reflect the preferences of each as between FGRs
and FHs.

Suppose we start from an initial position *K*, with the current relative price
at which FGRs exchange for FHs represented by the slope of the line *AB*. The
insurance company has more FGRs than FHs; the retired person more FHs.

By concentrating our attention at *K*, we can see that this is not an
equilibrium market situation. The insurance company values FHs relative
to FRGs more highly than the market (as shown by the slope of *AB*). It will
therefore exchange in the market some of its FGRs for FHs with the retired
person. As it does so, the market rate at which FGRs exchange for FHs falls.
Equilibrium will occur on the contract curve at a point between *L* and *M*.
This point will be the position where for *both* the retired person and the
insurance company the marginal rate of substitution of FGRs for FHs is

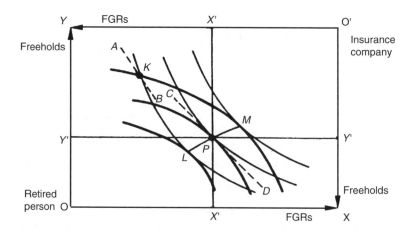

Figure 3.1 Increased satisfaction through the exchange of real property assets

equal to the market rate at which FHs exchange for FGRs. Suppose this new rate of exchange is represented by the slope of the line CD. Then the equilibrium position will be P. Thus exchange in the market has: (i) allocated supply so that the retired person has OY' FHs and OX' FGRs, and the insurance company has $O'Y'$ FHs and $O'X'$ FGRs; (ii) made both the retired person and the insurance company better off, since at P each is on a higher indifference curve than at K.

(2) To INDICATE CHANGES IN DEMAND FOR LAND RESOURCES AND INTERESTS
If, for instance, house-occupiers switch their demand from rented to owner-occupied houses, this will be shown (see Figure 3.2), other things being equal, by a relative rise in the price of houses for owner-occupation, *up* from OP to OP_1 (a), compared with houses for renting, *down* from OR to OR_1.

Similarly, in our earlier examples of interests, a relative increase in the demand for the insurance company's 'with-profits' policies would result in it having a greater preference for FHs compared with FGRs. This would be reflected in a change in the slope of its indifference curves (they would become more horizontal), and the new equilibrium position would be at a relatively higher FH price.

Increases or decreases in demand result mainly from changes in the following.

(a) *Expectations of future yields* resulting from, for example, a change in the price of the final product (where land is a factor of production), a possible switch in government policy (for example, relaxation of rent control or less restrictive planning), or expected changes in the rate of growth of the economy or in the rate of inflation;

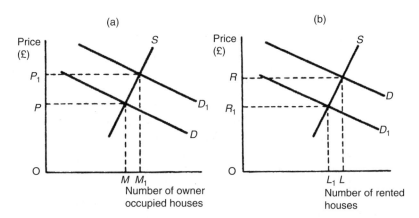

Figure 3.2 A change in demand from rented to owner-occupied houses

(b) *Taxation*, for example, tax concessions to owner-occupiers but not to renters, favourable treatment of charities (where relief from income tax leads them to favour high-yield rather than growth assets);

(c) *Income or tastes*, so that a resource or interest becomes more desirable for personal reasons – for example, more leisure increases the demand for golf courses and bowling and fishing facilities;

(d) *Institutional factors*, such as the costs of transferring assets being altered, or funds becoming more difficult to obtain in an imperfect capital market.

(3) To induce supply to adjust to changes in demand

The supply of interests in real property can change by:

(a) *Developing real property*, either by the adaptation of existing buildings or by constructing new buildings. Thus, in Figure 3.2(b) as demand switches from rented to owner-occupied houses, the price falls to OR_1, and supply contracts from OL to OL_1, LL_1 being sold for owner-occupation (expanding supply there by MM_1). Eventually, new equilibrium prices are established, OP_1 in the owner-occupied market and OR_1 in the rented market.

(b) *Changing existing interests*, with no physical alteration in the property. For example, assume that, initially, freeholds are selling at £200 000, whereas similar ninety-nine-year leases are making £160 000 and their FGRs are just over £4000. An increase in the demand for freeholds drives up their price to £240 000. Dealers could now buy FGRs and leaseholds separately, marry the two, and make a profit upon sale of the single freehold. As a result, the prices of FGRs and leaseholds (through the increased demand) would rise, and that of freeholds (through the increased supply) would fall. This would continue until a new set of equilibrium prices had been established, say freeholds £220 000, leaseholds £170 000 and FGRs £5000. On the other hand, an increase in the demand for leaseholds and FGRs could lead to the division of freeholds.

These amalgamations and separation of interests are continually taking place in all sections of the real property market in response to people's preferences. A property developer, for instance, has often to marry the FGRs and the shop leases on a given site in order to secure the freehold for development. Similarly, an agricultural estate may be formed out of many separate farms. On the other hand, interests may be separated. A property company may originally have intended to retain the whole of the freehold interest in a development. But a rise in demand, resulting in a higher price for freehold investments, may induce it to sell a part-share to an institution, reinvesting the proceeds in a new development.

Of course, such changes take time to complete (see Chapter 4), and are subject to the imperfections of the real property market. Moreover, efficient adjustment to changes in demand and supply assumes that all interests are divisible and that there is a perfect capital market. Neither is true.

Office blocks come in large 'lumps' (though the emergence of property bonds, property unit trusts and 'securitisation' has helped to overcome this difficulty). Imperfections of the capital market may prevent a full response to preferences regarding interests. Thus if a building society will not give a mortgage on a freehold flat in the centre of a town, the would-be purchaser could be forced to go to a modern semi-detached house in the suburbs (see p. 333). Or if the government is seeking to reduce its spending, PACE, its agency, may be forced to lease premises instead of buying out-right. Finally, government restrictions on supply (such as planning controls) or interference with the price mechanism (such as rent control) obstruct the efficient operation of the market economy. Thus an equilibrium situation takes a long time to be achieved, by which time new factors are likely to have arisen, producing a change of direction towards a new equilibrium.

(4) To indicate changes in the conditions upon which land resources can be supplied

Improved techniques in constructing high-rise buildings, for example, may make flats cheaper compared with low-rise houses and flats. Thus in Figure 3.3 the supply curve moves from S to S_1. This is signalled in the market by a fall in the price of high-rise flats from OP to OP_1.

(5) To induce demand to respond to changes in the conditions of supply

As a result of the fall in the price of high-rise flats, demand for them expands from OM to OM_1 (see Figure 3.3). Demand for low-rise houses therefore decreases from D to D_1 (see Figure 3.4) with an actual contraction in supply of MM_1. These changes simply illustrate the fact that prices of substitutes move in the same direction.

(6) To 'reward' the owners of land resources

Rewarding the owners of land resources is a by-product of the market. Such rewards are of two main kinds.

First, there is the return on capital invested. When a person looks for a certain return without risk (for example, FGRs) then the return corresponds closely with the opportunity cost – what his capital could have earned in the best alternative (such as government stock). There is therefore little 'profit' element in such a return.

But the yield from a land resource usually extends far into the future. Being a fixed factor its reward is dependent upon demand and is thus largely in the nature of 'economic rent'. It can be high, for example, to people who own land banks before an increase in demand; or it may be negative, for example, to builders who have bought land banks before a slump. In short, this second type of reward, 'super-normal profit', arises because of the risk attached to any fixed factor.

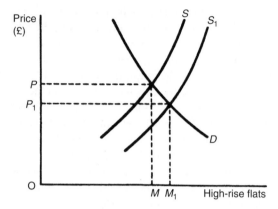

Figure 3.3 The effect of a change in the conditions of supply on price

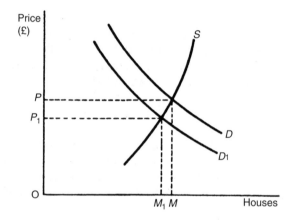

Figure 3.4 The response of demand to changes in the conditions of supply

Conclusion

The function of the real property market is to establish a pattern of prices and rents so that, given sufficient time (the long period), land resources are allocated according to their most profitable ('highest and best') use relative to other land resources. This occurs because competition in the market induces owners to switch resources to that use which yields the highest net return. For example, agricultural land is used for housing, a house is divided into flats or changed to offices, and, in time, sites are cleared for redevelopment. Indeed, in chapter 14 we show how the market, in allocating resources between competing uses, establishes patterns in land use and land values.

Of course, efficiency of the market economy may be impaired because the conditions stipulated in Chapter 1 do not hold. But, given competitive conditions, the creation of different interests in real property is the response to differences in individual preferences. Although we have illustrated the argument in terms of the main forms of interest, we must recognise that there is a wide variety of interests meeting individual preferences, for instance, through restrictive covenants. When looked at in this way, we have to acknowledge how well the market performs its task, allowing just a small change in price to reflect individual preferences. In contrast, the state is likely to be rigid, so, for example, council-house tenants may not be able to keep a dog or paint the front door to the colour of their own choice even if willing to pay slightly more rent. And, even more important, if land is taken over by local authorities how will it be allocated among its different uses to obtain the maximum net benefit possible?

Summary

The main categories of property interests are:

1. Freeholds
2. Leaseholds
3. Freehold ground rents
4. Mortgages

   Buyers and sellers of real property are either occupiers, who demand property for its use; or investors, who regard property as a store of wealth; or both.

   The functions of the real property market are:

- To allocate existing real property resources and interests
- To indicate changes in demand for land resources and interests
- To induce supply to adjust to changes in demand
- To indicate changes in the conditions upon which land resources can be supplied
- To induce demand to respond to changes in the conditions of supply
- To 'reward' the owners of land resources

   The overall function of the real property market is to establish a pattern of prices and rents which results in land resources being allocated according to their most profitable ('highest and best') use.

Review questions

1. Explain the difference between 'freehold' and 'leasehold'.
2. Why are 'Freehold Ground Rents' similar to an investment in gilt-edged securities (with relatively low returns)?
3. Explain how property can be seen as both an investment and consumer good.
4. How does supply of real property adjust to changes in demand?
5. What is the primary function of the real property market?

Recommended Reading

J. Harvey, *Modern Economics*, 7th edn (London: Macmillan, 1998) chs 3–5.
J. E. Manser, *Economics: A Foundation Course for the Built Environment* (London, E&FN Spon, 1994).
M. Newell, *An Introduction to the Economics of Urban Land Use* (London: Estates Gazette, 1977) ch. 1.

CHAPTER 4

The Pricing of Land and Land Resources

After studying this chapter you will be able to:

• **Explain the concept of 'economic rent'**
• **Show how a demand curve for land can be determined**
• **Explain and illustrate how the interaction of demand and supply will lead to an equilibrium market price or rent**

4.1 Land as a whole

Undeveloped land, or 'pure' land, refers solely to natural resources and space. Thus land as a *whole* – that is, the earth's land surface – can be regarded as being fixed in supply. Increasing such land by reclamation from the sea involves so much investment of capital that it is more appropriate to view it as an addition to capital goods rather than to land.

This idea of land as a whole being fixed in supply has been important in past discussions of cost and value. With man-made commodities, including capital goods, price is a function of demand and supply and, in so far as supply is influenced by cost of production, price itself is influenced by cost. But since land as a whole is a fixed supply provided by Nature, the earnings of 'pure' land are determined solely by demand.

Thus in Figure 4.1 *POMN* represents the earnings of land when demand is *D*, and $P_1 OML$ when demand is D_1. In fact, however small the earnings, the total supply of land is still the same. We can say, therefore, that its opportunity cost is zero. Hence all the earnings of land as a whole are an

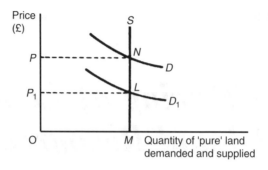

Figure 4.1 Economic rent

excess over opportunity cost. They represent *economic rent*, that part of the earnings of a factor which results from it having some element of fixity of supply (in economic terms, the return arising because supply is not perfectly elastic).

Certain points should be noted as regards this general statement.

(1) To say that the earnings of land are a surplus over opportunity cost does not mean that payments do not have to be made for land. Price still performs the vital function of rationing scarce supply among *competing* uses. This is necessary to ensure that, in each location, land is put to its most profitable use according to the preferences of consumers and society.

(2) It follows from (1) that the supply of land can never be regarded as fixed from the *viewpoint of any one use* (unless it can only be used in one way). Additional supplies can always be bid from other uses if the proposed new use has a higher value than the existing use.

(3) The productivity of land can usually be increased in response to additional demand by using it more *intensively* by the addition of capital.

(4) The fact that the earnings of land as a whole are entirely demand-determined is important from the point of view of taxation – land will still be there, no matter how high the tax. In other words, a tax on pure land has no disincentive effect on the supply of land. Economic rent can be taxed away entirely. This is the basis of taxes on land, such as petroleum revenue tax, a development land tax (see Chapter 22).

Nevertheless the following points must be remembered.

(a) Unless all forms of land use are taxed equally, the pattern of land use will be distorted. Whether such distortion is on balance good or bad can only be decided by: (i) a comparison with the inevitable distortions produced by alternative taxes; (ii) its connection with spillover benefits and costs; (iii) one's political views.

(b) Costs of production include normal profit – that is, what is necessary to keep the entrepreneur in the current line of production. But the size of normal profit may be blurred, and taxes may overlap super-normal profit and fall on normal profit. Thus, as first mooted, the petroleum revenue tax was too high, and oil-drilling companies threatened to withdraw from further operations since it cut into the normal profit required to cover the risk involved. The government therefore had to modify its proposals.

4.2 The commercial rent of land

Commercial rent is simply a periodic payment for the hire of land. Normally, there is competition for land between the different potential users. The rent of land, therefore, as with other factors of production, is determined, in the absence of any government interference, by the interaction of demand and supply.

Demand

Let us assume that:

(a) the land under discussion is homogeneous;
(b) buyers are only interested in maximising private utility or money returns;
(c) conditions of demand and supply do not change – for example, as regards sources of raw materials, transport facilities, public utilities, building technology;
(d) a long-period situation prevails, in that firms can vary the quantities of all factors employed;
(e) the output at which profits are maximised is known.

Here we are concerned with *occupation* demand, either as a consumer good or as factor of production (see pp. 30–1). We shall concentrate on the latter.

In order to maximise profit, the equilibrium output must be produced at the minimum possible cost. The demand for land as a factor of production is a *derived demand* – it is wanted for the contribution it can make to a final product. Moreover, it has to be combined with other factors, labour and capital, to produce the goods that are wanted. Thus the quantity of land which a firm demands depends upon: (i) its productivity; (ii) its price relative to other factors; and (iii) the price of the final product.

In determining the demand curve for land, therefore, three main problems have to be answered: (1) How does a change in the price of land relative to other factors affect the demand for land? (2) How will a change in the productivity of land in a particular use affect demand? (3) How will a change in the price of the product affect the demand for land in that use?

The isoquant technique can be applied to solving these problems. In Figure 4.2 EP_{10} and EP_{20} are isoquants showing all the different

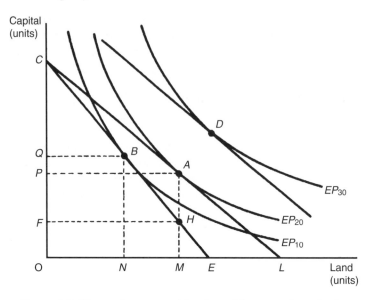

Figure 4.2 The optimum combination of factors of production

combinations of land and capital which will yield outputs of 10 and 20 units of accommodation respectively. According to the profit-maximising output (which we will assume to be EP_{20}), there will be a minimum given outlay on factors of production. Spent wholly on land it would buy OL units; spent wholly on capital it would buy OC units. The slope of the budget line CL indicates the relative prices of land and capital.

The cost-minimising factor combination for the EP_{20} level of output is OM land plus OP capital. Any other combination would yield less than 20 units of accommodation (that is, it would fall below EP_{20}). At A the marginal rate of technical substitution of land for capital equals

$$\frac{\text{Price of land}}{\text{Price of capital}}$$

If the profit-maximising output had been EP_{30} a larger money outlay would have been required, but, given the same land and capital prices, the slope of the budget line would remain unchanged. Here the cost-minimising point would be D.

The following points should be noted.

(1) If the price of land were to rise so that the same money outlay as before now buys only OE land, it will produce a new budget line CE and a new cost-minimising combination of ON land plus OQ capital. Thus the rise in the price of land has had two effects: (i) more capital is now combined with less land than before; (ii) because less land can be bought with the given outlay,

the level of output has been reduced from 20 units to 10 units of accommodation.

(2) An increase in the productivity of land will produce a new isoquant for 20 units, as shown by the dashed line EP'_{20} (see Figure 4.3). The same output (20 units) can now be produced for a smaller minimum outlay – the budget line is nearer the origin – by increasing land from OM to OS and by decreasing capital from OP to OR.

(3) The smooth continuity of the isoquant denotes that factors are infinitely divisible; as regards land, this means that the homogeneous plots are infinitely small. Moreover, our analysis assumes that the quantity of land can be adjusted. Suppose, however, that when the price of land rises from CL to CE (Figure 4.2) the quantity of land remained at OM. This would produce a new position at H (only HM capital could be afforded on the given budget), with a product of something less than EP_{10} (say 8 units of accommodation) because land is having to be employed too extensively.

(4) Suppose, through an increase in demand, that the price of the standard unit of accommodation rose. The new profit-maximising output would now be larger than EP_{20}, say EP_{30}. At this output more capital and more land would be demanded even at the same relative prices.

We can sum up by saying that a fall in the price of a factor (in this case land) will lead to an extension of demand (the demand curve slopes downwards), whereas an increase in its productivity or an increase in the price of the product will lead to an increase in demand for the factor (the demand curve moves to the right). The sum of the demands for land of the individual firms will give the industry's demand for land.

The equilibrium market price

As regards supply, when the rent for land in a particular use rises, it will be surrendered by less profitable uses. In short, the higher the price, more will usually be supplied; there is an upward-sloping supply curve (see Figure 4.4).

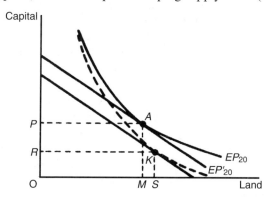

Figure 4.3 The effect on the demand for land of an increase in its productivity

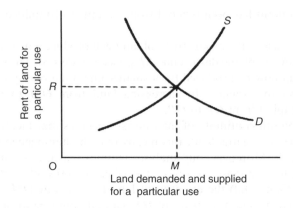

Figure 4.4 The determination of the commercial rent of land

The interaction of demand and supply will give an equilibrium market rent *OR* for this type of land. Competition will have ensured that at this rent it goes to the highest and best use.

Non-homogeneous land and economic rent

So far we have assumed that all land is homogeneous. We shall now relax this assumption. In practice, land varies in quality. Thus *agricultural land* differs in fertility, climate, altitude, topography and accessibility to the market.

Consider a piece of land which produces 8 tonnes of wheat per hectare. There will be less fertile land, but, we will assume, such land will still be used for growing wheat provided it yields 4 tonnes per hectare. This latter land just earns its *transfer cost*, the minimum it has to earn to keep it in its present use, and is thus said to be marginal as regards wheat-growing. In contrast, the 8 tonne land yields 4 tonnes per hectare above the marginal land; this extra yield is an *economic rent* resulting from its greater fertility.

The same argument applies to *urban land*. Different characteristics, for instance, accessibility, the physical condition of the site and institutional restrictions (development plans and covenants), give rise to differential rents. Shops in Oxford Street and offices in the City of London all earn a high *economic* rent as a result of the high *commercial* rents which they command. Economic rent accrues to any factor which is fixed in supply, and is determined by demand. Thus if the demand for shops in a district increases, an existing shop let on a lease earns a *profit rent* until the next rent review. This profit rent is economic rent, and can be capitalised in the form of a premium should the lease be sold.

4.3 The pricing of land resources

Whereas land refers to natural resources, land resources can be defined as the total natural and manmade resources over which possession of the earth's surface gives control. That is, land resources are equal to the natural content of land plus any improvements attaching to or incorporated in the land. Indeed, when we talk about a transaction in land, we are usually referring to land resources. In agriculture, for instance, land would normally include the farmhouse and buildings, the fences and water supply, while a freehold residence is the land plus all the fixtures on the land – the house, conservatory, fish-ponds, swimming pool, fences, and so on.

Supply, price and the time period

Price in the market is determined by demand and supply. In economic analysis it is usual to allow for the fact that changes in supply take time by dividing time into three main periods (see Figure 4.5).

In the 'momentary' period, no adjustment of supply is possible (S_m). In the 'short period' supply can be altered by engaging more variable factors (S_s). Eventually, however, supply can be increased by adding to fixed capital, thus combining the factors of production in their best proportions (the 'long period', S_l). Thus if demand increases from D to D_1, the price of the product changes from OP to OP_1, OP_2 or OP_3 (corresponding respectively to the above periods).

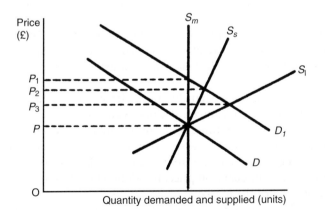

Figure 4.5 The effect of time on the conditions of supply

4.4 The dominance of stocks over flows

The relative size of stocks and flows

While not incorrect, the general analysis of the formation of price over time suffers from two main weaknesses when applied to individual goods.

(1) THE TIME TAKEN TO ACHIEVE THE LONG-PERIOD SITUATION VARIES
CONSIDERABLY
The full response of supply to a rise in the price of buildings usually takes a very long time. The various interests in a site required for redevelopment have to be amalgamated (usually by acquiring leases), planning permission has to be obtained and any compulsory purchase orders subjected to time-consuming procedures. This means that, when applying the usual time-period analysis to land resources, we have to recognise that for a considerable period of time we are virtually dealing with a fixed stock. Thus changes in demand will tend to be more significant than changes in supply in determining market price.

(2) NO ALLOWANCE IS MADE FOR THE SIZE OF STOCKS OF EXISTING GOODS
RELATIVE TO FLOWS OF NEW GOODS COMING ON TO THE MARKET
With most goods we do not have to pay much attention to this. Because their life is relatively short, existing goods (the stock) have to be replaced frequently by new supplies (the flow over a period). This is true even of consumer durable goods, such as washing-machines, refrigerators and motor-cars.

Take cars, for example. Other things being equal, any increase in the demand for cars will, in a free market, push up the price. Extra imports may help to meet this additional demand. But if manufacturers consider that the higher price is likely to be permanent, they will eventually add to plant so that the supply of cars coming on to the market increases. This flow of new supplies will be significant relative to the supply coming on to the market from existing *stocks*, and will thus be a main determinant, with demand, of price.

But the position is somewhat different with certain goods, for example, ships, aircraft, and land resources. Because such goods are so durable, stocks of them accumulate over time. As a result, new flows on to the market (additions, say, per annum) are small or insignificant in comparison with the supply to the market coming from existing stocks. As a result, *new* supply has relatively little influence on price; for all practical purposes, supply from old stock dominates the market.

Two qualifications, however, should be made. First, it is the turnover of old stock which is really significant (see below). Second, over the years accumulated flows affect the size of stocks, and have their effect in this way. But the possibility of this is very limited in developed city centres.

Price is therefore largely determined by demand; new supplies follow this price rather than have much influence in determining it. The position is summarised in Figure 4.6.

An illustration from housing

Since buildings have a long life, the stock of *owner-occupied* housing units in the UK is approximately 25 million. The turnover of this stock (about 5 per cent or 1 250 000 units) is large relative to the flow of *additional* units being produced each year, about 180 000. Indeed in areas (like Greater London) which are surrounded by a green belt, most houses coming on to the market are from the existing stock of houses.

In such a situation demand determines the price of houses. For example, let us assume an increase in the demand for living accommodation. In the short run existing dwellings are used more intensively, for example, by a decrease or disappearance of the number of vacant dwellings, an increase in subtenancies, a doubling-up of families, an increase in the number of persons per room. Eventually, this will cause the prices of owner-occupied houses and rents of existing accommodation to rise.

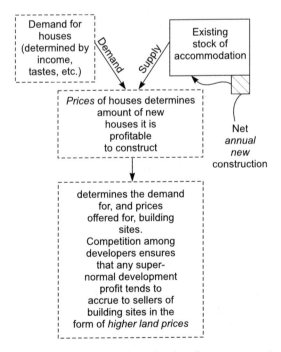

Figure 4.6 The dominance of stock of real property on its price

But since the flow of new houses on to the market is insufficient to affect significantly the supply, this higher price of existing houses will represent the price of *all houses* in the market. Any newly built house which comes on to the market will be sold at the higher price. In other words, the price of new houses is determined by the price at which existing houses sell.

The price paid for land for new housing is thus the residual between what the new house will sell at (determined by the demand for old houses) and what it costs to build, including normal profit. Take, for instance, a builder bidding for a spare site in London on which to erect a house. Suppose similar old houses are selling for £240 000, and that he estimates that it will cost him £160 000 (including his normal profit) to build. He can therefore afford to bid £80 000 for the land and indeed will have to do so if he is to secure it in competition with other builders.

Because houses take time to build, this is a situation which exists in all localities in the short period. Where building land is available, however, the high price offered for existing and, therefore, new houses will encourage builders to erect new houses, and this will continue so long as the cost of new houses on to the market will be sufficient to influence the stock of houses, and the price of old houses will tend to fall. This is most noticeable in districts where the supply of building plots is plentiful, for example, in new towns, overflow towns (Swindon, Ashford and so on) and the fringe land of certain towns where planning permissions have been freely given to permit expansion. In the long period, therefore, these new flows affect the price of old houses, and when the prices of old and new houses coincide, the cost of building new houses does affect the price. But it may take a very long time before this situation happens and, where cities are surrounded by green belts which cannot be built on, the price of houses will tend to be dominated by demand.

Corollaries of the foregoing analysis

(1) Current construction costs are not relevant in determining prices and rents of real property

Such costs include the price of land, building materials and labour costs, and the cost of builders' borrowing, for example, on overdrafts.

As regards the price of land, it is sometimes stated, for example, that the high cost of land is responsible for high house prices, thus limiting home ownership. Our analysis gives scant support to this view. An increase in demand for houses causes the price of old houses to rise. This enables builders to bid more for land – up to the difference between what they can sell a new house for (the price of similar existing houses) and the cost of building (including normal profit). Thus, in our example, if the price of houses rose to £320 000 and building costs remained unchanged, £160 000 could now be paid for the land.

Of course, to the individual builder, the price of land is a cost; as with building components, he has to pay the going competitive market rate to obtain it. But the 'individual' view that land prices should be controlled because they are 'bad' puts the cart before the horse. What we have done is to examine the underlying factors – the demand for houses – which determine the price of land from the point of view of builders as a whole.

Empirical support of the above analysis is contained in the *Digest of Building Land Prices 1974* (published by *Estates Gazette* and the House Builders' Federation). In 1972 the average price paid for land on housing estates was £25 000 an acre. In the last quarter of 1973 it had fallen to £21 000, and builders who had acquired land banks at 1972 prices were showing a loss. The reasons for the fall in land prices were the fall in house prices and the rise in costs. The *Digest* comments that current conditions make it clear 'that land prices are determined by house prices rather than the other way round' – an example of the inductive method of establishing an hypotheses as opposed to our deductive method.

Three other points should be noted.

(a) It is what could be the builder's super-normal profit which represents the maximum he can bid for land. Unless this is sufficient to attract land from its next-best use, such as agriculture, he cannot build.

(b) Since the price of land is determined by the demand for housing, controlling its price artificially would not result in house prices falling.
Instead, the surplus return would simply go to somebody other than the land-owner, for example, the first purchaser, or local authorities who acquire land compulsorily at existing use values. Furthermore, it would upset the allocative function of the market whereby the equilibrium price ensures that scarce land goes to its highest and best use. Artificially low prices, maintained by some form of price control, would lead to a 'wasteful' demand for land in less profitable uses.

(c) As the price of houses rises, land costs form a greater proportion of that price. Thus, in our earlier example, when the house sold for £240 000, the land cost formed one-third of that price; when the house rose to £320 000 through increased demand, the land cost rose to one-half.

Similarly, we have to ask whether a rise in *the cost of building materials and labour* will put up the price of houses in the short period. The answer is that, where building land is earning an economic rent (that is, its price is above its 'transfer' or next-best use), a rise in building costs has no effect on the current price of houses. Since the supply of houses comes mainly from existing stock, their price in the market is determined by demand. A rise in building costs therefore simply means that the builder has a smaller margin to bid for the land. Thus, in our original example, had building costs risen by £20 000, his maximum bid for land would have been only £60 000.

Price changes support this argument (see Table 4.1). Whereas in 1987–8 average construction costs rose by approximately 10 per cent, the price of

Table 4.1   Index of house prices, land prices and construction costs, 1987–2001

	Average price of new dwellings mortgaged by the Nationwide Building Society, UK, 1993 = 100	Average price of private sector housing land, England and Wales 1985 = 100	Average construction cost in public sector house-building, England and Wales 1995 = 100
1987	89	174	86
1988	114	231	95
1989	123	227	99
1990	119	199	98
1991	109	200	92
1992	104	177	88
1993	100	187	90
1994	102	196	101
1995	102	205	100
1996	103	212	102
1997	111	220	106
1998	126	237	109[*]
1999	135	280	113[*]
2000	155	330	118[*]
2001	168	410	122[*]

[*]Great Britain

Sources: *Construction Statistics, Department of Trade and Industry;*
Housing Statistics, Office of the Deputy Prime Minister;
Nationwide House Prices Bulletin.

new dwellings rose by 28 per cent, and the price of housing land by 33 per cent as builders acquired land in anticipation of a future rise in house prices. On the other hand, in 1989–90 when the price of new dwellings fell by 3 per cent and construction costs by only 1 per cent, the price of housing land fell by 12 per cent as builders had to release surplus land acquired in the previous two years.

The effect of a rise in the *rate of interest* must be considered from the viewpoint of both the builder and the house purchaser. On the supply side, the builder has to pay more for his overdraft, but this will affect only what he can bid for the land, not the house price. It is on the demand side that the rise in the rate of interest has the major effect – the higher cost of borrowing on mortgages leads to a decrease in demand, and thus the price of houses will tend to fall!

(2) A TAX MAY BE IMPOSED ON THE ECONOMIC RENT OF LAND RESOURCES
The government can impose a tax on land resources up to the level of economic rent they earn and this will make no difference to their supply. It should be noted, however, that land resources include capital. If the tax should be so large as to overlap the transfer earnings of capital or normal profit, further building will not take place.

(3) DEVELOPERS CAN BE REQUIRED TO COVER SOME OF THE SOCIAL COSTS OF PROJECTS
A different type of 'tax' – planning gain – may be imposed (see pp. 412–14). So long as it does not cut into normal profit, a local authority can, as a condition of planning permission, require developers to include in their schemes either houses (which are usually less profitable than offices) or improvements to the infrastructure, such as sewers. The first is largely on political-social grounds; the second can be regarded as covering some of the social costs of the scheme.

(4) AN INCREASE IN TRANSPORT COSTS WILL INCREASE ECONOMIC RENTS AT THE CITY CENTRE
Increased transport costs or road congestion will make houses on the periphery of a city a poorer substitute for houses at the centre. This will diminish the extent to which the increase in new flows of houses can be significant compared with the existing stock. Thus the difference in economic rent between the centre and the periphery will increase as house and therefore land prices rise at the centre, and will tend to persist.

Summary

Land as a whole can be regarded as fixed in supply (although this is not true from the viewpoint of any one use). As a result, all the earnings of land as a whole are an excess over opportunity cost or 'economic rent'.

A fall in the price of land will lead to an extension of demand (the demand curve slopes downwards); while an increase in the productivity of land, or an increase in the price of the product of land, will lead to an increase in demand for land at all prices (the demand curve shifts to the right). Supply of land for a particular use will be increased as its price increases (the supply curve slopes upwards).

Changes in supply take time and so the supply curve of property becomes more elastic the longer the time period. The commercial rent of land is determined by the interaction of demand and supply and competition ensures that at this rent the land is put to its most profitable use.

Property and land resources are durable and so stocks of them accumulate over time. As a result, new supply is a small proportion of total stock and, therefore, has little influence on price. Prices are then largely determined by demand.

Review questions

1. Are land resources fixed in supply?
2. Why would a tax on pure land have no disincentive effects on the supply of land?
3. Explain, using a diagram, how supply of property can become more elastic in the long-run.
4. Why are there long time lags in property supply?
5. What is meant by 'planning gain'? Give an example.

Recommended Reading

J. Harvey, *Modern Economics*, 7th edn (London: Macmillan, 1998) ch. 22.

J. E. Manser, *Economics: A Foundation Course for the Built Environment* (London, E&FN Spon, 1994).

D. Myers, *Economics and Property: A Coursebook for Students of the Built Environment* (London: Estates Gazette, 1994).

M. Newell, *An Introduction to the Economics of Urban Land Use* (London: Estates Gazette, 1977) ch. 15.

CHAPTER 5

Investment in Real Property

After studying this chapter you will be able to:

● **Compare the investment characteristics of different interests in real property**
● **Describe the various types of investor in property**
● **Explain the role of real property investment in portfolio management**
● **Explain how property earnings can be capitalised**

The economist distinguishes two meanings of the word 'investment':

(a) expenditure on the purchase of *existing* assets – for example, shares of a company, or an interest in an existing (perhaps tenanted) office block;
(b) expenditure on the *creation of new* fixed assets – for example, the construction of North Sea oil rigs, or the development of a new office block.

Thus property investment is an example of the first meaning and property development is an example of the second.

Because land resources are durable, rights existing in them have a long time-scale and, although there may be management costs, no problem exists in storage. Property rights, like stocks and shares, are therefore demanded as investment assets. Indeed, as we shall see, the real-property market can now be regarded as a part of the wider investment asset market. It is in the sense of holding assets as a store of wealth that we use the term 'investment' in what follows.

Even so, as shown in Chapter 2, real property as a whole does exhibit features which distinguish it from other assets.

5.1 Special investment characteristics of different interests in real property

The broad objectives of investment are to preserve or enhance the real value of the asset and to receive a flow of income over time. We therefore begin by describing in outline the extent to which different interests in real property fulfil these objectives, and the priorities of the main investing groups.

As we saw in the previous chapter, different interests in real property really represent different bundles of rights. However, like stock exchange securities, they can be classified according to their broad *investment* characteristics: 'equity' interests – for example, freeholds; 'equity-loan' interests – for example, freehold ground rents with significant reversionary prospects; 'loan' interests – such as leaseholds, freehold ground rents with distant reversions, and mortgages.

Each type of interest will now be examined from the point of view of investment.

(1) Freeholds

The holder of a freehold, whether owner-occupier or investor, takes the full financial risk of ownership. If the rent increases – for example, through scarcity or inflation – he gains; if the rent falls – for example, through deterioration of locality – he loses. A freehold is, therefore, an 'equity' interest, equivalent to the ordinary share in a company.

When purchased as an investment, freeholds are usually subject to a lease granted by a previous freeholder. The purchaser receives the rack-rent (full annual rental which a property could achieve were it to be let out to rent) under the lease and the reversion at the end of the lease. But to obtain the full equity interest there must be provision for frequent rent review; otherwise the freehold bears a closer resemblance to a leasehold interest.

Freehold investments usually involve some management: for instance, collecting the rent and ensuring that the tenant observes the terms and covenants of the lease. There may also be maintenance obligations, such as external repairs. Such management costs have to be deducted from the rent received to ascertain the net income.

Like ordinary shares, freeholds differ in quality and this is reflected in their yields. Briefly, the yield, that is the net annual income return expressed as a percentage of the market price of the asset, depends upon: (i) the purchase price; (ii) the current rent; (iii) the prospect of future rent rises as a result of increased demand for the type of property or because of inflation; (iv) the frequency of rent reviews; (v) the type and condition of the property; (vi) the strength of the occupier's covenant; (vii) management costs, (viii) development possibilities; and (ix) estimates of future changes in government policy, for example, as regards depreciation allowances.

Demand for prime properties – for example, city-centre shops and modern first-class offices – by institutional investors is keen and they have the funds necessary for what are mostly expensive purchases. As a result, yields on such freeholds are low (shops 7 per cent, offices 6.25 per cent), and, until recently, below the yield on long-dated government securities (see Table 5.2). This *reverse yield gap* implies that the difference was expected to be made good by future rent increases.

In contrast private persons have to consider the cheaper secondary properties. Nor can they overcome the difficulty by borrowing, since insurance companies and merchant banks are reluctant to lend against secondary property. The result is that such properties are sold on a much higher yield (8–11 per cent).

In practice, yields differ slightly on the different types of freehold property. Thus prime shops have a lower yield than offices, while the latters' yield tends to be less than that on industrial and residential properties. We can explain this by considering the characteristics of the main types of property.

(a) *Shops* Location is all-important in determining the yield on shops. Generally speaking the best high street positions are occupied by the multiples, their values being enhanced by complementarity with one another. The main reasons for the low yield on prime shops are:

(i)   the supply of such sites is limited by purely spatial considerations;
(ii) multiples, the fastest-growing outlet of the retail trade, are willing to pay high rents for these sites;
(iii) the goods sold have a high income elasticity of demand, thereby ensuring growth in turnover; and
(iv) the institutions seek such investments because occupiers have excellent covenants and the rental rate of growth has been the highest of all types of urban development.

Even a short distance from the prime shopping location rents fall off considerably, while potential rent growth is not nearly so good. Hence yields on secondary shops are about double those on prime shops.

(b) *Offices* Prime office blocks appeal to the institutions with large funds to invest, because they can often be let to a single tenant providing an excellent covenant, thereby reducing management costs.

Between 1989 and 1994, however, during the recession, amalgamations of firms, and reduced staff requirements because of the introduction of IT, led to an over-supply of offices, resulting in falling rents, over-renting and reduced prospects for future increases. Furthermore, this has highlighted the problem of obsolescence through technical advances and changes in working practices. Hence, though the institutions are still buying modern office blocks, it is the property companies which are acquiring the older properties where there are opportunities to add value by management expertise or even redevelopment

(c) *Industrial factories and warehouses* Industrial premises tend to be less popular as investments than other types of property. The reasons are:

(i) rents are usually more affected by economic depression;
(ii) many factories are built for a special purpose, and if they have to be relet difficulty may be experienced in finding a similar tenant, or, alternatively, expense is incurred in adaptation;
(iii) changes in techniques of production and handling goods can make the factory obsolete – for example, greater eave height may be required for fork-lift stacking in a warehouse; and
(iv) the intensive use of industrial premises leads to more rapid depreciation than with other properties, though tax reliefs give some compensation.

The result is that the current yield on industrial premises is 7–13 per cent. Nevertheless, there are indications that newly built B_1 premises are becoming more popular as investments (see p. 244). These are of simple construction, on the ground floor only, have large clear spaces, roof lighting and office accommodation attached, and are easily adapted to different uses. Furthermore, they can be written off as depreciation for tax purposes, and may carry special tax allowances.

(d) *Residential* For a number of reasons residential property usually shows the highest yield:

(i) rent increases tend to lag behind the current market rent;
(ii) costs of management, for example, through frequent rent collection from many tenants, tend to be relatively high; and
(iii) the cost of repairs, for which the landlord is usually responsible, tends to be heavy.

However, recent relaxation of the legal constraints on rent increases and repossession (see pp. 337–8) have made residential property a more attractive investment proposition, particularly for the private investor.

(e) *Rural estates* In the UK the two main types of tenure for farms are tenant farming and owner-occupation.

Where a rural estate is let, the landowner (investor) usually provides fixed capital (such as buildings, roads and drainage), while the tenant is responsible for working capital (such as implements, livestock, fertilisers) and labour. But there are no rigid rules. With complete freedom of contract, the arrangement reached would be the one that maximised the joint earnings of the two parties. In practice, ignorance, inertia and even obstinacy of one party may reduce free bargaining.

Tenant farming, once predominant, has declined markedly since the Second World War, and today accounts for less than 20 per cent of all holdings in England and Wales. The Agriculture Holdings Act 1948 made it difficult to give a tenant notice to quit, and the right of succession was extended to relatives working on the farm by the Agriculture (Miscellaneous Provisions) Act 1976. Though a revision of rentals is possible every three years, they remain somewhat below the free market level. Investors' income is therefore low, and many farms were sold to owner-occupiers. To halt the contraction in the number of tenanted farms, the Agricultural Tenancies Act 1995 provided for the terms of new farm business tenancies to be decided by free bargaining between landlord and tenant.

Until recently, agricultural land has proved an excellent hedge against inflation, with steady rent increases and above average capital appreciation, chiefly as a result of buoyant demand brought about by:

(i) rising prices of agricultural products through the EU's Common Agricultural Policy (CAP) and the devaluation of sterling in 1986 and 1992;

(ii) the appreciation in the value of additional sources of income, such as woodlands, mineral workings, sporting rights, which now form part of the total investment value of an estate;

(iii) the prospect of possible urban development;

(iv) owners who have sold land for development at very high prices re-investing the proceeds in farmland to take advantage of the 'roll-over' concession for capital gains tax;

(v) when Britain joined the EU British farmland was cheap compared with prices in other EU countries;

(vi) a nil rate of inheritance tax on farmland;

(vii) the social standing which land-ownership gives in a rural community, and the satisfaction of walking round a rural estate compared with a block of offices; and

(viii) a rise in the value of the residential and amenity elements of many farms.

As a result, institutions (chiefly insurance companies and pension funds), together with rich individuals and farming investment companies, held some farmland in their investment portfolios. But, as a result of the fall in the price of farmland in 1984 and the uncertain prospects for agriculture, the institutions have liquidated most of their holdings.

All the factors mentioned in Chapter 2 which differentiate real property investments from other investments are accentuated in the rural estate market; (i) not only is each estate unique in its size and position, but it differs in topography and fixed capital; (ii) the rural estate market is highly localised; and (iii) many estates change hands by private treaty and therefore at undisclosed prices, with demand being influenced by non-economic factors, such as family considerations. Thus the rural estate market tends to be imperfect.

(2) Leaseholds

A freeholder may rent the premises he owns to somebody else. The usual practice is to grant a lease for a fixed number of years in return for a capital sum (a 'premium'), or a rent, or a combination of both. These leases have value and can be exchanged in the market.

At the end of the given period the property reverts to the freeholder, and then the value of the lease to the lessee is zero. Thus if a premium has been paid for a lease, the purchaser should accumulate a sinking fund by putting aside a part of the income received during the period of the loan. Since such sinking-fund provision has to come out of income after tax has been paid, only pension funds and charities, who pay no tax on income (see pp. 60–1), are not penalised. As a result of the restricted market, yields on leaseholds tend to be higher than those on comparable freeholds.

(3) Freehold ground rents

Freehold ground rents (FGRs) refer to the annual payments received on long leases. Originally they were mostly charged on land leased for development, but they are now received for flats sold on long leases. Since they are small relative to the full value of the developed site upon which they are secured, the income is certain. Thus where reversion is distant, FGRs are comparable with irredeemable or very long-dated government stock although, being less liquid, yields are higher, particularly if management is involved (as with FGRs on flats).

Because of inflation, freeholders granting long leases have insisted on provisions for periodic revision of the ground rent or for profit-sharing or for some combination of both.

When reversion is less than 50 years, an FGR increasingly assumes equity characteristics, for its reversionary value will tend to rise. Its price will tend to be higher if it has a special value to a particular person, such as the current lessee of the property or a property developer who wishes to assemble land for future development.

(4) Mortgages

Mortgages are long-term money loans secured on real property, with interest payments being prior charges. Thus the risk of non-payment of interest or of capital is small. Unlike leaseholds, capital is repaid, and so no sinking fund is necessary. In effect, therefore, mortgages are similar to debentures or government bonds, and their yields tend to move together. On the other hand, because of inflation, mortgages on commercial and industrial properties are less attractive to the financial institutions, who now prefer to retain an equity interest – for example, through part-ownership, sale-and-leaseback or profit-sharing provisions.

5.2 Investors in real property

Investment in real property is carried out by private persons, private trusts and the institutions – insurance companies, pension funds, charities, property companies, property bond funds and property unit trusts. To some extent each has different objectives, and so their preferences differ.

(1) PRIVATE PERSONS
Anybody who purchases a property rather than renting is an investor. The satisfaction or return received should at least equal what could be obtained if, instead, premises were rented and the money invested elsewhere. For example, a person may rent rather than buy a shop either through lack of capital or because it is considered that the money can be more profitably employed in carrying stock, and so on.

Owner-occupiers, for example, shop-owners, farmers and householders, are holding wealth in the form of real property. They enjoy a full equity interest – income or satisfaction from the use of their property, and normally a hedge against inflation.

Other private persons investing in real property usually have only limited funds. Thus their direct investment tends to be restricted to dwellings and secondary shops. Indirectly, however, they can invest in prime shops and offices by buying property bonds or shares in property companies or unit trusts specialising in quoted property companies

(2) INSURANCE COMPANIES
By and large, life-insurance companies try to match assets to future liabilities, and this largely determines the spread of their portfolios as between short-term and long-term fixed-interest investments and equity holdings.

The post-war trend of insurance companies' asset holdings has been away from fixed-interest securities towards ordinary shares and, until 1980, towards property (see Table 5.1). In order to give endowment and life-insurance policies an 'inflation-hedge', companies introduced 'with profits' policies. As a result, until 1980, they increased their holding of property, concentrating, like other institutions, on office blocks on prominent sites in important commercial centres, shops in peak trading positions of key regional towns, and industrial property which is well located with regard to the motorway network.

Most property is acquired by direct purchase, but because of a shortage of the right type of property many institutions have participated directly in development, usually in conjunction with development companies, property companies and construction firms.

Table 5.1   Changes in the distribution of assets of insurance companies, 1968–2002

	Assets (% of total)					
	1968	1978	1984	1989	1997	2002
Short-term assets	1.4	6.0	2.6	6.8	5.7	7.2
Government securities	26.9	27.0	24.4	12.3	15.9	2.5
Ordinary shares	22.4	28.0	40.1	19.1	41.8	49.6
Preference shares and debentures	19.2	5.7	3.7	4.2	15.3	15.2
Overseas securities	–	–	–	15.0	12.1	14.9
Loans and mortgages	15.8	6.9	3.5	3.0	1.2	0.3
Land, property and ground rents	10.3	19.7	16.7	7.1	6.3	6.9
Other assets	4.0	6.7	9.0	32.5	1.7	3.4
Total	100.0	100.0	100.0	100.0	100.0	100.0

Insurance companies find it advantageous to own properties directly rather than through shares in property companies because:

(a) direct investment in property gives the company more control than an investment in property company shares;

(b) a substantial holding of the shares of a property company (necessary to exercise some control) may be more difficult to dispose of than a first-class building;

(c) the prices of buildings have tended to be less volatile than the prices of property company shares;

(d) the high gearing of a property company is of little advantage to an insurance company, which always holds part of its assets in fixed money terms; and

(e) holding shares in a property company represents an inefficient way to invest in property, since corporation tax is deducted from the profit attributable to dividend, whereas the insurance company pays a lower tax rate on life income.

Insurance companies still hold a part of their assets in mortgages as an alternative to fixed-interest-bearing stock.

(3) PENSION FUNDS

Pension funds now compete strongly with insurance companies and property companies for first-class properties, since the inflation-hedge helps to retain the real value of the accumulated pension funds.

The smaller pension funds invest in property indirectly through *pension fund property unit trusts*, whose trust deeds limit membership to pension funds and charities enjoying tax exemption. Such trusts afford the advantages of property investment without management problems. The larger funds, however, prefer to purchase and manage their own properties. The disadvantage of holding shares in property companies is even greater for pension funds than for insurance companies since pension funds do not pay tax on income or capital gains (see also p. 60) but since 1999 have been unable to reclaim tax credits on shares held.

(4) CHARITIES AND TRUSTS

Charities and trusts are concerned not only with income (from which periodic distributions are made) but also with retaining the real value of trust funds. Consequently, although they pay no income tax, they cannot invest entirely in high-yielding securities. For example, the Church Commissioners, who pay clergy stipends from investment income, endeavour to preserve the real value of that income by holding a part of their portfolio in equity interests, including property and farmland.

Unlike most institutional investors, charities receive little 'new' money for investment each year. They are therefore constantly reviewing their existing portfolios to see what possible adjustments could best serve their beneficiaries, both present and future.

(5) PROPERTY COMPANIES

Property investment and development companies have grown considerably since 1945, largely reflecting the boom in urban redevelopment. Most tend to be highly geared, their capital consisting of a high proportion of loans to ordinary shares. Properties owned provide the security against borrowing, while interest charges are covered by regular rents. High gearing is beneficial to the few ordinary shareholders when profits are good, and it makes it easier to retain control.

Today many non-property companies, such as Barclay's Bank or Blue Circle, have recognised the additional returns made possible by more active management of their properties. To this end a subsidiary company is formed – for example, Barclay's Property Holdings or Blue Circle Properties.

The larger companies tend to specialise in office blocks or prime shop properties, and a few (such as Slough Estates) in industrial property. Residential property investment is confined mainly to smaller companies, many of which engage in 'break-up' operations, selling houses and flats to sitting tenants or, when vacant possession is obtained, to owner-occupiers.

(6) FOREIGN INVESTORS

Overseas investment in UK property (particularly in central London) has increased considerably since the fall in property prices through the recession and the 1992 devaluation of sterling. Foreign banks have also been active in funding such purchases.

(7) PROPERTY BOND FUNDS

The person wishing to invest in property is faced with the snag of having insufficient funds to buy prime property, the kind which has shown the greatest capital growth. The property bond fund, a comparatively recent innovation, partly succeeds in overcoming this difficulty. Subscribers buy a number of units in a fund which invests the money in first-class property. Thus Abbey Life, now part of Lloyds TSB, had over £200 million invested in offices, shops and industrial property in the major cities of Britain, and also in Belgium, Holland, France and West Germany. Agricultural estates are also held. In this way the holder of property bonds has a wide spread in first-class property, with the value of the bonds varying directly with the value of the properties held. In conjunction with their agents, these funds take an active interest in the management of their properties, revaluing them at fixed intervals.

(8) PROPERTY UNIT TRUSTS
A similar principle operates with those unit trusts which specialise in property (for example, Cornhill Property Share), but in order to avoid management commitments, such unit trusts use their funds to buy shares in property companies or in companies such as hotels which are concerned with property.

(9) BUILDING SOCIETIES
Building societies can be regarded as institutional investors, since they are an important source of loans for house purchase. Their activities are analysed in Chapter 18.

As we shall see, demand for property as an investment asset has a considerable effect on its capital value and, through this, influences the supply of different types of property. We have to ask, therefore, what determines the level of yield on the different types of real property assets? Having answered this question, we can examine the influence of investment demand on the flow of different types of property on to the market.

Two aspects of property yields have to be considered:

(a) the *level* of yield, which reflects the relationship with general investment yields and is thus established within the context of national economic trends, government policy and comparative risks;
(b) the *pattern* of property yields.

Each will be discussed in turn.

5.3 The overall level of yield on investment assets in general

At different times all asset yields move in the same direction; it seems that the 'bench-mark' upon which they are based rises or falls. The question we have to answer, therefore, is: How is this bench-mark determined?

Alternative ways of holding assets

People can hold assets in many different forms – for example, money, bonds, debentures, shares, land, houses, paintings or antiques. All except money yield either a flow of income or direct satisfaction.

On the other hand, only money is perfectly liquid: that is, it can be changed into some other form without delay, cost or possible capital loss. The yield forgone by holding money is thus the opportunity cost of being perfectly liquid.

Questions of risk apart, a person will arrange his 'portfolio' of assets according to the emphasis he puts on liquidity as opposed to yield. If he wants complete liquidity, he will hold money; if he prefers some return, he holds other assets. There is a whole variety of assets to choose from. Figure 5.1 shows some examples.

In order to eliminate complications arising because assets differ in liquidity and risk, it is assumed that the only asset other than money is undated, fixed-interest government bonds. This gives us a model in which there are only two kinds of asset in which wealth may be held – money and bonds (see Figure 5.2).

The determination of the price of 'bonds'

Let us assume that, at any time, there is a given stock of money and a given stock of bonds available for holding as assets. This stock of money will equal the total supply of money (cash and bank money) in the economy less the amount demanded by persons and businesses for normal buying and selling operations.

Money	Building Society deposits	Treasury Bills	Debentures and mortgage loans secured on real property	Irredeemable bonds and freehold ground rents with distant reversions	FGRs with early reversions	Shares in companies	Freeholds

Figure 5.1 Alternative forms of holding assets

Figure 5.2 Holding assets as an alternative between money and 'bonds'

Now the price of bonds, as with other commodities, is expressed in terms of money. And, in our simple asset market, equilibrium will occur where, given the stock of money and of bonds and the preferences of the public for holding one or the other, a money price of bonds is established at which the public is willing to hold just the amount of bonds and money available. At any other price there would be no equilibrium. If, for example, the bond market price were below the equilibrium price, demand would exceed supply. In other words, there would still be some people preferring to hold money rather than bonds. As they switched, the price of bonds would rise until nobody wished to switch further. This would be the equilibrium price.

It should be noted that the equilibrium price of bonds can be viewed as the equilibrium rate of interest (yield) on bonds, since the two are inversely related. A 5 per cent bond (that is, one paying annual interest of £5 per £100 nominal value) will in fact be yielding a return of 10 per cent if its price on the market falls to £50. Conversely, should the price rise to £125, the bond yield would fall to 4 per cent.

This simple model explains the determination of the rate of interest, the 'bench-mark' for yields on the whole spectrum of assets. It should be noted that it is a 'stock' rather than a 'flow' theory. The justification for this is that neither the stock of money nor the stock of bonds is subject to great variations except over considerable periods of time. The supply of money is controlled by the government; the flow of bonds (new issues by borrowers) is small compared with the existing stock of old bonds. Current borrowing will thus have little effect on the 'bench-mark' rate of interest. It is therefore the supply from the existing stock of bonds, together with demand, which determines the price of bonds at any one time. The price at which new issues are offered is determined by the current price at which old bonds are being traded. The situation is parallel to that of the housing market (see pp. 47–8).

5.4 The pattern of yields on different assets with particular reference to property assets

The structure of interest rates and asset prices

We can now relax the assumption of a single income-bearing asset, bonds. In real life, wealth can be held in a range of assets differing in lender's risk, income yield and liquidity.

Lender's risk may relate to income or capital. A very short-term investment (say, in a Treasury Bill with only a few weeks to repayment) will be almost completely riskless so far as capital is concerned but provides no guarantee that the money repaid can be reinvested to obtain the same income yield, since short-term rates of interest may have fallen in the meantime. In short, such an asset would be capital-certain but income-uncertain. On the other hand, a long-term investment yielding a fixed money return (such as an FGR) is income-certain but capital-uncertain, since its market value will fall if interest rates generally should rise. Other assets such as shares in speculative mining concerns may be both income-uncertain and capital-uncertain.

What will be the condition of equilibrium for asset prices? Depending on: (i) the expected net income yield; (ii) the degree of risk as regards income and capital; (iii) liquidity (ease and cost of marketing); (iv) the asset preferences of the general public with respect to (i), (ii) and (iii); and (v) the relative stocks of each asset (including money), the answer is suggested in our simple money and bonds model. There will be some equilibrium pattern of asset prices and associated yields such that, after taking into account all transaction costs, nobody feels he can gain by switching between assets. With any other pattern some switching will be profitable and prices will change until there is equilibrium.

Real property assets can be slotted into this asset structure. Like the investor in stocks and shares, investors in real property will appraise an estate or investment for the same qualities specified above. In addition, there may be conditions which apply to property interests in particular, especially possible changes in government monetary and fiscal policy and attitudes to legal constraints and taxes on real property.

Thus a more realistic model of an asset market would be:

Money (M)
Treasury Bills (T)
Debentures or bonds with a fixed repayment date (D)
Irredeemable bonds (B)
Ordinary shares (S)
Mortgage loans secured on real property (Mo)
Leasehold investments (L)
Freeholds (FH)
Freehold ground rents (FGR)

Deductions from the model

We can deduce a number of propositions from this model:

(1) Since money is included in the asset pattern, any change in the economy's total supply of money, unaccompanied by a compensatory change in the transactions demand for money, will alter M. It will thus have a disequilibrating effect on the existing pattern of asset prices.

Suppose the monetary authorities were to increase the overall supply of money in the economy by open-market operations. If they buy Treasury Bills, M increases and T decreases; if they buy bonds, M increases and B decreases. In both cases the pattern of asset prices and yields is affected. Thus if the monetary authorities buy Treasury Bills, their yield will fall, and consequent switching operations will reduce all short-term rates. The prices of longer-term assets are also likely to be affected, though the speed and extent of the change will depend on market expectations. If the fall in short-term rates is expected to be reversed in the near future, there will be little profit in switching to long-term securities. In these circumstances, prices of short-term assets may rise considerably without inducing much change in long-term asset prices. On the other hand, if the change in short-term rates is regarded as a shift by the monetary authorities towards a permanent lower level of short-term rates, switching operations will be more pronounced, and long-term asset prices will rise in sympathy.

Thus expectations, and uncertainty with regard to them, blur the edge of any formal analysis of the asset market. Consider freehold investments as an example. To an investor, a freehold investment has two main aspects – the rent income and a 'growth' element depending on prospects of future increases in rent and capital value. Should monetary policy cause short-term interest rates to rise, the yield factor alone would dictate some switching out of freehold investments, bringing yields into line. But such selling is unlikely if expectations of growth are strong. Such expectations may be due to inflation, and if people think that the monetary authorities' raising of short-term rates is unlikely to be effective in controlling inflation, the prices of freeholds could be pushed up: that is, freehold yields may fall even though short-term rates are rising.

(2) The equilibrium pattern of prices will be affected by people's expectations of income from the various assets and their estimate of future capital appreciation. Thus an institution investing in a freehold showing a current yield of 6 per cent with five-year rent reviews must anticipate a compound growth in rent of 8.35 per cent per annum over twenty years to match a current return of 13.65 per cent on undated $2\frac{1}{2}$ per cent Consols.

People's attitude to risk will also affect the pattern of asset prices. Thus prices in a market dominated by widows and orphans seeking income-certain investments (such as government stock) will be different from one dominated by speculative investors primarily interested in capital gains (such as shares in oil-prospecting companies).

(3) Because all assets are, in varying degrees, substitutes for one another, a change at any point affects the equilibrium pattern and will result in switching until equilibrium is restored.

The extent of the change will vary according to the degree of substitution, close substitutes experiencing a greater movement than poor substitutes. For example, a switch from irredeemable government bonds to ordinary shares offering prospects of capital growth will lead to a fall not only in the price of bonds but also in the price of, say, FGRs with distant reversions. Similarly, the rise in the price of ordinary shares will be extended to freeholds since these, too, are likely to be affected by factors making for capital growth.

The prices of intermediate assets will move in sympathy according to their substitutability, on the one hand for government bonds, and on the other for ordinary shares. Eventually a new equilibrium pattern of asset prices will be established where there are no opportunities for profitable switching. Generally, property yields move in line with non-property yields. Of course, this consistency does not imply equality of interest. Differing risks, investors' asset preferences and cost of switching will all be reflected in the final equilibrium pattern of prices and yields.

The pattern of property yields

From the above analysis, it follows that in principle it is unrealistic to separate investments in real property from other investments. Although real property assets may incur extra costs of acquisition and management, they are not a homogeneous group of assets different from other assets in the market. Thus investors seeking income stability and certainty will regard FGRs and bonds as good substitutes for each other, while investors looking for capital-growth prospects will see more affinity between shares and freeholds than between shares and debentures. In other words, it is more informative to regroup our assets as follows:

$$[M \quad T \quad \mathbf{Mo}] \qquad [D \quad \mathbf{L}] \qquad [B \quad \mathbf{FGR}] \qquad [S \quad \mathbf{FH}]$$

where the bracketed groups each contain close substitutes having similar yields, and the *real property assets* (in bold type) are interspersed throughout the whole pattern. If, however, we wish to concentrate on property assets, we can extract from the above groups to give their pattern of yields. In real life the above assets would vary considerably even within particular categories – leaseholds, for instance, having different maturity times.

The complete investment decision

So far we have looked at interest in property as investments competing with other types of asset. But having decided on his broad strategy, an investor has to consider the detailed attributes of *similar* investments. Thus those who have decided to invest in ordinary shares must weigh up the respective merits of different companies. Similarly, if freeholds are preferred, a choice has to be made between the different properties being offered on the market.

Thus portfolio management consists not only of switching between different types of investment in general but also between particular investments within the same class.

The role of flows on to the asset market

After a disequilibrating event, equilibrium in our 'stock' model of an asset market was restored solely by switching operations. This was justified because the size of the stock of old securities dominates any new flows.

In practice, however, we must recognise that flows are continually coming on to the market in the form of new borrowing (which necessitates the issue and sale of new assets). This has two effects. First, flows tend to reinforce the switching of *existing* assets to restore an equilibrium pattern. This is because any additional supply of new financial claims through borrowing will tend to come from those sectors currently favoured by investors. Second, over a very long period of time, flows on to the market have a cumulative effect on the size of the stock, and thus affect the yield in the long term.

The effect of imperfections in the asset market

In a perfect asset market:

(a) there would be complete knowledge of prices and opportunities prevailing in every part of the market;
(b) there would be no barriers, such as dealing costs or day-to-day management obligations, to hamper switching operations or to put pressure on the form new flows (borrowing) should take;
(c) assets would be so divisible that they could be bought by many buyers each having a small amount of funds;
(d) investors would act solely on the basis of financial gain.

Given these conditions, the asset market would be a single market in which an equilibrium pattern of prices and yields would be established reflecting the size of the stock of different types of asset relative to investors' preferences.

In practice, perfection is not realised. Thus the high denominations in which Treasury Bills are issued mean that they can only be purchased by the institutions. In addition, there are the costs of buying and selling assets: for example, stamp duty, broker's commission, transfer stamp, and so on.

With real property assets, imperfections of the market are even greater (see Chapter 2). As a result, the prices of many real property assets, such as freeholds and leaseholds, may respond only very sluggishly to a change in another part of the asset market. Above all, certain characteristics of real property interests present barriers to investors wishing to move out of stock market assets. Thus, although Table 5.2 shows a correlation over time between yields on real property and other assets, those of the former tend to be higher than those of the latter. For instance, FGRs show a higher yield than long-term government bonds, while the yield of multiple shops is higher than that of ordinary shares except when the stock market is disturbed by special events or when the rate of inflation is high.

The main characteristics of real property interests which make for these higher yields are as follows:

(1) They are *less liquid*, as there is no central market comparable with the Stock Exchange.
(2) They are *less homogeneous*, so that the services of a valuer and solicitor are required, and transactions take time to complete while the title to the property is investigated.
(3) They are often *not divisible* into small and uniform units, thereby excluding direct purchase by the small investor (though 'unitisation' is helping to overcome this difficulty).
(4) Most interests *require management*, a function outside the experience and time of many investors. To pay for the services of an agent, a higher yield is required.
(5) Real estate is subject to *specific legislation* (such as rent controls, planning requirements) which may increase transactions costs and uncertainty regarding expected income.

5.5 Asset yields over time: an empirical study

The model

The previous section has developed a model explaining how yields on property assets are determined over time. While it emphasises short-term variations, it can also deal with long-term secular changes in yields.

As regards *short-run* yields, it is basically a stock theory. The main influence on the overall yield of assets lies in changes in the demand for money. Thus an increased desire to be liquid will result in the yields on all assets rising, including property yields. Suppose the initial impact is on undated government bonds: an increase in the demand for money will lead to a fall in the price of bonds and thus a rise in their yield. Bonds will now be cheap relative to property interests, particularly FGRs, thus giving a relatively higher yield. The holders of property interests will thus tend to switch into bonds. As this occurs, the price of bonds will rise and the prices of property interests will fall, until a new equilibrium set of relative prices is established such that nobody wishes to switch any further.

Table 5.2   Allsop & Co. yield tables 1960–94

Year end	Prime Offices	Prime Shops	Prime Ind/Whs	Secondary Shops	Prime Retail Whse	FTA All Share dividend yield	UK Clearing Bank Base Rate	Av. Building Soc. Rate	Long Term Benchmark Bond	Retail Price Index (base = 13.1.87)
Rent reviews commenced										
1960	7.00	5.50	10.00	7.00		5.00	6.00	6.00	5.60	
1961	7.00	5.50	10.00	7.00		4.75	6.50	6.28	6.50	
1962	6.00	5.50	10.00	7.00		5.50	5.25	6.61	5.40	
1963	6.00	5.50	10.00	7.00		5.75	4.00	6.27	5.50	
1964	6.50	5.50	10.00	7.00		5.00	6.00	6.16	6.10	
1965	6.50	6.00	9.00	7.50		5.25	6.50	6.63	6.20	
1966	6.50	6.00	9.00	7.00		6.00	6.50	6.95	6.40	
1967	6.50	6.50	9.00	7.50		6.50	6.00	7.20	6.90	
Sterling devaluation										
1968	7.00	7.00	9.00	7.50		5.75	7.50	7.46	7.60	
1969	6.50	7.00	8.75	7.50		4.50	8.00	8.08	8.50	
1970	7.50	7.50	9.00	8.00		5.00	7.50	8.58	9.30	
1971	8.00	7.00	8.50	7.00		5.75	6.00	8.59	8.30	
1972	5.00	6.00	7.50	7.00		4.00	6.00	8.26	9.60	
1973	5.00	5.75	7.50	9.00		4.50	11.00	9.59	11.90	
Oil crisis and serious inflation										
1974	7.50	7.50	10.00	13.00		10.00	12.00	11.05	17.00	
1975	6.25	6.25	9.00	9.00		6.74	10.50	11.08	14.80	
1976	6.25	5.75	9.00	8.00		6.10	11.19	11.06	15.00	
UK oil on stream										
1977	5.75	4.75	8.00	8.00		5.71	8.79	11.05	10.90	
1978	4.50	4.25	7.00	7.00		5.62	9.17	9.55	13.20	

All-time high interest rates										
1979	4.50	3.75	6.75	6.50		5.70	13.92	11.94	14.70	
1980	5.50	4.00	7.25	9.00	10.00	6.45	16.33	14.92	13.90	
1981	5.00	3.75	7.25	9.00	10.00	6.39	13.29	14.01	15.80	
1982	5.00	3.75	7.75	9.00	9.00	5.26	11.92	13.30	11.10	
1983	5.00	3.75	7.75	8.00	8.00	4.75	9.79	11.03	10.50	
Thatcherite growth										
1984	5.00	3.75	7.50	8.00	8.00	4.62	9.69	11.84	10.60	
1985	5.00	3.75	7.50	7.00	7.50	4.65	12.25	13.47	10.50	
1986	6.50	4.00	8.50	7.00	7.50	4.02	10.92	12.07	10.50	
1987	6.00	4.25	8.00	7.00	7.25	3.47	9.75	11.61	9.50	101.90
Inflation: recession										
1988	6.00	4.50	7.50	7.00	7.00	4.33	10.06	11.05	9.30	106.90
1989	6.00	5.00	8.00	8.00	6.75	4.22	13.83	13.65	10.00	115.20
1990	8.00	5.75	9.50	10.00	7.00	5.00	14.84	15.16	10.00	126.10
1991	8.50	5.00	8.75	9.00	9.50	4.93	11.68	12.47	9.73	133.50
UK leaves ERM										
1992	8.75	5.25	9.00	9.50	9.00	4.60	9.92	10.60	8.80	139.40
Growth resumed										
1993	7.00	4.50	7.50	7.75	7.00	3.59	6.00	8.00	6.75	141.00
1994	6.00	4.50	6.75	8.50	6.50	4.02	5.75	7.90	8.65	144.40
1995	6.25	5.00	7.00	8.50	6.50	3.85	6.75	7.92	8.29	150.60
1996	6.00	4.50	7.25	8.50	6.00	3.78	5.75	6.83	7.95	158.80
1997	6.50	4.00	7.00	8.25	5.50	3.37	7.00	7.70	6.90	159.30
1998	6.00	4.00	7.00	8.00	5.00	2.80	7.50	8.50	5.87	163.50

Source: Allsop & Co.

Two refinements, however, should be noted. First, because of the imperfections of the property market, there may be a time lag before property yields are brought into line with the rest of the market. Second, since the total value of property interests is small relative to stock market investments, changes in demand for the latter are likely to dominate the asset market. Only in abnormal circumstances, for instance, as in 1980–3, is the property market likely to initiate changes in yields.

Once the overall trend of asset yields has been established, variations in the yields between assets can be explained by differences in the demand for the different types of asset (see p. 64) and the relative supply situation. For example, the low yields on prime shops and offices are the result of the high demand of institutions coupled with their relatively limited supply.

In the *long run* the yield on an asset will be affected from the supply side through the accumulation of flows over time. If the price of equities is relatively high (yields low), selling shares will represent the cheapest way for firms to raise capital for expansion. If this continues over a considerable time, the accumulation of these flows will have a significant influence on the stock of equities, so that, other things being equal, their price falls (yield rises).

Investment yields, 1938–60

The long-run trend over the period 1938–60 was for yields on assets to fall until 1949, and thereafter to rise.

The inter-war period was dominated by the depression. Because government stock offered certainty of yield compared with equities and most property interests, its yield was consistently lower. Furthermore, under Chancellor Dalton's 'cheap-money' policy (1945–9), the money supply was increased and, with no change in liquidity preference, the price of government bonds rose, Consols, for instance, yielding only around 3 per cent.

However, in 1949 Dalton's policy broke down. Investors considered that the high price (low yield) of Consols could not be maintained. As they began to sell, their expectations were self-justified. Yields rose, and in 1951 Bank Rate was raised. The year 1949 therefore represents the watershed; since then there have been fluctuations around an upward trend in asset yields.

Initially, however, the yield on fixed-money-interest-bearing assets (including FGRs) was still low in comparison with equities and freeholds. Earnings on ordinary shares and property were rising with the general increase in prosperity and the gradual dismantling of controls. Historically, too, yields on equities had always tended to be higher than the yields on government stock because of the greater risks involved. This risk factor dominated until 1959. Thereafter the yield on ordinary shares, and eventually on freeholds, became lower than the yield on Consols. We have the phenomenon of the 'reverse yield gap', a situation produced by inflation.

Inflation and the pattern of asset yields, 1960–2003

Inflation has dominated the yield on assets since 1960 (Table 5.2). First, it affected relative yields, people requiring sufficiently high yields on 'money' bonds to allow for a fall in the value of money. In contrast, over a long period, equity interests offer some hedge against inflation. At first, ordinary shares were favoured, but investors, particularly the institutions, saw the advantages of prime property. By 1972 the yield on offices was little more than that on equities, and on agricultural land it was lower. It should be noted, however, that the figures shown in Table 5.2 apply only to prime properties, those favoured by institutions. The shortage of these properties tended to force down the yield considerably in comparison with secondary properties, though, as substitutes, these too experienced some fall in yields. Second, inflation led to restrictive government measures to protect the balance of payments. Rates of interest rose; earnings on shares and property looked less rosy. In such circumstances yields on assets generally rise.

Political crises, too, tend to produce short-term rises in yields. Not only do they create uncertainty about future earnings, especially as government measures usually involve increased taxation, but people generally seek to be more liquid. Asset prices therefore fall. The movement is accentuated if previously a speculative position had been built up.

This is illustrated by the events of 1971–4. The Heath government, intent on growth, increased the money supply. This made spending easier, the effect being felt on the asset, house and consumer-durable markets. Asset yields fell, as did the real rate of interest, that is, the nominal rate less the rate of inflation.

But inflationary pressure forced the government to take counter-measures, including in November 1972 a freeze on business rents which sparked off a liquidity crisis in the property market. When the oil crisis in late 1973 gave a further twist to inflation, pessimism spread to the Stock Exchange. In both markets people had invested in expectation of continually rising prices, and this speculative position led to larger falls than would otherwise have occurred.

The pattern was repeated in the 1980s. High interest rates to combat inflation led to recession in 1979–82. Thereafter until 1987 asset prices recovered strongly, boosted by the growth in national output, a fall in the annual rate of inflation to 2 per cent, the collapse in world oil prices and a fever of 'take-over' bids. But renewed inflation forced the government to raise the rate of interest in stages from 1988. How this affected the economy generally, and the property and construction industries in particular, is described in Chapters 8 and 19.

As a result of the rate of inflation being held at close to 2.5 per cent since 1995, it is now accepted that the UK has entered a period of low inflation. Residential property prices have risen dramatically since 2000, however, and there have been fears that this could undermine the government and Bank of England strategy on inflation as housing costs soar and homeowners spend from their rapidly increasing equity. Returns on all UK property were much greater than those for equities or UK gilts in the period 1998–2001, as can be seen in Table 5.3.

5.6 The effect on the real property market of the demand for land resources as an investment

Occupation and investment demand

We have said that real property interests are wanted for (a) *occupation*, because they yield utility or profit, and (b) *investment* – that is as a means of holding assets – and as such are regarded as alternatives to other types of asset. But investment demand cannot be completely separated from occupation demand, since the amount of rent paid will affect the capital value of the interest just as the size of the dividend paid on an ordinary share affects its price.

Demand and supply in the asset market will generally produce equilibrium prices and yields for all the various assets. There will thus be a given 'acceptable yield' for each different kind of property interest which, in its turn, will be partly dependent on the yields of comparable stock market assets. In other words, the price of a land resource will depend heavily upon the price of substitute assets in the 'asset market'.

Table 5.3   Nominal returns on equities and gilts 1970–2001 (% per year)

	UK property	UK equities	UK gilts
1970–2001	11.8	14.4	11.4
1970–1980	14.9	12.8	9.2
1980–1990	11.8	18.5	14.0
1991–2001	10.5	11.4	10.4
1996–2001	12.6	6.9	9.3
1998–2001	11.1	0.5	3.8

Sources: ATIS REAL Weatheralls, Investment Property Databank, Barclays Capital.

As an example of such a substitute asset, let us take a blue-chip ordinary share, such as Unilever. Such a share has (i) actual current earnings, (ii) prospective earnings, and (iii) an inflation-hedge based largely on (ii). People bid in the market for it according to how it compares with other assets, such as gilt-edged stock and alternative blue-chip shares. Now, while the size of the earnings on a Unilever share is relevant, the important point is that such earnings are capitalised at the rate of yield which is acceptable on a Unilever share *compared with other types of asset*. If earnings double, but 'acceptable yield' remains unchanged, the price of the share will double; if earnings remain unchanged, but 'acceptable yield' is halved, the price of the share will likewise double.

Similarly with land resources. Office blocks are wanted by investors, chiefly institutional ones. Their current earnings are capitalised at a rate which reflects their likely future earnings and their inflation-hedge *compared with alternative assets*. This capitalisation rate may enhance their value considerably *irrespective of actual earnings* – that is, irrespective of the demand for occupation purposes.

Centre Point, a controversial office block development in London, provides an example. Here two factors served to increase its value to at least £45 million in 1972:

(a) earnings potential increased as rents rose because of occupation demand for offices; and
(b) acceptable yield on prime office blocks fell from 6 per cent to 4 per cent (note also that some of this investment demand may be speculative, driving up the price and lowering the yield still further).

Suppose Centre Point cost £15 million to build (including normal profit) and that potential current earnings were £900 000 a year. Therefore, if the going rate at which office blocks are capitalised is 6 per cent, its capital value would be the same as its cost, £15 million.

If now the rent doubles to £1 800 000, the capital value of Centre Point will increase to £30 million.

Now assume that, with this higher rent, the acceptable yield on office blocks falls from 6 per cent to 4 per cent. The capital value of Centre Point will now be £1 800 000 times 25 – that is, £45 million.

The effects of changes in the capitalisation rate

Changes in the rate at which earnings are capitalised have important effects on the real property market.

First, they influence the relative supply of the different types of property. The resources of the construction industry are diverted into office-building rather than into properties, such as rented flats, which are capitalised at a lower rate.

Second, they increase the cost to the public sector of its own construction (for example, of roads, schools, hospitals) since resources have to be bid away from producing high-priced offices. For this reason, in times of rising property prices, there tends to be a proportionate falling off in gross fixed capital formation in the public sector.

Third, they can have adverse effects on the working owner-farmer. Suppose a farmer owns 500 acres which he bought by means of a loan for £200 000, that is £400 an acre, some twenty years previously. If the rate of interest which he has to pay is 15 per cent, he must make at least £60 an acre per year (after all other costs and normal profit have been covered) to justify his capital outlay.

Now suppose that the Church Commissioners decide to invest in land. They buy 3000 acres which they let at £60 an acre, the going rate. But it is the yield which they are prepared to accept on this investment which is of vital importance. Suppose this is 5 per cent. Other institutions in the market will accept a similar yield, and competition forces the price up from £1 200 000 (originally £400 an acre) to £3 600 000 (that is, £1200 an acre).

This has important results for the working owner-farmer.

(a) He has a windfall capital gain – though this is of doubtful value unless, with his family, he is retiring from farming.
(b) It could raise the amount of inheritance tax payable on death should the present 100 per cent relief on farmland be reduced.
(c) As a result of (b), there is a tendency towards fragmentation of agricultural estates.
(d) Because the capital outlay is prohibitive, tenant farmers are unlikely ever to become owners of large farms.
(e) Until 1988 farms became increasingly owned by institutions since the working farmer could not compete with them in the market. However, with the decline in medium-term prospects for agriculture, the institutions have sold many of their farms (see p. 57).

Summary

Investment is both purchase of existing assets (e.g. property investment) and the creation of new fixed assets (e.g. property development). Property investment can be made in freeholds, leaseholds, freehold ground rents and mortgages.

Investors in real property include private persons, insurance companies, pension funds, charities, property companies, foreign investors, property bond funds, property unit trusts and building societies. Property investment is one of a number of possible asset investments that can be made. Other possible investments include government bonds (gilts) and equities (shares). A portfolio of assets may well contain some of each type of investment. Since 1996, property has out-performed both gilts and equities in terms of return on capital invested.

Review questions

1. What determines the yield on freehold investments?
2. Explain the advantages and disadvantages of the main types of freehold investment.
3. Explain what is meant by 'reverse yield gap'.
4. How has the pattern of UK asset yields changed in the last fifty years?
5. Explain why the yields on real property interests may be higher than those on other assets.

Recommended Reading

P. Ambrose and B. Colenutt, *The Property Machine* (Harmondsworth: Penguin, 1975).

P. N. Balchin, J. L. Kieve and G. H. Bull, *Urban Land Economics and Public Policy*, 5th edn (London: Macmillan, 1995) ch. 4.

M. Ball, C. Lizieri and D. MacGregor, *The Economics of Commercial Property Markets* (London: Routledge, 2001).

M. Brett, 'Who does what in property', *Estates Gazette* (27 January 1990).

N. Enever, *The Valuation of Property Investments* (London: Estates Gazette, 1977) chs 2–6, 11 and 13.

W. D. Fraser, *Principles of Property Investment and Pricing*, 2nd edn (London: Macmillan, 1993).

PART III

DEVELOPMENT

CHAPTER 6

The Development Process

After studying this chapter you will be able to:

- **Explain how and why development takes place**
- **Explain the functions of a developer**
- **Show how development takes place for economic reasons and how it ensures efficient use of land resources**
- **Illustrate different methods of project evaluation**
- **Explain the economic rationale for intensity of site use**

6.1 The nature of development

Why development takes place

Over time the demand for land resources changes, brought about by changes in the size, income and tastes of the population, the rate of growth of economic activity, methods of transport, techniques of production and distribution. On the supply side, existing buildings wear out or become less suitable to present uses, and the cost of constructing new buildings or adapting old buildings changes. Development is the response to such changes.

Indeed, the development process may itself be dynamic, one development generating development elsewhere. Thus a house-owner who gives his property a face-lift may stimulate his neighbours to do likewise. As a result, demand increases for nearby houses which can be improved, and eventually a whole neighbourhood may be upgraded, a process often referred to as 'gentrification'. Similarly a comprehensive replacement of large houses by blocks of flats can lead to the redevelopment of a shopping centre in order to serve the needs of the increased population.

As a result of such changes in the conditions of demand and supply, some structural change of buildings is usually necessary. This may take different forms:

(a) *modification of the existing building* through refurbishment (for example, new office or shop layouts) or conversion (for example, houses divided into flats, offices converted into residential apartments);
(b) *redevelopment*, where existing buildings are demolished and replaced by new ones;
(c) *new development* through outward expansion on undeveloped land (for example, suburban housing).

All these usually require planning consent. As a rough yardstick, therefore, development covers those projects which entail planning consent.

The importance of development in the UK economy

While the figures in Table 6.1 include depreciation, they nevertheless indi-cate the relative importance of development in the UK economy for 2001.

Development in the private and public sectors

In the *private sector* development is carried out by (i) occupiers, or (ii) specialist developers, or (iii) by financial institutions, property companies or construction firms working through the price system.

The advantage to the occupier of initiating his own development is that he obtains a building which is tailor-made to his individual requirements. But

Table 6.1   The importance of development in the United Kingdom, 2001
(current prices)

(a) Gross Domestic Product		£988 014 m.
(b) Gross Fixed Capital Formation		£162 244 m.
(c) Gross Fixed Capital Formation in:		
(i) dwellings	£25 537 m.	
(ii) other buildings and structures	£43 837 m.	
		£69 374 m.
(d) (c) as a percentage of (b)		42.8
(e) (c) as a percentage of (a)		7.0

Source: The United Kingdom National Accounts (The CSO Blue Book).

development involves know-how and highly specialised skills not usually found in the main business of the occupier, and only a few firms are large enough to have their own property division responsible for development. Most occupiers wishing to develop their own property, therefore, compromise by employing a specialist developer, such as Bovis. They submit a specification of their requirements for a building, and the developer endeavours to meet these on previously agreed terms.

Irrespective of whether the development is carried out by the occupier or a specialist developer, the same basic decisions and calculations have to be made, for (given competition) each has to pay the full opportunity cost in order to secure a site.

Public-sector development accounted in 1998 for 8.3 per cent of total development, but the percentage varies from year to year. Most public development decisions are taken on a mixture of political, social and economic grounds. Public development therefore tends to fluctuate both with the politics of the government in power and the current overall requirements of its stabilisation policy. In Chapters 6–10 we concentrate on commercial development in the private sector, analysing in particular how it functions within the price system. Chapter 11 is concerned with public development decisions.

6.2 Problems of the developer

Functions of the developer

The commercial developer may be defined as an entrepreneur who provides the organisation and capital required to make buildings available in anticipation of the requirements of the market in return for profit. This definition emphasises that the developer is essentially an 'entrepreneur' accepting the unsheddable risks of producing for an uncertain demand. Consideration of his functions will reveal not only his major problems but also the risks involved.

(1) HE RECOGNISES THE POTENTIAL FOR DEVELOPMENT
In essence this means (i) estimating future demand for alternative uses of existing land resources (see below), and (ii) calculating the cost of building for new uses. From among these different uses he must choose the scheme which will produce the maximum net return subject to the constraints involved: for example, the availability of finance, planning and building requirements and legal restrictions in the title or use of the land.

His initial assessment will cover the physical nature of the site (soil-bearing, drainage, slope), the availability locally of adequate construction capability, and, if residential, social amenities (schools, shops, health services and so on) and environmental aspects (open spaces, trees, compatible land uses nearby).

Thus the developer bears the uncertainty of the scheme. On the demand side, returns may be less than estimated, the result, for example, of economic depression, increased taxation or new rival projects. On the supply side, planning permission may be delayed, construction costs escalate or the cost of finance rise.

(2) HE ASSEMBLES THE SITE

This involves buying the proprietary rights over the land as they become available until the whole site has been assembled. But there may be difficulties in acquiring certain interests which exploit the monopoly power inherent in their unique situation. As we shall see in Chapter 10, this can involve collaborating on a partnership basis with the local authority – but with some loss of profit to the developer.

Again he may, by improving accessibility, enhance the value of a site. Usually this involves providing a road. But British Gas and Bud Developments paid much of the £50 m. extra cost of diverting the extension of the Jubilee Line to take in Greenwich so that a derelict 276-acre site there could be developed profitably.

Assembling the site and the actual construction take time. This exposes the developer to a possible fall in the profit estimated; for example, the government may restrict office development or construction costs may escalate. In any case, he has to allow for certain costs additional to those of acquiring the land and construction. These additional costs can be divided into *ripening costs* and *waiting costs*.

Ripening costs arise through holding land in anticipation of profitable future development. They cover the interest on capital tied up, plus any speculative element which has been paid for the land above its current use value in the hope that eventually planning permission for a higher use will be forthcoming.

Waiting costs are incurred, even when the land already has planning permission, because construction takes time and it is necessary to span the period before revenue from the development is received. Such costs, therefore, include professional fees and interest on stage payments.

(3) HE OBTAINS THE NECESSARY PLANNING PERMISSION

This involves negotiating with the local authority to secure the most profitable scheme.

After checking the statutory development plan and other documents, such as Planning Permission Guidance Notes (PPG) of the Department of the Environment (ODPM), the developer will probably make contact with the local planning officer. Not only will this acquaint him with the authority's thinking, but it can be a valuable public relations exercise in that it indicates a willingness to co-operate.

Naturally the developer will seek the maximum possible flexibility in the planning conditions in order to meet the requirements of prospective purchasers or tenants. On the other hand, since interest charges on finance for the site are accruing, he may be forced to compromise in the interests of speed.

The authority may provide a *planning brief* for the specific site or group of related sites. This indicates probable constraints and the authority's requirements regarding density, layout, building type and materials. Often these views are the result of previous unsuccessful planning applications. Alternatively, the brief may accompany the *outline* planning permission in which case it is really a *design brief*, since it covers the design details which have to be submitted within three years.

(4) HE ARRANGES FINANCE (SEE CHAPTER 8)

(5) HE GETS THE PROJECT BUILT
This includes avoiding as far as possible extra costs through delays in construction or modification of the original design.

(6) HE ARRANGES THE FIRST LETTING OR SALE OF THE DEVELOPMENT
The developer may retain the whole or part of the development. Retention of a development provides asset backing for future borrowing and a steady rental income which serves as a cushion against *a slump* in receipts *from new developments* (as in 1991– see Chapter 9). On the other hand, the developer has now to manage the property, becoming in part a property company. In practice, the decision on retention may hinge on the availability of finance. For instance, an insurance company might only lend for a commercial development on condition that upon completion it obtains the freehold interest.

With large projects, these functions are likely to be performed by a team of specialists consisting of an architect, quantity surveyor, letting agent, and so on. At their head is a project manager, who may be the developer himself. Indeed today insurance companies and property bond funds may not only supply the finance for development but also fulfil the uncertainty-bearing role of the developer by directly employing such a team to find, evolve and carry out development schemes.

The rationale of development

Development is necessary to ensure the efficient use of land resources. In the main the life of a building ends not because the structure is physically worn out but for *economic* reasons. Sometimes operating costs exceed revenue and, because there is no alternative use, the structure is abandoned, as, for example, in the case of Cornish tin mines. More usually the site can be used more profitably. As we shall see, the developer who can put a site to its most profitable use can make the highest bid for it. Thus, given a competitive price system, land resources are used to their greatest efficiency. However, it is important to note that the developer's bid is based solely on his private benefits and costs. Externalities may justify government interference in the development process.

The decisions of the developer

The basic question which the developer asks is: Will the value of a replacement building exceed the value of the present building plus the cost of rebuilding? If so, redevelopment will be profitable. In order to arrive at this fundamental decision, the developer has to:

(1) choose between development projects;
(2) estimate demand for different developments;
(3) decide on the quality of the building;
(4) calculate how intensively the site shall be developed;
(5) estimate how much he can bid for the site;
(6) obtain finance;
(7) decide whether to develop alone or in partnership with a local authority.

The first five decisions are examined in this chapter, and the last two in Chapters 8 and 10 respectively.

6.3 Choosing between capital projects

Basic difficulties

The development of land resources involves present capital expenditure in return for an anticipated flow of future benefits. Where, as usually happens, capital funds are limited, or where only one development is possible on a given site, projects are said to be 'mutually exclusive'. It is essential, therefore, to choose the project whose value exceeds the cost of the factor inputs used by the greatest amount. This means that projects have to be 'ranked'.

Ranking, however, poses problems. First, with different projects, benefits are received and costs incurred at different points of time. Second, the future is uncertain. Third, benefits and costs, particularly in the public sector, may be difficult to measure. In this chapter we concentrate on methods of dealing with the first two difficulties. Chapter 10 considers the third.

Table 6.2 Differences in capital projects

Project	Initial capital cost (£000)	NAR (£000)			Terminal value
		Year 1	Year 2	Year 3	
A	100	50	50	50	Nil
B	100	100	10	–	Nil
C	100	–	50	120	Nil
D	100	100	50	–	Nil

Differences in capital projects

Capital projects can differ as regards (a) initial outlay; (b) phasing of capital expenditure; (c) size of expected yields; (d) timing of future yields; (e) certainty of yields; and (f) estimated life and terminal value (if any).

Table 6.2 illustrates four hypothetical projects. It is assumed that (i) such projects are competing alternatives; (ii) all have the same initial expenditure which covers the total cost of the project; and (iii) there is no terminal value. But they differ as regards the size and timing of expected yields. To simplify, we deal in terms of future net annual revenue (NAR), that is, the gross annual return (for example, from rents) less annual management, maintenance and repair costs. NARs are assumed to be net of tax and to accrue at the end of each period.

Methods of evaluation

Projects can be evaluated by different methods which vary in complexity. In general, the simpler ones are only preferred where special considerations apply.

(1) COMPARATIVE COST
Here a straight comparison is made between the initial capital costs of projects – which may be the determining factor when funds are limited. Otherwise it suffers from the obvious weakness that it fails to take into account the size and timing of NARs; all projects in Table 6.2, for example, being rated equally.

(2) CUT-OFF PERIOD
This method chooses a period by which the initial cost must be recouped. If in our example this period were two years, all projects except C would be acceptable, preference being given to D on account of its higher total yield. The difficulty is that project C is rejected solely because returns, although

considerable, accrue late in its life. Nevertheless, using a cut-off period to choose D could be justified – for example, if D hinges on an innovation which cannot be protected by patent and is likely to be copied by other firms within two years or if political uncertainty or financial coustraints necessitated recouping the initial cost within two years.

(3) PAY-BACK PERIOD

Here investment options are ranked according to how long income yields take to recoup the initial outlay. In our example, both B and D achieve payback in year 1. This method can be justified where uncertainty as regards future cash returns – for example, for a small firm lacking diversity – or obsolescence of equipment is marked, for then a possible quick exit must be borne in mind. But it fails to take account of: (i) differences in the timing of yields earned before the pay-back date; (ii) yields earned after the pay-back date. On the latter count, for instance, D is obviously superior to B.

(4) AVERAGE RATE OF RETURN

This can be calculated in various ways.

(a) Adding the NARs, dividing by the years of the project's life, and expressing this average as a percentage of the initial cost. For D this would be:

$$\frac{150}{2} \times \frac{100}{100} = 75 \text{ per cent}$$

and for C:

$$\frac{150}{3} \times \frac{100}{100} = 50 \text{ per cent}$$

(b) Obtaining a *net* average rate of return by adding the NARs, deducting the initial capital outlay, dividing by the number of years, and expressing this net average yield as a percentage of the initial outlay. This gives:

$$D = \frac{150 - 100}{2} \times \frac{100}{100} = 25 \text{ per cent}$$

and

$$C = \frac{170 - 100}{3} \times \frac{100}{100} = 23 \text{ per cent}$$

This method has two main disadvantages. First, it depends upon the number of years chosen. If, for instance, in Year 3, D had an NAR of 20, it would cease to rank above C, although its overall profitability had

increased! Thus the method produces a bias in favour of short-term investments having high yields. Second, it ignores the pattern of yields, higher
earlier *NARs* being treated the same as low later ones.

The major criticism of the above methods is that they fail to take into
account both the number and the timing of yields. Other things being equal,
the greater the number of *NARs*, the more profitable the investment. Similarly, early *NARs* have the advantage that they can be reinvested. The
number and timing of yields are allowed for by the *net present value* and
the *internal rate of return* methods described below.

(5) NET PRESENT VALUE

Here the future *NARs* of the investment are discounted at a target rate of
interest (see pp. 157–61) to give their present value. The net present value
(*NPV*) of the project equals the sum of these discounted *NARs* minus the
capital cost of the project. For example, if we take 8 per cent as the rate of
interest for discounting, the present values of the *NARs* of project *A* are:

$$\frac{50}{1.08} + \frac{50}{(1.08)^2} + \frac{50}{(1.08)^3} = 128.9$$

Thus the net present value is 28.9.

Ranking the above projects according to *NPV* would give: *C* (38.1), *D*
(35.5), *A* (28.9) and *B* (1.2). All show positive *NPV*s and are therefore
acceptable, but if borrowing was subject to a limit, the rule would be: accept
all schemes from the highest *NPV* downwards until the capital budget has
been exhausted. In general,

$$NPV = \sum_{t=0}^{t=n} \frac{B_t}{(1+i)^t} - \text{capital cost}$$

where *B* is net benefit (*NAR*), *i* is the target rate of discount and *t* the life of
the project in years. A project is profitable where $NPV > 0$.

It should be noted that:

(a) The *NPV* of a particular investment depends upon the rate of discount
used: the higher the rate of discount, the lower will be the *NPV*.

(b) Where projects differ in their patterns of *NARs*, the ranking of projects
can depend upon the rate of discount chosen. For example, comparing
projects *C* and *D* for rates of discount of 8 per cent and 20 per cent gives
the information contained in Table 6.3.

The reason for the reversal of ranking when the rate of discount increases
to 20 per cent is that *NARs* for *C* are realised later in the project's life, and
the higher rate of discount penalises later benefits more heavily. Alternatively, we can explain the situation by considering the rate of interest at
which earlier *NARs* can be reinvested to provide a sinking fund to cover the
cost of the project. Since project *D* has earlier *NARs*, raising the rate of

Table 6.3 NPV at rates of discount of 8% and 20%

	8%	20%
C	38.1	4.2
D	35.5	28.0

interest at which these can be reinvested means that eventually they out-weigh *C*'s larger, but later, *NAR*s.

(6) YIELD – THE INTERNAL RATE OF RETURN (IRR)
This method involves finding that rate of discount at which all future *NAR*s from the project would have to be discounted to make their sum equal to the initial capital cost. More generally:

$$\sum_{t=0}^{n} \frac{B_t}{(1+r)^t} = K$$

where *B* = net benefits, *r* = the *IRR*, and *K* = the initial capital cost.
    For example, for project *A* we have:

$$\frac{50}{1+r} + \frac{50}{(1+r)^2} + \frac{50}{(1+r)^3} = 100$$

where *r* equals the *IRR*.
    This is found either by solving the equation for *r* or, more practically, by trial and error using valuation tables. Thus using *PV* of £1 tables (single rate, no tax), discounting at a rate of 24 per cent gives a *PV* of £99.1 (too high a rate), while 23 per cent gives £100.6 (too low a rate). The rate to give *PV* of exactly £100 can be obtained by interpolation: it is 23.38 per cent, say $23\frac{1}{2}$ per cent. A similar process gives the *IRR* for the other projects: $B = 8\frac{1}{2}$ per cent; *C* = 22 per cent, D= 37 per cent.
    The advantages of the *IRR* method are:
(a) No rate of discount has to be specified (as with *NPV*), since *r* is deter-mined by expected *NAR*s.
(b) It conforms with the more usual business practice of comparing rates in order to assess profitability. All projects are profitable if their *IRR*s are greater than the appropriate borrowing rate of interest. But if projects are mutually exclusive or there is a budget constraint, they have to be ranked, which can still be done according to their *IRR*s.
(c) No substantial recalculations are necessary should the cost of borrowing change.
(d) It is easier to take account of risk than with the *NPV* method since the margin between the *IRR* and the appropriate borrowing rate of interest will indicate whether there is sufficient to cover risk.

Nevertheless, where a choice has to be made between different projects, the *IRR* ranking may differ from the *NPV*s. This happens where the *NPV* is calculated at a low rate of discount, for here, in comparison, the *IRR* discriminates against later-benefit projects, as follows.

Since the *IRR* is calculated for an $NPV = 0$, it must always be greater than a rate of discount which produces a positive *NPV*. We can illustrate this by calculating the *IRR*s for projects *C* and *D* from Table 6.2. *D* (37 per cent) ranks above *C* (22 per cent). This confirms the *NPV* ranking (Table 6.3) for a rate of discount of 20 per cent of *D* (28 per cent) and *C* (4.2 per cent). The reason is that a 20 per cent rate of discount is fairly close to the *IRR*s.

However, a discrepancy arises when the rate of discount diverges considerably from the *IRR*s. At a rate of discount of 8 per cent, *C* (38.1 per cent) is ranked above *D* (35.5 per cent Table 6.3).

To guard against such a discrepancy when using the *IRR* method, the correct procedure would be to compare the *incremental* yields of *C* and *D* – their different cash flows. *D* has an *NAR* of 100 in Year 1, whereas *C* has an *NAR* of 120 in Year 3. That is, with *C*, an effective outlay (income forgone) of 100 yields 120 in two years' time. This is equivalent to a yield of 9.5 per cent, whereas *D*'s initial 100 can only earn the market rate of 8 per cent when reinvested. Thus *C* is preferable to *D*.

Calculation of an incremental yield is also necessary when the capital costs of projects differ. If one scheme is cheaper but has a higher yield, it is necessary to calculate the incremental (marginal) yield on the additional sum invested. For example, if there were no constraints on borrowing at 10 per cent and only one building could be erected on a site, it would obviously be more profitable to invest in a project costing £15 million and yielding 15 per cent than one costing £150 000 and yielding 100 per cent! On the other hand, allowance would have to be made for the tendency of risk to increase with the size of an investment.

The conclusion is that we should test projects by both *NPV* and *IRR* methods to ensure that they do not differ. In general, the *NPV* method is safer. In effect it chooses the market rate of interest at which to invest early benefits, whereas the *IRR* assumes that early benefits can be reinvested at the rate of return on the project, a somewhat higher (and more doubtful) figure.

Allowing for risk and uncertainty

So far we have treated expected future benefits and costs as if they will actually occur. In practice, however, they are not certain, and in assessing projects allowance has to be made for the risk of forecasts being wrong. How should this be done?

In economics it is usual to distinguish between *risk* and *uncertainty*. With the former there is a known probability distribution. With uncertainty (which arises, for instance, through a change in consumer's demand or a change in technology), the 'law of large numbers' does not apply. However, the methods described below, with the notable exception of the application of probability distribution, apply equally to both risk and uncertainty.

Most methods in general use can best be described as 'rule of thumb'.

(1) For very risky projects, a *cut-off period*, for example, three or four years, can be adopted (see p. 87).
(2) A *percentage addition* to costs or a *percentage reduction* in benefits can be made where these are uncertain. In practice, however, this method really provides only for over-optimism, and there are risks apart from this.
(3) A *risk premium* can be added to the discount rate when calculating present values. That is

$$NPV = \sum_{t=0}^{t=n} \frac{B_t}{(1+i+p)^t} - \text{capital cost}$$

where p is the risk premium. Not only is this method simple, but it also penalises distant returns, where uncertainty is considered to be greater, more heavily. However, this presents difficulties because: (a) it is unlikely that risks are so orderly as to be constant in each year; (b) the risk premium penalises projects where benefits are mainly received late in life; and (c) it gives the decision-maker no guide as to how large the premium should be.

Where the *IRR* method is used, it has to be judged whether the estimated yield provides sufficient margin to cover the risk involved.

More systematic ways of allowing for risk are:

(4) Applying the mean of the *probability distribution* for the different risks involved, for example, the probability of a building project exceeding the stipulated completion date. The difficulty here is that while two distributions can have the same mean, they may differ significantly in their dispersions.
(5) Making a *sensitivity analysis*. For example, where there is doubt over the exact rate of discount which should be applied to future *NAR*s, different discount rates can be used to indicate how a change in the rate would affect the viability of the project. The method can be applied to other variables, such as occur in construction costs or changes in the future rate of inflation. It is thus possible to highlight the more sensitive variables and the degree to which the profitability of a project could be affected by even minor variations in a single component of the total calculation. On the other hand, a sensitivity allowance is limited in the number of variables it can embrace for otherwise the range between the

Table 6.4 Uncertainty and the returns on projects

	Possible NPVs (£m)		
Project	Optimism Best	↔ Medium	Pessimism Worst
A	14	7	4
B	17	8	2

best possible outcome and the worst could be so wide as to provide little real guidance to the decision-maker.

(6) For uncertainty, *rule of choice* can be formulated for different degrees of certainty. The rule chosen depends upon whether the planner is optimistic and can afford to take risks, or whether he is pessimistic and cannot take a chance on possible bankruptcy. In the former case the rule would allow him to maximise the possible return, while with the latter he would seek the best possible minimum return.

For example, Table 6.4 gives possible outcomes at different degrees of optimism for two different projects, A and B. Thus the most optimistic outcome for A is 14 and the most pessimistic is 4, whereas for B the most optimistic is 17 and the most pessimistic 2. It is likely that a large firm (such as Wimpey) having many projects or capital reserves can afford to be optimistic. It therefore adopts a policy of 'maximax' by choosing project B. On the other hand, a small firm with fewer projects and less capital reserves would have to take a more cautious view. If an *NPV* of £4 m is necessary to cover building costs, it must choose project A, since the worst possible outcome of B could lead to bankruptcy.

While 'games theory', of which the above is an example, may provide no definite solution to the problem (as for the large firm above), it does allow the developer to consider uncertainty possibilities in a logical form.

6.4 Estimating demand

The *NPV* of a development indicates to the developer the likely value of the completed project. Since the *NPV* depends upon the stream of future *NARs*, demand for the type of building and its operating costs both now and in the future have to be estimated.

The problem of estimating demand for a small, single development differs somewhat from that of a city-centre project. We can illustrate this by concentrating on shop developments.

Single development

With a single development, a guide to the likely selling-price can be obtained from current market information. If, for instance, enquiries from estate agents reveal that, in the same shopping area, a prime shop unit with vacant possession sells for £200 000, the developer has a yardstick for his own project, since this price has been reached in a market where buyers and sellers have taken into account present and estimated *NAR*s. Similarly, a recently-agreed market rent of, say, £16 per square foot of shopping space would reflect the current *NAR*.

The developer would adjust such prices to his own particular project by allowing for differences in location, nearness to multiples, complementarity with similar shops, occupation rates (if a specialist shop) and features such as layout, storage facilities and staff accommodation. Consideration would also have to be given to the possibility of similar new developments rivalling his in the near future. Some indication could be obtained by an examination of the development plan and of the register of outstanding planning consents and current applications.

Other adjustments could cover how quickly the type of shop sells or lets and the adaptability of the lay out to selling different goods as demand changes or to introducing new techniques of retailing.

City-centre projects

In the past, shopping areas have developed along high streets on a shop-by-shop basis. But post-war new town projects, comprehensive redevelopment of city centres and suburban growth of the more prosperous towns have necessitated planning in advance the size and layout of shopping areas.

The developer has first to estimate the overall demand for shopping facilities, both current and future. The major influence will be the number of people likely to fall within the catchment area of the shopping centre. Furthermore, the structure of this catchment population must be analysed as regards its age, composition, household formation rates and socio-economic groupings. Census information should help with these details.

Other influences on demand include the current national economic climate and the possibility of future changes in the rate of growth, inflation, the interest rate and government policy. And, since the value of a shopping complex relies heavily on the economy of its immediate location, a similar analysis must be carried out for both the region and the town, especially as regards the level of employment, whether the employment has a stable base or is largely dependent on one industry or employer, and the likelihood of future expansion through the influx of new industries.

One approach to estimating the demand for a shopping centre and its power to attract retail spending from other centres is as follows.

The size of the *shopping space* must be related to estimated overall demand for shopping facilities and the extent to which there is a present deficiency.

In practice, this demand is usually expressed in terms of the *total value of retail turnover*. From turnover in existing shopping centres, a floor-space ratio (*FSR*) for each particular type of shop can be obtained, using the formula

$$FSR = \frac{\text{Units of floor space}}{\text{Turnover in current prices}}$$

This known *FSR* can then be applied to the forecast retail sales of the new shopping centre: floor space required = FSR × forecast retail sales. Since each type of retail shop will have a different *FSR* (jewellery, for example, with its low physical turnover will have a higher *FSR* than groceries), the total floor space requirement will be an aggregate of the floor space requirements of all shops in the shopping area calculated according to their individual *FSR*.

While this technique can provide a rough guide to estimating shopping space, it has three main weaknesses. First, it depends on the accuracy of the forecast of total retail turnover. Second, the 'units of floor space' in the formula will itself be dependent on shop rents. If these are high, increased turnover may be met by more intensive use of existing floor space rather than by adding to it. Third, the method ignores the power of a new shopping centre to attract customers from a rival centre.

Reilly's law of retail gravitation covers this last problem. Examining shopping habits in the USA in the 1920s, W.J. Reilly concluded that, as a general rule, two cities will attract retail spending from the area between them in direct proportion to the size of the city's population and in inverse proportion to the square of the distance to the city from any particular point in the area between. Thus a city of 320 000 population located four miles from the intermediate area will attract twenty times as much trade from it as a rival city of 49 000 located seven miles away; that is:

$$\frac{320\,000}{16} : \frac{49\,000}{49} = 20 : 1$$

We can apply the theory to derive the retail catchment area of a city. Supposing we have a smaller town of population P_1 and a larger town of population P_2, there would be some point between them where a household would be indifferent whether it shopped in town 1 or town 2 (see Figure 6.1). According to Reilly's law, the location of such a point is determined by the formula:

$$\frac{P_1}{(d_1)^2} = \frac{P_2}{(d_2)^2}, \text{ that is } \frac{\sqrt{P_1}}{d_1} = \frac{\sqrt{P_2}}{d_2}$$

But $d_1 + d_2 = D$, the distance between the two cities, so the last expression can be written:

$$d_2\sqrt{P_1} = (D - d_2)\sqrt{P_2}$$
$$= D\sqrt{P_2} - d_2\sqrt{P_2}$$
$$d_2\sqrt{P_1} + d_2\sqrt{P_2} = D\sqrt{P_2}$$

Dividing through by $\sqrt{P_2}$, we have

$$d_2\frac{\sqrt{P_1}}{\sqrt{P_2}} + d_2 = D$$

$$d_2\left(\frac{\sqrt{P_1}}{\sqrt{P_2}} + 1\right) = D$$

$$d_2 = \frac{D}{\frac{\sqrt{P_1}}{\sqrt{P_2}} + 1}$$

Thus d_2 locates the watershed of city P_2 as regards its 'pulling power' relative to P_1 and is defined once we know D, P_1 and P_2.

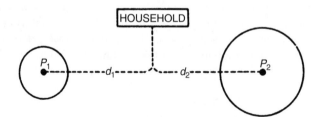

Figure 6.1 Reilly's law of gravitation

Though this crude formulation illustrates the basic technique for evaluating shopping developments, refinements are necessary. Because a city's power of attraction rests on spending power rather than on just its population size, consideration has to be given to the composition of the population (for example, by age group and working proportion), its earning capacity (for example, whether they are skilled workers), government subsidy policy within the district and the spending habits of different income groups. Ease of transport between the intermediate area and the centre is also relevant.

More important, dynamic factors must be taken into account. Thus some allowance would have to be made for future population growth. Above all, a new, large shopping centre may generate its own growth. For example, specialist shops may so enhance the reputation of such a centre that it will grow more rapidly than smaller centres in the area.

Not only the size but also the *layout of a new shopping centre* must be planned carefully. With a single shop development, the subsequent provision of a municipal car-park nearby or the opening of a 'big name' store next door would increase revenue-earning capacity.

In contrast, with a comprehensive city-centre development, such external-ities are under the developer's control. That is, externalities can be 'internal-ised' to maximise the value of the total area. This means relating the shopping area to public transport and car-parks, and then siting shops in order to secure *complementarities*, referred to later in Chapter 14 as 'special accessibility'.

Such complementarities arise because retailers of a certain type can achieve enhanced turnover by trading next or close to retailers of a similar or compatible type or even of a completely different nature. It is therefore essential to secure the optimum 'tenant mix' (sometimes referred to as 'merchandising') by planning the size, shape and location of shops in order to maximise the value of aggregate turnover, for this in turn should maxi-mise rentals.

The developer is likely to start from the key retail outlet, such as the department store or supermarket. Secondary magnets, such as banks and the Post Office, are then located, and multiples positioned between them. The object is to generate movement of shoppers around the whole centre by avoiding the creation of dead spots through the concentration of too many important magnets in one area. The remaining space is then allocated to the specialist shops, such as jewellery, shoes, cameras and clothing, having regard to their complementarity preferences. Thus food stores prefer to be located together, with the specialist shops, such as delicatessen and patis-serie, being close to the supermarket. Other trades, such as stationers, hairdressers, florists, restaurants and toy shops, are less demanding, but they add colour and variety to the centre and so have to be carefully located in order to secure the overall objective.

Since different types of shop have different requirements as regards window space (cameras, jewellers), show space (furniture), customer-circulating space (clothiers) and storage space (ironmongers), merchandising demands detailed planning in advance, especially if there is to be flexibility to meet future changes in requirements.

6.5 Optimum construction outlay

Revenues are determined not only by the use to which a site is put but also by the capital outlay on the building erected. Questions to be answered are:

(1) What refinements should be incorporated in the building?
(2) To what extent should higher initial capital costs be incurred in order to save future maintenance costs?
(3) How intensively should the site be developed?

As we shall see, the answers to these questions all hinge on the principle of equating marginal revenue and marginal cost. More specifically, any addition to construction outlay must be at least covered by the addition to *NPV* from the resulting higher net revenues. We shall discuss the first two questions in this section; the third, and most important, in Section 6.6.

The quality of refinements

When deciding on refinements, such as lifts and air-conditioning in offices, the basic question is: How much will such refinements add to revenue? If the enhanced *NPV* exceeds the cost of installation, such refinements should be incorporated.

Capital costs as opposed to maintenance costs

For most buildings there will be some possibility of trading off higher initial construction costs against reduced maintenance costs. Here again the same marginal principle applies.

If higher initial building costs lead to lower future maintenance costs, *NAR*s will be greater than for a building costing less. We therefore have to choose that combination of construction costs and discounted *NAR*s which will yield the highest *NPV*. Here the rate of interest and expectations of future wage-rates would be major determinants. A high rate of interest penalises projects whose returns are received further in the future, such as a building with initial capital costs. Thus a high rate of interest operates in favour of a low-capital/high-maintenance building. On the other hand, maintenance costs tend to be labour-intensive, and if wage-rates are expected to increase more than other factor rewards it would give an advantage to the dearer, low maintenance-cost building.

However, over and above these considerations, the imperfection of the capital market may impose a budget restraint so that a cheaper building has to be erected.

6.6 The intensity of site use

Buildings as the addition of capital to land

As well as determining the best use of a site, the developer has to decide how intensively it shall be developed. If, for instance, the most profitable use of a large suburban site is for housing, to what density should the houses be built? Or, if an office block is to be built in a city centre, how many storeys upwards (given no government restrictions) shall it go? In economic terms, how much capital shall be combined with the site?

Although the two decisions – most profitable use and capital-intensity of development – are arrived at simultaneously, we shall simplify the analysis by assuming that the best use has already been determined, confining the immediate discussion to capital spending on the actual building.

Combining capital with a fixed supply of land

Since we are dealing with a particular site, we can regard land as a fixed factor. To simplify the explanation, we shall assume that the project has a life of one year and that all returns are received at the end of the first year. (The obvious example of this in practice would be where a non-renewable one-year lease is held on a vacant site).

The problem now resolves itself into the familiar one of applying units of a variable factor, which we shall term 'capital', to a fixed factor, land. It is assumed that:

(1) All costs of developing the site – material and labour costs, ripening and waiting costs, legal fees and normal profits – are capital costs.
(2) The capital unit may be an unspecified physical amalgam of materials and labour with the return and cost likewise unspecified (see Figure 6.2(a)). Alternatively, we can be more precise, defining the capital unit as £100-worth of capital factors, with the cost of this unit for the year thus being £100 + the going rate of interest (see Figure 6.2(b)).
(3) There is perfect competition in both the capital and product markets. Thus all the capital the developer requires can be obtained at a given price, and the product sells at a given price per unit. The latter means that the marginal physical product curve can be regarded as the marginal revenue product curve since *MRP* equals *MPP* times the price per product unit whatever the output. The *MRP* is *net*, operating costs having been deducted.
(4) A site is being developed for offices, with one suite of offices occupying one storey. It is assumed that the height of the office suite makes no difference to the rent, and so, following from (3), each suite lets at the same rent.

(5) There are no government controls on height, and developers are free to bid for the site.

As extra units of capital are applied to the fixed site, the law of diminishing returns eventually comes into operation, and the *MPP* of capital falls. This is because building upwards incurs extra costs; for example, a more expensive substructure is necessary, labour costs per unit rise with height, and lifts and fire escapes have to be provided. Thus the return on given additions to capital eventually decreases, giving a downward-sloping *MRP* curve (see Figure 6.2). Since all capital can be obtained at a given price (assumption [3] above) the *MC* curve is horizontal.

Development of the site will take place up to the point where marginal revenue equals marginal cost: that is, to where the *MRP* of a unit of capital equals the cost of a unit of capital (*OB* in Figures 6.2(a) and 6.2(b)). The building reaches its optimum height, i.e. the development is complete, when *OM* units of capital have been applied to the site.

6.7 The amount which can be paid for the site

In Figure 6.2 total proceeds of the development will be *AOMC*, and the total capital cost *BOMC*. In practice, the developer will have plans of the optimum building to be constructed, and he can obtain preliminary cost estimates based on these plans. In addition, he will have to cover waiting and ripening costs, extra costs arising from the operation of escape clauses, overheads and normal profit. All costs will be included in *BOMC*. Thus the maximum which he can pay for the land is the residual, *ABC*, the shaded area.

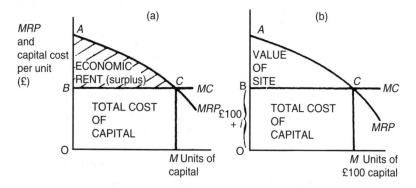

Figure 6.2 Applying capital to a fixed site

Corollaries

Certain corollaries follow from our assumptions and analysis.

(1) If offices were the only or the best use to which the site could be put, *ABC* would represent the demand price for the site. Thus if the site were 1000 square metres in size, its demand price would be £*ABC*/1000 per square metre. *Competition among developers would ensure that this price was in fact bid.*

(2) Suppose, however, there was an alternative use (for example, a departmental store) with greater productivity. This would be shown by the higher *MRP'* curve (Figure 6.3) giving a larger residual surplus. The developer who recognised this use could bid more for this site. Thus competition ensures that the site goes to its most profitable use, for this has the largest residual surplus.

(3) Competition also ensures that the site is developed upwards to the point where $MR = MC$, where *ABC*, the bid for the site, is a maximum. Thus, not only does the site go to its most profitable use, but the type of building upon it is the one which secures the highest possible yield – having regard to the cost of alternative sites (see below).

(4) A *higher building* and a *higher site price* will result either from a rise in the *MRP* of capital or from a fall in the rate of interest.

A rise in the marginal revenue productivity of capital from *MRP* to *MRP'* (Figure 6.3) could occur through: (i) an increase in the marginal *physical* product as a result of improved techniques (such as self-service selling) or increased productivity of the construction industry; (ii) higher revenue – for example, from increased prices of the existing product supplied by the building or from a new higher use as the demand for another good increases or planning permission is granted. The height of the building increases from *OM* to *OM'*.

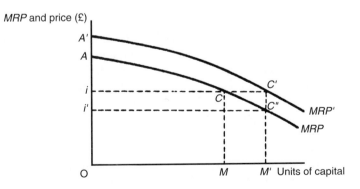

Figure 6.3 The effect of change in the productivity of capital or in the rate of interest on the height of a building and on site value

A fall in the rate of interest would lower the cost of each capital unit – for example, from Oi to Oi^1 again increasing the height of the building from OM to OM^1 (using the MRP curve).

Similarly, the *price of the site* will rise from AiC to $A'iC'$ when MRP rises to MRP' or from AiC to $Ai'C'$ when the rate of interest falls to Oi'.

(5) From the viewpoint of the individual developer, land is a cost; he has to pay the competitive market price in order to obtain it. His argument therefore runs as follows: 'The higher the price of land, the more I have to economise in its use. Thus a site has to be used more intensively by applying more capital per square metre. High land prices have caused high buildings.'

Now while this may be quite true from the viewpoint of the individual, our analysis of the *land market as a whole* turns the argument on its head: (i) where demand, as reflected in the rent attainable, is high, the use capacity of land is high; (ii) this means that a highly intensive use of land is profitable; and (iii) because high building is profitable, land values are likely to be high.

Relaxation of the one-year-life-project assumption

We can now relax our assumption that the project has a life of only one year. Provided that we assume that the price of capital and the price of the product do not change over time, the above solution holds, for yields can be discounted back to their present value according to the year in which they are obtained and then added together. The area $AOMC$ in Figure 6.3 will now represent the value of the aggregated discounted yields throughout the estimated life of the project.

The extensive use of land

By building higher, the developer is in effect saving on the cost of land. But diminishing returns mean that the cost of obtaining a given addition to revenue increases. Thus the developer will only build an extra storey so long as this is cheaper than acquiring extra land. In other words, there is a 'margin of building' in terms both of intensive use (adding an extra floor) and of extensive use (adding extra land).

Suppose the demand for office suites in a district increased. A developer could respond either by adding a storey to a building or by building a ground-floor suite on undeveloped land. The alternative adopted would be that which cost less to produce a given addition to revenue.

In practice, competition for land for different uses will ensure that, in the long run, development everywhere will be pushed to the point where the

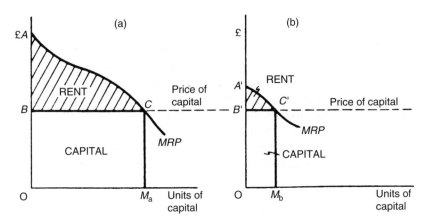

Figure 6.4 The intensive and extensive use of land

marginal return to capital is equal to the marginal cost of capital for every site. Thus in Figure 6.4, plots of land of the same size are developed for (a) the city-centre site by the addition of capital OM_a, and for (b) the suburban site by the addition of OM_b. In the first case the rent is ABC, and in the second $A'B'C'$.

To sum up, it is the strength of demand, represented by MRP (Figure 6.4) which determines simultaneously both land prices (the shaded areas) and density.

6.8 The choice of development project

Where only one project is possible on a given site, the developer has to choose the one which is most profitable – that which yields the highest NPV. The answers to the questions considered above will provide the essential data for comparison purposes – the expected $NARs$ from different projects, how $NARs$ fall as the height of the building increases, the initial capital cost and subsequent maintenance costs.

Having done their calculations, developers compete with each other to obtain the site. The developer who can recognise the most profitable use (often described as the 'highest and best use') can make the highest bid. As a result, given perfect knowledge, a competitive price system and no external costs or benefits, the site is used in the most efficient way.

Summary

Development takes place in response to changes in the demand and supply of land resources. It includes modification of existing buildings, complete re-development and new development on greenfield sites. Development is an important part of overall UK investment and a significant part of GDP.

Developers perform a range of functions, acting as entrepreneurs who recognise development potential and bear the risks of the project. A variety of different methods are available to developers to enable them to evaluate development projects. The developer's decision on intensity of site use is subject to the law of diminishing returns – basically units of a variable factor (capital) are applied to a fixed factor (land) up to the point where the *MRP* of a unit of capital equals the cost of a unit of capital.

Review questions

1. What factors influence the decision to redevelop land and buildings?
2. What are the main functions of the developer?
3. Explain the basis of a project evaluation based on net present value.
4. Explain how risk and uncertainty can be coped with in evaluation of development projects.
5. Use a diagram to explain what determines the intensity of site use in a development project.

Recommended reading

D. Chiddick and A. Millington (eds) *Land Management: New Directions* (London: E. & F. N. Spon, 1984) section 5.

J. Harvey, *Modern Economics*, 7th edn (London: Macmillan, 1998) chs 10, 11 and 22.

Mainly for Students, 'Merchandising', *Estates Gazette*, vol. 239 (4 September 1976) p. 740.

M. Newell, *An Introduction to the Economics of Urban Land Use* (London: Estates Gazette, 1977) chs 2, 3, 5 and 11.

A. Parker, 'Tenant Mix', *Estates Times* (28 April 1989).

J. Ratcliffe, *Urban Estates Management* (London: Estates Gazette, 1979) chs 7–12.

W. J. Reilly, *The Law of Retail Gravitation*, 2nd edn (New York: Pilsbury, 1953).

M. Roberts, *An Introduction to Town Planning Techniques* (London: Hutchinson, 1974).

K. E. Way, 'Viability in Property Development', *Estates Gazette*, vol. 239 (4 September 1976) p. 705.

CHAPTER 7

The Timing and Rate of Redevelopment

After studying this chapter you will be able to:

- Explain how the timing of redevelopment is an economic decision
- Show how changes in property demand can affect rental income
- Show how changes in property supply can affect operating costs
- Explain how a change in the rate of interest is likely to affect the development decision

7.1 The timing of redevelopment

When does redevelopment take place?

Where land is already developed by having a building on it, fixed capital is embodied in the land. Such capital has no cost in the short period; as a result, redevelopment to a new use, which requires expenditure of further capital, usually occurs only after a considerable period of time.

In general terms redevelopment takes place when the present value of the expected flow of future net returns from the existing use of the land resources becomes less than the capital value of the cleared site. We have therefore to calculate the present value of the land resources in their current use and compare this with the value of the cleared site. Our method of arriving at both values follows the present value method. It is assumed that over the period under consideration there is no change in the value of money. But it should be noted that the rate of discount used for calculating present values has, over the last three years, been related to an interest rate which will keep the yearly inflation rate at 2.5 per cent.

The present value of the land resources in their current use

It must be emphasised that we are seeking to establish a *capital* value. Since this depends on the *net* returns expected to be earned in future years, such returns must first be estimated and discounted to the present and then aggregated in order to arrive at the present capital value.

(1) THE EXPECTED NET ANNUAL RETURNS FROM CURRENT USE

The net annual return (NAR) during any given year of the life of a project is the difference between the gross annual return (such as the rental received) and the operating costs (including repairs and maintenance). Since we are dealing with the future, both the gross annual return (GAR) and the operating costs are estimates – shown diagrammatically in Figure 7.1.

As the years go by GAR is likely to decrease because: (i) where there were super-normal profits accruing to the initial development, they will encourage similar developments, and this will lower future returns – for example, from rents; and (ii) expectations are subject to greater uncertainty and risk the further one looks ahead. Offsetting these, complementary developments may come along, thereby exerting an upward pressure on rents.

In contrast, operating costs rise as the years go by because: (i) the structure deteriorates physically; and (ii) the older the building, the less adaptable it is to new technical requirements, such as modern office machinery, parking for car shopping.

(2) DISCOUNTING AND AGGREGATING NARS TO OBTAIN PRESENT CAPITAL VALUE

The NARs for the whole of the future life of the building have to be discounted to the present and then aggregated in order to obtain the present value of the land resource in its current use (see Figure 7.2).

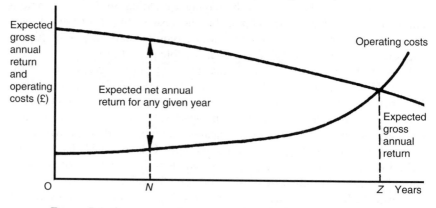

Figure 7.1 Gross annual returns and operating costs over time

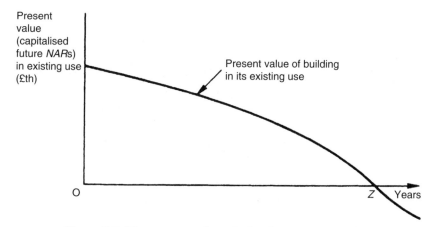

Figure 7.2 The present value of a land resource over time

In Figures 7.1 and 7.2 *NAR* and present capital value both become zero after *OZ* years. If no redevelopment has taken place by then, the land resources are left derelict, as with Cornish tin mines and Welsh slate quarries.

This can be summarised as:

$$P = \sum_{t=i}^{n} \frac{R_i - O_i}{(1 + r)^i}$$

where:
P = value of property in current use
n = period when *GAR*s can be earned in current use
R_i = *GAR*s from i to year n
O_i = operating costs, excluding depreciation, from i to year n, and
r = rate of discount

The value of the cleared site

At any one time, the value of the cleared site is equal to the present value of the most profitable alternative use *less* the cost of clearing the site and rebuilding for this new use (see Figure 7.3).

(1) THE PRESENT VALUE OF THE MOST PROFITABLE ALTERNATIVE USE
This is obtained by the procedure used for calculating the present value of the current use: (i) the future *NAR*s in the best alternative use are calculated; and (ii) these *NAR*s are discounted to the present and aggregated to give a capital present value, DD_1 in Figure 7.3.

It will be observed in Figures 7.2 and 7.3 that in year 0, when the existing building was constructed, the present value in the current use (*OP*) was

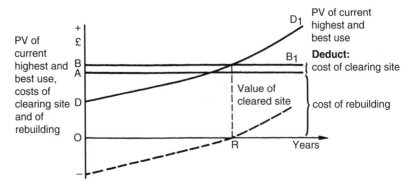

Figure 7.3 The value of the cleared site

greater than the present value in the new alternative best use (*OD*). It was for this reason that the land went to its current use. From then on, however, the value of the alternative use (*DD₁*) rises. This occurs for two main reasons. First, changes in the conditions of demand and supply (discussed later) mean that a new building, being specifically designed for the new use, will earn higher *NAR*s. Thus an old office building will give way to one that is air-conditioned and has the structure and space suitable for modern office equipment. Second, any new building would probably have a longer time horizon than the old building (which has already run a part of its life) so that there would be more future *NAR*s to aggregate to obtain its present value.

(2) DEDUCTION OF THE COST OF BRINGING THE SITE TO ITS ALTERNATIVE USE
From the present value of the best alternative use at any one time, we have to deduct: (a) the cost of demolishing and clearing the site (*AB* in Figure 7.3); and (b) the total cost of rebuilding for the new use, including ripening costs and normal profit (*OA*). For simplicity, we have assumed that costs (a) and (b) both remain constant over time. *BB₁* represents the sum of (a) and (b).

The present value of the cleared site is thus the difference between *DD₁* and *BB₁* in any given year. In year *O* the value of the best alternative use would be only just below that of the chosen current use, for then each was competing for a cleared site. However, once a site has been allocated to a given use and has had a building erected upon it, any new use has the additional handicap of demolishing and rebuilding. Thus, until year *R* the value of the cleared site is negative.

Using the previous notation, and assuming that *R′* and *O′* to refer to the best alternative use, and

C = the value of the cleared site
D = the cost of demolition and clearing the site
B = the cost of rebuilding to the new best use, we have:

$$C = \sum_{t=0}^{n} \frac{R'_i - O'_i}{(1+r)^i} - D - B$$

(3) REDEVELOPMENT OF THE SITE

By combining Figures 7.2 and 7.3 in Figure 7.4, we can show when redevelopment takes place. From year R the value of the cleared site is positive and increasing and eventually in T exceeds the present value of the building in its current use. Thus redevelopment takes place in year T, when $C = P$ (the value of the cleared site equals the current use value).

It should be noted that in year T the building is still *technically* efficient, for it can earn a *NAR* until year Z. However, in year T it becomes *economically* inefficient because resources can be switched to a new use having a greater value. Thus we can define the economic life of a building as that period of time during which it commands a capital value greater than the capital value of the cleared site.

7.2 The rate of redevelopment

Method of approach

The diagrammatic model can be used to analyse all redevelopment situations.

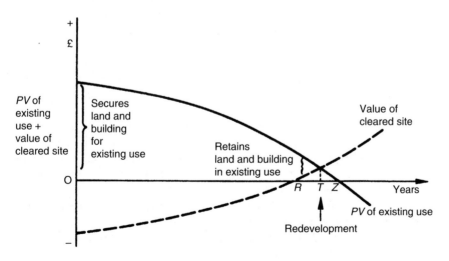

Figure 7.4 The timing of redevelopment

By way of illustration, we shall examine the *rate* of redevelopment. The rate of redevelopment will depend upon changes which occur over time in the relationship between:

(1) the present value of the existing use of the land resources;
(2) the present value of the best alternative use;
(3) the cost of rebuilding.

It will be accelerated if (2) increases relative to (1), or if the cost of rebuilding falls. It will be retarded if opposite changes occur. What we have to consider, therefore, are the factors affecting (1), (2) and (3).

Present value depends upon expected future *NAR*s and the rate at which they are discounted to the present. This rate will be common to both existing and alternative uses. We can thus concentrate on the *NAR*s of each, the difference between *GAR* (*rentals*) and *operating costs*. Rentals are concerned largely with changes on the demand side, operating costs with changes on the supply side.

Changes on the demand side affecting rental income

Let us assume that the current use of a site in the city centre is large residential houses and that the best alternative use is offices.

A change in the *demand for large city-centre houses* can arise through changes in: (i) tastes (such as a switch in preferences towards flats or smaller suburban houses); (ii) real income (for instance, people tend to move out-wards to more spacious gardens as their income increases); (iii) the distribution of income (for example, higher taxation of the rich forces them to vacate expensive city-centre houses); (iv) the price of substitutes (such as cheaper suburban houses); (v) transport costs or facilities (for example, fare increases or the building of a motorway or underground railway); (vi) mortgage terms; (vii) complementary activities (such as new schools or golf courses in the suburbs); (viii) government policy (for example, making planning permission to convert large houses to flats conditional upon the provision of off-street parking).

Similarly, rents from offices, the alternative use, would be affected by changes in both occupation and investment demand. Thus a rise in *occupation demand* for professional services or for offices in city-centre positions would increase rents, while government dispersal policy would tend to decrease them. But since *NAR*s depend largely on *expected* future rentals, *investment demand* would increase the capital value if such rentals were expected to increase. Put in an alternative form, the current yield on offices would be capitalised at a lower rate for investment purposes, thereby increasing the capital value of offices.

Changes on the supply side affecting operating costs

Basically the same considerations apply to both houses and offices, but we shall illustrate the former. With houses, operating costs may change because: (i) maintenance costs and repairs change – for example, builders' charges may rise, or repairs may be curtailed (as, for instance, in the twilight zones of towns); (ii) technical improvements may allow conversions to a more intensive use, so flatlets may become economically viable as a result of cheaper partitioning and the development of compact units incorporating a sink, refrigerator and electric cooking facilities; and (iii) government policy may alter – for example, improvement grants will reduce conversion costs, whereas more stringent fire-precaution regulations will increase them.

The effect on the rate of redevelopment of a change in the rate of interest

A change in the rate of interest is unlikely to have equivalent effects on both the present and alternative use.

First, at any given time a part of the physical life of a building has passed. Thus the years of future yields are fewer, and its present capitalised value is less. In contrast, the next-best-use building has not yet begun its life, so that there are more yields to be capitalised. This means that a rise in the rate of interest will favour the present use since it applies to fewer future yields. In other words, it will reduce the value of the next-best use more than that of the current use.

Second, a higher rate of interest will increase ripening and waiting costs, thus decreasing the present capital value of the next-best use.

Figure 7.5 illustrates how, for the above reasons, a rise in the rate of interest brings about changes in the position of the capital-value curves of the present and next-best uses. The net result of a rise in the rate of interest is to retard redevelopment from year T to year S; a fall in the rate of interest would tend to accelerate it.

Third, in addition to a rise in the rate of interest, the imperfection of the capital market may mean that certain forms of development may encounter additional penalties. Thus house purchasers tend to rely more on borrowed funds than do insurance, industrial and property companies. For instance, insurance companies have a net inflow of premium income, while large firms can usually borrow temporarily from a bank when the rate of interest seems high, funding the loan later when the long-term rate has fallen. In contrast, house purchasers will find that a higher rate of interest will reduce the maximum loan available through the building societies' and banks' income/repayment ratio constraint on lending.

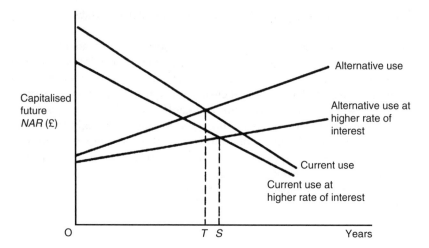

Figure 7.5 The effect of a rise in the rate of interest on redevelopment

Building costs

Redevelopment will be accelerated by a fall in real building costs because this will increase the value of the cleared site. Such a fall may occur through increased productivity in the construction industry or improved technology, for example, in the building of high-rise office blocks. In contrast an increase in building costs will retard redevelopment.

Relaxation of the assumptions of a perfect market and perfect competition

Conditions in the real world may affect the pace of redevelopment:

(1) Imperfect knowledge, immobility of factors, or just inertia, may mean that it takes time for profitable redevelopment to get under way.
(2) Imperfections of the capital market may affect the type of development. For instance, houses may be built instead of a block of flats because selling the former on completion gives the developer an earlier cash flow.
(3) Legal restrictions, such as a covenant prohibiting the building of a particular type of shop, may postpone redevelopment until another type of shop becomes competitive with the current use.
(4) There may not be perfect competition in the supply of sites. Thus publicly owned land might not be offered for sale, while some owners of sites essential to the complete development exercise their monopoly power in the price they demand
(5) Government policy, particularly as regards planning, may prevent redevelopment for certain uses. On the other hand, the exercise of

compulsory purchase powers may make it easier to combine interests and so accelerate development – for instance, for slum clearance. Other examples of government policy affecting the rate of development are taxation policy (for example, residential and commercial buildings cannot be written off as depreciation), improvement grants (which encourage the modernisation of owner-occupied or rented, older, residential properties), and the Leasehold Reform Acts of 1967,1993 and 2002 (which, by enabling owner-occupiers to purchase the freeholds of their leasehold interests, have made it virtually impossible to retain estates intact for future comprehensive redevelopment).

Summary

Redevelopment takes place when the expected value of the expected flow of future net returns from the existing use of land resources becomes less than the capital value of the cleared site. The rate of redevelopment depends on the relationship between the present value of the existing use, the present value of the best alternative use and the cost of rebuilding. An increase in the rate of interest is likely to retard development because its effect on present values of the alternative use will be greater than its effect on the present value of the current use.

Review questions

1. **Why are operating costs of buildings likely to rise over time?**
2. **Why are property returns (rents) likely to decrease over time?**
3. **Explain the determinants of the rate of redevelopment of land resources.**
4. **Show how demand changes can affect the rental income from a property; and how supply changes can affect operating costs of a property.**
5. **Explain why a rise in the rate of interest is not neutral in its effects on the present value of existing and alternative uses of a land resource.**

Recommended Reading

J. E. Manser, *Economics: A Foundation Course for the Built Environment* (London, E&FN Spon, 1994).

D. Myers, *Economics and Property: A Coursebook for Students of the Built Environment* (London: Estates Gazette, 1994).

CHAPTER 8

Finance for Development

After studying this chapter you will be able to:

- Explain what is meant by 'creating an interest' in real property
- Describe how imperfections in real property markets affect property development finance
- Describe the main sources of short-term finance
- Describe the main sources of long-term finance

8.1 General considerations

Principle of financing real property development

Development needs finance: (i) to cover the development period; and (ii) to purchase the finished development either for occupation or to hold it as an investment. The former is usually referred to as a 'short-term' or 'bridging' loan, and the latter as a 'long-term' or 'funded' loan. There are thus usually three main participants: (a) the *borrower*, that is, the developer (who may also be the long-term holder); (b) the *lender of short-term finance*, such as a clearing or merchant bank; and (c) the *provider of long-term finance*, usually a bank or institution such as an insurance company or pension fund.

The method of raising finance, whether short-term or long-term, is based on the principle of creating an interest in the real property. The owner can use the property simply as security for a bank loan (which can be regarded as a short-term mortgage). Alternatively, he can sell a definite interest. For instance, the owner of the 'fee simple absolute' of a particular property may

114

lack the capital necessary to develop. He might obtain this against a rent charge. Or the owner-occupier of a shop or farm may wish to raise additional working capital. He could do this by 'sale and leaseback'. The creation of an interest enables the lender to obtain an income from a property without having to occupy it.

The essential point to note is that, for the person creating the rent charge or selling and leasing back his property, the form chosen represents, *other things being equal*, the most preferred way of raising capital. Similarly for the lender: the particular interest created, a rent charge or leaseback, represents the best way of using capital.

Market imperfections

However, 'other things being equal' assumes that in the market: (i) there are a number of competitive lenders; and (ii) there is always a 'price' represented by the rate of interest at which a would-be borrower can obtain funds as an alternative to selling an interest.

In practice, these conditions do not hold. First, the borrower may be faced with a monopoly lender, as occurs, for instance, with the small developer who has to rely mainly on a bank. Thus a speculative builder might find that the conditions of a loan are more or less the same from all banks, being limited to one year only. As a result, he has to watch his cash-flow position carefully. This may even force him to build houses, which can be sold as they are completed, rather than a block of flats.

Second, property often consists of 'large lumps', an office block costing, say, £50 million to build and a city-centre redevelopment considerably more. In such cases finance is usually secured by negotiation between principals, and the precise terms will reflect their relative strengths in bilateral bargaining.

Third, government policy may influence the terms of a loan. For example, the switch to using base rate changes as the major weapon for suppressing inflation could mean that lending on variable rate terms is preferred, with a loan at a fixed rate having to carry a risk premium to cover a possible future rise in base rate. Similarly, taxation affects property finance. Corporation tax and capital gains tax leave smaller profits for ploughing back into future developments. Exemption from income tax means that leaseholds have advantages for certain purchasers, such as charitable trusts (see p. 61), while capital gains tax may discourage 'sale and leasebacks'.

Thus the main effects of these market imperfections are:

(a) Interests may be created which would not have been had the market offered alternative sources of finance. Thus a sale and leaseback may be preferred to a mortgage simply because it provides finance to the full value of a property as opposed to only two-thirds.

(b) Particular conditions can be imposed by the lender as an alternative to charging a higher rate of interest.
(c) Since funds cannot always be obtained when needed or on terms which suit the borrower, finance plays an important role in the timing, quantity and type of development undertaken.

The response to market imperfections

A study of property development since 1945 reveals no hard-and-fast ways by which capital is raised. Rather, it demonstrates the ingenuity of developers in obtaining funds as conditions have changed in the capital market, usually as a result of changes in government policy. Thus in the 1960s when the 'Big Four' banks were required to limit their lending, property developers turned to merchant banks, foreign banks and even finance companies who had previously specialised in hire purchase.

Sources of capital also alter as the requirements of lenders change. This may be due to a policy adjustment – for example, insurance companies sought equity interests with the introduction of 'with-profits' policies. On the other hand, it may simply be the result of an adjustment in an institution's portfolio of assets. Thus, as a hedge against inflation, a pension fund may increase its lending for property development in return for a part-share in the freehold interest. This means that a developer should organise facilities with three or four alternative sources.

What follows, therefore, is simply a broad survey of the different arrangements which may be made to raise finance. In practice, new devices are continually being invented to meet changes in market conditions. Indeed, each project tends to attract its own financial structure, the exact terms being finely tailored to suit the particular preferences of both borrower and lender.

8.2 Short-term finance

Sources of short-term finance

A developer needs *short-term* finance for the development period in order to purchase land, meet ripening and waiting costs and pay the building contractor and professional consultants. The period usually extends from one to three years, but for comprehensive developments it can be much longer. With the latter, the developer may rely on rolling over short-term loans; more usually, longer-term finance from the institutions will be required from the start.

The distinction between short-term and long-term finance in property development reflects *risk*. The greatest risk is during the construction period, the least when the building is completed and occupied. There is thus a difference in the terms and rate of interest charged.

In many respects short-term development finance can be likened to the working capital of industry, for such capital covers the production period until the finished good is sold. Thus the sources of short-term finance for development tend to be similar to those for businesses in general.

Short-term finance is obtained mainly from the banks – the clearing banks, merchant banks and the UK subsidiaries of foreign banks. All are concerned with the liquidity, security and profitability of the loan.

Collapses in the property market in 1973 and 1990 have highlighted the risk to a bank of being locked in as a lender of 'project finance', where the sale of the finished building is the sole means of repayment. The tendency now, therefore, is to put more emphasis on *liquidity*, that is, regaining quickly the money lent should there be a collapse in the property market (see Chapter 9).

First, therefore, the bank assesses the development company's capability and financial background. Has it a record of previous successful developments? Has it managed to retain some of these? If so, what is its gearing and overall cash flow? Can it be relied upon to complete the project?

The quality of the project will also be examined as regards its location, design, and so on – but, more importantly, as to its saleability in a weak market. And, where a loan is offered, it will be structured to the nature of the project (for example, site assembly, working capital for construction), and limited from one to three years. Thus a loan for an industrial warehouse development would be for a shorter period than a loan for an office block, since the former usually takes less time to complete. The object is to give the borrower sufficient flexibility, while still exercising a measure of control over the project.

For *security*, a *clearing bank* limits the loan to about two-thirds of the cost of the development, usually determined by its own valuer. This may present a difficulty for a small entrepreneur, such as a housebuilder or minor office developer with few supporting capital resources, so that he is advised by the bank to consider less costly and risky projects such as refurbishments. Any super-normal profit could provide the equity for more ambitious schemes later. Alternatively, where his own bank declines to lend, there is just a slight possibility that a loan can be arranged through a *property insurance broker* (see p. 121).

In contrast, the well-established property company is at an advantage. Not only may its existing property holdings provide collateral, but net revenue from them may cover interest payments on the new loan. Even so, it will limit its collateral as far as possible since uncommitted property can be used to support later borrowing. Where a loan is confined to the specific project it is known as a 'non-recourse' loan; where other assets of the company or parent company can be called upon, it is a 'recourse' loan. usually the final agreement lies between these two – a 'limited recourse' loan.

A large property company may wish to form a subsidiary company to carry out a particular development, but limiting its equity commitment to an initial 5 per cent of the finance required. A bank would advance, say, 80 per cent of 'senior debt'. The balance of 15 per cent – 'mezzanine debt' – could probably be obtained by arranging cover against loss with an insurer who specialises on loans secured against commercial property.

Loans from a bank can be by either overdraft or term loan. Whereas the overdraft is cheaper, a term loan gives the developer greater security. But with both the rate of interest can fluctuate. A developer may therefore prefer to raise short-term finance through a *merchant bank*, whose lending limits may be up to four-fifths of the value. Although the interest rate charged may be a little higher, it can be fixed for the whole period of the loan, enabling development costs to be forecast more accurately.

As regards *profitability*, it must be recognised that, whereas the institutions, the ultimate purchasers, base security on the completed and occupied buildings, the banks have to base theirs on their assessment of the project and their knowledge of the developer. This risk must be reflected in what it earns over and above the 'opportunity cost' of a safe return on the money market. Moreover, unless there is some provision for varying the rate charged, this risk margin can be eroded should short-term interest rates rise.

8.3 Longer-term development finance

Major developments

Since construction finance on a two-year basis presents difficulties for major developments such as a shopping centre or a large office block, it is now usual for the institutions to provide long-term finance from the start. Similarly, when the developer is building for an occupying institution, the latter may make all the financial provision.

This financing of the development process by the institutions has been encouraged by the increasing competition to secure prime property investments, and their provision of development finance may hinge on there being some degree of equity participation in the completed building.

The actual arrangement may, therefore, take many forms, with an increasing degree of final equity, as follows.

(1) PRIORITY YIELD
Here the institution agrees a minimum yield with the developer, say 6 per cent. If the developer's ability is such that he can achieve a yield of $7\frac{1}{4}$ per cent, the institution allows him to keep the capitalised $1\frac{1}{4}$ per cent difference as his profit. Should there be a yield in excess of $7\frac{1}{4}$ per cent, the institution would require a share to enable it to relate risk to profit.

Priority yield provides a high incentive for the developer to keep costs to a minimum and to let the project as quickly as possible.

(2) SALE AND LEASEBACK

The essence of the leaseback is that the freehold with the benefit of planning consent is sold to an institution which then advances the development costs at a fixed rate of interest. If the development is not let within, say, six months of completion, the developer receives a balancing payment in return for either entering into a leaseback or providing a leaseback guarantee at an agreed base rent. This balancing item represents the developer's profit and is based on a certain yield to the institution of about $7\frac{1}{2}$ per cent. If costs rise or completion takes longer than expected, the developer makes up the difference from his balancing item.

Once letting to an occupational tenant is achieved, the lease is surrendered or the guarantee extinguished. Thus this form of a sale and leaseback is somewhat akin to a mortgage. If the rent secured is in excess of the base rent, provision is made for the institution to share in the enhanced value.

(3) PROFIT EROSION

A variation of the straight leaseback is the profit-erosion method. Where the developer is reluctant to commit himself to a potential 25-year-lease liability, he stakes his profit by agreeing to the institution's drawing the base rent from the balancing item. Should the balancing payment become exhausted, the developer's interest ceases and the institution takes over full letting responsibility.

Since under this method the institution accepts a greater risk, it requires a slightly higher yield.

(4) CO-OPERATION BETWEEN THE DEVELOPING COMPANY AND THE OCCUPYING INSTITUTION

If the developing company has a successful record, an institution may accept fuller participation in the project, providing both the short-term and long-term finance. The institution acquires from the developer a legal interest in the site, grants him a licence to build and meets the development costs. In return, it receives interest on the sum advanced and, when complete, occupies the building at a rent calculated on an agreed percentage of the total cost of development.

(5) JOINT COMPANY

The developer and the lending institution can form a joint company, shares being held in agreed proportions. This enables the institution to acquire a major equity interest in modern developments which may be in short supply. Moreover there is a secure return on the finance advanced. On the other hand, only interest payments are a deductible item in assessing corporation tax, so that dividends on shares are reduced by the tax. This is a disadvantage to non-tax-paying institutions such as pensions funds and charities.

(6) DIRECT DEVELOPMENT BY THE INSTITUTION
The tax disadvantage of the joint company has in recent years induced many institutions to accept the full risk of carrying out developments themselves. Usually a developer/consultant is engaged and paid a project management fee, calculated either as a fixed percentage of the construction cost or related to the eventual profit of the project. Not only does this allow the institution to influence the design and specification of the property and the quality of the tenant but, as the property is being obtained at source, it is likely to show a 1–1.5 return above current market yields.

8.4 Long-term investment finance

Repaying short-term finance

With short-term finance being quite expensive, the developer will start building as soon as possible after the site has been acquired and get the building completed quickly. He is then able to realise his profits, either by selling the development or holding it as an investment,

A developer who realises all his profit as soon as possible by selling the completed project is really a property trading company. Ideally he would sell during the construction period. Suppose, for example, that the development is an office block with a capital cost of £4 million. A merchant bank makes the developer a short-term loan of £3 million, leaving him to find £1 million (including interest) from his own resources. The developer finds a tenant and pre-lets at a rent of £500 000 a year which, on a 10-year-purchase basis, gives a capitalised value of £5 million. He can now sell the project as an investment to an institution on an initial payment, with the balance being paid as the development proceeds, giving him a profit of £1 million.

However, it is likely that a successful property development company will wish to retain some of its better developments, or at least an interest in them, as an investment. To do this, it needs some form of 'holding' agreement in the development finance arrangements and long-term finance.

Finance through equity capital

Finance can be divided broadly into *equity capital* and *loans*. Equity capital is obtained by ploughing back profits or by selling shares. Except for well-established and fairly large companies, the former is unlikely to provide sufficient capital to purchase developments of high value. On the other hand, raising capital by the sale of shares is really open only to a public company, and usually a minimum of £50 million must be raised to make a public offer or 'rights issue' an economic proposition. Though this sum may present no obstacle to a successful developer, equity financing has three main disadvantages.

First, the cost of this type of finance depends largely upon the current popularity of property-company shares on the Stock Exchange. If these are selling on a low-yield basis relative to fixed-interest-bearing bonds, new equity can be obtained on favourable terms and give owners of existing shares a capital gain. But the opposite may apply, especially at a time when the company is requiring funds urgently.

Second, since shares carry voting rights, increasing the number of shares could mean that the control of the company passes out of the hands of the original owners and make it more difficult to contest a hostile take-over bid.

Third, property companies are particularly suited to 'high-gearing', that is, having a high proportion of fixed-interest loans to ordinary shares. Since rents are regular, fairly certain and, with inflation, likely to rise, fixed-interest charges are covered by a steady income flow. Moreover, the property itself provides security for the loan. The alternative of raising funds by increasing the number of shares, referred to as diluting capital, simply means that any rise in profits has to be shared with the additional shareholders and is therefore only used to the extent that loan finance is unavailable or that too high a gearing may be detrimental to the share price.

Yet though a straight loan in money terms is preferred by a property company, the imperfections of the capital market may restrict its choice. For instance, to guard against inflation, many institutions may lend only on some form of equity-loan basis (see below), while the smaller company will probably find it advantageous to work through a specialist *property finance broker* having close connections with insurance companies and other lending institutions. He deals with specific propositions on a fee-paying basis and advises on the relative merits of the different offers of finance for the proposed project.

Methods of raising long-term finance

Since long-term finance is secured on completed buildings, capital is much safer. Moreover, the margin between interest payable and rental income provides an indication of the security of the loan. Thus long-term finance is usually available on easier terms than short-term development finance, and is tied closely to the current yield on long-term government securities.

(1) Mortgages

Ideally a developer would prefer to obtain a straight loan from an institution, covered by a mortgage on the completed development. At one time it was usual for the capital to be repaid at the end of the mortgage period; nowadays, in order to protect themselves against inflation and rising interest rates, lending institutions tend to require periodic repayments of the loan which can then be reinvested.

The difficulty for the developer is that he may not have a sufficient cash flow to cover the interest charge plus the capital repayments, especially as the latter are not chargeable to income for taxation purposes. Thus whether a mortgage loan is feasible depends upon (i) the timing of future revenues with respect to outgoings, and (ii) how the lender requires repayment of capital. Figures 8.1 and 8.2 illustrate two possibilities.

In Figure 8.1 the developer's flow of revenue is quite adequate for servicing the loan, and this in spite of the fact that the lender requires repayment of the capital by equal amounts during each year of the loan.

In Figure 8.2 the borrower has negotiated more favourable terms. With equal yearly sums to cover both interest and capital repayments, the latter is smaller at the beginning of the loan. In spite of this, however, the developer's cash flow is insufficient to service this total yearly sum simply because, in relation to required interest payments, gross revenues are small in the earlier years of the project, though they are expected to increase over time, either through increased demand for this type of development or through inflation.

In practice, the deficiency in cash flow may be substantial. If, therefore, the developer does not already have income from other property to cover the shortfall, he has to rethink his financing along one of the following lines. These alternatives, used to avoid early capital repayment, are usually acceptable because they offer the lending institution some form of equity participation as an inflation-hedge, the extent of this involvement depending largely on the requirements of its investment portfolio.

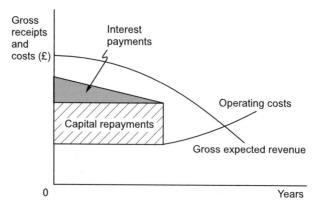

Figure 8.1 Viable mortgage terms

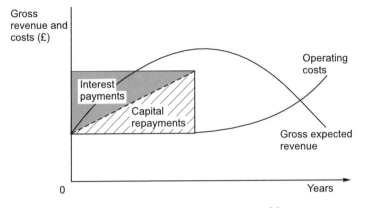

Figure 8.2 Mortgage terms not viable

(2) MORTGAGE DEBENTURE

Here an advance is made against the security of a particular property but with the lender having a recourse against the assets of the company or parent company. An advance is usually limited to two-thirds of the value of the *completed* development, but capital repayment is not required until the end of the loan period. While such a straight loan may suit the borrower, it provides no inflation-hedge. Lenders may therefore add some form of equity-participation condition, such as the option to convert the debenture into share capital at a future date. Alternatively, the return on the loan may be in the form of a rent charge.

(3) RENT CHARGE

A rent charge simply gives the lender a charge on the rents of the property. This can provide an inflation-hedge by linking the charge to rising rents, but legal remedies for non-payment are less satisfactory than for a mortgage or lease. If the rent charge is unpaid, the lender may enter into possession and collect rents until the debt is recovered, when the property reverts to the owner. With a mortgage or lease, however, proceedings can be taken for forfeiture should the tenant persistently fail to fulfil his commitments.

Government sources of capital

Apart from the private-sector sources of finance described above, government funds are also available, *Regional Selective Assistance*, partly funded by the EU's structural funds can cover up to 15 per cent of the cost of buildings in Assisted Areas. The *Regional Development Agencies* can draw on the *Single Regional Budget* to promote local forms of regeneration. In the remaining *Enterprise Zones*, new and existing firms enjoy exemption from general rates and 100 per cent capital allowances for corporation and income tax for expenditure on industrial and commercial buildings (see p. 409). In housing, housing associations obtain capital through the Housing Corporation, while renovation grants for dwellings over 10 years old are available to owner-occupiers, landlords and tenants subject to a financial resources test.

Summary

Short-term development finance is required to cover the development period. Long-term development finance is required to purchase the finished development either for occupation or to hold it as an investment. The method of raising finance depends on the creation of an interest in real property (such as a rent charge). Sources of short-term development finance include clearing banks, merchant banks and foreign banks. Long-term finance comes from institutions (such as insurance companies), the occupying institution, equity capital (obtained by selling shares) and in some circumstances from government funds.

Review questions

1. What are the main sources of short-term development finance?
2. Describe the types of arrangement that may be entered into by developers in order to obtain long-term finance.
3. Explain why 'sale and leaseback' arrangements might be affected by changes to stamp duty on commercial leases which were made in the 2003 budget.
4. Explain the advantages and disadvantages of raising development finance by selling shares.
5. What is meant by 'high gearing'?
6. Why are property companies suited to high gearing?

Recommended reading

M. Brett, *Property and Money* 2nd edn (London: Estates Gazette, 1998).

Centre for Advanced Land Use Studies (CALUS), *Urban Renewal* (London: CALUS, 1972) ch. 6.

J. Harvey, *Modern Economics*, 7th edn (London: Macmillan, 1998) chs 6, 24–7.

J. Ratcliffe, 'Types of financing', *Architects' Journal*, Supplement (22/29 August 1984).

CHAPTER 9

The Impact of Finance on the Commercial Property Market

After studying this chapter you will be able to:

- **Explain the causes of major fluctuations in commercial property and housing markets during the last fifty years**
- **Show that property is a major part of the UK financial structure**
- **Explain the repercussions of the 1989–91 property crash**
- **Describe the current property market in terms of the returns from different sectors**
- **Speculate on future prospects for real property markets in the UK**

This chapter examines fluctuations since the Second World War which have occurred in the provision of commercial property, mostly in response to free market forces. In contrast, the housing market has been dominated by government interference, and the consequences are analysed in Chapter 17.

We concentrate on the two major market collapses of 1973–4 and 1989–91. The latter was the major upheaval, and the property industry has taken a long time to adjust to the new market conditions which it gave rise to.

But it poses serious questions. Why did it occur? Was there nothing to be learned from the 1973–4 collapse? Or alternatively, is it possible, as a guide to future policy, to identify common features which serve to undermine steady, sustainable growth?

9.1 The property market in the 1950s and 1960s

The aftermath of the Second World War

During the war years, what was left of the construction industry could do no more than carry out first-aid repairs to those bomb-damaged buildings still capable of being put to effective use. As a result when the war ended the industry was faced with the mammoth task of reconstructing whole city centres and rebuilding on derelict bomb sites.

The demand for new buildings opened up opportunities for a new breed of property developer, some of whom had originated as estate agents and had the foresight to acquire derelict sites at bargain prices.

Initially their activity followed the traditional principle: if the prospective yield of the finished building exceeds the rate of interest at which finance can be borrowed, there is the possibility of profitable development. The shortage of modern office and retail buildings resulting from the war, together with a low rate of interest, meant that their profits were high and attracted other developers.

On completion, the developer could choose either to retain the development or to sell it on to an institution, chiefly an insurance company or pension fund. Both were seeking prime properties for their investment portfolios to take advantage of rising rents and to provide a hedge against an increasing rate of inflation. Initially institutions bought from a developer on a long lease. Later, seeking a share of the profits, they provided the funds for the construction period on a profit-sharing arrangement or even formed a joint company with the developer.

There were only occasional and minor hiccups in the upward trend of property prices, usually because the government, to reduce imports, had to raise base rate. In 1964, however, it resorted to physical control of new office development.

An institution-led investment boom 1971–2

In 1972 the Heath government decided to expand the economy and the money supply was increased. Much of this new money found its way into the property market via the clearing banks, which could now compete openly with the merchant banks. Between 1970 and 1973 bank lending increased from £71 m. to £1332 m., with most of the increase going to property companies.

There was no lack of demand, the institutions were willing to buy all completed developments. Not only was 3.5 per cent an acceptable rate of return on prime property investments but, with a shortage of office space for occupation purposes, rents doubled within two years, thereby enhancing capital values still further. Between 1964 and 1974 the value of the Centre

Point office block in London soared from £10 m. to around £60 m. even though it remained empty (see p. 75).

9.2 The collapse of the property market 1973–4

The market's vulnerability to external events

The price of property freeholds now contained a large element of speculation, with loan repayments not covered by rents in the expectation that deficits could be safely rolled over until covered at the next rent review.

The first check on optimism occurred in November 1972 when, as part of its strategy to combat inflation, the government froze commercial rents. In the following summer a steep rise in the world oil price gave a further twist to inflation and a loss of confidence in sterling. The government's growth policy came to an end.

The rise in interest rates which followed was catastrophic for developers. Buildings under construction fell in value, the situation being aggravated by rising construction costs and completion delays. Worse still, depositors with the fringe banks withdrew their money since they could obtain higher returns elsewhere, e.g. in local authority short-term loans. These banks could, therefore, no longer roll over loans to developers.

The storm might have been ridden out had the rent freeze not been renewed. The institutions now reappraised property as an investment, for continually rising rents, upon which their policy had been founded, appeared doubtful. The crisis in confidence, as institutions stopped buying, engulfed both developers and banks, particularly the fringe banks. While property prices were rising, the liquidity risk of borrowing short and lending long for property development and acquisition seemed negligible. Now, when the banks wanted their money back, borrowers could not sell the property against which they had borrowed. But the banks themselves had been far too liberal as regards 'deficit financing' by property companies – lending, for instance, at 14 per cent on controlled residential property showing a current yield of less than 5 per cent. As property prices tumbled, even the original lending base of four-fifths' valuation was not covered.

Many major developers and property companies failed. But, in order to protect depositors and the integrity of the banking system as a whole, most of the fringe banks were rescued by a support operation, known as the 'Lifeboat', mounted jointly by the 'Big Four' clearing banks and backed by the Bank of England.

Anti-property sentiment produced two further blows. First, to deal with the windfall profits made by developers, in December 1973 a development charge on first lettings was imposed. This was a tax on capital gains before they were realised, but it was so ill-defined as to suggest that the Conservative government did not really know what it was doing. Second, in March 1974 a new Labour government came to power. Residential rents were frozen, and there was no easing of the restrictions on business rents. As a result, an orderly property market ceased to exist.

The wider repercussions

What the government had failed to realise when introducing its hotch-potch of measures was the extent to which property had become a vital part of the UK financial structure. The collapse in property prices involved a large part of the City. Not only could insurance companies pay less in bonuses on life and annuity policies but also pension funds could not keep pace with inflation. The value of the assets of many banks also fell. Thus the liquidity crisis in property affected Stock Exchange optimism and share prices tumbled, Worse still, this loss of confidence occurred when world events were revealing the underlying weaknesses of the British economy.

The assumption behind the creation of the Bank of England's 'Lifeboat' was that the crisis was simply a short-term one of confidence: given breathing-space, properties could be sold off in an orderly manner, and confidence restored. But throughout 1974 high interest rates necessitated increased borrowing by the secondary banks, and this forced the sale of property. Thus the government, following pressure by the Bank of England and the institutions, announced in December 1974 that control on business rents would end. This partially lifted uncertainty surrounding property values, and confidence in first-class property as an investment was gradually restored.

The property collapse of 1973–4 has been described in some detail because important lessons could have been learned from it. Instead in less than a decade the same basic mistakes were being repeated.

9.3 The 1989–91 property collapse

A period of consolidation

As the institutions once more began to buy prime properties, an orderly property market was re-established by the end of 1975. But the secondary market remained dull, largely because many development and property companies were still selling to repay the banks. In addition, the banks themselves were following a much more conservative lending policy, re-inforced by the Labour government's strict control of the money supply.

As regards development, finance was still available – at a price – for base rate remained high. The difficulty lay in finding projects to give a profitable return on a borrowing rate of around 15 per cent. Moreover, apprehension as regards future profitability resulted from (i) doubts as to whether rents would continue to rise at their previous rates, (ii) the uncertainties resulting from the Community Land Act 1975, (iii) the introduction of the development land tax, 1976, and (iv) the recession shortly after the Thatcher government took over in 1979.

The recovery in development activity

The demand for property recovered strongly from the mid-1980s onwards. This was the result of: (a) the rapid rate of growth in the economy; (b) expansion in the service industries; (c) the demand for large modern offices to house information technology equipment and Stock Market personnel following Big Bang in 1986; (d) the relaxation of planning controls; (e) changes in the User Classes Order 1987, and the advent of business parks, science parks, out-of-town shopping centres and retail warehouses; (f) the explosion of consumer credit and spending. All added up to a major increase in the demand for space and in rental growth, inducing investors to buy buildings at ever-lower yields in anticipation of this continuing.

To respond to the increased demand, property developers needed credit – and this was forthcoming, as follows.

The banks' lending policy

Initially the banks followed a fairly cautious lending policy, usually limiting loans to about 65 per cent (80 per cent on rare occasions) of the value of the property and for a period of no more than five years, with actual advances geared to various stages in the completion of the project. Covenants were tailored to the risk exposure they were prepared to accept and to provide an 'exit' should the development turn sour for some unforeseen reason. The individual development loan was usually in the range of £5 m.–£20 m.

One important feature of development schemes in the 1980s was the vast increase in their complexity and size: London Bridge City, Broadgate and Canary Wharf, were all over 2 m. square feet of office space. While a loan of £100m. would be considered on its merits, few banks would accept this degree of risk-exposure on their own and so they usually invited others to join in funding the project. Such a syndicate also allowed small banks to participate in high-quality developments.

As a rule of thumb, banks also limited their risk by restricting their loans on property to some 30 per cent of their total lending, with development funding accounting for about half the property portfolio. Sometimes, as an alternative, risks were spread by insuring the 'top slice' of loan where this was above 60 per cent.

A bank-led finance development boom

In Chapter 8 we described the conventional method of financing property development through forward funding by an institution. Usually the development was pre-let, thus making it a sound investment even before construction started. Often the buyer was the same institution which had provided the initial finance, for insurance companies and pensions funds were eagerly seeking an equity interest in first-class property, especially easily-managed office blocks which, with rising rentals, provided a hedge against inflation and real growth. Property companies, too, often retained some of their developments to increase income from their own investments.

From the early 1980s, however, the institutions became less enamoured with property as an investment and so had no need to seek prime properties for their portfolios. Instead they considered that shares had better growth prospects (which proved true of the early 1980s but meant that they missed out on the property boom of 1985–9). Pension funds, for instance, reduced the proportion of their assets in property from 21 per cent in 1979 to 9 per cent in 1989.

However, the withdrawal of the institutions from financing commercial development did not bring about a decline in construction activity, for the void was filled in various ways, chiefly by the banks where a number of factors induced them to follow a less-cautious lending policy. The government's change in the method of monetary control (from minimum liquid asset requirements to varying the rate of interest) allowed them to expand their deposits, and financing property development provided a welcome home for their surplus funds. Moreover, the removal of controls on exporting capital by the world's leading economies allowed overseas banks and their financial conglomerates, particularly US and Japanese, to offer loans. In contrast, the merchant banks, so severely mauled in 1974, largely confined their participation to pure investment lending and underwriting, and avoided holding any major element of development debt in their own loan portfolios.

The emergence of the developer-trader

Not only did the replacement of the institutions by the banks in financing development represent a move from investment-led to debt-financed development, but the approach and nature of the developer also changed. With the earlier developer the building was pre-let and the long-term investor was in place before construction started.

In contrast, the 1980s developer, often an individual rather than an institution, had as many projects in the pipeline as he could obtain finance to initiate them. During the early part of the boom he found little difficulty in managing to sell at a profit. The bank would then be repaid, and further projects embarked on. Such a developer-trader flourished in the ethos of Thatcher free enterprise.

Proposed projects brought forward by euphoric developers met a ready response from the banks, who competed with one another and with foreign rivals by designing new loan packages. The role of the banker changed from that of conservative risk-manager to a target-achieving seller of loans, with the loan officer rewarded with bonus payments. 'Limited recourse loans' restricted the banks' ability to recall debt, and going even further, 'non-recourse loans' isolated a particular project from the overall financial profile of the borrower as regards, for example, debt and covenants existing on other projects. This really meant that a parent company could not be called upon to cover any default on a loan by an offshoot company formed simply to carry out a particular development. In effect, the lender, not the borrower, took all the risk and was the loser if the development turned sour.

To make it easier for developers to obtain funds, merchant banks were joined by other financial intermediaries – specialists in 'structural engineering finance'. By 'creative finance' and 'mezzanine' finance, loan schemes were tailored to obtain the maximum initial finance, usually by allowing the difference between interest payments and rental returns to be carried over to the next rent review when it could be paid out of higher rents.

As an alternative method to bank lending in raising capital, preference shares were offered to investors. If successful, this source was more attractive than selling ordinary shares at a heavy discount, for this diluted the equity portion.

Between 1985 and 1990 yearly bank lending to property companies increased in money terms from £7 bn, to £38.9 bn with overseas investors (mostly American and Japanese banks) providing some 40 per cent. By 1990 the banks' total property debt amounted to approximately £500 bn. Yet property analysts had previously cautioned that an excess of space over demand, particularly in the office sector, could develop.

Factors which triggered the 1989–91 crash

Just as there were special factors which stimulated the boom, so other conditions arose which triggered the slump. The banks had looked at property development solely from the supply side, treating developers not as entrepreneurs, but as manufacturers of floor space. Scant regard was thus paid to the fact that they were lending in a highly speculative market. If, say, the interest charged is 15 per cent and the yield from rents 6 per cent, even if loans cover only 70 per cent of the value of the property, it still leaves a shortfall if rents do not go on rising. Then asset cover is diminished as capital values decline, and the banks find that the escape routes provided by their loan covenants including collateral are insufficient to avoid a loss.

Such a check on rental growth occurred both on the demand and the supply sides. The rate of inflation started to rise, almost doubling to 7.7 per cent between 1987 and 1989, causing workers to seek wage rises in excess of this. The rate of interest was raised in stages, the banks' base rate reaching 15 per cent in October 1989. This had the effect of halting firms' investment plans and squeezing consumer demand, especially as house mortgage rates rose to 15.4 per cent.

Nor was there any follow-through in demand to the expansion of financial services following deregulation in 1986. Confidence was eroded by the Stock Market crash in October 1987, and later the general economic recession reduced demand for both workers and office space, especially in the City of London. The levying of VAT on rents of new buildings added to the gloom for banks, building societies and insurance companies (see p. 414), since they were unable to reclaim it.

Furthermore, the introduction of the Uniform Business Rate in 1990, although phased in, left many firms, especially retailers, with smaller profits (see p. 425). Moreover, such profits had already been squeezed by the downturn in consumer spending. Wherever it was possible, therefore, retailers cut back on their existing floor space.

The situation was aggravated on the supply side. Just as demand was falling, new floor space, both retail and office, was coming on to the market as developments in the pipeline were completed. Thus by the end of 1991 some 30 per cent of the City/Dockland office stock was vacant. Office rents fell by over 20 per cent, and the gloom spread to the retail sector. The decline was most marked in London and the south-east, but also rippled outwards.

When a highly speculative market exists, anything which administers a shock to confidence has a disproportionate effect, especially when the market, as with property, is highly sensitive and responsive to monetary conditions. The result, therefore, was a cumulative slump in which the housing market was also caught up (see pp. 348-9). Developers were left with expensive land banks and unfinished buildings on their hands.

The banks' falling asset cover and their response

Some property and development companies played for short-term relief from their cash-flow problem by capitalising interest payments below the line in order to avoid showing a serious fall in profits in their annual accounts. But this 'creative accounting' and any restructuring of borrowing could only afford a breathing-space while alternative sources of long-term funds were investigated.

The trouble was that half-completed buildings, and even buildings which could not be let, were unsaleable. The resulting fall in asset values left developers with insufficient cover for their borrowing with the banks. Thus the choice for the banks was whether to call in the receivers for interest defaulters and to write-off losses or to restructure loans in order to protect the funds already committed until the climate for selling completed developments improved. Generally, though a few major companies were forced into bankruptcy, the banks followed the restructuring course, but at a price to the borrower.

9.4 Lessons which need to be taken on board from the two collapses

The 1989–91 property market collapse was the most severe in living memory. But its basic causes were essentially similar to those of the market's failure in 1973–4, thereby underlying the rather cynical observation that 'the only thing we learn from history is that we learn nothing from history'. If instead we are to profit from past experience, it is important to recognise the circumstances which can eventually give rise to market instability.

First, the over-optimistic expectations of developers were supported by borrowed funds. But the loans advanced were only short-term. Thus to cover a construction period of two or more years, it was absolutely essential that they could be rolled over.

Second, the lending institutions failed to adhere to the recognised principle of sound banking – not to borrow short in order to lend long without adequate security as cover for regaining liquidity. All lenders – secondary and merchant banks in 1971–5 and the clearing and foreign banks in 1985–9 – failed to recognise the vulnerability of their loans to the inadequate security provided by unfinished or unlet buildings. In comparison, the developer-trader or a company buying property by deficit-financing had, should there be a downturn in the market, little more than the lender's money to lose. Insurance companies, too, by underwriting mortgage indemnity policies, were party to the over-lending, and building societies provided funds for commercial development although they had little real experience in this field.

Thus the lending institutions were exposed to unforeseen shocks: the world reaction to the rise of the oil price in 1973 and the hike in interest rates to curb mounting inflation in 1989.

To a large extent the banker's lack of caution was inexcusable for in 1987, two years before the property market collapse, Lloyds bank economists had predicted in their Economic Bulletin a deteriorating economic situation ahead which would result from a serious balance of payments problem. Nor should it have been necessary for the Governor of the Bank of England to warn the banks in October 1989 that their £40 bn lending on property looked excessive. More heed should also have been given to property analysts who were cautioning that an excess of space over demand, particularly in the office sector, could develop in the near future.

Nor can valuers be held blameless for they failed to appreciate the inadequacy of relying on historic comparables instead of making some attempt to suggest likely future relevant economic trends similar to those covered by analysts of Stock Exchange securities.

But the major responsibility for both collapses rests with the Conservative governments in power at the time. Both expanded monetary demand in pursuit of growth. Yet they failed to recognise the resulting incipient inflationary pressure and had no effective or coherent policy to deal with it before it got out of hand.

The 1972–3 measures of the Heath government – a rent freeze and a development charge which bit into normal profit – were inadequate, ill-defined and, above all, misguided in that they failed to appreciate the major part played by the property industry in the overall functioning of the economy. Nor did the Labour government, which took over in March 1974, help to restore confidence with its antipathy towards property and its proposals to rationalise land by a Community Land Act.

Similarly the seeds of the 1989 collapse were sown in Lawson's 1988 budget. Fearing deflationary consequences from a collapse in security prices on Wall Street, he cut income tax. In the event Wall Street quickly recovered, and his decision simply added to an already surging aggregate monetary demand.

9.5 Repercussions of the property collapse

Apart from 1973–4, the property industry in 1985 had enjoyed forty years of growth, underpinned by increasing real incomes, inflation, rising rents and the expansion of pension and life insurance funds looking for long-term investment. But, with the 1990 crisis, property entered uncharted waters against a background of static real income, unemployment of $2\frac{3}{4}$ m., a developing world-wide recession, a government determined to hold down inflation by adjustments in the rate of interest, and institutions already switching from property to other assets in their investment portfolios.

The immediate effects of the collapse have already been described. But it also altered many of the basic conditions upon which property development and investment had hinged over the previous forty years. It is to a consideration of some of these more important repercussions that we now turn.

(1) A REVISION OF THE VIEW OF THE INSTITUTIONS REGARDING PROPERTY AS A LONG-TERM INVESTMENT
The annualised return on a property holding depends on the rent received and the acceptable yield in competition with substitute investments. Thus if the rent rises and the competitive yield remains unchanged, there is an increase in capital value which, added to the rent, gives the annualised rate of return on the original cost.

In the recession, rents fell and yields rose. From 1991–4 and after 1997 the reverse yield gap – the amount by which the yield on gilts exceeds that on property – disappeared. For secondary properties it was possible to obtain a margin of earning capacity above the cost of borrowing.

Attention is now focused on the fact that the demand for property is derived from the use to which it is put. In short, occupation demand is a crucial element in the value of a property. In the boom, large office developments in particular seem to have been prompted more by their yield as an investment, with supply responding more to the availability of finance than to the likely demand of potential tenants.

Too little weight, too, was given to the illiquidity of property or to the fact that much of the new office supply would be tied to a single industry – financial services.

Even before the downturn, many institutions had started to reduce the property content in their investment portfolios, considering that equities offered better long-term prospects. The property crisis reinforced this view. Thus the Church Commissioners, following a 20 per cent drop in the value of its £1.5 bn commercial property portfolio together with losses on its development programme, decided to reduce its property weighting from 70 per cent to less than 50 per cent.

Moreover, with the government apparently determined to hold the rate of inflation at 2.5 per cent, the inflation hedge attribute, which applied particularly to retail properties, was of far less significance. By 1993 *net* institutional investment in property had fallen to £500 m., only a quarter of what it had been in 1982.

Since the mid-1990s property has made a sustained recovery. Nominal returns have been close to their long-run average at 12 per cent per year, but inflation-adjusted returns of over 9 per cent have only been bettered at the high point of the 1980s' boom. Since 2000, investment markets have been dominated by the fall in the stock market, giving successive years of negative returns on equities for the first time since 1973–4. One consequence of the stock market slump has been that today (2003) property ranks as the UK top asset class performer over the last 9 years.

(2) REVISION OF THE LEASE STRUCTURE

The typical 'institutional' lease prior to 1989 was the 25-year full repairing and insuring lease with 5 year rent reviews on an upward-only basis. Such a lease on a prime property let to a good covenant presented an institution – for example, a life insurance company – with a secure long-term investment for meeting future commitments together with a hedge against inflation.

With rents rising consistently, such terms were acceptable to a tenant since strong competition for properties meant that, should there be a wish to end occupation, the lease could easily be assigned, often for a premium. Furthermore, against this background, the lessee was willing to concede '*privity of contract*' (that is, the original lessee is liable for fulfilling the terms of the lease even after assignment, should the new occupier default).

The 1990 collapse of property changed the relative strengths of landlord and tenant for with supply of all types of property exceeding demand, negotiating strength moved in favour of the tenant. Thus, at best, rents tended to remain static, the over-rented being protected from falling only by the upward-only condition; at worst, the tenant, hit by recession, was forced into liquidation, leaving the landlord with empty premises and a difficult letting situation ahead.

Consequently on renewals or new leases the tenant has been able to exploit his improved negotiating position. New leases today are usually for a shorter period of about 15 years, with a possible fitting-out and rent-free period, and rent reviews and even break-clauses every five years – a useful negotiating ploy at a rent review for it threatens the landlord with a possible rent void should the tenant quit.

The fall in rents also meant that many properties on earlier leases were 'over-rented'. This focused attention on 'privity of contract'. With rising rents, possible default by the new tenant was acceptable since the property could soon be re-let, possibly at a higher rent. Now it could result in the assignor being landed with a considerable financial liability. The Landlord and Tenant (Covenants) Act 1995, therefore, limited liability to the first assignment only.

What are the likely possible effects of this new type of lease on property investment?

First, there is a change of emphasis on criteria. At one time it was considered that the virtue of a property depended on location, location, location. Now the security of the covenant – the tenant's standing and his ability to pay the rent and to fulfil other conditions such as repairs and insurance which the lease stipulates – have an enhanced importance.

Second, the new lease may reduce the willingness of institutions to invest in property. The lower security offered together with the added uncertainty through the occupier's exposure to a harsher economic background may strengthen the trend towards reducing the proportion of portfolio funds held in property.

(3) New sources of finance for property development
The withdrawal of the banks from development finance meant that developers have had to go into the market in search of funds. There were two major problems. First, how could property companies which were just keeping their heads above water fund their debt to avoid sinking into liquidation? Second, in view of the vast amount of capital now required for so many modern development projects, what changes in the nature of the debt are necessary to attract lenders?

Short-term finance.   One source was to tap the money markets direct by issuing *commercial paper*. This is a very short-term IOU sold by the borrower at a discount on the commercial paper market where there are investors looking for a home for surplus cash. The period could be for 40 days to three months, though by rolling-over on the market it could be regarded as a medium-term source of finance up to £50 m. As commercial paper is un-secured, the standing of the borrower is very important.

Longer-term finance.   In order to bridge the period from the start to the completion and sale of the project, a developer could contact a specialist finance firm who might be able to arrange the necessary bridging loan for non-speculative, preferably pre-let, projects. Thus with a *'defer and accrue'* plan the lender agrees to advance, say, 85 per cent of the value on completion, possibly with the rate of interest 'capped' – that is, the ceiling is fixed, but not the bottom. The developer knows exactly what he can spend and may, if he so wishes, hold on to the property as an investment. This type of funding might be more suited to a building society wanting comparatively little risk.

Where a bridging loan is not available, a property company could find that its only option is to appeal to shareholders to provide funds through a *'rights' issue*. This dilutes capital and is thus not really a satisfactory method for a property company, which in normal circumstances should be able to finance property acquisition and development by debt, with profit going to share-holders.

A *sale and leaseback* would be preferable and could be tailored to suit the future requirements of the property company. The seller realises the capital tied up in his property in exchange for a stream of rental payments. The purchaser, possibly a bank, has no wish to hold on to the property indefin-itely. Although provision will be made for periodic rent increases, the bank is quite willing to include an option to re-purchase the property at, say, five-year intervals. The bank has the benefit of tax allowances on capital expend-iture, and these allowances can be set off against profit from other business. The cost of funds charged to the borrower can thus be kept relatively low.

Convertible mortgages offer another alternative whereby the borrower provides the lender or investor with equity in the scheme in return for a higher loan advance and reduced obligations. The amount of equity at stake is determined by the investor's required internal rate of return and the expected level of capital growth offered by the property.

Many modern development projects are so large that the finance required presents difficulties regarding size and illiquidity. Thus an alternative which is currently gaining favour is for the finance to be provided by some form of *syndicate*. A syndicate can be formed for a specific project, with each member accepting the risk and sharing the profit according to the size of this contribution.

'Unitisation' of a property goes one step further, its value being divided into a number of small units and often covering different projects. By buying units the investor can spread his risk, while liquidity can be achieved by selling units on the market. The main snag is the difficulty and cost of frequent valuations. On the other hand, with an Authorised Property Unit Trust (APUT), there is the advantage that now tax is paid only at 23 per cent, not 35 per cent as previously.

The method developed in the USA for raising the large amount of capital required for modern projects is *securitisation* e.g. through Real Estate Investment Trusts (REITS). In essence this involves segmenting the mortgage into bonds carrying different levels of risk in order to appeal to the preferences of as many different types of investing institutions as possible. In doing so it gives access to global markets, being particularly suitable to the Japanese, for example, who wish to lend while avoiding as much risk as possible. Yet at the same time there is the possibility of considerable flexibility, for different types of bond can be packaged according to the requirements of the buyer. Thus though large sums can be raised, the weighted average cost of the financing is lower.

Furthermore, the issuer may be able to finance a number of projects in one securitised offering. Since bonds are tradable in the way that bank debt is not, they offer greater liquidity. Indeed as property securitisation in Europe grows, eventually a global securities market is likely to develop.

Finally, though most of the debt is packaged in the form of bonds, the developer retains the freehold and thus full management control. This allows him to exploit his expertise and market knowledge to obtain the growth which accrues to the equity interest.

The return of the banks and institutions.   By 1994 the banks had made such a strong recovery in their finances that they had surplus funds to lend. Nevertheless they have followed a conservative policy, concentrating their lending on investment properties where there is little risk when loans mature.

But in any development there is an element of speculation. In the past it was covered by pre-letting or the likelihood of the eventual rent being higher than that at which the project was originally costed.

The present tendency is for risk to be spread more equally between the developer and institution. In place of the pure developer-trader, the present-day developer is more of an 'enabler', simply assembling a development project for a specified fund or occupier. Provided he has an established track record, an institution may then, for the major share of the profit, provide the funds. But it will have to be a prime property offering a current yield covered by a fairly guaranteed current market rent. Apart from such schemes, however, development activity will remain sluggish, the institutions preferring alternative investment assets.

(4) AN EXTENSION OF VALUATION OBJECTIVES

Until recently valuation technique has concentrated almost exclusively on ascertaining the current open market value (OMV) of an individual property by comparing its location, physical characteristics, rent, covenant and other tenure conditions with those of fairly similar properties having a recently-traded price. This emphasis on an individual appraisal of a property based on historical data recognises the fact that, though to a degree each interest may be uniquely different from others, there are often characteristics which afford a measure of substitutability. Even so, such a valuation is limited by the infrequency of transactions and the paucity of information regarding those which do take place, thereby depriving the valuer of essential market evidence for lettings and rent reviews.

In contrast, there is, within the broad types of stocks and shares, a large measure of homogeneity. Moreover, through frequent dealings on the Stock Exchange and modern information technology, investment analysts are provided with an up-to-date valuation of each individual share, bond, and so on. Furthermore, knowledge is now worldwide. Nor is the current price of an interest based solely on the merits of its past performance: the microeconomic factors of demand and supply in its particular market and changes in the macroeconomic variables of the wider economics will also affect its price. Both micro and macro considerations play an important role in the securities market. In short, the current price also reflects an assessment of the risk from all possible changes which can occur in the future.

The collapse of the property market in 1989 has caused valuers to reflect on the part they played in fuelling the preceding boom. Their OMVs were based on the assumption that the economic conditions underlying the price of comparables would remain constant. As a result some valuations were so inaccurate that they gave cause to legal redress. Should more weight have been given to the implications for property of wide shifts in the economies of the UK and the world at large?

Hence what is now being mooted is that the valuer of property (which is, like securities, a long-term investment) should similarly make an estimate of future price movements, even to the extent of containing within his report a sensitivity analysis. In short, he must go further than the micro-level analysis of individual market returns of comparables, to view the wider shifts and currents in the major economies of the world, as already happens in the world market in securities. Indeed this requirement is already recognised in the newer concept of the 'estimated realisation price' (ERP) which, while still requiring precise definition, does hint at an assessment of the possible risk element in property's future price movement.

The demand for land and real property is closely related to the level of real national income and the cost of borrowing. With houses, demand depends mainly on the level of monthly personal income relative to mortgage repayments. For commercial and industrial property, demand depends on net profitability; that is, it is a derived demand, similarly dependent on the current level of income and on the cost of borrowing.

To be more specific, consideration would, for example, have to be given to the rate of growth of national income, the success of anti-inflation policy, possible changes in the rate of interest, the ability of firms to maintain and increase exports, and the government's likely attitude to tax levels and the type of tax favoured. Such important questions must be based on reasoned analysis, not reliance on a 'hunch'.

It is essential, therefore, that valuers of real property have a knowledge of how the level of activity is determined, how the main macro-variables are related and how changes in them can affect the economy as a whole. Such knowledge provides insight into the current position, and from there some peering into the future is possible. The objective cannot be complete accuracy – even the Treasury model cannot achieve this. Rather it should indicate possible future cyclical movements, and the application of macro-economic theory to information currently available should reduce the margin of error. As external circumstances change over time, so the forecast needs to be amended. Cyclical booms and slumps affect the rate of development and the allocation of funds to the property sector. An expanding economy will probably require new factories, warehouses, shopping facilities and improved housing. Similarly an increase in the inflation rate may prompt the government to raise the rate of interest, and bring into question whether the present level of activity can be sustained.

Valuers must not be reactionary to this new approach. The reason why they were not sufficiently far-seeing in the mid-1980s was largely because, like many others, they have in the past tended to 'rubbish' the analytical approach of economists. For example, that a serious balance of payments problem was developing had been forecast in 1987 by Lloyd's Bank economists in their monthly Economic Bulletin – two years before the property market collapsed, yet neither valuers nor even the banks themselves managed to appreciate its full macro implications, especially as regards likely government measures to rectify the situation.

Canary Wharf

The history of Canary Wharf epitomises the nature of the crisis and the subsequent recovery. The construction of this office tower block, the flagship of the Docklands regeneration complex, was nearing completion when the demand for offices collapsed. The interest payments incurred by its parent Canadian company, O & Y, forced it into liquidation, and the creditor banks, led by Lloyds, had little option but to administer the complex.

A fall in City of London office rents, increased demand from an expanding financial services sector and bargain purchases by Japanese and German investors in particular brought stability to the London office market. At an initial rental of £18 per square feet, Canary Wharf was therefore able to let its own offices as they were completed.

The rise from 1993 of office rents in general enabled Paul Reichmann, the developer of Canary Wharf, to obtain new overseas backers and buy back control from the banks. It must be emphasised that the Canary Wharf complex was part of the scheme to regenerate the dockland area, with the government providing aid in tax concessions and improvements in the infrastructure (including the extension of the Jubilee Line) at an estimated

£2650 m. Today 7 m. square foot out of the complete scheme of 13.5 m. have been completed, and major tenants are coming forward at rents approaching £40 per square foot in order to secure the rate-free concession before the Enterprise Zone status comes to an end. The City of London now recognises Canary Wharf as a major competitor.

The Canary Wharf scheme was expected to break even by 2000. This prospect enabled Paul Reichmann in March 1995 to float on the open market 25 per cent of the equity, at a price which valued Canary Wharf at £2.3 m.

The secondary property market   While proposed major developments outside London, for example, the redevelopment of Southampton's surplus dockland, have also gone ahead, the secondary market has failed to establish definitive comparables. The collapse of property prices left most buildings over-rented, and so there were few rent reviews to establish a level of post-crisis rents.

Prices achieved at auction would suggest market rents should show a yield of around 10 per cent, giving a margin of 3 per cent above the cost of borrowing to cover administration costs and profit, with any capital gain regarded as a windfall bonus.

How housing was affected by the 1989–91 collapse is described in Chapter 18.

9.6 The commerical property scene in 2003

Rates of commercial property return have been good since the mid-1990s: 1995–3.5 per cent; 1997–15.0 per cent; 2000–11.5 per cent; 2002–10.0 per cent; and the projection for 2003 is 6.0 per cent and 2004, 7.5 per cent. The retail sector is expected to show the highest return (retail sales rose at the end of 2002 and retail rents continue to rise) and office property the lowest. Demand for offices has fallen steadily since 2001 due to job losses and the technology bust. Commerical property rental growth slowed in 2002 because of weakness in the corporate sector and this is expected to reduce capital values in 2003 while at the same time exerting upward pressure on yields. Recent falls in the stock market to a 7-year low may help to sustain investor interest in property, however, because it is seen as a safe haven for investors battered by worldwide stock markets in free fall and savers who are being offered ever lower interest rates. There is still a positive yield gap between property and gilts but, possibly fortunately given past experiences, a reluctance to embark on speculative development unless significant pre-lets can be secured.

Summary

The institution-led investment boom of 1971–2 was fuelled by speculation and rising capital values for commercial property. This was brought to a sudden end by the government freeze on commercial rents in November 1972, and a rise in interest rates. The subsequent collapse of the property market had far-reaching effects because of the extent to which property had become a vital part of the UK financial structure.

During the 1980s development schemes greatly increased in complexity and size. Commercial and foreign banks financed a speculative development boom which led to an excess of space over demand by 1990. When interest rates were raised to curb inflation, both investment and consumer demand fell sharply. The result was a cumulative slump in both the commercial property and housing markets.

While valuable lessons have been learned from these two severe property downturns, and new financial instruments have been devised to finance development, there is no guarantee that the current strength of the property market will continue unchecked. Strong demand conditions and low inflation, however, mean that the 2003 situation is very different from that of 1973 and 1989.

Review questions

1. Explain the major reasons why there was a commercial property market collapse in 1973–4.
2. Explain the major reasons why there was a property slump in 1989–91.
3. What new sources of finance for property development have arisen since 1991?
4. Assess the performance of property as an investment asset since 1996.
5. What reasons are there for believing that the current property 'boom' will not be followed by a crash?

Recommended reading

M. Ball, C. Lizieri and D. MacGregor, *The Economics of Commercial Property Markets* (London: Routledge, 2001).
M. Brett, *Property and Money*, 2nd edn (London: Estates Gazette, 1998).
O. Marriot, *The Property Boom*, 2nd edn (London: Estates Gazette, 1990).

CHAPTER 10

Comprehensive Redevelopment

After studying this chapter you will be able to:

- **Explain the nature of comprehensive redevelopment**
- **Explain the economic basis of the development decision**
- **Explain the reasons for co-operation between local authorities and private developers in undertaking comprehensive redevelopment**

10.1 The nature of comprehensive redevelopment

Why certain redevelopment has to be 'comprehensive'

Comprehensive redevelopment takes two main forms: (i) slum-clearance, occurring mainly in the 'twilight' zones of older towns; and (ii) city-centre redevelopment, providing modern shops and offices.

In both cases, redevelopment, like the planning of New Towns, has to be comprehensive rather than piecemeal. First, the scheme is so large that only a unified plan can arrange complementarities. Thus slum-clearance can link houses with local shops, schools and open spaces, while city-centre redevelopment can achieve complementarities between offices and shops. Second, the most advantageous scheme usually involves organising the infra-structure to improve accessibility through a redesigned road system, better transport termini, off-street parking facilities and pedestrian precincts, and to provide public services, such as civic offices, libraries, open spaces and even a new sewer system.

Post-war growth in comprehensive development

For a variety of reasons, the second half of the twentieth century saw an upsurge in the scale of slum-clearance and city-centre redevelopment.

(1) War bombing, which devastated large areas of many towns, provided the opportunity for complete redevelopment.
(2) Housing conditions, particularly in the 'twilight zones', were unacceptable to the new philosophy of the Welfare State.
(3) Redevelopment of many town centres had become economically viable, the value of the cleared sites exceeding the value of the buildings in their current uses. The reasons for this change in relative values were:
　(a) full employment and economic growth had increased spending power, benefiting shops (particularly multiples selling goods having a high income-elasticity of demand) and 'service' industries as opposed to the older basic industries;
　(b) the growth in government services, the special cable requirement of the new information technology (IT), and the desire of prosperous manufacturing firms for prestige offices increased the demand for first-class office accommodation in large buildings;
　(c) a retailing revolution towards supermarkets and multiple stores;
　(d) improved accessibility for the new car-shopper – for example, through better road systems and parking facilities – added to the profitability of new shopping centres;
　(e) investment demand for prime properties by the institutions pushed up capital values.
(4) Local authorities began to take a wider view of their planning functions, moving from a restrictive approach towards the more positive objective of maximising net social benefit. Many authorities therefore initiated urban renewal to achieve the greater social benefits of a comprehensive scheme as opposed to individual piecemeal development. Added to these benefits were the financial advantages of increased rateable value and, except in periods of economic stringency, government assistance towards the cost since urban renewal accorded with the new Welfare State philosophy.

10.2 Comprehensive redevelopment by private enterprise

The functions of the developer in comprehensive redevelopment can be undertaken by private enterprise or a local authority. Each has its own particular strengths and weaknesses.

Advantages of development by private enterprise

Development by private enterprise, whether by a development company, property company, construction firm or even an insurance company, has the following advantages:

(1) sole responsibility for the development rests with the developing company. This results in quick decision-making, effective administration and rapid completion;

(2) since it accepts all the risks and is dependent upon the profitability of the scheme, the company is competitive in its approach;

(3) expertise has probably been acquired in previous developments, whereas a local authority developing a city centre may only be undertaking a one-off project;

(4) a developer with a record of successful projects can usually obtain finance;

(5) where a single private developer is responsible for the complete project, many social costs and benefits will be allowed for in the scheme evolved; for example, accessibility and complementarity are recognised and promoted since these add to profitability.

Moreover, the local authority can impose its own ideas, both in prior consultations and through its planning requirements.

Disadvantages of development by private enterprise

Not only does the individual developer undertaking a comprehensive scheme run into practical difficulties but his objectives may also conflict with the interests of the local authority. We shall deal with each problem in turn.

Comprehensive redevelopment encounters obstacles in acquiring many separate interests. First, interests have different owners and, particularly with leases, expire at different times. Indeed, fragmentation of ownership has been increased through the breaking up of estates under the Leasehold Reform Acts of 1967, 1993 and 2002. Second, the developer is not buying interests in a perfectly competitive market. A development may be held up by one owner refusing to sell or using his monopoly power to exact an exorbitant price. Eventually the local authority may have to be asked to invoke its powers of compulsory purchase.

Furthermore, the private developer cannot change the existing layout of roads in order to produce a better development. Thus either the development conforms to an ossified road structure or the help of the local authority has to be sought to modify it.

More important from the point of view of the optimum use of land resources, the objectives of the developer and the interests of the local authority may not coincide.

First, in order to maximise his profit, the private developer prefers to undertake only the profitable parts of the scheme – offices, shops and possibly residences – leaving the local authority to provide the unprofitable infrastructure – sewers, roads, transport facilities, public conveniences, schools, and so on. Though such capital expenditure will eventually secure extra revenue through increased rateable values, the local authority, in buying land for the infrastructure, is forced to pay a market price inflated by private developers competing for the highly-profitable sites. Redevelopment by the local authority avoids this difficulty. However, should it not wish to assume this responsibility, an alternative solution is to negotiate 'planning gain', where consent for planning is conditional upon the developer meeting some of the infrastructure cost (pp. 412–14).

Second, unlike the private developer, the local authority is vitally concerned with social costs and social benefits. This is not to say that these are ignored when a private developer is responsible for the complete scheme for as noted above, he can, by 'internalising externalities', enhance its overall profitability. In any case, the local authority can impose its own ideas through its planning requirements. But in certain circumstances the local authority may be *forced* to initiate redevelopment. Rebuilding houses in a twilight zone, for instance, may be unprofitable for private enterprise (for example, because of competition from subsidised housing). In contrast, the local authority must consider the external costs of *not* clearing slums.

Third, only the local authority is in a position to initiate comprehensive redevelopment where the originating motive is to provide a new road system.

10.3 Redevelopment by the local authority

Should not therefore the local authority assume the entrepreneurial role and itself be wholly responsible for urban renewal? Here again there are difficulties.

(1) Administrative functions are being undertaken by a body which, through its planning powers, also acts in a quasi-judicial capacity. There is thus the danger that the authority, in order to enhance the commercial prospects of its own project, will refuse planning consent for development elsewhere.
(2) In taking responsibility for development, the local authority, which is basically a political body, may be motivated by civic pride or political dogma rather than by economic considerations, especially where intangible costs and benefits are difficult to measure in money terms.
(3) It has to be asked whether the organisation of a council – through departmental chief officers, committees and council meetings – is appropriate

for commercial decision-making and maintaining the impetus of large development schemes. In contrast, the private developer can make quick decisions as he monitors the scheme throughout the construction period.

(4) Since the local authority is probably concerned with only a one-off scheme, it may find difficulty in obtaining scarce development specialists for, unlike private enterprise, it cannot offer long-term contracts at the high salaries such specialists command.

(5) In accepting the role of risk-bearing, the local authority takes responsibility for possible losses. Should an authority accept such a risk when a private developer is willing to do so?

(6) Central government restrictions may mean that the local authority could not raise sufficient finance for the scheme.

10.4 Partnership arrangements between local authorities and private developers

Co-operation between local authorities and private developers

Although in the past many successful comprehensive redevelopments – for example, Regent Street and Grosvenor Square – have been carried out by private enterprise, today both the private developer and the local authority recognise that neither can function satisfactorily independently of the other. Thus co-operation has evolved, usually through some form of partnership arrangement whereby the local authority and other parties, particularly the developer, participate in the scheme and share in the common proceeds.

The exact terms of the partnership will vary according to each party's commitment, relative bargaining power and degree of integration desired. On the one hand, the developer may need the compulsory purchase powers of the authority; on the other, the local authority wants the developer's expertise and sources of finance (usually through an institution) – virtually a 'Private Finance Initiative' (PFI) many years before 1992 when this was officially presented as the follow-up to privatisation (see p. 385).

Usually the local authority *acquires the land and provides the infrastructure*. The site, or parts of it, are then leased to individual developers. This method has advantages to the local authority: (i) less capital outlay than if it were responsible for developing; (ii) less responsibility for development decisions, since these are decentralised among the individual developers; (iii) retention of overall control of the development plan; (iv) the cost of the infrastructure can be covered from the proceeds of the sale of leases; (v) an equity interest can be retained by periodic reviews of the ground rent (perhaps as a proportion of the full market rent) and through the reversion of the land at the end of the lease.

Alternatively, the local authority can form a *joint company* with the developer. Even so, possible problems have to be anticipated and solutions agreed. First, there must be a fair and generally understood procedure for selecting the developer to be involved in the joint company. Second, the basis for sharing the equity must be decided – for example, in proportion to land-ownership, or to the original capital contributed or to the initial ratio of ground rent to rack rent. Third, institutions who have provided finance may also require a share of the equity.

In general, whatever the form of partnership, there must be a governing framework sufficiently precise to cover areas where the avoidance of disputes is essential for the progress and future management of the development, while still allowing the developer to proceed on a basis which is free from undue restriction and control.

Steps in the formation of a partnership scheme

Let us assume that the initiative comes from the local authority. The authority provides a plan showing the area for development and the means of access, and indicates what it requires in the scheme. Developers are then invited to participate in the proposed development. The authority checks on the ability of those who accept, and chooses about half a dozen to prepare an outline submission including the financial basis upon which they would proceed.

Usually developers attend before the authority and enlarge on their ideas. One developer is then selected, and detailed discussions are held on the type of development as well as the financial terms.

Co-operation along these lines has certain advantages. First, the two parties get a better understanding of each other's requirements, so that they can evolve a scheme which is mutually satisfactory. Second, the local authority can weigh up the pros and cons of requiring the developer to provide certain civic amenities at his own expense, particularly as regards its effect on the return on capital invested in acquiring the site. Third, the selected developer can undertake detailed surveys of demand in order to assess the shopping and office space required and the community and recreational facilities which can be supported. Fourth, the local authority can assemble the site, using its powers of compulsory purchase where necessary. This overcomes extortionate price demands for critical sites and should reduce the time taken to assemble the complete site.

As a result of these detailed negotiations, a *building agreement* and *form of lease* are drawn up. The building agreement is the basic document, defining the precise contents of the scheme. Accompanied by a set of plans, it sets out how the cost of those parts of the scheme for which the authority is responsible are to be determined and whether any buildings are to be erected by the authority.

The *form of lease* covers the terms upon which the local authority will lease the site to the developer upon completion of the development. It deals with (i) the period – normally about 125 years, (ii) the ground rent, and (iii) the respective responsibilities of the local authority and the developer for the future maintenance of the project.

Ground-rent terms can vary, but the dominant aim will be to allow the authority to participate in the profits of the scheme. Nowadays this goes much further than fixing a ground rent with periodic rent reviews to guard against inflation. Usually local authority leases combine: (i) a basic ground rent at a level which gives the developer a satisfactory yield on his total capital expenditure, for example, 2 or 3 per cent above the basic borrowing rate: and (ii) rent-review provisions. The latter may be complicated by the fact that not all units may be let immediately. Moreover, there is the problem of whether the ground rent should vary in its proportion to rack rent over time. It is argued that since the developer took the initial risk and that this increases with time, he should derive a greater income from the project as time goes by. Thus the proportion of ground rent to rack rent should remain constant and not increase. Finally, if the institutions providing finance want a share of the equity, it complicates the rent-review clauses.

For shopping centres in particular, provision has to be made for *cleaning, security and maintenance*. However, making the local authority responsible may lead to inadequate services, since these centres require higher standards than the ordinary streets. The solution could be to appoint a shopping centre manager, who would be a joint appointee of the authority and tenants and funded by them.

To sum up, the authority and the developer want an attractive town centre, the authority primarily to provide a local amenity, the developer to obtain a successful commercial investment. Both aims can be achieved provided both parties feel the contract is fair and that in its operation one party is not seriously disadvantaged in an unforeseen way.

The future

The government's resolve to control the overall level of public sector spending to avoid running a Public Sector Net Cash Requirement (PSNCR) puts tight limits on its grants and lending to local authorities, and even imposes a ceiling on their spending from their Council tax proceeds and what they can borrow through the market. Thus future comprehensive city-centre development is likely to have to rely on the private sector providing the necessary finance through a PFI as well as managing and completing the agreed scheme. Such, for instance, was the arrangement for the redevelopment of Birmingham's central shopping area, the Bull Ring.

Summary

Slum-clearance and city-centre redevelopment are examples of comprehensive redevelopment. Such major schemes require a unified plan in order to achieve complementarities, for example between shops, offices and transport links.

Private enterprise schemes have many advantages of efficiency and finance, but may suffer because local authority help is required with compulsory purchase and road layout. Moreover, private enterprise schemes will undertake only profitable parts of the development, leaving the local authority to pick up the bills for necessary infrastructure. Development by local authorities is possible but suffers from institutional and bureaucratic difficulties and finance may be difficult. As a result co-operation has evolved in partnership arrangements between private developers and local authorities who share the proceeds. Such partnerships are becoming more common through PFI schemes.

Review questions

1. Why do some redevelopment schemes need to be comprehensive?
2. Explain the advantages and disadvantages of comprehensive redevelopment by private enterprise.
3. Why are local authority–private enterprise partnerships likely to be successful?
4. Identify the stages of formation of a partnership scheme.
5. Explain why PFI schemes are likely to become more common in future comprehensive redevelopments.

Recommended reading

A. W. Davidson and J. E. Leonard (eds), *Urban Renewal*, Property Studies in the United Kingdom and Overseas, no. 3 (London: Centre for Advanced Land Use Studies, 1972) ch. 6.

Department of the Environment, *Report of the Working Party on Local Authority/Private Enterprise Partnership Schemes* (London: HMSO, 1972).

J. Ratcliffe, *Urban Land Administration* (London: Estates Gazette, 1978).

CHAPTER 11

Public-Sector Development: Cost–Benefit Analysis

After studying this chapter you will be able to:

- **Explain the concept of potential pareto improvement**
- **Describe the principles of cost–benefit analysis**
- **Explain the limitations of cost–benefit analysis**
- **Analyse the difficulties of choosing an appropriate discount rate**
- **Give examples of use of CBA in actual land-use decisions**

11.1 The functions of cost–benefit analysis (CBA)

Welfare and 'Pareto optimality'

The object of an economic system is to allocate scarce resources in such a way that society's welfare is maximised (see Chapter 1). But since welfare is subjective to the individual person it cannot be quantified in absolute terms. Thus only in the narrow Pareto sense – where at least one person is made better off without anyone being made worse off – can we assert that the reshuffling of resources will result in a *definite* welfare improvement.

For practical purposes, however, this requirement is too restrictive. Securing benefits for some persons almost invariably incurs costs to others. We can allow for this by saying that a *potential* Pareto improvement exists when those who gain from a change can fully compensate those who lose. The improvement is only 'potential' because welfare may be affected by the inherent income redistribution underlying the change when compensation is not actually paid (see p. 160).

Property development represents a reallocation of resources to increase welfare. In the private sector it takes place through the market system; in the public sector decisions have a political content, but a technique referred to as cost-benefit analysis (CBA) may be used to impart objectivity. Whichever method is used, it must be evaluated on the welfare test: does it allocate resources to produce a Pareto-optimal situation? That is, is it one where it is impossible to increase welfare by a further reshuffling of resources?

Weaknesses of the price system

With the price system, individuals indicate their preferences in the market. The demand curve reflects the benefit expected to be received from different quantities of goods and services. Similarly, the costs of supplying these quantities are shown by the supply curve. Resources are allocated on the basis of the equilibrium price which results.

But, as we indicated in Chapter 1, the market economy can achieve the maximum net benefit for society only under highly restrictive conditions, and then subject to the existing distribution of income. The facts that such conditions do not apply in real life and that welfare could possibly be increased by redistributing income provide grounds for government inter-ference in the market mechanism.

The nature of government decision-making

Action by the government may take the form of regulation (such as building regulations to reduce fire hazards), taxes or subsidies (such as grants towards the maintenance of historic buildings) or by the government itself providing goods and services. It is with the last that we are chiefly concerned in CBA. Government responsibility for roads, bridges, airports, parks, amenity land, new urban areas and housing means that decisions have to be made as regards the allocation of land and land resources. Is investment in a new motorway justified? Which site should be chosen for a new airport?

The difficulty is that, since many public-sector goods are provided free or below market-price, indications of the desirability of investment through the price system are either non-existent or defective. Moreover, allowance has to be made for 'spillover' benefits and costs. For instance, the usual cost-revenue criterion may be inappropriate when there are unemployed resources, for then the real cost of government spending to employ them may be zero, especially if there is a strong 'multiplier' effect. The government, too, may have to pay more attention than the private sector to the wishes of unborn generations to achieve inter-generational equity. Therefore, some other basis of decision-making usually has to be adopted.

Government decisions may rest mainly on subjective political considerations. For example, in order to obtain a 'social mix', council housing may be provided in an expensive residential area. Such a procedure, however, has serious defects in dealing with public investment. First, the one-person, one-vote principle does not weight votes according to the intensity of welfare gained or lost. Thus, the simple majority decision might allow two voters marginally in favour of a scheme to outvote one who strongly opposes it, in spite of the fact that the sum of their benefits is less than the costs inflicted on the single opponent. Second, political decisions are essentially subjective. Economic efficiency in resource allocation requires that objective criteria should be used as far as possible. Third, the extension of government involvement in the economy has increased the burden and complexity of public-sector decisions. Many would argue that decentralisation of decision-making is desirable.

The role of CBA

CBA is a technique which seeks to bring greater objectivity into decision-making. It does this by identifying all the relevant benefits and costs of a particular scheme and quantifying them in money terms so that each can be aggregated and then compared.

In particular, CBA is likely to have its main use in the public sector where (i) price signals are inadequate to guide investment decisions; (ii) 'spillover' benefits and costs are important because of the magnitude of the schemes; and (iii) the welfare of unborn generations has to be allowed for – for example, by conservation measures.

11.2 The principles of CBA

Quantifying in money terms

Since welfare is subjective to the individual, it cannot be measured cardinally in order to aggregate the welfare of individuals. The nearest we can come to surmounting this difficulty is to say that benefits are commensurate with willingness to pay (*WTP*) in terms of money. This can be justified as follows.

A consumer maximises benefits from his expenditure when:

$$\frac{MU_A}{MU_B} = \frac{P_A}{P_B}$$

If, for instance, the marginal utility (*MU*) of the last unit of *A* is five times that of the last unit of *B*, he will buy an extra unit of *A* provided that the price of *A* is less than five times the price of *B*. Thus benefits derived are indicated by *WTP*, that is, the sum of money which a person will pay for a good or service rather than go without it. Thus the area under a market demand curve measures aggregate individuals *WTP* or, in other words, aggregate marginal benefits.

In Figure 11.1 DD_1 is the demand curve. Assume that average costs are constant: the supply curve *PS* is thus perfectly elastic. The price will then be *OP*, and people will buy *OM*. Benefits derived equal *DOMR*, but total expenditure will be *POMR*, giving *consumers' surplus* of *DPR*. Consumers' surplus should therefore be included with benefits, especially with large indivisible projects. But for goods which are bought in quantity in the market, calculating consumers' surplus would involve ascertaining and aggregating each demand curve for each consumer. Because of the difficulties involved in obtaining a complete demand curve, it is usual to value the benefits in terms of total expenditure.

Benefits have to be compared with the costs of obtaining them – that is, the cost of the factors which have to be diverted from the best alternative project (*POMR* in Figure 11.1). In practice, the supply curve may not be perfectly elastic but rising, indicating average cost increases as output expands. Some factors earn economic rent, the aggregate of which is known as *producers' surplus*. This too should be included as a net benefit. But, for practical reasons, costs, like benefits, are measured in terms of quantity times price. If benefits exceed costs, the project should go ahead (but see p. 175).

A simple public investment problem

Assume that a large area of sandy beach can be reached only by a narrow lane branching off the main road some five miles away. As a result, visitors, even though they are mostly local, find it necessary to travel to the beach by

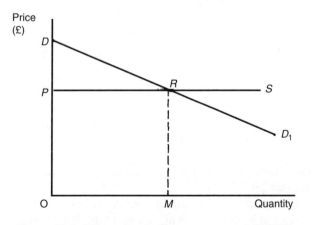

Figure 11.1 Measuring 'willingness to pay' (WTP)

car. No parking is permitted on the approach lane, but the local farmer has converted a field adjacent to the beach into a car-park.

A parking fee is charged which the farmer feels maximises his profits. The car-parking fee is £1, at which 10 000 cars park annually, leaving considerable spare capacity. The only cost, which is incurred irrespective of the number of cars parking, is £2 000 for two attendants employed for four summer months to collect parking fees and clean the toilets. The farmer is currently seeking to sell the car-park and is asking £80 000 for it.

Because the lane to the car-park is so narrow, all waiting is prohibited by double yellow lines each side. The council has to employ two wardens, costing £5000 a year, to ensure that the no-waiting restriction is observed. Even so, frequent hold-ups mean that the return journey averages 32 minutes.

The council estimates that if it took over the car-park and made parking free, the cars using the park would increase by 10 000 a year. The increased visitors would require extra toilets costing £20 000, but these could be supervised and cleaned by the existing two men, since they would not be needed to collect parking fees. The extra traffic would also necessitate widening the approach lane at a cost of £170 000. After the road improvements the return journey to the beach would take only 20 minutes. It is estimated that the 12 minutes saved is worth 20 p per car journey. Moreover, the two traffic wardens would no longer be necessary.

For the council the scheme has a further advantage: enlarging the town's recreation park some eight miles distant at a cost of £50 000 need no longer be proceeded with, since people are likely to prefer the beach once car-parking is free.

Finally, it is assumed that there is full employment and no inflation.

The CBA approach

In all cost-benefit analysis it is necessary to:

(1) *List all relevant items.* These will include spillover effects of the proposal, such as the cost of extra toilets and road-widening, the saving on the extension to the town's recreation park. Care must be taken to avoid double-counting: thus the farmer could not include the loss of his land and the loss of parking fees, because the former is simply the capitalised value of the latter.

(2) *Value expected benefits and costs,* deciding whether any allowance is to be made for the more distant future.

(3) *Discount the future flow of benefits and costs* in order to obtain their capitalised present value. This involves choosing an appropriate rate of discount (see pp. 170–4).

(4) *Appraise the project* by setting off aggregate benefits against aggregate costs. This can be done either according to the Pareto criterion of seeing

how different parties gain or lose, or by a direct comparison of additional benefits and additional costs.

The Pareto balance-sheet

The parties to this public investment in a car-park are the farmer, the existing parkers, the additional parkers and the taxpayer. What are their respective gains and losses?

The *farmer* receives £80 000, but loses a net income of £8 000 a year.

Existing parkers save £10 000 a year on fees, and 12 minutes on the return journey valued at £2000 a year.

New parkers have so far provided no firm indication of the value of car-parking benefits to them. It is therefore necessary to estimate their *WTP*.

Figure 11.2 depicts the situation.

Since the farmer is a monopolist, his demand curve will be downward-sloping; let us assume it is linear. We know that, with free parking, the demand would be 20 000; thus the demand curve cuts the quantity axis at this point. The farmer's marginal revenue curve will also be linear. Because $MR = 0$ at point M, elasticity of demand at A is equal to 1, and therefore $DA = AD_1$; and $OM = MD_1$. We know that all the farmer's costs are fixed costs; thus $MC = O$ up to full capacity of the car-park, and therefore MC is coincident with the quantity axis up to this point.

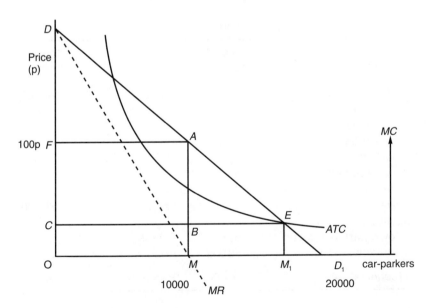

Figure 11.2 Demand for car-parking

The farmer will maximise his profits by charging car-parkers 100 p (OF), appropriate to 'output' OM where $MR = MC$. At this price, there are 10 000 parkers.

Assuming a 10-year purchase, we obtain a Pareto balance sheet (Table 11.1).

With free parking total demand would be 20 000 and the *WTP* of new parkers would be measured by the area AMD_1, equal to £5000 a year. The saving in time through the road improvements also provides these new 10 000 parkers with an extra benefit of £2000 a year.

Taxpayers have to bear the costs of the investment: £170 000 for widening the road and £20 000 for the additional toilets. But there are gains: £50 000 is saved through not having to enlarge the town's recreation park, and the two traffic wardens at £5000 a year will no longer be required; since full employment has been assumed, they can find jobs elsewhere.

Annual future revenues and costs have to be discounted to the present to obtain their current capital value. Let us assume a discount rate of 10 per cent and that these perpetual flows are valued on a ten years' purchase basis. We therefore have the Pareto balance-sheet shown in Table 11.1.

Since those who gain can compensate those who lose and still show a net increase in benefits of £20 000, the local authority should undertake the project. It should be noted, however, that the viability of the scheme arises only because spillover benefits, chiefly the saving on enlarging the town's recreation park, have been included.

Table 11.1 A Pareto balance-sheet

	Gains (£)		Costs (£)
Farmer			
Sale proceeds	80 000	Profit lost	80 000
Existing parkers			
Fees saved	100 000		
Time saved	20 000		
New parkers			
Parking benefits	50 000		
Time saved	20 000		
Taxpayers		Land	80 000
Saving on:			
town park extension	50 000	Toilets	20 000
traffic wardens	50 000	Road widening	170 000
Total benefits	*370 000*	*Total costs*	*350 000*

Additional benefits and costs approach

In practice, CBA usually concentrates only on net *additional* benefits and costs (Table 11.2). The net increase in benefits is still, of course, £20 000.

Possible constraints

A CBA is itself a commodity having costs and therefore should not be undertaken if these are likely to be greater than the possible net benefits where these are not certain.

But even if CBA shows a favourable balance, the project may run up against obstacles. Thus the council's car-park scheme above could only go ahead if funds were available. In practice, there may be *budget constraints*. Public-sector borrowing may be limited or financing the scheme through taxation may be difficult. Where there is a budget constraint, projects have to be ranked and available funds apportioned between them so as to secure the maximum net benefit possible. This ranking problem was discussed in Chapter 6.

Some projects may be subject to *legal constraints*, involving easements, covenants or even the responsibilities of public bodies as laid down by statutes, for example, for common land. A costly and time-consuming private bill procedure may be necessary in order to proceed with the scheme.

More important, the project may encounter *administrative or political difficulties*. Where more than one local authority or public body is involved, they may be motivated by different interests or political views. Thus the National Trust would probably oppose an electricity scheme which took pylons over land for which it was responsible.

Finally, the project may be opposed on *distributional* grounds, being deemed to benefit the rich to the exclusion of the poor. For instance, if it were located in a prosperous region rather than one of high unemployment, it could conflict with government regional policy.

Table 11.2 CBA net additional benefits and costs

	Benefits (£)		Costs (£)
Existing parkers	100 000	Road-widening	170 000
New parkers	50 000	Land	80 000
Costs saved:		Toilets	20 000
Parkers' time	40 000		
Traffic wardens	50 000		
Town's recreation park	50 000		
Total	290 000		270 000

Difficulties with a CBA

Our simple example of the car-park obscures conceptual and practical difficulties which are inherent in any CBA. These include:

(a) allowing for the distributional effects of a project;
(b) adjusting market prices to allow for indirect taxes, price controls, and so on;
(c) estimating the 'willingness to pay' for intangibles which are not priced in the market;
(d) incorporating intangibles;
(e) choosing the appropriate discount rate; and
(f) providing for risk and uncertainty in estimates of future benefits and costs.

We now examine these in more detail.

11.3 The problem of distributional effects

It would be rare for a public project to qualify on the strict Pareto principle of some gainers but no losers. We can adapt the car-park scheme above as an example. Suppose the farmer knows the demand curve, DD_1 (see Figure 11.2). His costs as stated are all fixed, with the average total cost curve a rectangular hyperbola (ATC) and the marginal costs nil up to the point of capacity (MC). Profits are maximised at a parking charge of OF (100p) with the number of cars restricted to OM (10 000), where $MC = MR$. Now assume the council faces the same demand curve and the same cost conditions. It could purchase the site from the farmer and extend car-parking to OM_1, charging price OC where revenue just covers the same total costs. This produces a net benefit increase given by the triangle ABE. Moreover, since the farmer has been fully compensated in money, no initial problem of income redistribution arises.

However, in our original example, car-parkers, although willing to pay, were given the benefit free, the cost being borne by taxpayers. The former gain; the latter lose. There is thus some redistribution of income.

The difficulty is that the gainers may be rich people having, as is generally assumed, a lower marginal utility of income than poor people; on the other hand, the losers may be poor people with a high marginal utility of income. In the car-park project, for example, the gainers were car-owners who had sufficient leisure time to take a trip to the beach, whereas the losers, the taxpayers, may include many old people who could ill-afford an increase in their council tax.

Because there is no cardinal measure of utility, we cannot completely over-come this difficulty of income redistribution. But it is possible to deal with it up to a point. If the change in income redistribution is small relative to the net benefit gain, it can be ignored. Alternatively, a weighting system, which will necessarily have an element of subjectivity, can be used. Thus, to assess the welfare of the car-park scheme, we should apply a low weight to the richer car-parkers' benefit and a higher weight to the poorer taxpayers' losses in order to reflect their relative differences in marginal utility of income.

This problem of distributional effects crops up in various forms. Country-lovers may lose pleasure through electricity pylons intruding on the landscape. If they are fully compensated, there is no loss of income so the problem of measuring their marginal utility of income does not arise. The difficulty (a frequent one) of identifying such losers means that compen-sation is not actually paid, and there are thus distributional effects. Simi-larly, when comparing the benefits of a project to future generations with its costs to the present population, some allowance should be made for the fact that future generations are likely to have a higher income.

11.4 Adjusting market prices

CBA expresses benefits and costs in money terms. To do this it has to give a price to identifiable units. This raises two problems.

(1) Where a good is traded in the market, to what extent can we use the market price?
(2) If there is no market for the good, for example because 'free riders' cannot be excluded, how can we ascribe a price to it?

In this section we are concerned with the first problem; the second is considered in Section 11.5. In order to avoid complicating the discussion, external benefits and costs will be ignored.

Possible deficiencies in market prices as reflecting opportunity costs

Where market prices reflect the true opportunity cost to society of employing resources in a particular way (assuming no externalities), they can be used to estimate the cost of a project.

However, in the real world it has to be recognised that prices in the market may not accurately reflect opportunity cost. This may be the result of imperfect competition, indirect taxes and subsidies, or controls which interfere with the free operation of the market mechanism. In these circum-stances it is necessary to consider whether some adjustment is both desirable and practical to produce a set of *shadow prices* for the CBA calculations.

Imperfect competition

Under perfect competition, price = marginal revenue = marginal cost = the cost of an additional unit of the good to society. Where there is imperfect competition, however, price is higher than marginal revenue, though the latter is still equated with marginal cost. Thus, price exceeds marginal cost which measures opportunity cost to society. Similarly, in factor markets the value of the marginal product at the quantity employed is higher than the factor reward when the firm is a monopsonistic buyer of factors.

Suppose in our example of the car-park that the tarmac for the road was supplied by a monopolist. In order to maximise his profits, he would charge price *OP* per tonne (see Figure 11.3). On the other hand, marginal cost would be only *OC* per tonne. We should thus value the tarmac at *OC*, the opportunity cost for this amount.

There are, however, two major difficulties. First, there is the practical one of estimating marginal cost. Second, there is the conceptual problem of the 'second best'. Given that the 'first-best' allocation of resources by marginal-cost pricing in all markets is unattainable, do we ensure a 'second-best' solution by adopting marginal-cost pricing solely in the public sector? We cannot be certain. If, in the existing situation, there is the same degree of distortion between price and marginal cost in all markets, adopting

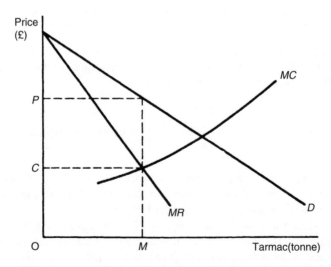

Figure 11.3 A monopolist's price and marginal cost for a given output

marginal-cost pricing in only one part of the economy could lead to an allocation of resources further from the Pareto optimum. In short, while there may be a single optimum position given all the essential conditions for Pareto optimality, there may be many 'second-best' possibilities, and if only the 'second best' is obtainable in practice we may be making things worse by tinkering with the system in the hope of attaining what is really impossible.

It should also be noted that marginal cost is not acceptable when, in a situation of decreasing costs, total costs are not covered. It has been suggested for such a case, therefore, that the principle of a two-part tariff pricing system should be followed, a sum being added to marginal cost by way of a fixed standing charge (pp. 398–400).

Indirect taxes, subsidies and market controls

Opportunity cost is represented by factor cost (that is, cost *less* indirect taxes, plus subsidies). It is argued that market prices should be adjusted by subtracting indirect taxes (for instance, for petrol saved by the construction of a motor-way) and adding subsidies (for example, for the value of agricultural produce lost). The snag with this procedure, however, is that taxes 'deducted' in this way should really be 'recouped' on other goods, thereby distorting *their* prices. There is thus a case for calculating benefits and costs at current market prices.

Similarly, physical controls such as rent control may keep prices below market price. Such controlled prices cannot therefore be used for CBA purposes.

Moreover, prices may be distorted by controls elsewhere – for example, through quotas. Suppose, for instance, that a land-reclamation project allowed a dairy farm to be established. In valuing milk it should be remembered that its price of is largely the result of the EU's agriculture policy of restricting supply by quotas. Similarly, prices of imports may be artificially lowered by a protection policy aimed at maintaining a higher exchange rate than that which would prevail in a free market.

Should adjustments be made to market prices?

Although market prices may not reflect true opportunity costs, the obstacles to making the necessary adjustments are formidable. The cost of obtaining the information needed may be too high to be worth while, and consistency in the adjustments made would be difficult to attain throughout both the public and private sectors.

Because of such problems, some economists have rejected correcting market prices. Others, however, consider that adopting a straight marginal-cost pricing rule gives consistency to accounting procedures and corresponds more closely to the costs which CBA is seeking to measure.

11.5 Pricing non-market goods

Market prices may not be available. This occurs with the following goods.

(1) *Community and public goods*, where 'free riders' cannot be excluded (examples are street-lighting, land, radio programmes) or where it is decided to make no charge (for instance, for public parks or bridges). Here the cost is covered by taxation which is unlikely to reflect true 'willingness to pay'.

(2) *Intangible externalities*, such as noise and congestion cost, human lives saved, the pleasure derived by passers-by from flowers and trees in private gardens or from a walk in a park.

Since both enter into CBA calculations, it is necessary to ascribe notional prices to them so that benefits and costs can be quantified in money terms. But formulating such 'shadow' or 'surrogate' prices faces formidable difficulties, as the following specific examples reveal.

Recreation

In our example of the car-park we were able to estimate the benefits (*WTP*) of a trip to the beach from an existing market. However, for many recreational facilities – such as the Lake District, Hadrian's Wall, the National Gallery – there has been no previous market. How, then, do we derive a demand curve?

One method would be to devise a questionnaire in which people state how much they would be willing to pay for the facility. Nevertheless, difficulties may arise in obtaining a representative sample, while replies may lack accuracy because of respondents' subjectivity.

A second possibility is to adapt prices from a parallel facility where charges are made, for instance, for admission to the grounds of a stately mansion. But for many activities, such as fell-walking, such an alternative is not available.

The usual method, therefore, is to see how demand varies with travel costs, both in money and time. The greater the distance travelled for such recreation, the greater the travel costs; thus demand should fall with distance. To allow for differences in density of population in the catchment area being studied, the number of trips per thousand of the population for different zones is derived. Suppose the following figures are obtained:

Zone	Trips per 1000 population
1	300
2	100
3	60

To simplify, let us assume that: (i) travel costs from zone 1 average £1; (ii) an outward movement to zones 2 and 3 each adds £1; and (iii) there are 1000 people in each zone. Thus if travel costs represent the price, we can derive a demand curve as follows:

Price (£)	Trips made from zone			Total trips
	1	2	3	
1	300	100	60	460
2	–	100	60	160
3	–	–	60	60

From the demand curve we can estimate *WTP*.

This approach, although based on revealed market behaviour, presents difficulties:

(a) What should be the unit priced – whole-day trips, half-day trips or hours spent enjoying the facility?
(b) If the car is the main mode of travel, then the number of trips should be related to every 1000 *car-owners* of the population.
(c) Some allowance ought to be made for the average number of persons brought by each car.
(d) Where the journey is made by car, the assessment of cost presents problems. If the car is used mainly for business, then only the marginal cost (chiefly for petrol) will be the real cost of the journey. On the other hand, if the car is used exclusively for recreation, a proportion of overheads should also be included.
(e) At what price should travel time be valued (see below)?
(f) How should costs be adjusted if the actual journey to the facility also gives pleasure?
(g) How is the cost to be apportioned if more than one recreation centre is visited on the journey?

Valuing time saved

Transport improvements usually result in reducing the time spent in making a journey. What price do we put on this benefit?

Where it is working time saved, for example, by deliveries by lorry, and it results in extra work being done, the employer's valuation should be accepted: that is, it would include savings on overheads as well as on wages.

But time saved may simply mean that people get to work quicker, thereby increasing their leisure time. For people who choose how many hours they work, the marginal utility of leisure and work time would be equal, so that again time saved should be at the earning rate. But for most people a straight choice between an extra hour's work and an extra hour's leisure is not available. In practice, therefore, leisure time has to be valued arbitrarily as a proportion of the earning rate, and in fact 25 to 50 per cent is usually taken as being the value of time saved.

An alternative approach is to take the value which people put on time indirectly when they incur higher costs in order to save it. This value may be indicated in different ways:

(a) People may pay a higher price for their housing in order to be nearer their work. The snag here is that the higher price may reflect quality differences or nearness to non-work facilities.
(b) The route chosen may reduce time but at a higher cost, such as the toll paid to cross an estuary by ferry. To be accurate, however, the assessment would have to be confined to regular users having perfect knowledge.
(c) Car-drivers may trade speed against petrol consumption, and so on. However, they may not know the exact extra cost involved, may enjoy driving at speed, or choose their speed for safety considerations.
(d) One mode of travel may be faster than another but more expensive – for example, a taxi as opposed to a bus. Comfort considerations, however, may enter into such a choice.

Some allowance should also be made for the fact that as productivity increases over time so will the wage rate; thus the value of leisure time will tend to increase over time.

Human life

Such projects as road improvements reduce deaths and accidents; others such as airports may increase them for people in the vicinity. How can a money value be given to human life? More specifically, how do we value loss of life? Here again there are alternatives, each presenting its own difficulties.

First, the present value of future expected earnings can be calculated, with additions for suffering endured and the grief experienced by the family. However, this ignores the consumer's surplus a person enjoys in spending his income.

The second alternative measures the present value of *net* output of the dead person, that is, the flow of future earnings less consumption. This method, however, presents moral difficulties, for it implicitly assumes that society's objective is maximising total GNP. Fortunately, society does not require a person to justify his existence on economic grounds. People living on state pensions are not disposed of because their death would represent a net gain to society! Society takes into account human feelings.

A third method assesses the value placed on human life by society through its political decisions. For instance, if compulsory safety-belts costing £X saved in total Y lives, the value of human life is at least £ $\sum X / Y$. However, the fundamental objection to this approach is that it is a circular argument: the economist should really be justifying the cost of compulsory safety-belts in terms of the value of lives saved!

A fourth measure, the sum for which a person insures his life, does not measure the value of life, but simply reflects a man's concern for his family's future in the event of his death. A bachelor, for instance, might have no life insurance, but he still values his life! Or life insurance may simply be the condition for obtaining a mortgage.

A fifth measure may be derived from people doing dangerous jobs. But information about risks may be incomplete and the labour market may be imperfect.

The real difficulty with all these methods is that they break with the criterion for a potential Pareto improvement: that there is still a gain after all losses have been compensated for. The second method highlights this snag, for the fact that society could gain from the death of a retired person arises simply because the latter receives no compensation for the loss of his life. Since such compensation is probably infinite, any project which saved one life would cover its costs!

However, it must be remembered that, in practice, we are not concerned with *one* person's certain death. What we have to compensate for is the extra *risk* of death to which all affected persons are exposed, for example, as the result of the increased traffic of a new airport. Those concerned are: (i) the additional air passengers; (ii) their relatives; and (iii) people living around the airport. The value of the risk to the first can be disregarded, since it can be assumed that travellers have allowed for this in buying an air ticket. Indeed, as regards the third group, care must be taken to avoid double-counting, since compensation may already have been carried out through the price system – for example, in a lower price for houses near the airport which has induced residents to accept the risks involved. Otherwise, an insurance figure can be accepted as the necessary compensation required by the second and third groups except that, since people tend to underestimate, this figure may be somewhat inadequate.

11.6 Dealing with spillover effects and intangibles

Spillover effects present practical problems. Which spillovers should be included? In aggregating costs and benefits, how much weight should be attached to the shadow prices of intangibles compared with true market prices?

The problem of which spillovers should be included is concerned, first, with the difficulty of distinguishing between real changes and distributional effects, and, second, on deciding the cut-off point.

Real changes and distributional effects

Real changes are those that affect the performance of other inputs (for example, an additional large office building in the City of London could increase traffic congestion and thus lower the efficiency of road transport) or the pleasure of others (for instance, a motorway creates a noise nuisance to nearby residents). Obviously such effects should be taken into account.

Distributional or transfer effects refer to those effects of individual projects which result in shifts in *prices* to other parties. Thus an increased demand by tourists for hotels in London will lead to higher wages of catering workers, not only in hotels but also in restaurants and cafés. Are these effects part of the cost to society of increasing hotel services? Consider what happens. The higher wages of catering workers will cause restaurants and cafés to reduce their demand for them. Each restaurant itself will now earn a lower economic rent, while variable factors will drift to more profitable uses. But what all this means is simply that maximising consumers' economic welfare has pointed to a better 'basket' of products from a reshuffling of resources. Although painful for some, such readjustments must occur in a changing economy. In any assessment of the costs and gains of public development, there is no reason why the government should consider distributional effects except that, on grounds of equity, it may feel some compensation is called for.

Similarly, does an allowance have to be made for changes in the prices of substitute and complementary goods and services which result from some public development? For example, road and rail transport are to some extent substitute products. If the government, by instituting a new road-building programme, reduced the economic viability of the railways, should this be allowed for in assessing the economic viability of investment in new roads? A private monopolist with many lines of production would obviously take into account such interactions when introducing changes. Should not the government do the same? Quite apart from the obvious difficulty of trying to trace the endless chain of effects throughout the whole field of government action, the answer is not entirely clear. The action of the monopolist may not be the appropriate criterion for the maximisation of consumers' economic welfare since there may be other spillover effects which he does not take into account. Thus the government may require the price of North Sea gas to be raised relative to that of coal in the interests of full employment, conservation of reserves and a long-term fuel policy dependent on coal reserves.

It is easy to be tidy and logical in theory but far harder to implement ideas in practice. In real life it may be extremely difficult to sort out real effects from distributional effects. For example, if a by-pass road isolates formerly thriving shopkeepers and involves them in loss of trade, does this represent a real cost or simply a transfer item? Seemingly the latter, for the physical productivity of shopkeepers has not been altered. Or has it? It could be argued that in this case planning has so affected the locational pattern of shop services that production potential has suffered because they are now in the wrong place. If we accept this reasoning, such losses must count as real effects which should be included in any reckoning.

In most cases these effects are not likely to be of great significance and are often offset by changes in the opposite direction (for example, in the case of the new road, production potential elsewhere may increase through being more advantageously located).

To sum up, the gains and costs of a project should include the value of any real spillovers. But changes in prices which merely reflect relative changes in the conditions of demand and supply are beside the point. Thus, in choosing between alternative public projects, the government should not act like a giant monopoly, seeking to maximise overall profits from its many activities, but should assess each case on its merits, taking into account real spillover effects. Pure redistribution effects are outside the question of economic efficiency, though the government can make a political decision to allow for them on the grounds of equity.

The cut-off point for spillovers

In considering spillovers there is also the difficulty of deciding the cut-off point and whether any allowance should be made for unforeseen costs and benefits.

In Figure 11.4, for example, a motorway is built from *A* to *B*. Do we include only the benefits of travellers from *A* to *B*? It is likely, however, that it could reduce congestion for travellers from *B* to *C* and from *E* to *B*. Indeed, such routes could be extended, so where do we stop? The further we go, the more difficult it is to distinguish all beneficiaries. Moreover, certain spillovers have to be decided by reference to what would generally be regarded as 'reasonable'. Thus while environmental spillovers from the motorway would certainly qualify, the envy which some people not owning a car might feel as they saw others using the motorway to get to the seaside would have to be excluded.

Nor can all spillovers be foreseen. The motorways around Los Angeles have saved the white-tailed kite from extinction. The reason is that the shrubs and grass of the broad shoulders and central dividers provide relative safety for mice and lizards, the staple diet of the kite, for no man in his right mind ever sets foot in these areas. Alternatively, there could be unforeseen external costs. The Aswan Dam, for instance, reduced the flow of fish food

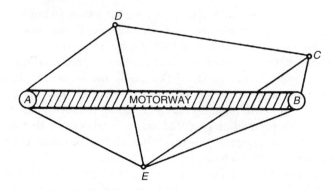

Figure 11.4 Effects of a motorway on surrounding roads

from the Nile into the Mediterranean, giving rise to the real costs of fewer fish and, by affecting the livelihood of fishermen, having distributional effects. Moreover, since this was not confined to Egyptian fishermen, it raises the problem of whether, in a world where countries are becoming increasingly dependent on one another, spillover effects should be limited to the national economy.

The weighting of intangibles in aggregating benefits and costs

In so far as there is perfect competition, market prices at factor cost reflect true opportunity costs. In comparison, shadow prices are derived indirectly, and to that extent are somewhat suspect. Should we therefore, when aggregating, treat market and shadow prices equally? The difficulty becomes more real when shadow prices form a high proportion of total costs and benefits. Thus, in our example of the car-park, the £70 000 benefits obtained by new parkers was based on an estimated demand curve derived from the price paid by existing car-parkers. Should this shadow price represent an overestimate of 30 per cent, the scheme would not be viable. Actual CBAs have shown the crucial margin of error is usually much smaller. Thus, while the Roskill Commission (1970) estimated that the Cublington site for the Third London Airport would be £158 to £197 million cheaper than Foulness, only a 1 per cent error in total benefit or total cost figures could have made Foulness the lower-cost site.

11.7 Choosing the appropriate discount rate

The 'real' rate of interest

If we postpone current consumption, resources can be used for investment in capital equipment. This produces greater output in the future: that is, there is

growth. The gain is increased future consumption. We can thus speak of a
rate at which current consumption can be transformed into future consumption. Starting from consumption C_0 this is shown by the transformation
curve TT_1 in Figure 11.5.

However, future consumption is valued less highly than present consumption. This is because (i) people generally suffer from myopia; (ii) future
income is less certain since there is always the risk of death; and (iii) future
income is likely to be greater than present income, and thus the marginal
utility of present income is higher. This preference which people generally
have for present as opposed to future consumption is referred to as *time
preference*, and is shown by the indifference curve SS_1.

A function of an economic system is to bring people's time preference into
line with the actual opportunity cost of transforming current consumption
into future consumption. Given a perfect market, perfect competition, perfect
knowledge and no externalities, the free market system can produce a rate of
interest which achieves this. We shall refer to this as the 'real' rate of interest.

In Figure 11.5 the transformation curve TT_1 shows that if XT is not
consumed but invested, consumption in year 1 can increase by MK. That
is, the net productivity of capital, k, equals:

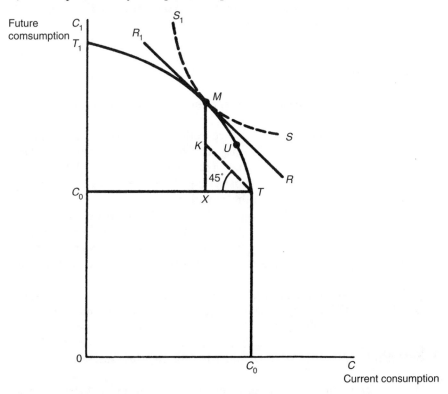

Figure 11.5 The determination of the 'real' rate of interest

$$\frac{MK}{XT} = \frac{MX - KX}{XT} = \frac{MX - XT}{XT} = \text{slope of } TT_1 - 1 \text{ at } X$$

Similarly, SS_1 can be regarded as a society indifference curve between C and C_1. At any point the marginal rate of substitution of C_1 for C is equal to the slope of SS_1. Since, however, people prefer C to C_1, this slope will equal $1 + s$, where s is the weighting to be attached to C compared with C_1. But s is really society's rate of time preference, and so $s = $ slope of $SS_1 - 1$.

Given our assumptions, the market will produce a unique or 'real' rate of interest, i, represented by the slope of RR_1, which equates the time preference of society (the individuals comprising the market) with the profitability of available investment opportunities. This means that $i = s = k$. In Figure 11.5 equilibrium occurs at M, where TT_1 just touches SS_1 the highest indifference curve attainable by society.

Any other point on TT_1 would put society on a lower indifference curve. Thus point U represents underinvestment compared with society's time preference, for the opportunity-cost rate of return is greater than the time-preference rate required. This disequilibrium between investment and saving would cause the rate of interest to fall until there was equilibrium with RR_1 at point M, where the net productivity of investment would be in line with society's time preference.

Complications

In practice, the conditions necessary for a unique, equilibrating rate of interest are not fulfilled.

First, many different rates exist, reflecting differences in risk (the small private company would have to pay a higher rate of interest than a large public company) or in imperfections in the capital market (the only source of funds to the small private company may be a bank, whereas the large company could float a loan on the capital market).

Second, money rates of interest may be affected by monetary influences as opposed to being determined solely by real forces – the return on investment and time preference. Monetary influences would include external pressure on the exchange rate or changes in the demand for money for liquidity purposes.

Third, actual money rates of interest may be higher than RR_1, the real rate, because the reward for saving is reduced by taxation and inflation.

Selecting from the rates offered in the capital market

With different rates to choose from, which is the most appropriate for assessing public-sector projects?

One view is that discounting should be at the rate of interest at which the government can borrow to finance such schemes: that is, the yield on long-term gilt-edged securities. However, the government borrowing rate tends to be low because it is a 'riskless' rate. But public projects such as *Concorde* are not free from risk, and the rate of discount should reflect this. Even if the project is financed from taxation, the opportunity cost is the rate which the tax-payer could have obtained had the money been left with him to invest.

Therefore, it is argued that because resources for investment are not unlimited, the opportunity cost of a public project is the equal-risk project in the private sector which has to be forgone. Thus the appropriate rate of interest is what a large public company would have to pay for funds to finance such investment – for example, the current debenture rate.

Only if lower risk is inherent in public projects should a lower interest rate be used. It can be argued that this lower risk does in fact exist. Because so many public projects are undertaken, risks are spread: losses on one project can be averaged out by gains on others. Thus the government (as it were) carries its own insurance. Moreover, not only are risks spread over projects but also the cost of any error in estimation is distributed among so many taxpayers that the actual risk borne by each is so small as to be acceptable. Thus discounting projects at a slightly lower rate than in the private sector is justified.

Projects financed out of taxation

It should also be noted that many projects are financed, not out of borrowing, but out of taxation. Here the true opportunity cost of capital would necessitate tracing the taxes back to their source and discovering the value of them to the original owners. Suppose, for example, that firms paying corporation tax could obtain a 25 per cent rate of return by ploughing back their profits. This would be the opportunity cost of capital raised by such taxation. Alternatively, if taxes force firms to borrow in order to carry out investment, then the opportunity cost of funds to the government is the cost of such marginal, private market borrowing. A study conducted in the USA using 1956–7 data produced an opportunity cost of funds raised through taxation equal to approximately double the bond rate prevailing at the time. No comparable study has been done in Britain, but in similar conditions it would be likely to produce a 'target' rate of interest for evaluating publicly financed projects much higher than the rate on gilt-edged securities.

The social time preference rate

Apart from allowances for differences in risk between public and private projects, the problem is complicated by time-preference considerations.

First, society's time preference is not the same as the sum total of individual time preferences. It can be held that individuals suffer from myopia, a deficient 'telescopic faculty', so that they fail to appreciate how much they would benefit from future as opposed to current consumption. This difficulty is covered where society acts for individuals.

Second, society as a whole is an undying institution, and the government, which is responsible for society's decisions, is therefore concerned with the welfare of future generations, making decisions (as it were) on behalf of those still unborn. Such decisions are of particular importance when a project has an 'irreversible' cost, such as the demolition of a historic building, the destruction of the natural beauty of the Lake District, the complete exhaustion of a mineral stock or the wiping out of a particular species of animal, bird or plant. As the Green Party puts it: 'We do not inherit the land from our fathers; we borrow it from our children.' Thus in comparison with individuals, who have a limited time horizon, society has a lower time preference.

Both the above arguments therefore give further justification for discounting public projects at a lower interest rate – the 'social time preference rate' – than that arrived at through the market.

Providing for risk and uncertainty through the rate of interest

Although all the usual methods of allowing for risk and uncertainty in appraising projects can be applied to public-sector schemes, the above discussion suggests that one based on choosing an appropriate rate of interest will be the one usually followed. In practice, governments fix a minimum rate of return which must be achieved for public-sector investment to be acceptable.

However, if public projects are discounted at a lower rate than in the private sector, this will divert resources towards public investment: for example, producing electricity from nuclear energy (a public project) rather than from natural gas (mainly private-sector investment). This is shown in Figure 11.6, where differences in risk and time preference between the private and public sectors are shown in the transformation curves and indifference curves respectively. The equilibrium real rate of interest is therefore lower in the public sector (LL_1) than in the private sector (RR_1). As a result, investment in the public sector is greater (X_1T) compared with the private sector (XT).

11.8 An appreciation of the role of CBA

Applicability of CBA in the public sector

It is essential, since resources are limited, that public-sector expenditure obtains 'value for money'. The difficulty is that financial criteria may be

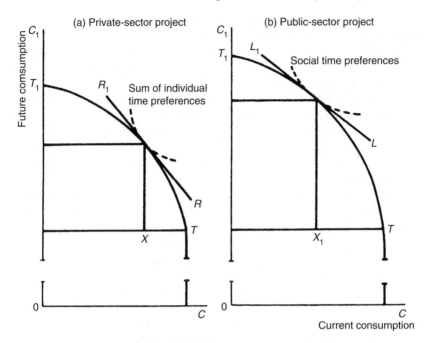

Figure 11.6 The allocation of investment resources between public-sector and private-sector project

either non-existent or inadequate for assessing the viability of projects. CBA is designed to assist such decision-making. Public projects often involve the allocation of land resources; thus the technique of CBA can be applied to evaluating planning applications, comprehensive redevelopment proposals, motorway construction, the siting of an airport, and so on. In particular, it can ensure that full allowance is made for spillover benefits and costs.

Limitations of CBA

Nevertheless, as our analysis has indicated, CBA runs up against conceptual and practical difficulties. These weaken its effectiveness as a tool for decision-making. The following considerations are of particular importance.

First, CBA cannot be used where political decisions dominate. For instance, how much is spent by Britain on defence may depend upon subjective views as to the possible role of the Armed Forces in support of foreign policy and to what extent such expenditure can be trimmed in order to extend the social services. Similarly, proposals for comprehensive education are advanced, at least partly, on the subjective grounds that they promote a more integrated society, while expensive local authority housing may be provided in areas of high land values, such as Hampstead, in order to achieve a 'social mix'. Although social factors can be identified, it is often impossible to measure them satisfactorily.

Second, CBA may be difficult to apply to certain decisions. Consider, for instance, a local authority which has £2 m. to spend on a swimming pool. The decision rests between: (i) one swimming pool of Olympic standards which, while it could also be used by local people, would bring prestige to the town; (ii) three smaller swimming pools, suitable for inter-school galas; and (iii) six very small pools specifically designed for children learning to swim. The advantages of each are largely immeasurable by CBA techniques, the result being that councillors will have to decide subjectively by voting at a council meeting.

Similarly, a firm CBA decision cannot be applied to a project involving irreversible decisions, such as the survival of a species of animal or plant. In such cases it is impossible to estimate a current economic cost, since it would deny future generations the opportunity to choose.

Third, CBA cannot deal objectively with the redistribution of income which results from a project.

Fourth, CBA encounters formidable difficulties both in measuring and aggregating intangibles. Its validity is enhanced as the number of values obtained directly from the market increases, particularly if they are determined under conditions of near-perfect competition.

Fifth, there is always the problem of the cut-off point in deciding the benefits and costs to be included. The viability of a project could rest on this decision, and interested parties may be tempted to extend the cut-off point in order to justify their particular preferences.

Finally, what passes as CBA is often in reality merely a 'cost-effectiveness' study comparing different methods of achieving a given end. CBA should not only examine the method of achieving an objective but should compare the likely returns from alternative uses of the same resources. Thus, in the Roskill study, the decision to build a third London Airport had been predetermined; the Commission merely examined the costs and benefits of alternative sites.

Conclusion on the role of CBA

CBA provides a rational technique for appraising projects where market information is either non-existent or deficient. But it must not make false claims for objectivity by dealing in precise sums. Though it is an aid to decision-making, it is not a substitute for it. Its role is to present systematically all the information relevant to a decision, indicating the weight which can be placed on the accuracy of the calculations submitted. Drawing up such an agenda ensures that the claims of rival pressure groups are assessed and that all the relevant issues are fully debated before the ultimate political decision is taken.

Examples of the use of CBA in actual land-use decisions

Though CBA as outlined above can be used in all public investment decisions, it has particular application to the allocation of land resources, where externalities are likely to loom large. Thus CBA studies have been undertaken for:

(a) the construction of the M1 motorway
(b) the siting of the third London Airport
(c) the resiting of Covent Garden Market
(d) town planning: Cambridge
(e) urban expansion: Ipswich
(f) a shopping centre: Edgware
(g) a Severn barrage for tidal generation of electricity.

11.9 Cost–benefit studies of the New Covent Garden Market

In 1961 a statutory public authority – the Covent Garden Market Authority (CGMA) – was created with the initial task of acquiring the properties of the wholesale horticultural market of Covent Garden located in central west London.

Two separate cost–benefit studies of resiting the old market at Nine Elms (south-west London) were commissioned by the CGMA.

The first was undertaken by A. J. Le Fevre and J. F. Pickering (1972), who used 1973 as the base year for their figures. They estimated that as a result of the growing direct links between the multiple retail chains and growers and the trend towards 'convenience' foods, the volume of trade passing through Covent Garden Market in 1973 would be only 75 per cent of that in 1959–60, and in 1981 it would be only 66 per cent. This assumption was then used as the basis for assessing future labour and equipment requirements.

Figures for the main costs and benefits were as shown in Table 11.3. Certain items are not given because the costs and benefits were assumed to balance within the heading. Nor did the study claim to be fully comprehensive – reduced congestion costs, environmental effects on residents and the loss of the individual character of the old site were considered to be of too small a magnitude to affect the general conclusion.

Discounting costs and benefits at 8 per cent (the current test rate for public-sector investment), and allowing for some reduction in annual equipment costs after 1981, gave an *NPV*, under assumption (a) of a 10 per cent reduction in the labour force, of £7.6 m.; and under assumption (b) of a 25 per cent reduction, of £6.03 m. Thus Le Fevre and Pickering concluded that on the basis of the assumptions made, 'the investment of

Table 11.3 1972 CBA of re-siting Covent Garden Market

Costs	(£)
Land and building	30 m.
Capital equipment (assumption (a)) } see below	100 000 p.a.
(assumption (b))	260 000 p.a.
Benefits	
Sale of old site	10 m.
Saving in:	
Labour costs:	
assuming (a) a 10% reduction in the labour force	142 000 p.a.
assuming (b) a 25% reduction in the labour force	338 000 p.a.
Transport costs	207 000 p.a.
Waiting costs	705 000 p.a.
Wastage	126 000 p.a.

£30m. in a new market at Nine Elms falls a long way short of proving a viable investment.'

How has this conclusion been borne out in practice? The New Covent Garden Market transferred to Nine Elms in 1974 and the Covent Garden Market Authority commissioned Professor J. H. Kirk and Mr M. J. Sloyan to ascertain the position in 1976 after nearly two years of operation. As a preliminary to assessing their study, however, it should be emphasised that Kirk had previously disagreed with the conclusion of Le Fevre and Pickering, chiefly on the grounds that they had underestimated the value of the old Covent Garden site (which he had put at £23 m., resulting in an estimated net gain rather than a loss).

Valuation of the 15-acre Covent Garden site was complicated by the delay in deciding planning use and the listing of some 250 buildings. But, largely on the basis of a sale of 4.6 acres of land adjacent to the old market hall at the end of 1974, Kirk and Sloyan (1978) estimated the value of the released land at Covent Garden as £24.3 m. Their other figures were based on costs actually incurred during the two years' operations and on empirical studies. For easy comparison with the Le Fevre and Pickering analysis, their figures are set out in Table 11.4 under similar headings.

Using an eight-year purchase basis, Kirk and Sloyan estimated the annual value of the old site as £3 m. The project therefore produced an annual return of £5.7 m. on an outlay of £36.2 m., equivalent to just under 16 per cent, an acceptable yield. Alternatively, if we discount the total annual *net* benefits of £2 724 000 at 10 per cent (a higher figure being chosen for 1976) the scheme shows an *NPV* of approximately £15 m.

Table 11.4 1978 CBA of re-siting Covent Garden Market

Costs	(£)
Land and building (net of the cost of that part of Market Towers let to non-market users)	36.2 m.
Capital equipment	600 000 p.a.
Benefits	
Value of the old site	24.3 m.
Saving in:	
Labour costs	804 000 p.a.
Transport and waiting costs	1100 000 p.a.
Wastage and pilfering	1420 000 p.a.

It will be observed that for all items Kirk and Sloyan's figures are higher than those of Le Fevre and Pickering. This is partly due to the rise in prices between 1973 and 1976. But Kirk and Sloyan were able to base their figures on observed costs, and these would reflect the fact that the volume of traffic actually increased by nearly 10 per cent during the Nine Elms site's first year of operation (compared with Le Fevre and Pickering's assumption of a gradual reduction in trade).

Postscript

This example illustrates why, because of its inherent inaccuracies, CBA must be regarded as an imperfect tool. Although the initial CBA considered that investment in the new site could not be justified, in the event, New Covent Garden Market has proved economically viable – but for reasons other than those covered by the study.

Of the £36.7 m. owed to the Ministry of Agriculture in 1977, £13 m. was written off. The subsequent *appreciation of London office property* allowed Market Towers, the office block built on the corner of the new site, to be sold for £20 m. and the remainder of the debt was repaid in 1990.

In 1989 an independent privatisation study concluded that a sale of the site to a developer for office use would net £166 m., but this was only one of a number of options for its disposal. Consequently in 1990 the government decided that in principle the assets of the CGMA should be disposed of, but to date (2003) privatisation has proceeded no further and it still exists as a management agency. The CGMA's book value of the site in 1994 was only £4.8 m. and its operating profit for the year was £0.84 m. The estimate of the value of the Thameside site now varies between £30 m. and £60 m. according to the permitted office content.

Summary

If those who gain from a property development can *in principle* fully compensate those who lose then a potential Pareto improvement has occurred. In the public sector, cost–benefit analysis may be used to determine whether a development will lead to a potential Pareto improvement. In a CBA it is necessary to:

- List all relevant items – including externalities
- Value expected benefits and costs
- Discount future flows of benefits and costs using an appropriate rate of discount
- Assess the Net Present Value of the development – if it is positive then there is potential Pareto improvement

Difficulties arise at each stage of the CBA and especially in the choice of discount rate (which is often based on market rates of interest by default). Nevertheless, CBA provides a rational technique for appraising developments where market information is lacking.

Review questions

1. Give a property sector example of a potential Pareto improvement.
2. Explain how a cost–benefit analysis is undertaken.
3. Explain the concepts of *consumers' surplus* and *producers' surplus*.
4. Why is it that market prices are not available for certain goods and services?
5. Explain how using a lower rate of discount in the public sector than in the private sector can lead to problems.

Recommended reading

F. Barker and K. Button, *Case Studies in Cost–Benefit Analysis* (London: Heinemann, 1975).

Institute of Chartered Accountants in England and Wales, *Cost Benefit Analysis Study Pack* (London: 1994).

J. H. Kirk and M. J. Sloyan, 'Cost–Benefit Study of the New Covent Garden Market', *Public Administration* (Spring 1978).

A. J. Le Fevre and J. F. Pickering, 'The Economics of Moving Covent Garden Market', *Journal of Agricultural Economics* (January 1972).

E. J. Mishan, *Cost–Benefit Analysis*, 2nd edn (London: Allen & Unwin, 1975) part 1.

D. W. Pearce, *Cost–Benefit Analysis*, 2nd edn (London: Macmillan, 1983).

CHAPTER 12

The Economics of Planning Controls

After studying this chapter you will be able to:

- **Explain why private sector development may not be socially optimal**
- **Show how bargaining between affected parties can, in certain circumstances, resolve externality problems**
- **Explain why government intervention, in the form of planning controls, may be necessary**
- **Describe the planning procedure**
- **Explain the economic impact of planning controls**

12.1 Externalities

Definition

In the pure market economy, resource allocation is the result of the decisions of consumers and producers who seek to maximise the difference between benefits and incurred costs. We refer to these as *private benefits* and *private costs*.

But there may be benefits and costs – externalities – additional to those which are the immediate concern of the parties to a transaction and which are not provided for directly in the market price. A firm may decide to build a new factory on a derelict site in a depressed district. In doing so it confers external benefits – tidying up the site and reducing the cost of government unemployment benefit payments. On the other hand, should the factory be built in a predominantly residential district, it would incur external costs of heavy vehicle movement, noise, loss of visual beauty and so on.

The full *social benefits (costs)* are, therefore: private benefits (costs) + external benefits (costs). Thus if an economically efficient allocation of resources is to be achieved, externalities, provided they are not too trivial, must be allowed for.

Since the spatial characteristic of land in particular gives rise to considerable 'spillover' costs and benefits, it is appropriate if, before considering planning controls, we examine the nature of these 'externalities' and how they might be dealt with.

Diagrammatic presentation of the problem of allowing for externalities

To simplify, it is realistic to assume that, because the initiators are unable to collect payments from beneficiaries or the sufferers to extract compensation for the extra costs imposed on them, externalities are ignored by private decision-makers. This gives rise to a divergence between private net product and social net product.

In Figure 12.1, it is assumed that: (a) there are no external benefits; (b) the price of a house received by a developer is constant, that is, marginal revenue (MR) = marginal private benefit (MPB) = marginal social benefit (MSB); (c) the marginal cost (MC) of building a house rises with increased density. On private benefit/costs considerations alone, houses would be built to a plot density of M. But more intensive development gives loss of open space and so on.

MSC, therefore, exceeds MPC. Plot density should therefore be limited to M_1, in order to achieve optimal development where $MSB=MSC$.

It must be noted that a divergence between MSC and MPC merely shows that a problem exists. Further information (using, for example, the techniques of CBA) is required to provide a solution to the problem.

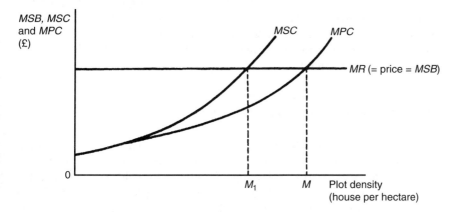

Figure 12.1 External costs and plot density

Externalities and the price system

This does not mean, however, that all activities giving rise to externalities should be subject to public control. Where people live in close proximity, some spillover costs are inevitable. Thus town-dwellers limit the open space available to one another and suffer a continuous hum of traffic noise. But people live in towns because of the advantages conferred and these include external benefits, such as agglomeration economies. Such benefits of town-life have to be set against the costs.

Nor should it be assumed that the price system completely fails to respond to externalities. Thus one property developer has responded to *environmental pressures* by providing a barn owl tower in a new office building to house the birds which were previously on the site.

Often externalities are reflected in the market price. Thus people will pay more for a house in a neighbourhood which has good schools, open spaces, shopping facilities, golf courses and road and rail communications. On the other hand, shops where traffic congestion is a serious problem will command a lower rent because trade will be adversely affected. Similarly with office rents: the necessity of having to pay employees an extra 'London allowance' to offset higher housing and travelling costs makes labour more expensive and induces some firms to seek an alternative location.

We also find externalities being 'internalised' by *private arrangements*. Thus a developer will attract shops to a shopping centre by making prior agreements with key retailers, and arrangements are made to concentrate small firms on industrial estates where they have some mutual interdependence. With residential estates, houses and flats may be sold subject to leases or convenants in order to secure external benefits (such as a satisfactory standard of upkeep, garden maintenance, and so on) or to avoid external costs (for example, excessive noise, car-parking nuisance, and so on).

Taking this a stage further, persons adversely affected by a new road proposal, such as routeing the M3 through Twyford Down, Winchester, may subscribe to a *pressure group* to oppose the scheme. More pervasively, some form of private trust, such as the Royal Society for the Protection of Birds or the Woodland Trust, may be established to deal with a general environmental externality.

Market provision for externalities by private negotiation

Where information and transactions costs are zero, bargaining between the affected parties should produce a price which reflects divergence of interest. Assume, for instance, that a developer **X** intends to build on a considerable part of the garden of a Victorian mansion which he has bought. Local residents, designated party **Y**, regard this development as a loss of amenity. **X** has two possible schemes. Scheme 1 is for a block of flats, and the higher the number of storeys (to increase the number of flats), the greater is the loss of amenity. Scheme 2 is for low-rise housing which still produces some loss of amenity according to the number of houses on the site.

The area under **X**'s curves in Figure 12.2 shows the total gain to the developer; that under **Y**'s curves shows the total loss to the residents. If there were no restrictions on development or no negotiation, **X** would adopt scheme 1, building flats, since the triangle *LOF* (a) is greater than the triangle *SOH* (b). But the residents' loss, equal to the area (la + lb), is greater than **X**'s gain. Thus it will pay them to 'buy off' **X** down to *OT* flats, where the net social gain equals area 1.

However, scheme 2 (limited to *OJ* houses) yields a larger net social gain, equal to area 2. To achieve this **Y** could offer up to (la + lb − 2a), **X** could also be better off since area 2 is greater than area 1, and would accept as little as (1 + la − [2 + 2a]). The difference between the two, (lb − 1 + 2), represents the benefit which can be achieved by negotiation, for lb equals a net social loss avoided (that is, a gain), −1 equals a gain forgone (a loss) and 2 equals a gain achieved (a gain). How this benefit is actually shared between the two parties will depend upon their respective negotiating skills.

It should be noted that were **X** to be made legally liable to compensate **Y** for the amenity costs inflicted, he would still develop to *OJ* where his marginal gain *JP* equals his marginal damages bill, but he would now be forced to pay for the full damages inflicted rather than possibly something less through skilful negotiation.

The need for government action

In practice, neither the market nor private arragements are likely to be adequate in dealing with externalities.

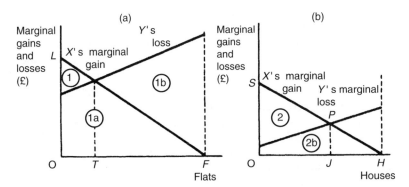

Figure 12.2 Allowing for externalities by bargaining between the affected parties

With the price system, there may be heavy frictional costs before a new equilibrium pattern of land values is established. How much congestion has to be suffered, for instance, while the price system solution is attained? Again, passively leaving the price system to deal with externalities may produce an inferior net social product (see below).

Similarly, private arrangements encounter obstacles. Not only may the costs be exorbitant relative to the benefits to be shared, but where 'free-riders' cannot be excluded, it may be impossible to organise sufficient collective bargaining strength to negotiate effectively. In any case, costs (or benefits) are often so far ranging – for example, the detrimental effects of exhaust fumes – that not all the losers (or beneficiaries) can be identified. Finally, uncertainty and selfishness may prevent a satisfactory solution by private action. However, where the individuals concerned have an identical interest on a specific issue, it is possible to arrive at an acceptable arrangement. Thus owners of the fishing rights on the Hampshire chalk-streams mutually agree to confine weed-cutting to three specified weeks during the fishing season.

Possible government action to allow for externalities

Because there are a variety of methods by which externalities can be allowed for in the allocation of land resources, the government can choose according to the particular case.

First, it may introduce a pricing system to bring externalities into the reckoning. For example, to deal with congestion, parking-meters may be installed, with even local residents charged for reserved parking permits.

Second, taxation and subsidies may take the idea of 'charging' a stage further. Thus it is suggested that prolonged roadworks by gas and water services, which cause serious traffic delays, should be deterred by taxation. Also, the rating of empty houses can be regarded as a tax imposed to offset the external costs resulting from homelessness and the overall shortage of accommodation. On the other hand, external benefits may be allowed for by subsidies. Government help towards slum clearance and housing falls under this heading (although alternatively it could be regarded as offsetting external costs). Other examples are the contributions and tax concessions made towards the costs of repairing ancient monuments and listed buildings and the sheep subsidies given to hill farmers in order to preserve the fell environment. In both cases, because private costs of upkeep exceed private benefits, rapid deterioration would otherwise result.

Third, externalities may be 'internalised' by the parties concerned combining or by widening the area of control. The National Trust, for instance, harmonises the interest both of farmers and walkers in order to secure maximum benefits from its Lake District properties.

Fourth, the government may itself assume responsibility for providing certain goods and services. This is usual when externalities are: (a) of national importance, for example, the Environment Agency can co-ordinate drainage, water supply and angling interests in order to maximise net benefits; (b) so extensive that only government authority can adequately allow for them – for example, providing a major airport; (c) cumulative, for instance, a slum area. Thus, if left to private enterprise, the clearance of a slum would take place in year *P* (Figure 12.3). However, a local authority could allow for the external benefits of such complete rebuilding – better health, less juvenile delinquency, an improved road layout, and so on. The capital value of such benefits would be added to the private enterprise's value of the best use, moving the cleared site value curve from *CC* to *CC*[1] and thus bringing redevelopment forward to year *L*.

Fifth – and frequently in the field of land resources – externalities may be covered by physical controls. Most evident are the consents required by law, currently the Town and Country Planning Act 1990. Their role in the allocation of land or real property resources is examined in what follows.

12.2 The planning procedure

Putting planning controls in place is accomplished in four main stages.

(a) *Planning Policy Guidance* notes (PPG) are issued periodically by the Department of the Environment, Transport and the Regions (DETR) to indicate important principles which should guide local authorities when they are considering planning applications. They are revised about every four years to reflect any change in current government thinking. Examples are PPG 6, proposing the limitation of new out-of-town

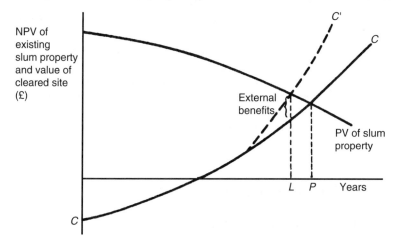

Figure 12.3 Allowing for externalities by the local authority rebuilding slum areas

shopping developments in order to provide the vitality of town centres, and PPG 13, emphasising the need to curtail road traffic movements in order to reduce earth warming through carbon dioxide emissions.

Appeals against a planning decision are to the Office of the Deputy Prime Minister (ODPM). They can be by:
 (i) written statements from both sides where a planning inspector decides after visiting the site;
 (ii) a public enquiry before an inspector, where witnesses can be called and cross-examined;
 (iii) for a major development, appeals are usually 'called in' by the Secretary of State for his own decision.

(b) A *structure plan* is drawn up by the county council. This envisages the broad lines of development by designating zones for different types of use. To be successful, a structure plan requires a preliminary *economic study* to assess the area's potential growth, the feasibility of alternative growth strategies, and the extent to which specific projects would be commercially viable within the overall plan. In short, such an economic appraisal at local level provides an objective basis for the physical redevelopment of the area, ensuring that environmental plans relate to an authority's real opportunities and not simply to its subjective development ambitions.

To allow for changes in government policy, the structure of local industry, improvements in the road network and technological advances in transport and construction, a structure plan must be reviewed on a rolling basis at regular intervals of about seven years.

(c) A *local development plan*, prepared by the district council, sets out more detailed policies to guide development in its area.

In metropolitan areas, councils produce unitary development plans which combine the functions of structure and local plans. Before any plan is adopted, local people can make representations of objections, usually at a local enquiry.

(d) *Planning consent* for a specific development which the developer has to obtain from the local planning authority – the district council – before he can proceed. In contrast to structure plans and building regulations which represent control by general regulation, planning consents are made on a case-by-case basis, though decisions are normally required to conform to the structure plan.

12.3 The rationale of planning controls

Incomplete arguments for planning control

Arguments often advanced to justify planning control are that it is necessary to: (a) secure a better environment in which to live; (b) ensure the most appropriate use of society's stock of land resources having regard to both the present and the future; (c) reconcile competing claims for the use of land.

But, without further qualification, each of these arguments appears somewhat superficial when subjected to economic analysis. Consider the 'better environment' argument. Naturally a more pleasant environment is something that everyone would like. But liking is one thing, achieving is another. Usually any improvement of the community's welfare in one direction imposes a cost in terms of something else that has to be forgone in order to achieve that improvement. That is, there is an *opportunity cost* of a better environment. A 'green belt', for instance, keeps land in agriculture – a lower use compared with housing – and also extends the journey to work of those city workers who live beyond it.

Similarly, with the second argument which suggests that if only our forebears had planned for the future, we should now enjoy a better urban environment – with a good road system, buildings having historic and architectural interest preserved, and an absence of slum tenements. But again this ignores the economic problem. Apart from the fact that our forebears did display considerable civic and social consciousness, they had to exist on an income considerably smaller than ours, and their planning provision for the future, though small by present standards, was probably the most they could afford.

As regards the 'reconciling competing claims for the use of land' argument, we have to ask why the price system cannot perform for land the allocative function that it does for other resources. Admittedly government authorities have to provide collective services, such as roads, reservoirs, parks, and so on, but these are no different from other resources, such as equipment for the armed forces, schools and hospitals, which are purchased through the market. Why cannot public demand for land operate through the price mechanism?

The above discussion must not be interpreted to suggest that planning is unnecessary. Rather it serves to emphasise that, for major schemes, the economist should be part of the entire planning process, rather than, as frequently happens, being called upon to analyse and appraise when the basic decisions have already been taken.

The need for planning controls

In practice the market economy, reflecting numerous individual public decisions, is not only capable of allocating land among competing uses but, as we have seen with development, does, *given certain conditions*, achieve maximum efficiency, both in the use to which a site is put and the type of building erected.

The key phrase, however, is 'given certain conditions' which, as explained in Chapter 1, do not always exist. As a result, the price system may not achieve full efficiency in the allocation of resources. It is appropriate, therefore, if we examine the part played by planning control in the context of a means of dealing with defects in the market economy.

What can planning control achieve?

Many developers are inclined to view planning controls as being negative, imposing frustrating conditions on their well-researched schemes. But, from the point of view of the community as a whole, planning controls can obtain positive benefits (subject to the condition that these exceed the administrative costs involved in applying them). Such benefits can be stated as follows.

(1) IMPROVED KNOWLEDGE
Decisions influencing the allocation of land resources through the market may be based on inadequate knowledge. At times, it can be argued, people may not be the best judges of their own welfare. For instance, their preferences expressed through the market might make inadequate provision for open space, such as parks and playing-fields. Through planning, a paternalistic policy allocates land to such uses. On the other hand, permission to build on cheap land near a motorway may be refused because the authorities consider that prospective purchasers of houses would underestimate the noise nuisance.

Again, in their present utilisation of land resources, individuals might make insufficient allowance for future needs. Governments, however, have a longer time-horizon (see p. 174). Thus they take measures to preserve buildings which have special architectural or historic interest. Indeed, the designation of green belts around towns may not only be necessary to safeguard amenity land for unborn generations, but could increase land values in the present. In Figure 12.4, original land values, shown by the curve LV, decrease regularly from the city centre outwards. With the introduction of the Green Belt, the land value curve shifts to LV^1, showing that the fall in the average value of land in the Green Belt is more than compensated by the rise in values elsewhere – even in the city centre – since accessibility to recreation and amenity land is now guaranteed. Thus houses adjacent to the Green Belt command a premium in their price representing this capitalised accessibility value, and this is recognised by the owners who resist any relaxation of Green Belt controls.

Inaccurate forecasts of future demand may also affect the efficient allocation of land resources. For example, in building on a particular site, the developer has a restricted time-horizon. But some consideration should be given to the extent to which demand is likely to grow in the future through population expansion or a rise in incomes. If, in fact, he underestimates future demand, the site will not be developed intensively enough; if he overestimates, it may be difficult to let units at an economic rent. The better information available to planners may avoid such mistakes: for example,

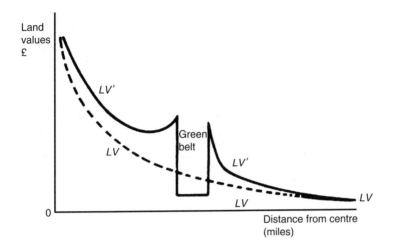

Figure 12.4 The effect on land values of the designation of a green belt

through a policy of density control. Similarly, with shopping-space, planning controls may be necessary to prevent too much being provided.

Imperfect knowledge may take the form of having to make decisions without being able to ascertain the investment plans of competitors. This can result in over-supply by the industry concerned and the inability to sell at the expected price. We can illustrate by office development in a city area. In Figure 12.5, D, D_1 and D_2 represent the demand curves for offices at different time periods, and S the long-period supply curve. In period 1, demand increases from D to D_1 but, because it takes some time for supply to expand to OM_1 the number of offices remains fixed at OM. Competition, therefore, leads to higher rents which rise to OP_1. Office developers respond

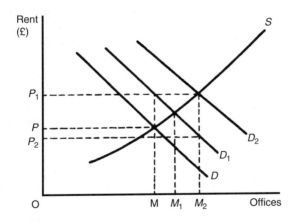

Figure 12.5 The effect of time lags in the supply of offices

to this higher price, starting to build offices irrespective of the fact that others are doing likewise. When all their building programmes have been completed supply has increased to OM_2. In order to clear the market, price has to fall to OP_2 unless demand increases to D_2 or inferior office accommodation is taken off the market. Here again planning can impose a scheme which co-ordinates the proposals of separate developers.

Uncertainty arising from imperfect knowledge of the intentions of others in a similar position can affect decisions on land use. This can be explained in terms of 'the prisoner's dilemma'. The police suggest to prisoner **A** that, in return for confessing and implicating his accomplice **B**, they will do their best to ensure that **A**'s sentence is limited to one year's imprisonment, although **B** will get five. However prisoner **A** senses that the police do not have a strong case and that, if neither confesses, there is a chance that they will both be acquitted. He has no means of communicating with **B**, and so his problem is to assess how **B** is likely to react to the same offer. Will he remain silent, relying on **A** to do likewise in order to give them both a good chance of going free? Or will he act selfishly and settle for one year, leaving **A** to do five years? This situation of the prisoner's dilemma can be related to owner's decisions on whether to improve their property in a run-down inner-city area. One owner is contemplating spending £20 000 on improving his property. If the owners of adjacent properties do likewise, there is a beneficial spin-off because the value of all properties would each increase, say to £30 000. On the other hand, if fellow-owners fail to renovate their properties, the first owner's expenditure could be largely wasted in terms of adding to the value of his property, since it may eventually have to be demolished. Although the planning authority also does not have knowledge of owners' intentions, it can create greater certainty by policy action – announcing a definite plan to renovate the whole area. This would stimulate owners to improve independently, secure in the knowledge that those who failed to do so would be brought into line.

Finally, it should also be noted that plans for future road developments and general regulations covering structure plans, zoning and building requirements all serve to eliminate much uncertainty, thus providing a framework within which developers can formulate their particular schemes.

(2) ALLOWANCE FOR EXTERNALITIES

The activities of individuals or groups may give rise to spillover benefits or costs to others. As shown earlier, in certain circumstances, externalities may be dealt with by 'internalisation' or agreement, or through the market mechanism. But where the total effect of the externality is important but spread so thinly that persons affected cannot be identified for purposes of co-ordinated action, state intervention is necessary. Those conditions apply in particular to land use. The type of building erected and the use to which it is put affect the welfare not only of neighbours but also of passers-by. Thus both the design of the building and its use are subject to public intervention through planning control.

In practice such control tends to concentrate on dealing with undesirable external effects, noise, smoke and congestion. *Zoning*, for instance, restricts land in certain parts of an urban area to a particular use. In doing so, it seeks to eliminate competitive uses of adjacent land, such as factories in residential areas or urban sprawl into the rural countryside. Planning decisions can also prevent the erection of buildings which do not harmonise with their surroundings resulting in a loss of variety in shopping centres or employment outlets.

But planning can also be positive, arranging complementary uses – for example, siting dwellings, schools, shopping facilities, car-parks and bus termini in strategic proximity, or encouraging the preservation of a listed building by granting an acceptable change of use.

(3) DEALING WITH IMPERFECT COMPETITION

Local authority planning backed by powers of compulsory purchase provides an overriding authority when the owner of a particular site stands in the way of a comprehensive development. Indeed, once the need for planning has been established, the logical step of allowing the planning authority to exercise powers of compulsory purchase makes coercion more acceptable since the authority has to give reasons. Similarly, the privatised utilities enjoy compulsory purchase powers under their own Acts to acquire private land or rights over it.

Planning powers may also be used to deal with underdevelopment of a site. For instance, the owner of a vacant half-hectare site in a built area may find it more profitable to restrict building to three executive town houses (*OA*, Figure 12.6), whereas the need of the district is for a more intensive development of smaller houses, a development which would result if building were pursued to the perfect competition position *OB* where price equals marginal social cost.

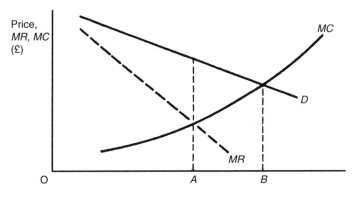

Figure 12.6 Restriction of the supply of houses on a given site by a monopolist owner

(4) THE PROVISION OF PUBLIC AND COLLECTIVE GOODS

The deficiencies of the market in supplying public and collective goods were examined earlier in this chapter. Since the provision of these goods, such as roads, bridges, car-parks and national parks, must be the responsibility of the state, and because they cover large areas or have location significance, some central planning is inevitable. Indeed this is all the more essential as there is often a near-irreversibility about land use, either on account of the cost of replacing a building, or the difficulty of unifying the different interests involved. Can we imagine, for instance, Hyde Park being created from an area covered by buildings?

Infrastructure services such as parks, sewerage, schools and water supply, also have to be integrated into a land-use plan for the area.

An overall planning authority has further advantages for dealing with the infrastructure aspects of land use. Thus if a private firm is entirely responsible for a development, it is restricted to working within the existing road scheme, the pattern of which was probably established before the coming of motor transport. In this way the road layout becomes ossified in an inefficient form. In contrast, co-operation between the private developer and a local authority having planning powers would allow the road system to be altered to meet the needs of modern transport and the environment generally.

(5) IMPROVING THE MOBILITY OF RESOURCES

For various reasons resources may be sluggish in responding to changes in demand or supply as indicated by the market. For instance, an increase in industrial activity in a given area may make it difficult to obtain extra labour because of a shortage of suitable housing in the district. Here the planning authority can help by ensuring that development proceeds in a balanced way, with housing being provided alongside permissions for new factory buildings.

Similarly in a depressed area labour may not wish to move because of social ties. The latter should be recognised by the planners as a benefit to be considered through the provision of an up-to-date infrastructure in the area and by making sites available to small firms.

(6) THE REDISTRIBUTION OF INCOME

Income redistribution is a political decision rather than an economic one, but problems of income distribution may be inherent in planning decisions. For instance, a householder who sells a part of his garden for development does so because there is a net benefit to him, but, because his action imposes uncompensated costs on his neighbours, they suffer a loss of welfare. Thus while the planning authority may consent to a development on environmental grounds, there can be distributional implications.

Indeed planning may go further, redistributing income as an active policy. For example, while there may be economic grounds for ear-marking dwellings for essential workers in city centres where the price of land is high, it also allows the poorer members of the community to occupy dwellings at a lower rent than would be established in a free market. More recently, planning control has been relaxed for building 'affordable housing' in rural areas.

Furthermore, planning decisions may redistribute income in favour of future generations – for example, by providing land for parks and recreation, preserving green belts and protecting historic buildings.

12.4 The pros and cons of planning controls as a means of government intervention

Justification for regulating by planning consents

The defects of the price mechanism may be offset by the government intervening in the market by adjusting its own supply and demand (for instance, by stockpiling agricultural produce and basic materials, locating its own offices in Development Areas, or placing orders with firms in areas of high unemployment), by taxing or subsidising certain activities (for example, imposing a higher rate poundage on commercial and industrial buildings than on dwellings; subsidising agriculture through rate relief) or by making regulations on a general basis (such as rent control; general building and fire precaution regulations). Why, therefore, should it interfere by planning control, which is basically on a case-by-case assessment?

First, a centrally-determined rate of tax would be general in its application and might not be appropriate for particular cases. Thus the external costs of a proposed development – such as extracting minerals in an area of outstanding natural beauty – may in total be so great that any tax imposed ought to be so high as to prevent such a project from being economically viable. But is it certain that this would happen? It is possible that the rate of tax decided centrally on an average basis would be so low as to enable the mineral extraction to proceed. In this particular case, therefore, the rule that an activity should proceed to the point where marginal social benefit equals marginal social cost would be breached. The difficulty is that the external costs incurred can vary in magnitude from one beauty spot to another for each differs in character and in the number of visitors it attracts. Taxation, however, would be applied to all on the same basis, perhaps even preventing mineral extraction where the beauty spot was of no outstanding quality and so remote that it was hardly likely ever to attract many visitors.

Parallel criticisms apply to minimum standard regulations, such as room height, window space, ventilation, and safety precautions. Not only do the minimum requirements tend to become the accepted normal standard of provision, but being decided centrally they impose rigidity. With buildings there must be flexibility to cover individual cases – for instance, a historic building where special features have to be preserved. Indeed, because all developments tend to be heterogeneous in character there is much to be said for controlling on a case-by-case basis rather than by general regulation.

Second, when granting planning permission, the local authority can impose special conditions covering the provision of public services, such as access roads and open spaces, a community centre, low-income housing units, and so on. Obviously the extent of such possible 'planning gain' through 'section 106' agreements varies from project to project. Planning on a case-by-case basis permits flexibility in the conditions imposed (see pp. 412–14).

Third, while some distributive effects are often inherent even in planning decisions (for example, countryside recreation facilities involving high transport costs benefit the rich more than the poor), intervention by taxation would be far more favourable to the rich, since they are in a better position to pay in order to proceed with a scheme.

Difficulties of control by planning

First, compared with taxation (where this is possible), planning lacks flexibility as regards individual preferences. This applies particularly to zoning through structure plans. For instance, married, female, part-time workers might be excluded from employment by transport costs and the time taken in travelling to a factory in an industrial zone. Thus a firm classified as 'industrial' and relying heavily on such labour might be prepared to pay additional rent (including a tax) for a site convenient for its employees, and this would be justifiable if the extra benefits to the firm exceeded the costs. Moreover, structure plans may impose rigidity since the highest and best use of a land resource can alter over time with income changes and transport developments.

Second, planning may take insufficient account of certain benefits which exist in the current land-use situation. Thus, in the past, structure plans dealing with the environmental problems of inner-city areas by complete rebuilding have not fully allowed for the loss of job opportunities in small firms which existed through low rents, the higher cost of travelling to work, the extra cost and inconvenience of obtaining odd-job services, the destruction of social contacts, the loss of community spirit and the elimination of variety – for example, in employment, shops and architecture.

Third, planning tends to overlook certain repercussions of the controls imposed. For instance, low-density housing requirements may mean that building for the poorer members of the community is confined to those parcels of land available for high-density development, with the result that its price per acre exceeds that of land for rich people's housing. Similarly design guides, such as the old Parker-Morris standards, impose an additional strain on maintaining the stock of second-hand dwellings. Secondary effects also occur when commercial developments are restricted in intensity (for instance, by plot ratios) in order to limit congestion. In practice the reactions of firms may actually increase movement. For instance, storage may be decentralised but the space vacated occupied by employees, while extra vehicles are usually needed to maintain contact between decentralised offices and the centre. In addition, public transport has to overcome the difficulty of serving more scattered destinations.

Fourth, planning tends to be negative in character. Thus, though it may prevent undesirable results, such as the despoliation of a beauty spot or excessive urban sprawl, planning controls in themselves do not lead to market forces initiating those schemes that the authorities would like to promote. For these the lead may have to come from the local council which nevertheless must always bear in mind that innovative private developers may propose superior schemes.

Fifth, case-by-case examination of applications for planning permission leads to delays in arriving at a decision, delays which are both frustrating and costly to the developer and wasteful in the use of land resources. The ODPM claims that 70 per cent of applications are decided within eight weeks, but this figure is weighted heavily by the number of minor changes, such as erecting a porch or building a garage, where the decision may be delegated to the planning officer.

Although 90 per cent of applications are given permission, there are still about 12 000 which each year go to appeal, with a 35 per cent success rate. Delays are more significant when the development is on a large site since then alternative schemes have usually to be considered and objectors may force a public enquiry. The Heathrow Terminal 5 Enquiry lasted from May 1995 to March 1999!

Finally, it must be remembered that the planning process itself uses up resources and so, like other activities, must only be undertaken to the point where the marginal benefit equals marginal cost. It is not therefore appropriate for dealing with only minor faults in the land and property markets.

12.5 The impact of planning controls

Though planning seeks to improve the working of the price mechanism, it does have repercussions on the urban land market and on the local economy, as follows.

(1) The value of an individual site

We can illustrate by considering how the value of a site is affected by the restriction of building density. In essence, such restriction limits the amount

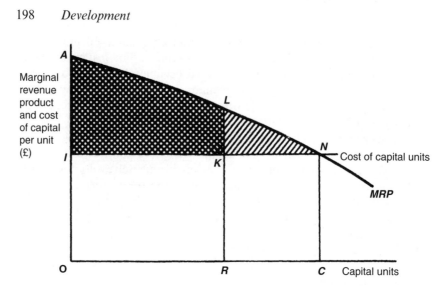

Figure 12.7 The effect of planning on the value of an individual site

of capital which can be applied to a given site. Thus in Figure 12.7 the restriction of density to *OR* reduces the value of the site from *AIN* to *AIKL*.

(2) The pattern of land values

Planning control – for instance, by zoning – alters the pattern of land values. For example, restricting the amount of land available for offices raises the value of existing office land and thus of any land which in the future is given planning consent for offices.

This is illustrated in Figure 12.8. In a free market the price of office land would be *OP*. Where planning controls restrict the supply to *OC*, the price would rise to *OP'*. But since another effect of control would be to free *CM* land for other uses, the price of land for such uses would be depressed.

(3) Overall land values

Maximising aggregate land values (but allowing for external benefits and costs) is an indication of the optimum use of scarce land resources. The Uthwatt Committee (1942) considered that planning merely shifted land values from one site to another with no change in the aggregate value.

But is this so? Suppose that in the redevelopment of a central urban area the town planner considered that more land should be devoted to workers' housing and less to offices and light industry. This means that the affected firms would have to develop elsewhere. But the efficiency of such firms could

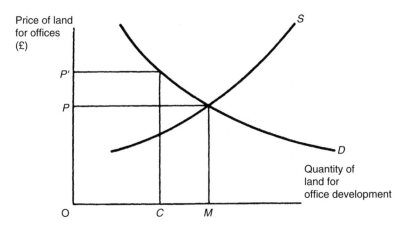

Figure 12.8 The effect of planning on the pattern of land values

be impaired if, through moving, they lost important advantages of accessibility to customers and of complementarity with other firms. In such circumstances the increase in land values of the sites to which firms moved would be less than the loss of values in the centre of the town.

Furthermore, it may not be valid to assert that increased social benefits would compensate for the difference. Moving firms to other locations could result in the loss of job opportunities for those workers not wishing to travel longer distances (for example, housewives and part-time workers) and for those too old for retraining. Moreover, firms remaining may have relied on complementary services from the firms which are moving, resulting in higher costs to them.

In such ways the value of land in the urban area could fall. Thus the town planner cannot assume that his decisions merely shift land values. They can affect aggregate value and hence allocative efficiency.

(4) Distributional effects

Though planning is mainly concerned with the allocation of land resources, it has both direct and indirect distributional effects which may clash with the economic efficiency objective.

The owner of land who obtains planning consent for development receives a windfall gain. On the other hand, where a restrictive land-release policy forces up the price of land, new purchasers – such as house-buyers – lose. Similarly, the grant of planning consent for a large supermarket could harm nearby shop-keepers.

Often the distributional effects are less direct. Where planning covers the provision of public goods – for example, transport developments, parks, schools, municipal golf courses – the tendency is for it to enhance the values of the better-class houses on the urban fringe. Similarly, a low-density plot ratio benefits the richer people who can afford a house with a large garden, while out-of-town hypermarkets or green belt recreation facilities are likely to be used more by people owning cars.

(5) Supplementary effects

Attention has already been drawn to certain repercussions of planning decisions, loss of job opportunities in the city centre, the destruction of social contacts, higher costs of travel, delays which increase development costs. Other supplementary costs include:

(a) the bureaucratic machine which has to administer planning;
(b) the possibility of planning blight settling on an area subject to proposals; and
(c) the growing practice of planning authorities to exact 'planning gain', even in the form of money payments, as a condition of granting consent (see pp. 412–14).

Nor must we forget that, subject to appeal to the Secretary of State, planning is ultimately controlled at the local level by committees of politically-motivated people.

Summary

Externalities are costs and benefits which are not provided for in market prices. It may be possible for such externalities to be accounted for by private bargaining arrangements. In most cases, however, it is necessary for governments to intervene in order to ensure that externalities are accounted for so that a socially optimal outcome is achieved. The planning system is one way in which government intervenes to try to ensure that the defects of the market are dealt with to achieve a social optimum. Planning control can be used to cope with a variety of problems such as:
- the need to preserve land resources for future generations
- urban sprawl
- factories in inappropriate locations
- monopoly ownership of land resources
- provision of public and collective goods

Review questions

1. What forms of government intervention are available to cope with externalities?
2. Why are planning controls necessary?
3. Show, using a diagram, the impact of planning controls on:
   (a) green belt land
   (b) an individual site for development
   (c) the pattern of land values
4. Explain the principal difficulties of control by planning
5. Describe the planning procedure

Recommended reading

A. W. Evans, *Urban Economics* (Oxford: Basil Blackwell, 1985) ch. 12.

J. E. Manser, *Economics: A Foundation Course for the Built Environment* (London, E.&F.N. Spon, 1994).

D. Myers, *Economics and Property: A Coursebook for Students of the Built Environment* (London: Estates Gazette, 1994).

B. Walker, *Welfare Economics and Urban Problems* (London: Hutchinson, 1981) ch. 10.

CHAPTER 13

The Construction Industry

After studying this chapter you will be able to:

- Assess the contribution of the construction industry to the UK economy
- Assess the efficiency of the construction industry
- Explain the structure of the UK construction industry
- Suggest ways in which productivity can be increased in the construction industry

13.1 The nature of the construction industry

Definition

In order to achieve consistency in national income calculations, industries are defined according to the Standard Industrial Classification. 'Construction' covers the erection, repair and demolition of all types of buildings and civil engineering structures. Specialist subcontracting finishing trades, such as asphalting, electrical wiring, flooring, plastering, roofing and plumbing are included, as well as the hiring of contractors' plant and scaffolding.

This definition recognises that building and civil engineering projects, unlike most other industries, are split into the separate operation of design, production and assembly. Architects and surveyors working on their own account are classified as professional services. The manufacture of components and materials, such as bricks, cement, timber, doors and windows, comes under 'manufacturing', and quarrying gravel and sand under 'mining and quarrying'. Thus the definition confines the construction industry to the *assembly* process.

This means that the contribution of the construction industry to GNP is the value added to the inputs of materials and services from other industries. In 2002 this amounted to £64 898 million, approximately 7.6 per cent of GNP. Sometimes, however, the full value of the output of construction firms is used and this includes the cost of materials and components. Such is the basis of measurement of Gross Fixed Capital Formation (expenditure on fixed assets), to which construction of buildings and dwellings contributed £69 374m. in 2001, nearly one-half of the whole (see Table 6.1 on p. 82).

The relationship between the efficiency of the construction industry and real property

Since the construction industry is concerned mainly with the construction, adaptation and maintenance of buildings, its efficiency is vital to real property.

First, an increase in construction efficiency will tend to accelerate redevelopment, for it is now relatively cheaper to provide a replacement building (see Chapter 7). Second, greater efficiency in construction will lead to a higher proportion of capital being combined with land. This is because capital, in the form of buildings, is made cheaper relative to land. As a result, if both factors are variable, capital is substituted for land. In other words, development is more intensive. This is shown in Figure 13.1; increased efficiency means that the price of capital falls from OR to $O'R$, shifting the budget line from RT to $R'T$. Consequently there is a movement to a higher isoquant and more capital, OC', and less land, OL', are employed, and more units are built for a given outlay.

Where construction is on a fixed site a better or higher building will be constructed (assuming no government planning or building limitations).

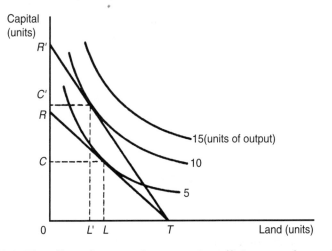

Figure 13.1 The effect of increased construction efficiency on the combination of capital and land in buildings

Greater construction efficiency raises the productivity of capital: in Figure 6.3 (p. 101) the MRP curve moves from MRP to MRP'. Since the price of capital (the rate of interest) does not change, the amount of capital applied to the site increases from OM to OM'.

Third, given no change in the overall demand for accommodation, greater intensity of development will tend to produce increased land values in the centre of the urban region compared with the periphery. In Figure 6.3 the rent that can be offered for a central site rises from AiC to $A'iC'$. In contrast, sites on the periphery (which are less capital-intensive) will benefit less from increased construction efficiency. This will be particularly true for office buildings, where high structures are more acceptable, than for shops and factories. Moreover, since with a given demand for accommodation a larger proportion of it will be satisfied by the higher buildings on central sites, the demand for peripheral sites will fall. In other words, the MRP curve of peripheral sites moves towards the origin, so that they are either developed less intensively in their current use or put to a lower alternative use.

Criticisms of the construction industry

At first sight, certain aspects of the construction industry would appear to indicate inefficiency – cumbersome pricing procedures, a high preponderance of small firms, the distribution of materials through builders' merchants, a large proportion of casual labour resulting in a high level of unemployment, the comparatively small increase in output per worker over time, a low level of mechanisation and a failure to adopt modern techniques of mass production.

Now, while some criticism is justifiable, much results from a failure to appreciate the diverse activities of an industry which ranges from large international companies performing all types of work to small, local, repair and maintenance firms. A study of the conditions of demand and supply relating to the industry reveals that its organisation is largely the response to economic factors. In other words, the critics are largely confusing technical efficiency with economic efficiency: they focus on the supply side, particularly as regards production methods, and tend to overlook the special aspects of demand.

13.2 The conditions of demand and supply in the construction industry

As a prelude to examining the organisation and production methods of the construction industry, it is essential to draw attention to the special features of the demand for and the supply of the product.

Demand

The particular features of demand can be summarised as follows.

(1) Because of differences of site, surroundings and users' requirements, most buildings, apart from speculative housing, are 'bespoke', tailor-made to the client's *individual specification*. To a large extent this determines the method of pricing (see later) and reduces opportunities for standardisation and thus of mass production.

(2) Since buildings are durable, nearly one-half of the value of the output of the construction industry is on *repairs and maintenance* (see Table 13.1).

(3) Because the products are mainly capital goods, they are expensive relative to income and are thus usually purchased through borrowed funds. Demand is, therefore, dependent upon the cost of *credit*. Thus controlling inflation through the rate of interest hurts the construction industry in particular.

(4) Demand is particularly subject to *seasonal and cyclical fluctuations*. It tends to be bunched in the spring and summer months. More serious, however, is the effect of periodic recessions since the industry accounts for one-half of Gross Domestic Fixed Capital Formation. As an investment goods industry construction is vulnerable to private-sector fluctuations in demand resulting from changes in expectations, a rise in the cost of borrowing or induced changes related to the level of income (the 'accelerator').

(5) *Government policy* is a further cause of unstable demand. Changes in taxes and subsidies can affect the rate of redevelopment. Of far greater significance, however, are the effects of virtually using the construction industry as one of the 'regulators' of the economy. Just over one-quarter of the work of the industry is for the public sector (see Table 13.1). Thus a cut in government spending bears heavily on the construction industry for the major impact is on capital projects such as new hospitals, roads, universities, local authority schools, housing, slum clearance and city-centre developments.

Table 13.1   Value of output of the construction industry, 2001 (£m)

		Private sector	Public sector	Infrastructure	Total
New Work					
	Housing	8797	1438	–	10235
	Other	17262	5330	7147	29739
Repairs					
	Housing	10989	6630	–	17619
	Other	10990	6109	–	17099
Total		48038	19507	7147	74692

Source: *Construction Statistics, Department of Trade and Industry.*

Table 13.2 and Figure 13.2 show how construction activity fluctuated over the period 1983–2001. In 1983–5 and 1990–5, there was spare capacity running at over 20 per cent.

Supply

Several distinctive features of the construction industry are also evident on the supply side.

(1) Not only is it an *assembly industry* but also its operations, like those of agriculture, are *consecutive*. In contrast, most manufacturing industries can carry out all their operations concurrently.
(2) Instead of production taking place in a factory, it occurs on the *site* of the *finished* product. This gives rise to problems of protection from the weather, storing materials, moving labour and equipment and supervision of work.
(3) For most jobs *the minimum technical unit is small*. Thus a traditional house can be built by two bricklayers, two bricklayers' labourers, two general labourers and a carpenter, with other tasks, such as plastering, electrical work and plumbing, being subcontracted. Even large jobs can be completed by a relatively small labour force by putting out the work to specialist firms, that is, by vertical disintegration.
(4) *Labour costs* form a high proportion, between one-third and one-half, of total costs. Skilled labour accounts for just over two-thirds of total

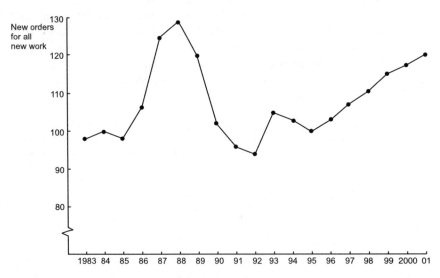

Figure 13.2 Fluctuations in construction activity 1983–2001; new orders for all new work (1995 = 100)

Table 13.2 Changes in construction activity 1987–2001, GB: selected activity indicators (1995 = 100)

	New orders: all new work	Output all work	Housebuilding completions	Brick deliveries	Cement deliveries
1987	125	96	113	149.7	120.6
1988	129	105	121	161.1	139.0
1989	120	110	110	135.7	140.9
1990	102	111	102	118.0	124.4
1991	96	103	96	106.0	102.1
1992	94	99	90	98.7	92.7
1993	105	97	93	106.9	93.0
1994	103	100	97	118.9	105.8
1995	100	100	100	100.0	100.0
1996	103	102	94	99.9	98.1
1997	107	105	94	104.2	100.3
1998	113	107	87	101.5	99.1
1999	102	109	90	103.6	98.9
2000	107	110	87	97.9	99.3
2001	109	114	86	96.0	94.8

Source: Construction Statistics, Department of Trade and Industry.

labour costs. Furthermore, although construction labour tends to be sheltered from international competition, the casual and cyclical nature of the work results in a high rate of unemployment. This is true even at the top of the boom, since there is often a time lag between the completion of one project and the start of another. As a result, unemployment in the construction industry forms a far higher percentage than unemployment of workers in general.

(5) The time lag between the response of supply to a change in demand can be regarded as a built-in mechanism likely to produce short-term fluctuations in activity (see pp. 191–2).

(6) Because construction takes time and the final product is usually specific to the customer, the Housing Grants, Construction and Regeneration Act 1996 details the stage payments which must be included in the contract.

13.3 Pricing the product

The construction industry can be divided into two groups: (a) contractors; (b) speculative builders. The nature of pricing the project differs accordingly.

(a) Contractors

Efficient pricing of a project would ensure that the requirements of the client are met at the lowest possible price. To achieve this the building should be constructed by the most efficient firm at a price which just covers total costs. This implies competition between firms.

It is not easy to assess whether price is competitive. While the estimates of quantity surveyors and the experience of architects on similar projects may provide some guide, comparisons cannot be exact, since most projects are different. To achieve individual pricing on a competitive basis, various methods are used.

(1) TENDER
The most common method is for firms to tender for the contract, the lowest tender, other things being equal, being successful. Certain points, however, should be noted.

(a) Competitive conditions in pricing the product require that many firms tender.

(b) In considering tenders account must be taken of the proven efficiency of firms. Normally the architect will advise. Ability to complete by a specified date is important. Moreover, under-pricing a project is not always to the advantage of the client. If the contractor runs into financial difficulties, delay results. Worse still, if another firm has to be engaged to complete, it may be in a strong position to exact a high price.

(c) Unlike manufactures, construction firms working on a contract are in effect working to a fixed price for their product *before* production commences. Thus, risk is incurred when tendering, for there is little possibility of adjusting the selling price (as in manufacturing) to cushion the effects of unforeseen difficulties.

(d) Since the construction process can cover a number of years, any fixed-price contract is, in time of inflation, fraught with danger. This risk is usually covered by the insertion of a 'rise and fall' clause to guard against cost increases. However, to some extent this reduces the contractor's incentive to shop around for the lowest-priced materials.

Tendering may be on an open-list or a selected-list basis. With *open tender* the project is advertised and any firm which wishes to submit a tender can do so on the basis of the plans and bill of quantities supplied. This method ensures the greatest degree of competition. On the other hand, it does involve firms in un-productive work, for only about 20 per cent of tenders submitted are successful, a cost which is eventually reflected in the price of projects.

Selected-list tender partly overcomes this defect. A few contractors whose past work has proved their competitiveness and capability are invited to tender. An additional advantage is that time is saved in awarding the contract so that work can start sooner. Provided new firms, especially those with more progressive methods, can be added to the list, and collusion between the fewer firms involved can be eliminated, the selected-list tender method still ensures competition.

(2) Negotiated contract

Though tendering promotes competition, it relies largely on a separation of the design and construction processes. Yet a building may prove just as acceptable functionally and aesthetically, and be constructed at a lower price, when the design allows for the special techniques, skills and equipment of a particular contractor. Such co-ordination can be achieved through a negotiated contract. With this, a single contractor is chosen for a given project without competitive tendering, and he consults with the architect even at the design stage. Indeed, a negotiated contract may be the only form of pricing possible when the work involves processes which only the particular contractor can carry out.

However, because the removal of competition could lead to a higher final price for the project (which can be on a fixed-sum, cost-plus or bonus basis), the selected contractor is usually chosen on the evidence of his previous tenders and work.

A development of the system of negotiating further contracts with a firm which has proved satisfactory is *serial contracting*. Where other buildings of the same type are to be erected, there is a legal understanding that the firm will be given a series of contracts once the first has been completed successfully. This enables the firm to plan large-scale economies, and should therefore result in keener prices.

(3) THE PACKAGE DEAL

Instead of appointing an architect, the client may go to a contractor offering an all-in comprehensive service from the design to the complete building at an inclusive figure. Thus the package deal is used mainly where a limited choice of design is acceptable – for example, for factories and farm buildings – but it may be extended to offices and local authority housing.

The package deal enables the client to be certain of the initial capital cost of the building, and it usually results in greater speed of erection and lower costs. However, these may be partly offset if the client has to engage a specialist surveyor to advise him, or if he requires changes during construction, for then the contractor can largely dictate his own terms.

A variation of the package deal is the *design and construct* contract. The client's professional consultant prepares a brief of the buildings required, often with site lay out plans. Each contractor then tenders on the basis of his own design and method of construction for that type of building.

(4) FEE CONSTRUCTION: MANAGEMENT CONTRACTING

Certain contractors, such as Bovis, have introduced a 'fee-construction' arrangement. The contractor and client negotiate a fee for management services, the client covering the construction costs. This reduces the contractor's risks, but brings the client and contractor into close relationship. Keeping costs to a minimum, however, depends upon the contractor's professional integrity and his hope of further business.

(b) Speculative builders

A speculative builder resembles a manufacturer in that he produces buildings, chiefly houses, in anticipation of demand. He is particularly active when demand is rising, and this is reflected in housing starts. His estimate of the selling price of the building will largely determine his bid price for the land. Since the building process takes time, the success of his venture will mainly depend upon the price originally paid for the land in competition with other builders. Rising house prices, with other costs fixed, will increase economic rent on the land, and thus super-normal profit. It must be remembered, however, that the volatility of house prices (often resulting from an unstable financial background) makes speculative building risky owing to the supply time lag (see pp. 191 and 379). Hence many small builders undertake it as a supplement to their main contract work.

Conclusion

Apart from the physical imperfections of the market, awarding contracts by competitive tender does promote competition, though past experience has revealed some collusion between contractors. With the negotiated contract and the package deal, imperfect knowledge and relative bargaining ability may influence the price.

Furthermore, it is necessary to emphasise that competitive prices will only prevail if, on the supply side, firms are of optimum size. This requires continuity of work, enabling them to operate at full capacity. As we shall see, it is the lack of such continuity which is one of the major causes of inefficiency in the construction industry.

13.4 The structure of the construction industry

The predominance of the small firm

Firms in the construction industry vary in size from the large civil engineering/building contractors, often undertaking such types of construction work as roads, bridges, office blocks, shopping centres and speculative housing estates, to one-man labour-only contractors such as bricklayers, plumbers, carpenters and jobbing maintenance firms.

Large construction firms can obtain the advantages of large-scale production. These include technical economies of specialised equipment and linked processes; commercial economies in buying materials; specialisation in management, such as their own surveyors and legal experts; the ability to raise finance on cheaper terms; and the spread of risks through diversification into many products, including international contracts. For small or even medium-sized contractors, spreading risks is difficult since a single contract may account for a large proportion of their work.

Nevertheless, the small firm predominates, those with less than twenty-five workers (including the self-employed) covering 98 per cent of all firms (see Table 13.3). On the other hand, such small firms account in value for only 40 per cent of total work.

This predominance of the small firm is a feature of all industries, including manufacturing. However, it is much more marked in the construction industry, a phenomenon common to other developed economies. The reasons are to be found on both the demand and supply sides.

Table 13.3   *The size and importance of private contractors in the construction industry, 2001*

Size of firm	No. of firms (thousands)	% of total	Value of work (£m)	% of total
Fewer than 25 employees	163998	97.6	6395.1	41.5
25–114 employees	3439	2	3052.7	19.8
115–599 employees	562	0.3	2672.3	17.3
600+ employees	124	0.1	3291.1	21.4
Total	168123	100.0	15411.4	100.0

Source: *Construction Statistics, Department of Trade and Industry.*

Demand factors favouring the small firm

Demand is characterised by the preponderance of relatively small contracts resulting from the individuality of the product (for example, the single house or extension where the minimum technical unit is small) and the importance of minor repair work. Above all, there are the fluctuations in demand, referred to earlier, which induce firms to remain small and flexible rather than burden themselves with disproportionately high overheads resulting from under-utilised specialist equipment.

Supply factors favouring the small firm

Since production is on site rather than in a factory, the difficulties of supervision are greater. Even where construction is on one site, labour is more dispersed. With a large firm carrying out work on many sites, the difficulties of management control are magnified. As a result, management diseconomies of scale may soon outweigh technical, commercial and other economies.

Moreover, vertical disintegration in construction through the employment of specialist firms results from the consecutive nature of the operations and the lack of continuity of the work for specialised equipment. Thus we have comparatively small firms contracting for pile-driving foundations, roofing, electrical work, heating and ventilation systems, lift installation, and so on. Such subcontracting has advantages to the main contractor, for (apart from saving on overheads) it makes estimating easier and reduces on-site supervision. On the other hand, it can increase the problem of co-ordinating the various construction operations.

Finally, as with other types of production, small businesses exist because the owner is prepared to accept a lower return in order to be his own boss.

Entry to the construction industry is fairly easy, as many jobs require little capital equipment or, if specialist tools and equipment are necessary, they can be obtained by hiring or subcontracting. Like most other businesses, however, builders find difficulty in obtaining capital to expand beyond a certain size, for their sources are, to all intents and purposes, limited to merchants' trade credit, personal savings, bank overdrafts and ploughed-back profit.

Many small builders try to operate on too small a cash flow, even though progress payments are received on an architect's certificate. Fluctuations in demand can prove financially crippling even for medium and large firms. Thus the rate of bankruptcies in the construction industry tends to be twice that of other industries.

13.5 Builders' merchants

The builders' merchant is the 'middleman' between the manufacturer of components and the builder. Few merchants now stock a full range of materials and components, and even the large chains hold only those having a high turnover. Instead we find specialisation: (i) stockists of heavy materials, such as bricks, breeze-blocks, cement, sand, aggregates, drain-pipes, and so on; (ii) merchants, including DIY stores such as B&Q, handling components for the later construction stages, such as baths, wash-basins and kitchen fittings, or for repair work, such as tiles, slates, guttering; (iii) specialist shops dealing in iron-mongery, glass, electrical equipment, glazed tiles, door fittings, and so on; (iv) local shops concerned mainly with finishing materials, such as wall coverings, paint, standard tiles and fittings, with their main customers being the 'DIY' enthusiasts.

Merchants also vary in size. There are regional chains, such as Jewson Builders Merchants Federation, and large merchants who often supply small merchants and retailers. But the specialist wholesalers and shops mentioned above tend to be small.

For builders' merchants, the cost of ordering, transporting, holding stocks and serving customers is high, for not only are materials and components bulky and often fragile, but many also have only a small turnover. Indeed, it has been estimated that an 18 per cent mark-up margin is required just to cover these costs. In addition, there are cash discounts and normal profit to be taken into consideration, so that the final mark-up on manufacturers' prices varies between 30 and 50 per cent.

Yet, in spite of such charges, the merchant continues to exist simply because he performs essential functions which result from the peculiar characteristics of the industry: the large number of small firms, the high proportion of repair work, the consecutive nature of the construction process, and the difficulty of storing materials on site. In short, he represents another form of vertical disintegration in the construction process.

Functions of the builders' merchant

The functions of the builders' merchant can be summarised as follows.

(1) ECONOMISING IN DISTRIBUTION
Where orders are small and numerous, it is more economic for manufacturers to distribute centrally through a wholesaler. Thus delivering in bulk to a merchant economises in transport and clerical work, while it is easier to assess the creditworthiness of a few established merchants than of individual builders. In his turn, the merchant breaks down the deliveries from manufacturers according to the requirements of the individual builder, usually economising in transport since one delivery to a builder may contain items from different manufacturers.

(2) HOLDING STOCKS
The merchant's function of holding stocks has advantages both to the individual builder and the materials' manufacturer. The builder is provided with an 'off-the-shelf' service, an important consideration where the demand for many jobs, such as repairs, cannot be anticipated, for it saves having capital tied up in storing components. Many merchants extend this service to larger projects. Because the consecutive nature of the building process gives rise to difficulties of storing materials and components on site, the merchant helps by phasing delivery.

Moreover, by holding stocks, the merchant enables the manufacturer to maintain the flow of components during periods of slack demand, thereby helping to stabilise prices. On the other hand, since the merchant does not fulfil the role of the dealer and speculate on future prices, fluctuations in the prices of building materials tend to be less than for agricultural products and minerals.

Finally, where materials, such as timber, have to be imported from abroad, the complications of foreign trade are shifted from the builder to the merchant.

(3) TRANSPORTING GOODS
By arranging transport, the merchant relieves the small builder of the need to own a lorry for moving dirty and bulky materials, such as gravel, sand, bricks and heavy components. This allows the small builder to carry fewer overheads, operating merely with a van or even his own car.

(4) GRANTING CREDIT
Builders are usually given at least a month's credit in purchasing supplies, though a tighter control is exercised when interest rates are high.

(5) GIVING TECHNICAL ADVICE AND PROMOTING NEW PRODUCTS

By dealing with a large number of builders, the merchant knows which materials are successful. Where a builder is free of an architect's specification or, as in jobbing and maintenance work, can use his own discretion, suggestions from the merchant may be helpful. The merchant is often assisted in selling new products by technical information supplied by the manufacturer.

On the other hand, there is a tendency for merchants to hold 'conventional' goods, especially where new products are more fragile.

Recent developments

Recent trends in the construction industry have tended to increase direct dealing between construction firms and manufacturers. The increase in the size of construction firms and the growth in the number of large projects, have meant that orders of sufficient size to interest manufacturers can be placed. Indeed, system-building uses components not normally stocked by builders' merchants. More manufacturers, too, are including installation in the price of their products, as with lifts, and heating and ventilation systems. Finally, many manufacturers have developed their own selling outlets – an example is Everest double-glazing which advertises in national newspapers.

High rates of interest can increase the costs of holding stocks. Merchants have often responded by amalgamations to achieve rationalisation of activities, while merchant chains tend to stock only standardised products having a short shelf-life, leaving it to smaller specialist merchants to hold other products.

13.6 Labour

Main characteristics

The construction industry employs some 1 557 000 people (2002), but of these only 968 000 worked as employees. There is a high proportion of skilled craftsmen (67 per cent) and of male workers (91 per cent). The main features of the work-force, however, are the number of one-man, labour-only subcontractors, the high rate of unemployment and the low productivity per worker compared with other industries.

LABOUR-ONLY SUBCONTRACTORS

Labour-only subcontracting predominates in house-building among carpenters, bricklayers and plasterers, who work either as individuals or in gangs. The main contractor provides the equipment and materials, paying the subcontractor for labour only. The advantages claimed are higher productivity, less site supervision and flexibility. But among other motives for its growth has been the desire of employers to reduce the burden of holiday and redundancy payments and training levies.

This labour-only subcontracting presents certain difficulties. In spite of regulations requiring up-front payment of tax, the government is faced with possible evasion. Because subcontractors work mainly on piece rates, they are unwilling to take on apprentices, the traditional means by which craftsmen are trained. Moreover, there may be uncertainty as to when the work will be performed and a failure to co-operate with other subcontractors. Finally, there is a tendency to neglect safety precautions, to waste materials and, with some gangs, to produce rushed, sub-standard work.

UNEMPLOYMENT

The rate of unemployment in the construction industry is usually between two and three times that of the economy generally. For instance, the rate of redundancy in the autumn and winter of 1993 was double that of manufacturing. The industry is vulnerable to all types of unemployment except that arising from a contraction of international demand.

Normal (or casual) unemployment results from the high labour turnover as projects are completed. While the small building firm works with a few, but fairly regular, local employees, the civil engineering contractor operates on a national basis, accepting contracts wherever they are available. Only key workers are retained for the different jobs; other workers are engaged locally and are paid off on completion of the project. Both at Christmas and Easter there is usually a two-week lay-off.

Frictional unemployment also occurs, some areas having surplus labour while others are suffering an acute shortage. The problem is not so serious with unskilled labour, Irish labourers, for example, moving to where they are required. But with skilled craftsmen there is both geographical and occupational immobility. Education and training of young workers is discouraged by the small pay differential between skilled and unskilled labour and the high rate of casual unemployment. To overcome the difficulty, the larger contractors try to retain skilled workers on a permanent basis, inducing workers to go to different sites by travel bonuses and lodging allowances.

The industry is also affected by structural unemployment, resulting from long-term changes in demand for the goods made in a region or changes on the supply side through the introduction of new techniques. When an area is depressed there is less demand for construction work. To some extent unemployment may be alleviated by government regional policy, new industries being attracted to the region by improving the infrastructure and providing modern factories. The construction work-force is therefore given more time to contract by natural wastage.

It is cyclical unemployment, however, which hits the construction industry particularly hard since it is producing capital goods (see pp. 379–82).

LABOUR RELATIONS AND PRODUCTIVITY

Productivity in the industry generally is discussed more fully in the next section. Here we consider labour relations: more precisely, obtaining the right quantity and quality of work from operatives.

The prevalence of labour-only subcontracting and the high rate of unemployment have led to fragmentation of trade unions, with only about one quarter of the labour-force being members. Most of these are employed by large civil engineering contractors and those local authorities which still employ some labour directly.

In the past, it is work on large sites that has suffered the most from poor site performance and industrial relations.

Various devices have been tried to improve the situation. Better working conditions, such as weather protection, heating and lighting, can help, but these are not always practicable. Improvement in the quality of management, especially as regards site supervision, has a greater impact. Personal supervision, where the principal works with his operatives, has been shown to increase productivity by 15 per cent. This, however, is not possible with large civil engineering contracts, and here experiments have been made in keeping to a few contractors (avoiding workers being disgruntled by the higher earnings of operatives employed by small subcontractors on piece-rates) and reducing the work-force of each site contractor to less than 500. This allows closer supervision, ensuring that materials arrive on time, reduces non-productive time (for example, by better time-keeping), encourages a better team spirit through closer contact between management and labour, and increases effort.

The latter can be promoted by special devices. Where possible, piece-work can increase productivity, but allowances have to be made for site difficulties and differences in mechanisation, and there must be some underpinning by a basic rate to allow for bad weather. Target-bonus schemes can also be introduced where work can be attributed to specific gangs. The difficulty is that to some extent such schemes can reduce management control over output and, unless all gangs keep in step, the flow of work can be upset. Finally, length-of-service payments may be made in order to decasualise labour with the object of improving labour relations.

13.7 Productivity

Increased productivity means that a given output can be achieved at lower cost – that is, the supply curve shifts to the right. The introduction of more and improved machines and the training of workers normally increase productivity in all industries over time. However, increases in productivity in the construction industry lag behind those in the economy generally, largely the result of the low level of mechanisation (see below).

One result of the slower growth in the construction industry's productivity is that the real cost of buildings tends to increase relatively to costs in general. Thus, given no change in demand for its products relative to those of manufacturing industries, an increasing proportion of national resources has constantly to be devoted to construction. Such reallocation would be accentuated if demand for construction projects increased relatively to other goods, because (for example) of a high income-elasticity of demand for houses, shopping facilities, schools and motorways, or through an increased rate of household formation.

How can productivity be increased?

In manufacturing, increased productivity has resulted chiefly from mechanisation, innovation and the creation of a large demand permitting mass production. The relatively lower increase in productivity of the construction industry suggests, therefore, that there has been less progress along these lines. Two questions have to be answered: Why should the construction industry be slower in adopting such methods? Can we expect improvement in the future?

13.8 Mechanisation

The average worker in manufacturing uses five times as much capital as the average construction worker. We have to ask, therefore: Why should construction be so labour-intensive?

Factors determining the substitution of capital for labour

Since mechanisation means providing workers with tools and power, it is really a substitution of capital for labour. The extent of such substitution depends upon: (i) how efficient firms are forced to be through competition; and (ii) the productivity and price of capital compared with the productivity and price of labour.

As we have seen, restricted local markets and imperfect knowledge may reduce competition for construction work. Nevertheless, some 50 per cent (by value) of such work is covered by fairly large contracts for which national firms compete by tender. Low mechanisation is therefore hardly the result of lack of competition.

It is necessary, therefore, to examine relative productivity and prices. Equilibrium will exist when capital and labour are combined to the point where their marginal rate of technical substitution equals their relative prices (see Chapter 1). In Marshallian terms:

$$\frac{MPP_{\text{capital}}(K)}{MPP_{\text{labour}}(L)} = \frac{\text{Price}_{\text{capital}}(K)}{\text{Price}_{\text{labour}}(L)}$$

As regards relative marginal physical productivity, that is, the rate at which MPP_k falls as capital is substituted for labour, we must consider both the short period, where labour is assumed to be the fixed factor, and the long period, where both factors are variable.

The short-period situation is depicted in Figure 13.3, where extra units of capital are added to a fixed supply of labour. Given perfect competition, the slope of the curve reflects substitutability. In project A, MPP_K drops off more slowly as capital is added because capital is a better substitute for labour than in project B. Thus a fall in the price of capital from OC to OC_1 leads to MM_2 extra capital being employed in project A but only MM_1 in project B.

The long-period situation can be analysed with the help of isoquants (see Figure 13.4). In Figure 13.4(a), because capital is poor substitute for labour, a given fall in the relative price of capital from C_1L_1 to C_2L_2 leads to only MM_1 capital being substituted for labour. In Figure 13.4(b) capital is a better substitute for labour and the same relative price fall leads to NN_1 extra capital being employed.

In short, a fall in the price of capital relative to labour should produce a substitution of capital for labour. But the extent of this substitution will depend upon: (i) how good physically is capital a substitute for labour; and (ii) the extent of the relative price fall.

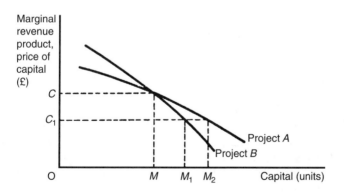

Figure 13.3 The substitution of capital for labour in the construction industry in the short period

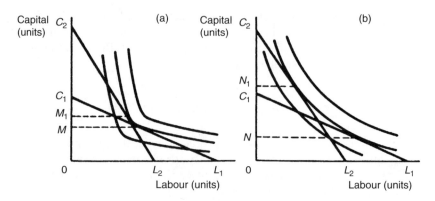

*Figure 13.4 The substitution of capital for labour in the construction
industry in the long period*

The possibility of physical substitution

When we examine the possible replacement of labour by machines in the
construction industry we find reasons why it is limited.

First, capital is not a good substitute for labour. Whereas a general
labourer is flexible in performing the consecutive jobs on a building site,
capital tends to be specific to one process. Nor is capital a good substitute
for skilled workers, such as plumbers, carpenters, bricklayers and electri-
cians, who form over one-half of the labour force.

Second, the nature of the work of the industry as a whole limits the
substitution of capital for labour. Over one-third of all work consists of
repairs and maintenance covering mostly labour-intensive jobs.

Third, two-fifths of new construction is high-rise building (mostly offices)
where there is already considerable mechanisation with capital equipment,
such as tower cranes, having replaced unskilled labour.

In practice, therefore, the substitution of capital for labour is only
possible for unskilled labour engaged in low-rise construction, that is, for
about one-half of the labour-force engaged in three-fifths of total *new*
work. Such low-rise construction is mainly traditional house-building,
where, as we shall see, the flexibility of the general labourer for performing many different jobs necessitated by the consecutive nature of building
operations makes him cheaper than specialist machines having a low rate
of use. Thus machinery is confined mostly to excavators for foundation-
digging and site-levelling, all-purpose transport (such as dumpers and
lorries) for moving soil and materials, and powered tools such as drills
and saws.

The price of capital relative to labour

For any given fall in the price of capital, therefore, the substitution of capital for labour would tend to be confined to about one-fifth of the industry's operations. But, even within this one-fifth, the conditions of the industry's work are such that the price of capital relative to that of labour tends to remain high. The low utilisation rate of specialised machines results from poor site organisation, delays and extra wear and tear due to bad weather, and the consecutive nature of building processes. It has been estimated, for example, that site utilisation of mixers is 30 per cent, of dumpers 66 per cent, water-pumps 26 per cent and excavators 70 per cent, though this can vary between jobs – cement-mixers, for instance, being more fully employed on road construction. Hiring machines or employing specialist firms for certain processes is not the complete answer to keeping down capital costs. Hiring is still relatively expensive because of a low hiring rate, which, for example, for mixers is 76 per cent, for dumpers 80 per cent, for water-pumps 56 per cent and for excavators 90 per cent. And vertical disintegration of processes, for instance, by obtaining ready-mixed concrete from a specialist producer, can increase the problems of dovetailing processes and of site organisation.

Added to this, the frequent and wide fluctuations in the level of activity in the construction industry increase the risk of expensive machines lying idle.

The low utilisation of machines, high wear and tear resulting from bad weather and the necessity of moving machines from site to site all tend to make capital expensive relative to unskilled labour. This, together with the low physical substitutability of capital for labour, accounts for the low degree of mechanisation in the industry.

The possibility of increasing mechanisation

It follows, therefore, that increased mechanisation depends upon a fall in the price of capital relative to labour or a rise in the physical productivity of capital compared with labour. Both are foreseeable possibilities.

First, a relative rise in wages, resulting from trade-union pressure or competition from other industries, would tend to produce a substitution of capital for labour. Thus bricks are now being delivered in packages or on pallets for mechanical handling.

Second, increased mechanisation could result if large firms, with their better organisation, became more important. For instance, improved organisation can reduce the high cost of a tower crane. Similarly, more large-sized contracts, such as for new towns or local authorities, give greater assurance that an expensive machine will be used to capacity.

Third, a movement towards larger components (for example, through offsite prefabrication) or towards high-rise buildings (for example, through the high cost of central sites, greater productivity in high-rise building or the relaxation of height limits) would necessitate cranes, and so on, for lifting.

13.9 Innovation

In broad terms innovation covers new labour-incentive schemes, improvements in organisation, and the use of standardised components. The first was considered in section 13.6; here we concentrate on organisation and standardised components.

Obstacles to innovation

The characteristics of the construction industry and the nature of the construction process present formidable obstacles to innovation. The preponderance of small, local firms means that knowledge of new and improved methods does not spread quickly. In any case, such firms, particularly house-builders, are often sheltered from competition. Even for other types of construction, differences in design, location and the degree of subcontracting make comparisons difficult, so that builders may not know whether new methods are cost-effective. Furthermore, with little significant change in the relative cost of factors, wide variations in the level of construction activity and the difficulties inherent in the piecemeal introduction of new methods where production consists of consecutive processes, there is little spur towards innovation. In addition there is an element of risk since faults in a new method (for example, the Ronan Point collapse in a block of flats, 1968) or in new materials (for example, the deterioration of concrete made with high alumina cement) may not show for some years later.

Organisation

Improving the organisation of the construction project can be examined with reference to the integration of the design/construction process and securing continuity of operations.

In Britain construction is marked by the diffusion of responsibility for the finished product. Although design and supervision are the responsibility of the architect, the main contractor is responsible for the actual construction. This division adds to the problems of organisation and site management.

Integration of the design/construction process requires the client, architect, quantity surveyor and main contractor to work closely together from the beginning. In this way the particular strengths of the builder can be harnessed and the most economic materials, consistent with the functional design of the building, chosen. The main snag of such integration of the complete process is that work cannot be put out to competitive tender.

Because construction consists of consecutive processes, careful programming is necessary to ensure continuity of operations, the arrival of specialist firms and materials on time and the best use of machines. However, the programme must have some flexibility. For example, inside work can be kept in reserve against bad weather, initial overtime limited so that there is scope for making good delays, and work outside the main programme, such as on garages and paths, held back in case delays occur through unforeseen difficulties.

Programming the basic processes can be tackled in a number of ways. It its simplest form it may simply mean planning operations around the task which takes the longest time, such as laying the foundations and building the main walls. Or the construction process may be based on ensuring that the minimum technical unit is fully employed – for example, about seven men in building a house, with other operations being subcontracted. A third method is to simplify the construction process by using new materials (such as ready-mixed concrete and light-weight concrete blocks for building), employing specialist firms and incorporating prefabricated units in order to reduce the number of operations on site.

Where the building is large or of a non-repetitive type, *critical path analysis* can be used to secure the efficient co-ordination of separate activities. Figure 13.5 shows in simplified form how this approach can be applied to the construction of a bedroom-garage extension to a house. The project is represented on an arrow diagram in which the arrows represent the different activities and the pattern of the diagram shows how these activities must be interrelated. This decides *how* the project must be carried out: all activities represented by incoming arrows must be completed before any of the activities represented by outgoing arrows can start. A second decision will then

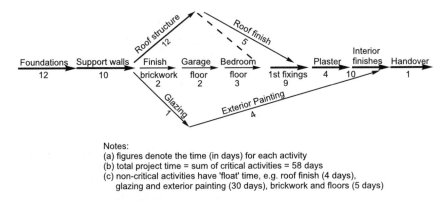

Notes:
(a) figures denote the time (in days) for each activity
(b) total project time = sum of critical activities = 58 days
(c) non-critical activities have 'float' time, e.g. roof finish (4 days),
   glazing and exterior painting (30 days), brickwork and floors (5 days)

Figure 13.5 Simple critical-path analysis diagram

cover how long processes will take to complete; but it should also be noted that only the critical path activities are worth expediting if an earlier completion is required.

Standardised components

The use of standardised components, such as windows, doors and roof trusses, reduces costs by allowing factory production and eliminating much craft labour on site. Factory-produced components are cheaper because they can be mass-produced with specialised tools, the organisation is on a permanent basis and does not need to be set up anew with each move to a fresh site, workers can be provided with cover from bad weather and with heat and light, and expensive skilled labour can be replaced by machines. In addition, the reduction in variety eases the stocking problem, while interchangeable spares make repair jobs cheaper.

Standardisation of components can be carried further by *dimensional coordination*, a systematic method of relating the size of components to facilitate their use together. It is based on a module of chosen dimensions which, in multiples and sub-multiples, provides the required sizes of all components, such as bricks, breeze-blocks, windows, doors, panels and floor slabs, in a logical progression. The advantages of dimensional co-ordination (which took a big step forward with metrication) are a reduction in the number of components, the elimination of wasteful cutting, and higher productivity through factory production and quicker assembly on site.

13.10 Mass production

The nature of 'industrialised building'

In manufacturing, one way in which costs have been reduced has been through the creation of a mass demand, usually by persuasive advertising. This has allowed the introduction of mass production yielding maximum economies of scale. Nevertheless, while the first requirement for this is a large demand, technical conditions of production must allow the process to be split into many separate operations so that specialist machines and workers can be employed continuously.

The construction industry has been based on what can be described as 'traditional building': that is, materials and components are purchased in the market and then assembled on site into buildings designed for particular or prospective clients. Recent trends have been towards substituting, where possible, 'system building'. This may simply refer to the incorporation in the building design of prefabricated components. More particularly, it may be limited to industrialised building, where (as far as possible) the whole building process from design to the finished product is based on factory techniques.

In essence *industrialised building* takes the form of designing a building in which the components, such as walls, ceilings, floor panels, cladding, concrete beams, and so on, are repetitive, thus allowing mass production under factory conditions with the advantages described above. Furthermore, since as much finishing work as possible is incorporated into the components, site work can consist mainly of assembly with no further work to be done. By this means it has been estimated that the building of a house can be reduced from 1800 man-hours by traditional methods to 900 to 1300 man-hours by industrialised methods, depending upon the particular system.

There are two main types of industrialised building: (i) 'open,' where the architect uses 'off-the-peg' components to achieve a design acceptable to the client; and (ii) 'closed', where design and components are one system, the manufacturer of the components also being responsible for the erection of the finished building. As far as possible, components are produced in a factory, though with closed systems they may be made on site.

To be successful, industrialised building must be able to compete costwise with traditional building methods. However, costs must be interpreted broadly, allowing for speed of building, subsequent maintenance costs, flexibility for future adaptation and special government aid towards research and development. The extent to which industrialised building can be cost-competitive depends upon conditions of demand and supply.

Demand

Industrialised building requires a demand which is both large and continuous. Thus in Figure 13.6, in order to secure the lower long-run average cost

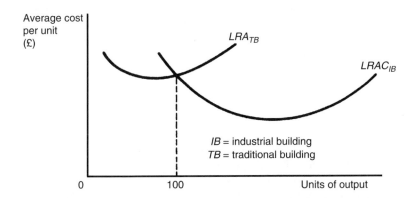

Figure 13.6 The minimum number of units to justify industrialised building

curve of industrialised building ($LRAC_{IB}$) resulting from design/construction integration, factory production of components and economies of scale, there must be a demand for at least 100 dwellings per period.

The difficulty is that, in the construction industry, total demand is simply an aggregate of small parcels: apart from new towns and local authority housing, approximately 90 per cent of all contracts are for less than 100 dwellings. Increasing the size of contracts would only be possible if the variety of buildings were restricted to a narrower range. Yet private clients, especially house-buyers, demand a building which is satisfying both functionally and aesthetically, since they feel that they are going to occupy it for a long time. Industrialised building, in contrast, is frowned upon as being uniform, a view mainly derived from the austere appearance presented by local authority flats which were subject to severe cost restrictions.

Demand for industrialised building therefore has to come from those clients where some uniformity of product is acceptable and where the highest and best use of the site is not impaired by the erection of a factory-built construction. This has meant that in the private sector the method has been most successful for factories, hotels, farm buildings, small garages, house extensions and garden sheds. Nevertheless, in the public sector, where 'need' rather then 'demand' is the dominant consideration (see p. 330), industrialised building has been significant in providing dwellings (particularly high-rise flats), schools (for example, the CLASP system – Consortium of Local Authorities Schools Programme), hospitals and universities. Even so, in 1971, their best year, industrialised dwellings accounted for only a third of the total of all new local authority and New Town dwellings completed.

Continuity of demand is a further requirement. Industrialised building involves capital investment, and this is likely to be uneconomic unless there is an adequate work-load over a number of years. Here the construction industry faces difficulties. First, particularly with regard to dwellings, the main product of industrialised building, tastes may change, as, for example, with high-rise flats (see below). Second, public-sector construction, the main outlet for industrialised building, fluctuates. Not only do political swings influence public-sector housing programmes, but the latter are a major victim whenever cuts are made in government spending.

Supply

Even if demand is sufficient to justify mass production, the method will only be adopted if it results in a competitive saving in costs of production. Yet, in spite of a government subsidy, industrialised building failed to gain an overwhelming advantage over traditional methods. The reasons for this were as follows.

(a) If skilled craftsmen and wet finishers are to be eliminated in the assembly process, the components of factory-built systems must have greater dimensional precision than traditional materials. But the greater accuracy of steel, plastics, wood and concrete slabs prepared under high pressure has to be weighed against their higher cost relative to bricks and concrete, especially as they are not as yet fully proven. Since materials account for about half the cost of a building and labour for one-third, a 25 per cent increase in the cost of materials would require a 37.5 per cent saving in labour costs just to break even.

(b) Factory-produced components increase transport costs through the extra journey of delivering them to the site and because they are usually bulkier and more fragile than the raw materials.

(c) A higher capital outlay is required, cranes for lifting being essential.

(d) Industrialised building tends to be inflexible. With traditional building, modifications are usually possible, both in actual construction and in subsequent use. In contrast, changes in industrialised building usually involve interference with the basic design. Thus, when experience necessitated new fire precautions for hospitals, they could only be incorporated in the industrially designed building at considerable expense.

(e) There is a tendency for industrialised building to eliminate the competition of tendering, a monopoly seller often being faced by a monopoly buyer with the price depending on their relative bargaining strengths.

(f) Traditional building can now make use of factory components through dimensional co-ordination.

Likely future trends

Industrialised building enjoyed a short-lived boom in the early 1960s, and by 1966 it accounted for 25 per cent of all dwellings (42 per cent of New Town and local authority housing). The Ronan Point disaster of 1968, however, produced a reaction against high-rise flats especially as regards the social disadvantages and certain constructional faults which emerged. Moreover, subsequent recessions in the construction industry have highlighted the risk of over-investment in fixed capital, thereby eroding any competitive advantage enjoyed by industrialised building. Finally, when unit cost controls were imposed in 1967, industrialised buildings could not keep within the prescribed cost maxima.

Three present trends are less advantageous to industrialised building. First, rising standards of living and the swing to owner-occupation have favoured traditional building to individual designs. Second, the easing of the back-log resulting from the Second World War and the swing towards renovation meant that there is now less emphasis on providing new dwellings quickly. Third, the high rate of unemployment in the construction industry has resulted in less stress being placed on increasing productivity. Today few blocks of flats of more than four storeys are being built.

On the other hand, possible future developments could renew interest in industrialised building. These include: higher land prices, which would encourage high-rise building; improved organisation and greater continuity of demand; a fall in the price of precision materials (such as plastics) relative to that of the traditional brick and concrete poured on site; a rise in relative wage rates or shortages of skilled craftsmen; a fall in the price of capital; and lower transport costs.

In the immediate future, however, such developments appear to be doubtful. Increases in productivity in the construction industry, therefore, are more likely to come from better labour relations, improved organisation and, above all, from the development of designs based on dimensional co-ordination incorporating, as far as possible, standardised, factory-made components.

13.11 The present situation and prospects

The construction process is subject to a high degree of uncertainty from changes in government policy, the peculiar wishes of clients, dependence upon the performance of subcontractors and frequent bottlenecks in the supply of materials, components and skilled labour. In addition, there are always possible delays in obtaining planning permission, bye-law approval and arranging finance.

The organisation of the construction industry reflects these difficulties. Contracting firms tend to exist solely as organisations capable of building and avoid committing themselves to one construction method or type of building. Instead adaptability is secured by adhering to simple and widely understood techniques and where a minimum of plant can be fully employed by redeployment among different jobs. Advantages of specialisation are largely secured by subcontracting.

Improvements in productivity are therefore likely to come chiefly from the development of higher management ability within individual firms and from innovations in the industry generally. The latter will rest largely on the standardisation and factory production of components, basing designs on dimensional co-ordination, and reconciling competitive tendering with integrated design and production techniques.

Nevertheless, the extent and speed of such innovations will depend upon the degree to which standardised components prove acceptable and the extent to which fluctuations in the level of demand generally can be eliminated. Harmonisation of linear dimensions of both components and design throughout the EU represents an important step in this direction.

Summary

In 2002 the construction industry contributed 7.6 per cent of UK GDP and employed more than 1.5 million people. Its efficiency is clearly of importance to real property since it is concerned with the construction, adaptation and maintenance of buildings. The preponderance of small firms, low productivity and high proportion of casual labour give an impression of inefficiency, but in fact the demand conditions of the construction industry result in these outcomes. Supply conditions are also distinctive with consecutive operations, production on site, small minimum technical unit size, high labour costs and time lags between demand change and supply response.

Construction is very labour-intensive and this is a major reason for low productivity. Output per worker could be increased by substitution of capital for labour but skilled labour is vital to the industry, and many jobs are relatively small and labour-intensive. Industrialised building was briefly popular in the 1960s, but demand for traditional buildings to individual designs has meant that this 'mass-manufacturing' approach to construction has not really taken off.

Review questions

1. Why is the efficiency of the construction industry important to:
   (a) the economy
   (b) real property?
2. Explain the special features of demand and supply which are likely to result in a preponderance of small firms in the construction industry.
3. Describe the methods of project pricing used in construction.
4. What functions do builders merchants perform?
5. How could productivity be improved in the construction industry?

Recommended reading

P. N. Balchin, J. L. Kieve and G. H. Bull, *Urban Land Economics and Public Policy*, 5th edn (London: Macmillan, 1995) ch. 10.
M. Ball, *Housing Policy and Economic Power* (London: Methuen, 1983) chs 3 and 4.

R. C. Harvey and A. Askworth, *The Construction Industry of Great Britain* (Oxford: Butterworth–Heinemann, 1993).

P. M. Hillebrandt, *Economic Theory and the Construction Industry*, 3rd edn (London: Macmillan, 2000).

J. Rafferty, *Principles of Building Economics* (Oxford: BSP Professional Books, 1991).

P. A. Stone, *Building Economics*, 3rd edn (Oxford: Pergamon Press, 1976).

PART IV

URBAN LAND USE

CHAPTER 14

Land Use and Land Values

After studying this chapter you will be able to:

- **Explain how the price of land is determined**
- **Explain Von Thunen's model of land use and prices**
- **Construct a land-price curve, showing the price of land at different distances from the central market**
- **Explain the determinants of urban land use**
- **Describe government policy in relation to location decisions of firms and households**

14.1 Introduction

Land-use decisions

Urban land use is determined by the various decisions made by *firms, households* and the *government* (primarily local authorities). Firms occupying shops, offices and factories have on occasions to decide whether to expand and, if so, whether to move or redevelop the existing site. Moreover, in a dynamic economy, new firms come into being and have to choose where to locate. Similarly, households decide where to live, and if many people move in a particular direction – for example, to the suburbs – it profoundly affects the character of urban land use. Finally, government authorities influence land use through the control of development, overall transport policy and the siting of roads, and by local authority house-building and comprehensive redevelopment.

Our first approach will be to assume a market economy where: (i) resources are allocated on the basis of prices, costs and profits; (ii) firms and households have preferences for settling in particular locations and these preferences are reflected in the price/rent they are prepared to pay for the use of land; (iii) owners of land sell/let to the highest bidder; (iv) knowledge of the market by buyers and sellers is sufficient to provide competition; (v) there are no dynamic changes, the transport system, transport costs, technology, and so on remaining unchanged; and (vi) there is no government interference in the market.

The determination of the price of land

The price of land, like the prices of other goods, is determined by the interaction of supply and demand in the market.

In the sense that the total *supply* of land is fixed, the price of land can be regarded as being determined by demand alone. Of more immediate concern, however, is the price and use of land in particular locations. Here again, for spatial reasons, land is limited in supply, especially land in the centre of an urban area. Nevertheless the supply of sites for any one use cannot be regarded as being completely inelastic, since alternative, although less-preferred, locations exist as we move outwards from the centre, the number of such sites increasing exponentially as the radius lengthens. Thus any increase in the demand for land of a particular type or for a particular use is capable of bringing forth additional supplies. Moreover, greater intensity of site use is possible, chiefly by the addition of capital to build upwards.

Demand by firms and households for a particular location depends upon the expected net revenue yield/utility. The price/rent is what has to be paid by a particular use to prevent the site going to some other use. That use which can outbid all others will secure the given site. In long-run equilibrium, therefore, land will, within the geographical and institutional framework and subject to the imperfections of the real property market, have moved to its most profitable use.

Since different locations have different use-capacities, a pattern of differential rents emerges. Furthermore, the pattern of land use reflects the competition between alternative uses for sites in the market. Thus land values and land use are determined simultaneously. Indeed we can extend the relationship to include intensity of use. The greatest demand will be for those sites having the greatest relative advantage. This is likely to make intensive development of the site profitable (see p. 99). Those users (such as offices) who can use the site most intensively will be able to pay the highest price/rent. Often, however, this results in a site having a split use – for example, shops outbidding other users for the ground-floor of a building, with offices or residences occupying the upper storeys.

Our initial task, therefore, is to examine what determines rent-earning capacity – the maximum amount which a particular activity can bid for land in a given location. In general, this bid will depend upon businessmen's profit-maximising decisions and households' utility-maximising considerations. The businessman will seek that location which maximises net gain, that is, the difference between receipts and costs, not simply the one which maximises sales revenue or minimises production costs. Similarly, a household seeks to maximise the utility advantage of a locality over costs of travel.

As a first approach we look at the model of land use and prices formulated in 1826 by Von Thunen, a German economist. This concentrates on differences in relative transport costs in different types of agricultural production.

14.2 Transport costs and location

Rent-earning capacity and transport costs

Von Thunen assumed:

(a) a boundless flat and featureless plain over which natural resources and climate are distributed uniformly;
(b) a central market;
(c) uniform horse-and-cart transport facilities to this central market;
(d) different foods can be grown, but since these differ in bulk, the cost of transporting them to the market differs;
(e) for each type of product, transport costs vary directly and proportionately with distance from the central market;
(f) different products have different cost patterns – for example, as regards transport and production costs;
(g) receipts from the cultivation of one hectare of land are the same for all types of product.

Given these assumptions, Figure 14.1 demonstrates the emergence of rent-paying capacity as a function of transport costs and thus of distance from market. Value and costs are measured vertically, the quantity concerned being assumed to be the product of one hectare. OC represents costs of production, but excluding the cost of transport to the market, at a production point which coincides with the central market. As distance from the market increases, so total costs are raised by the increased cost of transport along line Cc'. Since revenue at the central market place from the sale of the given quantity of the product remains constant at OR, rent or bid price per hectare (the difference between total revenue and cost) diminishes as distance from the market increases. Thus at distance Od the bid price is rb and at Od', $r'b'$. Ultimately a 'no-rent margin' for this particular product would

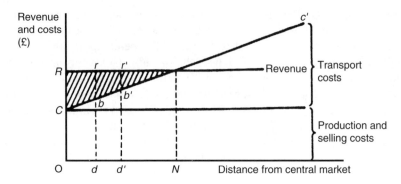

Figure 14.1 Rent-paying capacity as a function of transport costs

be reached at a distance of *ON*. If this were the only product, land at a greater distance than *ON* would be without value.

Where more than one product is possible, however, the bid price and the 'no-rent margin' will vary according to their different transport costs. This is illustrated in Figure 14.2 which assumes (for simplicity) two products, *A* and *B*. The product of a hectare of each is assumed to bring in the same sales revenue *OR* at the central market.

Product *A* (Figure 14.2(a)) has production costs of *OA*, and transport costs increasing with distance from the market. Thus *AA'* shows total costs at different distances from the market. In contrast, product *B* (Figure 14.2 (b)) has higher production costs, *OB*, but less steeply rising transport costs, giving total costs of *BB'* at different distances from the market. As a result, the 'no-rent margin' is reached at *L* for product *A* and at *M*, further from the centre, for product *B*.

Combining both in one diagram (Figure 14.2(c)), it can be seen that in the vicinity of the market *A* will support the higher rent bid (*AR* compared with *BR*). Competition between producers will ensure that land rent rises

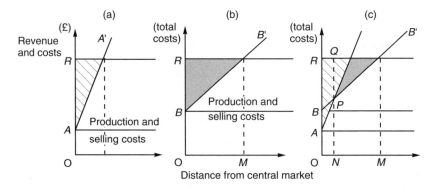

Figure 14.2 Transport costs of different products

to this level and that land will be used for the production of *A* to the complete exclusion of *B*. However, since transport costs are greater for *A* than for *B*, the advantage of *A* over *B* diminishes as we move further out, until at distance *N* both products support rent bids of *PQ* per hectare. At a greater distance than *N*, product *B* can support the higher rent bid and would thus outbid *A* for the land. Beyond *M*, neither *A* nor *B* would be produced.

Rent-earning capacity and land use

Figure 14.3 develops the analysis of Figure 14.2 to obtain a basic land-use model based on transport costs. The rent-earning capacity of the different land uses in Figure 14.2 is measured at increasing distances from 0; for example, the rent-earning capacity of product *A* in Figure 14.3 is simply the shaded area in Figure 14.2(a) turned anti-clockwise 180°; similarly for *B* (Figure 14.2 (b), and so on. Four uses of land are assumed instead of the two in Figure 14.2. *A* might be market gardening, *B* grain production, *C* root crops, *D* grazing. These examples are merely for illustrative purposes and assume that uses *A, B, C* and *D* bear the kind of relationship to one another so far as production and transport costs are concerned as that holding

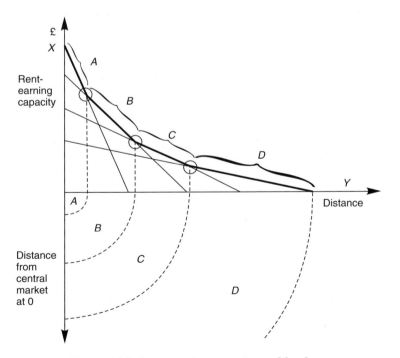

Figure 14.3 Rent-earning capacity and land use

between product *A* and product *B* in Figure 14.2. Thus *A* would represent the highest value use of land at the centre, but transport costs rise swiftly and so reduce the rent-earning capacity of *A* sharply as distance from the centre increases. *B* would be a 'second-order' use of land at the market centre, but since transport costs increase less rapidly than for *A*, it would, after a certain point, displace *A* as the most profitable land use. Similarly, *C* eventually replaces *B*, and so on.

If 0 represents the market centre, this land-use model gives four concentric zones about 0. One quadrant of such zones is indicated in Figure 14.3. The limit of any zone's use, say *A*, is not where its no-rent margin occurs, but where the land becomes more profitable in some alternative use.

Conclusions

Conclusions which emerge from this model are as follows:

(1) Land uses determine land values and not vice versa.
(2) Because of increasing transport costs, producers of goods having high transport costs relative to their value (weighty, bulky or perishable goods) will be able to outbid others for land at the centre. But the amount they can bid declines rapidly as distance from the centre increases, and eventually other producers whose goods are not so transport-orientated will be able to outbid them, and so on.

We thus have the thick *land-price curve XY* (Figure 14.3) showing the price of land at different distances from the centre, assuming each plot achieves its maximum bid price.
(3) With homogeneous land, the land-use pattern is one of concentric zones around the central market (Figures 14.3 and 15.1, p. 248), nearness to the centre depending on transport costs relative to value. This land-use pattern will be reflected in the pattern of urban land values.

14.3 Factors determining urban land use

Businessmen, we have assumed, locate their activities where they can maximise profits, and households live where they can maximise utility, that is, achieve the greatest residential benefits. But what determines profitability and utility? The answer is *accessibility* – the advantages of a particular urban location in terms of movement, convenience and amenity. It is helpful, however, if we examine the term under the headings of general accessibility and special accessibility.

(1) General accessibility

By concentrating on transport costs as *the* factor determining land values, Von Thunen tended to ignore the revenue-earning capacity of different locations. To a large extent this weakness can be taken care of by embracing transport costs within the wider concept of 'general accessibility' – the advantage of a particular location in terms of the movement costs (including time) it avoids and the revenue-earning capacity (including convenience) it affords. Thus firms require general accessibility to factors of production (particularly labour) and to markets, while households seek accessibility to work opportunities, shops, schools and recreational facilities.

Since general accessibility is largely dependent upon transport facilities, the Von Thunen model explaining the spatial pattern of land use and land values in an agricultural region can be applied to an urban area. With both firms and households, some users rate the importance of general accessibility higher than others. Generally speaking, most business users find that the centre of the urban area, the central business district (CBD) affords the greatest accessibility. Thus for offices, which are labour-intensive rather than land-intensive, the CBD is the focal point for the supply of labour, while for shops (particularly speciality shops such as jewellery, ladies' fashions, cameras, and so on which need to draw customers from as wide an area as possible) CBD locations give the highest revenue-earning capacity.

On the other hand, the CBD is limited spatially, and competition for sites there results in high prices/rents. Thus the advantages of accessibility have to be compared with the level of rent. For shops, accessibility to as many customers as possible is paramount and the revenue-earning capacity of ground-floor locations in the CBD enables them to outbid other users. Similarly offices, which are labour-intensive, find upper-storey locations present no great obstacles to accessibility and so they are able to outbid other users, such as factories and warehouses, which are land-intensive. Thus, as with the Von Thunen model, a pattern of land use and land values emerges with shops outbidding offices for central ground-floor locations, and offices outbidding factories and warehouses.

(2) Special accessibility – agglomeration economies

While general accessibility – the money, time and trouble costs of getting anywhere – affects all firms and households, location decisions may also be influenced by *special* accessibility resulting from external economies of concentration or complementarity.

External economies of concentration can take the form of a ready supply of trained labour (such as secretarial skills), common services (such as servicing office equipment), and reputation of the locality (for example,

Harley Street for medical specialists). At times, however, diseconomies of concentration, such as traffic congestion, may exercise a repellent effect, and eventually reduce the general accessibility of a locality.

Complementarity exhibits different aspects. First, personal contact with other specialists during the working day may be necessary (for example, advertising agencies and newspapers, money market dealers and banks). Second, shops selling comparison goods (for instance, ladies' fashions, antiques and works of art) can, by congregating together, tap each other's trading market and enhance the reputation of the locality for a particular good through the greater choice offered to customers. Third, consumer services (such as restaurants, cinemas, theatres, hotels) congregate in the CBD since they serve the workers and shoppers there, while hotels locate near major airports. Fourth, complementarity induces smaller shops to be near a dominant retailer (such as Harrods, Marks & Spencer, a Sainsbury supermarket) or may even bring together unlike activities (for example, shops selling gardening tools amidst City of London offices).

At times, complementarity may be negative, acting as a repellent (for instance, ladies' fashions shops would not locate in the 'red light' district of Soho).

Special accessibility often means that, within the pattern of urban land use produced by general accessibility, there is a 'clustering' of shops and activities such as ladies' fashions (Oxford Street), young people's fashions (Covent Garden), designer clothes (Sloane Street), bric-a-brac (Portobello Road), antiques (Fulham Road), cinemas and theatres (Leicester Square). Inasmuch as many special accessibility advantages are likely to be strongest in the CBD, they reinforce its general accessibility superiority.

As regards residential location decisions, both aspects of special accessibility, – concentration and complementarity – are relevant. Concentration of population promotes the provision of libraries, churches, schools and recreational and cultural facilities. Similarly for complementarity: not only does nearness to parks, golf-courses and open spaces enhance the residential attractions of a district, but often households prefer to live alongside others of the same social and cultural background, religion or race. As we shall see (p. 263), special accessibility is a factor in producing wedges of high-quality housing.

(3) Additional factors

Although urban areas tend towards the same broad structure of urban land-use, each exhibits its own particular variation. Factors producing such differences include the following.

(a) *Historical development.* While the land-use patterns of some towns are heavily influenced by location decisions made by the Romans or nineteenth-century industrialists, others (such as Milton Keynes) are clearly a product of twentieth-century planning.

(b) *Topographical features.* Physical aspects – rivers, mountains, plains, slopes, wind, climate and geology (subsoil) – often influence the location decisions of different activities. With some – for example, defences, docks and airports – natural site attributes are essential.

(c) *Size.* Only in large urban areas is it possible to support certain activities, such as opera, legal and medical specialists, many of which seek central sites. Similarly a firm may only be able to recruit sufficient highly specialised labour in a large town (see p. 276).

(d) *Imperfections of the capital market.* These may in practice prevent preferences being fully expressed in the market. Thus the willingness of institutions to fund office projects has weighted city-centre redevelopment in this direction.

(4) Dynamic change

Among other factors producing dynamic change are the secular *increase in real income* and *technical developments*. Both have an effect on the pattern of land values. Thus, on the *demand side*, the wide ownership of cars and freezers, together with new retailing techniques, largely account for the setting-up of out-of-town hypermarkets, retail warehouses and shopping centres, thereby increasing land values in the suburbs relative to the inner urban area (but see below). Similarly, factories and warehouses have been sited on new orbital roads outside the urban area, especially as they have become more land-intensive with the use of the flow method of production and mechanical handling of goods. The development of road transport has also resulted in residential infilling of land between the major transport routes of the urban area and in the movement of households towards the periphery. Indeed the movement has gone further, with new and expanded towns and sub-centres developing outside the major conurbations which are now shrinking in population.

The effect of technical developments on the location of offices is mixed. Improved lifts and air conditioning, together with new building techniques which reduce the cost of building upwards, make for more intensive development of the CBD. On the other hand, information technology and improved communications allow the majority of office procedures to be carried on at sub-centres (such as Croydon, Reading) and in the new business parks (see p. 244) or even by home sub-contracting.

In examining the effect of transport developments on the pattern of land prices, we must not neglect the *supply side*. An outward movement from the centre increases in a geometric progression the land surface which can be occupied. For example, if a transport improvement allowed a 30-minute journey to the centre to cover 10 miles instead of 5 miles in the rush-hour, the residential land available would increase from 78.54 square miles to 314.16 square miles. Thus while the increased demand for such land tends to raise its price, it could be offset by the larger number of sites available.

Much hinges, however, on the elasticity of demand for land. If this is unity, there will be no change in the amount spent on land. In practice, however, demand is likely to be elastic, as people prefer larger sites. While, therefore, we cannot forecast the final price change, we can say that the price of land in the suburbs will increase relative to that in the inner urban area as people move outwards (Figure 14.4).

The exception is likely to be the CBD where improved transport results in a larger catchment area for specialist shops – for example, the multiple chains – and specialised commercial activities such as services of an international character (for example, insurance, banking, financial and commodity dealing) and the head offices of large firms.

Summary

We can simplify the foregoing discussion by saying that basically there are three major determinants of the location of a particular activity: (1) accessibility; (2) environmental characteristics; and (3) rent. There is a trade-off of (1) and (2) against (3).

(4) Dynamic factors, chiefly the secular increase in real income and technical developments, also alter location. But of equal importance is:

(5) Government policy.

14.4 Government policy

The government, both central and local, influences location decisions through its policies on taxation, planning, parks, green belts and open

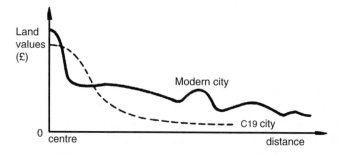

Figure 14.4 Changes in land price gradients

spaces, conservation, transport and traffic congestion, housing, schools, universities, public utilities, hospitals, and so on (see also Chapter 17).

We can cite a selection of three changes in government planning policy to illustrate how the market responds through developers' decisions on location.

Out-of-town retail developments

During the 1980s there was a relaxation of control by the government in accordance with its free enterprise philosophy. Planning authorities were instructed to be less rigid when considering applications for planning consent, and the onus was put on them to show why a proposed development should be refused: for example, for environmental reasons. In particular, the planning authority had to reflect carefully where a refusal to develop would entail economic loss.

One result of the easier planning controls was that the supply of retail outlets could respond to the increase in consumer spending. GNP showed an annual increase of over 4 per cent, and from 1981–8 retail sales increased at an average annual rate of 4.8 per cent compared with only 1 per cent in 1971–80.

In the city centre, shops were refurbished, and often covered shopping malls were built. But with the increase in car ownership and leisure time and the migration of people to the urban rural fringe, there was a growing demand for *out-of-town shopping facilities*. On the supply side, too, the increasing rents in the city centre and the growing traffic congestion prompted retailers to consider moving outwards. Sites near to orbital roads and motorway junctions were the preferred locations. Development took the form of shopping centres (consisting of a number of different shops in a central covered arcade), super-stores offering one-stop shopping and retail warehouses selling DIY, flat-pack and fixed furniture, carpets and floor coverings, electrical goods, motor accessories and other goods requiring a large selling area. Some of these developments have been combined in retail parks, which include in addition restaurants, banks, travel agents and, more recently, leisure activities and even swimming pools.

The User Classes Order (UCO) 1987

In addition to controlling the construction or alteration of buildings, planning legislation restricts the type of activities for which they can be used. But to avoid having to apply for planning permission every time there is a change in the nature or the intensity of an activity, the UCO was introduced in 1948 to group together similar uses, no consent usually being required for changes within each group. Periodically the UCO has been revised to reflect changes in the nature of economic activities.

Such a change was the switch from earlier types of engineering (such as cars, machines tools, heavy electrical equipment) to the light industry of high technology (for example, computers, micro-chips, electronics). This new light industry was radically different in its requirement from the older traditional industries for, in contrast to large factory sheds, it wanted smaller and cleaner premises integrated with the office requirements of the production unit.

Thus the UCO 1987 amalgamated the former light industrial use class with most of the activities under the existing office class to form a new category – a business use class, B_1. This prompted a major surge in development, with new manufacturing work space having a high office content. Added momentum was given to this change by a new General Development Order 1988 which allowed transfer without planning permission from B_2 (general industrial) to the new B_1. As a result former industrial buildings were converted to high-tech workshop/offices, especially on industrial estates on the edge of towns.

More important, however, was the emergence of a new concept – *business parks and science parks*. With the relaxation of planning controls, these were given a boost by technology changes which involved network computer systems and under-floor cabling.

Business parks have been carefully located, usually with good access to motorways and dual carriageways, but within easy reach of a main town.

Above all, they have been master-planned from conception with strict standards of control over architecture, parking, site density, landscaping and management. Most parks provide occupiers with a range of tenure options. Expansion can be provided for by taking in adjacent land or by moving to a larger unit on the park.

Large parks have on site such amenities as banking, shops, wine bars, hotels, pubs and sporting facilities. They are, therefore, more than a collection of individual businesses. They are mini-communities which in time, as UK traffic congestion increases, could develop into places where people live as well as work.

Since business parks are highly dependent on car travel, they are also likely to be affected by the new PPG 13 (p. 245). Though their response could be to develop, like the out-of-town super-stores, on sites well-served by public transport, there is also the possibility, given planning consent, of developing in tandem with a residential district, a policy already followed in Kent.

The concept of business parks has been applied to *science parks* which were originally located near university towns to forge formal links between university research and its development by business. Subsequently science park development was seen as a potential tool for the regeneration of traditional industrial areas.

More recently, the cuts in government funding per student for education have encouraged universities to see property development as a means of raising cash. Thus the objective of the original initiative has been superseded by their selling a commercial development under the science park banner.

The rejuvenation of town centres

Government policy was reversed in 1993, when concern at the decline in the vitality of traditional town centres led to a revised PPG 6 being issued by the Department of the Environment. This considered that the rapid development of out-of-town retailing, especially the large regional shopping centres, was mainly the cause, and future planning decisions would be required to take this into consideration.

This presumed discrimination against further out-of-town shopping development was reinforced by PPG 13. With the long-term objective of reducing carbon dioxide emissions, this advised that future planning policy should encourage people to work and shop near where they live, thus reducing trips by car.

These two government decisions on the lines of future development could eventually:

(a) lead to the provision of offices on or near railway stations;
(b) shift food-only super-markets back to the town centre;
(c) limit development of new out-of-town super-stores to sites well-served by public transport, possibly integrated with the new office location;
(d) encourage the provision of a home delivery service by these stores, especially as shopping through the Internet expands.

Summary

Supply of land for a particular use is not completely inelastic, so the price of land is not totally demand determined. Land values and land use are determined simultaneously by the interaction of supply and demand. The greatest demand will be for those sites which maximise net gain/profit (for businesses) or maximum utility (for households).

Von Thunen's model of land use and prices shows rent-earning capacity as a function of transport costs and thus of distance from the market. Using this premise it is possible to construct a basic land-use model based on transport costs. For homogeneous land, the land-use pattern is one of concentric zones around the central market.

Factors determining urban land use include:
- general accessibility
- special accessibility resulting from external economies of concentration or complementarity
- a variety of factors unique to a particular urban area
- transport and communications developments
- government policy

Review questions

1. Since the supply of total land is fixed, is it true to say that the price of land is determined by demand alone?
2. Explain, using a diagram, how the rent-earning capacity of land can be related to transport costs.
3. Explain how greater intensity of site use in the CBD is possible.
4. Why will land (in a perfect market) be used in the most profitable way?
5. How can the government influence the location decisions of households and firms?

Recommended reading

P. N. Balchin, J. L. Kieve and G. H. Bull, *Urban Land Economics and Public Policy*, 5th edn (London: Macmillan, 1995) chs 2 and 3.

A. W. Evans, *Urban Economics* (Oxford: Basil Blackwell, 1985) chs 2 and 3.

CHAPTER 15

The Pattern of Urban Land Use

After studying this chapter you will be able to:

- Use bid rent curves for different firms to explain their location in relation to the CBD
- Use bid rent curves for different households to explain their location in relation to the CBD
- Describe the broad pattern of urban land use
- Appraise various theories of urban structure including:
  - concentric zone theory
  - radial or axial development theory
  - cost of friction hypothesis
  - wedge or radial sector theory
  - multiple-nuclei theory
  - sector-zone theory

15.1 Location equilibrium for firms and households

Let us assume: (i) there are just two types of urban user, firms and households; (ii) all urban users would like to be near the centre of the town because it is the point of maximum accessibility; (iii) differences in transport routes and topography can be ignored.

By using the indifference technique of Chapter 1 we can explain the equilibrium location for both firms and households, but in order to allow for their different requirements, respectively profit and utility, we will deal with them separately.

(a) Firms

The assumption that the CBD is the point of maximum accessibility implies that there is no haulage of inter-city freight which is not based on the CBD – a situation applicable to the nineteenth century when railway stations were sited there.

Because the CBD affords maximum accessibility, rents there are highest. In deciding where to locate its operations, therefore, a firm has to trade off rent against accessibility, that is, distance from the CBD. Its equilibrium location will be the one which maximises its profit. There are two stages in the analysis.

First, we define lines of constant profit (similar to indifference curves and equi-product curves in Chapter 1). These iso-product curves (usually in this context described as 'bid rent curves') join points where the level of profit is the same at different distances from the CBD. Thus in Figure 15.1, starting from a given rent OA at the CBD, we can draw the straight-line bid rent curve AP_2, which joins points at which the firm would make the same profit as it moves outwards from the CBD, the loss of net revenue being exactly offset by the lower rent. Similarly, a higher initial rent OB at the CBD would result in a bid rent curve BP_1 further from the origin and depicting a *lower* level of profit than AP_2 since the firm is paying a higher rent to secure a CBD site.

Second, on the bid-rent-curve diagram, we impose the land-price curve derived in Figure 14.3 which shows *actual* market rents at an increasing distance from the CBD – applying it, however, to land use in the urban area.

The firm, having regard to market rents, will endeavour to locate on its highest bid rent curve, that is the one nearest the origin. It will therefore

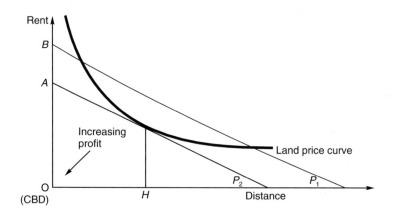

Figure 15.1 Bid rent curves and the location decision

locate at *H* where the land price curve just touches AP_2, for this will be the most profitable location at current market rents.

Some firms will place greater importance upon location than others. Those which value the CBD as the consumer market for their goods will have steeply falling bid rent curves (for example, L_1, L_2 in Figure 15.2) since a considerable fall in rent will be necessary to compensate for the loss of revenue as distance from the CBD increases. Similarly for firms which are labour-intensive, such as offices, proximity to the CBD could be crucial. All such firms, therefore, will seek to locate near the centre: for example, at *L*.

On the other hand, firms which are land-intensive, such as warehousing and manufacturing (especially those employing a ground-level flow method of production) will have less steeply-sloping bid rent curves, P_1 and P_2. These firms will thus locate further from the centre, at *P*.

The analysis indicates that the urban area will end where agriculture (the most land-intensive industry) is not outbid by other users. Even here, however, market gardening, where accessibility to the urban market is important and which is more labour-intensive, will tend to be located on the urban fringe to a greater extent than will dairy farming and cereal growing.

The fundamental weakness of the model stems from the assumption that the CBD is the only point having accessibility value. In doing so it: (a) ignores the development of orbital roads and motorways, which provide accessibility outside the CBD for inter-city freight movement by road haulage; and (b) fails to recognise that many firms require locations which give access to national and international markets. In addition the model overlooks the effects of planning control and subsidy and taxation inducements on location decisions.

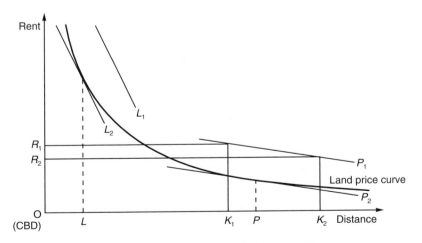

Figure 15.2 Bid rent curves for different firms

(b) Households

Whereas there is a very direct relationship between business demand for accessibility and the profitability of land use, residential demand for accessibility tends to be more complicated, depending on the utility of certain locations and even of particular sites expressed in terms of:
(a) travel time and costs related to distance from work, shops, schools, entertainment, cultural activities and recreational facilities; and
(b) non-monetary considerations such as space, fresh air, peace and quiet, locational prestige, neighbours and family ties.
Since both these aspects of residential utility come within our definition of accessibility – the advantages of particular locations in terms of movement and convenience – we can use the bid rent curve technique to analyse the main basic simplifying assumption that accessibility to work, shops, and so on involves travelling to the CBD.

But the non-monetary considerations mentioned above have an additional influence on households as they seek to maximise utility in deciding where to live. Though accessibility to the CBD is important, there is a pull to the suburbs, not only on account of the lower rent, but because accessibility to more house-space and garden, and to modern schools, playing-fields, parks, golf-courses and the countryside generally is greater than in the CBD. We shall concentrate on space, particularly space as regards the house and garden. For households, living near the CBD has the advantage of accessibility, but high rents restrict the amount of space which they can afford. Yet moving to the suburbs to obtain space and environmental advantages at the lower rent entails higher transport costs (in the form of fares, time and discomfort) in travelling to the CBD for work, speciality shopping, entertainment, cultural activities and central government services, such as the city administrative offices, library, polytechnic, art gallery, and so on.

It should be noted, however, that the monetary advantage of accessibility depends not only on *how much* a trip costs but also on *how often* the trip is made. Normally accessibility to one's regular work-place is of relatively high importance, since it usually involves at least five trips a week, outweighing trips for recreational activities.

In deciding where to live, therefore, households have to trade-off transport costs to the CBD against the extra space offered by the suburbs, that is, they have to choose between distance from the CBD and the level of rent. Simplifying the issues in this way makes it possible to obtain bid rent curves showing rents at various distances from the CBD which afford a household equal satisfaction. Thus the bid rent curve of the household is a location indifference curve corresponding to the iso-profit curve of the firm.

As with firms, we can impose on the bid-rent diagram the land price curve depicting actual market rents at increasing distances from the CBD. Each household will seek to be on the bid rent curve nearest to the origin and thus chooses that location where the land price curve touches the bid rent curve nearest the origin, since this location yields the greatest possible utility at current market rents (as in Figure 15.1).

The shape of the bid rent curve depends upon family tastes and disposable income. Family tastes will be influenced largely by the composition of the household, particularly the number of children and their ages. Since a young family will require space and access to schools, the transport costs of the breadwinner's daily trip to work in the CBD are relatively not so important. Such a family will tend to have flat bid rent curves such as UR_1 and UR_2 (Figure 15.3) and locate at R, whereas single people, old people, or families consisting mainly of wage-earners will tend to have the steeper bid rent curves at UP_1 and UP_2 and locate nearer the CBD, at P.

Similarly, households which have different incomes are likely to have differently-shaped bid rent curves. Those with low incomes cannot afford the transport costs of travelling to the CBD from the outskirts. Their demand, therefore, is travel-inelastic with respect to rent, and their bid rent curves UP_1 and UP_2 slope steeply downwards. In contrast, the higher-income households are likely to be travel-elastic since they can afford transport costs. Indeed at very high incomes travel is comfortable in chauffeur-driven cars with time being spent usefully in reading, dictating letters, and so on. This is reflected in flatter bid curves, UR_1 and UR_2.

In other words, as income increases, accessibility to work, except for the very rich, proves to be an 'inferior good', people preferring to spend more of their income on transport to obtain space and environmental advantages on the fringe of the urban area. The result is that lower-income households are located at distance OP from the CBD, where they occupy space intensively at high rents per square metre, whereas the high-income households are located at distance OR where they enjoy more space (because rents per square metre are lower) but incur increased transport costs.

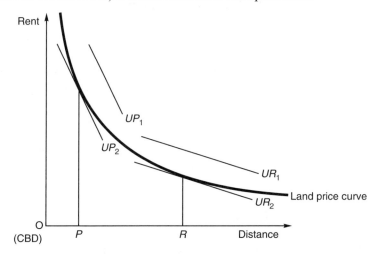

Figure 15.3 Bid rent curves for different households

An exception to the above is the very rich person who can afford and prefers to occupy one of the few houses having spacious gardens which still remain in the CBD.

Once again it should be noted that this 'trade-off' model of residential location is based on the following implicit assumptions.

(a) *All employment is in the CBD.* Though this was true of the nineteenth century, it is not so valid today. Nowadays people can often both live and work in the suburbs, usually involving lower travelling costs (in terms of time and comfort) than with CBD employment.

(b) *Transport costs are proportionate to distance in all directions.* In fact travel by car outwards from or across the urban area can be cheaper and quicker because less traffic is encountered. Similarly, public utilities in some cities charge fares irrespective of distance, thereby subsidising households in suburban locations.

(c) *Housing location is a function of income, rent and travel costs.* However, other considerations may influence choice – for example, proximity to relatives or people of the same social class or ethnic group, the desirability of a prestigious or generally attractive site, the avoidance of traffic congestion, noise and fumes from motor vehicles. The effect is to make neighbourhoods more homogeneous within themselves and more unlike other neighbourhoods (see pp. 264–5).

(d) *There is no government interference in the market* – for example, by planning control, local authority building.

Our basic model would have to be modified to embrace these real-life conditions.

15.2 Application of the Von Thunen model

The Von Thunen theory of location based on transport costs from a central market produces a pattern of concentric zones, each zone specialising in a particular type of agricultural produce. By substituting 'general accessibility' for 'transport costs' we can apply the Von Thunen model to urban areas.

The foregoing analysis suggests that firms will oust households from the CBD. The outcome will be a commercial zone of radius *OC* surrounded by a residential zone (Figure 15.4). Similarly, land values will fall from the centre to the periphery as indicated by the thick line *LP* which shows the highest bid at any point.

A general pattern of land use

Basically the locational pattern of land use in an urban area reflects the demand for and supply of sites. By a process of competition, a site will be

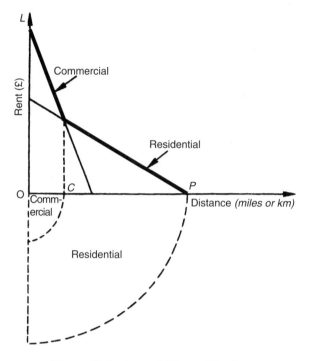

Figure 15.4 Accessibility and land use

secured by that use which can extract the greatest return from its accessibility advantages since it can offer the highest rent. Thus a broad zonal arrangement focused on the centre emerges because similar or functionally-related activities locate at the same distance from the centre of the urban area, with other uses being excluded (Figure 15.5). Allowing for its simplified assumptions, therefore, the Von Thunen model can explain: (i) the pattern of land use of the urban area; (ii) the fall in land values from the centre to the periphery; and (iii) how the urban area grows, since each zone tends to expand into the next as population and economic growth occur. The basic pattern eventually results – a separation between workplace and residence.

Any current pattern, however, is continually being modified through changes in: (a) the size and composition of the city's population; (b) the level and distribution of income; (c) technology, such as the development of road transport and information technology; (d) the social and economic organisation of community life – for example, TV, Sunday shopping, multi-car ownership; (e) government policy – for example, its presumption against further out-of-town shopping centres (PPG 6) and green belts; (f) the growth of the urban area.

In response to such factors, land use alters by: (a) adapting existing space – by, for example, dividing large houses into flats; (b) changing the type of

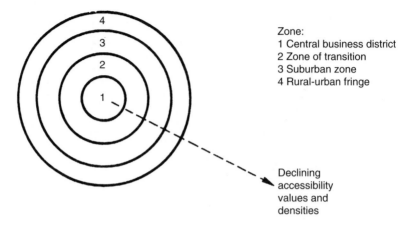

Figure 15.5 The broad pattern of urban land use

use, such as large houses into offices; (c) demolition and rebuilding; (d) infilling on vacant land within city boundaries ('brownfield' sites); (e) expanding outwards from the periphery into the open country ('greenfield' sites); (f) the development of dormitory areas – for instance, around railway stations – which eventually form separate nuclei, even eventually becoming part of the urban area as further expansion takes place.

In most urban areas it is possible to distinguish, in a highly simplified form, certain broad, but irregular concentric zones, as follows.

(1) THE CENTRAL BUSINESS DISTRICT

The CBD is the optimum location for shops, commerce and services for, as the focus of inter-city transport, it has the greatest accessibility.

But growth in the city's population and economy increases competition for the limited space available. The consequent rise in land values leads to changes in the CBD.

First, greater intensity of development takes the form of multi-storey buildings.

Second, the CBD moves outwards as shops and offices take over from other users – houses, for instance, being converted into offices, workshops, and so on with redevelopment eventually taking place. Thus the exact boundary of the CBD may be difficult to distinguish, as it often merges gradually into light industrial and residential uses.

Third, land use within the area develops on a functional basis. Thus retailing often becomes separated from office use, although offices do generate a demand for shops. Though the boundaries may be blurred, the entertainment area of large cities tends to be separated from shops and offices. Public administration, the central library, the main post office, the technical college, and so on are often found in the CBD.

Eventually functional sub-cores may emerge, such as in London, Bond Street (fine art), Whitehall (central government), Harley Street (doctors), while the ousting of residences by commerce results in an exodus of workers in the evening so that the CBD becomes a lifeless desert at night.

(2) THE ZONE OF TRANSITION

This zone contains a mixture of land uses. Historically it was largely the pre-1900 urban residential area characterised by the segregated speculative development of: (a) upper and middle-class housing in large units; and (b) terraced (and later tenement) housing for lower-income groups. Merging with the latter were small backyard industries which provided the main employment opportunities.

As commerce and retailing have taken over in the CBD, subsidiary activities, such as warehousing and wholesaling, have moved to the zone of transition. Other users include small workshops, printing, clothing and employment agencies, all of which are labour-intensive and often form a link between the office/retail core of the CBD and the outer residential fringe.

However, dynamic forces, such as population and income growth, mean that within the zone there is constant change. Warehouses are converted into offices or mail-order stores, while light manufacturing moves to modern factory premises on the outskirts of the urban area. More obviously, population growth results in the conversion of houses. Apart from a few high-income dwellings (such as Belgravia in London) large houses are converted into flatlets or letting rooms. The easier and cheaper it is to convert for new uses, the longer complete redevelopment will be delayed, for a rising capital value outstrips for a time the increasing value of the cleared site (see p. 110).

Frequently speculators, anticipating eventual redevelopment, buy buildings and simply let them out at a lower use, such as low-income, multi-family dwellings. Net revenue is enhanced by spending little on maintenance and repairs. As a result, neighbouring properties, reacting to this urban blight, also deteriorate. Thus slums grow, especially if redevelopment is frustrated by public policy, such as security of tenure, density controls and planning restrictions on the type of use.

(3) THE SUBURBAN ZONE

This zone has emerged during the past sixty years, being closely connected with the development of the electric train and later the motor-car, the latter giving rise to ribbon development along arterial roads. Residential uses at moderate or low densities predominate, but households are still within reach of urban attractions and employment. Clustering takes place near rail and road services, and there is some district segregation by socio-economic class. There is also a scattering of such facilities as schools, medical centres, churches and public houses. Open spaces, such as parks, golf courses, race courses, allotments and cemeteries abound, often occupying sites between radial route-ways.

Today many suburban areas are developing their own activities. The increase in the scale of urbanisation often means that it is no longer efficient to service a large city from the CBD. Thus large establishments, such as hospitals and universities, move to transport junctions or the outskirts, while industry, by locating in well-defined districts in the suburbs, can have transport links to the urban market while enjoying lower rents and easier expansion than in central sites. Above all, office development is increasingly taking place, sometimes creating satellite commercial centres, such as Croydon and Reading.

(4) THE RURAL-URBAN FRINGE

The influence of the city on land use extends far beyond the built-up area. People are willing to 'commute' to work in towns (especially the larger towns) from well beyond the suburban zone. Even those who choose to live in a full country setting are still mainly dependent on the towns for their livelihood.

Even agriculture responds to the influence of the city, for market-gardening and pick-your-own produce are prominent.

Location by function

(1) SHOPS

Goods sold by shops can be classified as: (i) speciality goods, such as jewellery, oriental carpets, works of art, ladies' fashions, musical instruments; (ii) shopping goods, such as furniture, carpets, coats, dresses, suits, cameras, radio and television; (iii) convenience goods, such as groceries, fruit and vegetables, confectionary, tobacco and newspapers, hardware. The type of good sold influences shop location.

Speciality and shopping goods are purchased infrequently and irregularly but account for a significant proportion of people's income and usually have a high income-elasticity of demand. The customer is prepared to travel some distance in order to compare goods. For their part, shops selling such goods depend upon a wide hinterland. With accessibility being so important, CBD sites are sought, especially those on the side of the wealthy residential sector. Since shoppers want to compare goods before buying, complementarity of location is also important. The prime sites are occupied by department stores, multiple chain stores and, because most shoppers are women (who take most note of window displays), by shops selling women's shopping goods. Variety chain stores and some convenience outlets (such as tobacconists) are usually nearby for they supply items incidental to the trip. Certain shops, for example, furniture and furriers, are towards the edge of the retail area, either because they require a large display area or because customers are prepared to seek out shops selling goods which are only bought occasionally.

Convenience goods are purchased frequently and at fairly regular intervals. Thus the location of such shops is close to either customers' homes or their place of work. The best sites are near railway stations or on major road intersections, such as the High Street. Such suburban shopping centres vary in size. Thus in Greater London they may include department stores, variety chain stores, specialist shops, banks, cinemas, life insurance and public utility offices. The smaller neighbourhood centres of about eight shops cater only for everyday needs – chemist, grocer, greengrocer, sub-post office, butcher, laundrette, newsagent-tobacconist-confectioner. Smallest in shopping size is the corner shop acting as a general store for nearby streets. Because they are selling convenience goods, such shops repel each other. Thus whereas two dress shops could be found next to each other in a large shopping centre, two adjacent butchers in a small neighbourhood centre would be unlikely.

Within an urban area, accessibility and type of shop are also correlated to sales turnover, shop rents and intensity of development, and all diminish outwards from the CBD. Indeed even within the central business area (and within some of the larger suburban centres) there is a correlation between distance from the point of greatest accessibility and land value. Department stores and other key traders, such as Marks & Spencer and Boots, occupy the most accessible and valuable locations, for they enjoy a high sales turnover and intensity of shopping. On the other hand, furniture and grocery shops are on the periphery of the centre, since turnover is less. Figure 15.6 shows a hypothetical rent gradient from the point of maximum accessibility to the fringe of the central business district.

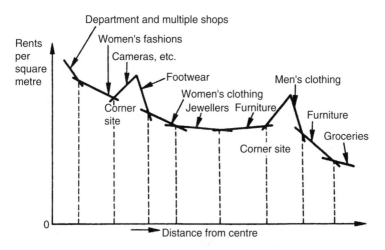

Figure 15.6 Accessibility, land values and type of shop in the CBD

The precise location of shops depends also upon the flow and character of pedestrian traffic, the current nature of adjacent development and the availability of vacant sites on the 'right side' of the street or on a corner.

The development of out-of-town shopping-centres disturbs the usual correlation between accessibility and sales turnover. For an out-of-town centre to be viable, accessibility must be high, yet values and sales turnover per square metre and intensity of development are low compared with central business areas. Apart from accessibility (proximity to ring-roads being beneficial), out-of-town centres depend on a large car-owning population, a large proportion of women working, the need to reduce shopping to one-stop buying, the availability of low-price sites for expansion (see p. 243), the provision of car-parks and the granting of planning permission.

(2) OFFICES

Whereas the site of a shop may mean the difference between business success and failure, office siting is more flexible. Indeed a location which affords general accessibility – through transport facilities for customers and employees – and special accessibility – through proximity to linked activities – is more important than the actual site.

Nevertheless, locating offices in the same part of the CBD used by shoppers has advantages. Offices can make use of valuable space above shops, thereby maximising values, since shopping space above the third storey is rarely viable in relation to central urban rents. Also offices increase retail sales, while retailers may provide certain services for offices – stationery, business machines and café facilities, for instance. On the other hand, there are advantages in locating offices in a separate central zone where there may be less noise, possibly less pollution, and more open space for car-parking and recreation. Indeed a recent tendency has been for many office activities (such as general administration, routine accounts and records) to move out from central areas to suburban and provincial locations. This separation of high-level management from routine administration has been made possible by better travel facilities, new communication technology such as fax and mobile phones, and changing use to B_1 class (see pp. 243–5).

Since many top-level decisions are based on personal contacts, head offices of large commercial and industrial firms require high accessibility and they therefore pay the high rents commanded by central sites. In contrast, offices attached to factories are subject to the broad influences determining industrial location.

The offices of the headquarters of professional bodies require fairly central locations but, though accessibility is important, they need not be as central as those of large firms. General – and to some extent, special – accessibility is not unimportant. Sites in historic squares or close to parks are favoured, for not only are rents lower than in the commercial centre, but they afford both a prestige address and an image of 'respectability'.

Branch offices of commercial and professional firms favour locations close to a residential population, the high streets of small towns and suburbs being popular. Except for estate agencies and building societies, such offices can occupy rooms above shops, and often congregate around railway stations and bus termini.

Local and central government offices tend to occupy less valuable sites on the periphery of the central business area. They may be sited in more central and prominent positions when a town-centre redevelopment scheme has been undertaken.

(3) INDUSTRIAL PREMISES

In manufacturing, the firm is much more concerned with selecting the town or city which offers the greatest overall location advantages rather than with the part of any one urban area which is ideally suited for its activity.

The actual location within the urban area will depend on the nature of the product, the scale of the market and the stage of development of the firm. For firms with a small localised market, for example, in printing or light engineering, an inner-city location may be preferred. When the market is wider, perhaps national or international, consideration must be given to transport networks. Industrial activity is increasingly moving to the edge of urban areas to take advantage of orbital roads and motorways, and to obtain more space to facilitate a flow method of production.

It has been argued that new firms will favour inner-city locations where second-hand premises are available at low cost and there is proximity to business services, markets and complementary firms. This is the *incubator hypothesis* that cities act as feedbacks for new firms which grow in this favourable environment until they are able to expand, substitute the external economies of an urban environment for internal economies of scale, and move out to a suburban location. However, evidence sheds doubt on the validity of the hypothesis. Changes in transport technology have resulted in wider locational choice, while the external diseconomies of congestion and poor environment have undermined the advantages of central locations for industrial activity. Hence the new type of industry has moved outwards to business and science parks (p. 245).

(4) HOUSING

Housing represents the largest use of urban land. There is a great variety of types, but redevelopment takes place relatively slowly compared with other uses. Except for occasional very high income and local authority housing, accommodation is, as we have seen, forced out of central areas by the expansion of business uses

Obstacles to the optimum use of land

Because of imperfections in the land market an ideal equilibrium of land use is never attained. In the first place, when demand changes there is a necessary lag in adjustment to need because of the fixity of investment in buildings. Moreover, any change in the transport system will affect the supply of available sites and the relative importance of sites within that total: for example, prior to the advent of the motor-car, development was tied to a limited number of routes (that is, the railways) and around any town or station by the limitations of horse-drawn transport. Motor vehicles enjoy greater flexibility of movement and this has expanded the potential radius of urban development.

Similarly, an improvement in building technology, say, one which enables multi-storey buildings to be erected more cheaply, will also have the effect of increasing the supply of buildings and enable more users to enjoy a central location if they can manage on the upper floors. More important are those restrictions on development due to government interference which may prevent (for example, planning permission), retard (for example, rent control), or make the cost prohibitive (for example, planning and bye-law requirements) for a use to obtain its optimum site. Here businesses must maximise their profits and residents their utility within the existing institutional framework.

15.3 Theories of urban structure

The major factors determining the locations of firms and households as outlined in Chapter 14 have been incorporated in various theories to explain the existing complicated pattern of urban structure. These theories vary in sophistication: broadly speaking, the more rudimentary concentrate on the influence of general accessibility while the more complex give greater weight to the other factors, particularly special accessibility – although general accessibility must be recognised as still being dominant.

Concentric zone theory

Although a concentric pattern of urban land use follows logically from the Von Thunen analysis, it was not until the twentieth century that research on actual patterns of land use emerged.

From an examination of the historical development of Chicago in the 1890s, E. W. Burgess (1925) developed the concentric zone theory. In contrast to the Von Thunen approach, however, Burgess's theory is descriptive rather than analytical.

In essence Burgess asserted that the typical process of urban growth is through a series of concentric circles expanding radially from the central business district. Somewhat similar to the pattern of Figure 15.5, five broad zones were postulated: (a) the central business district; (b) the zone of transition or inner ring; (c) the zone of factories and working men's homes, typified by a largely stable working-class population living in older houses frequently lacking in amenity; (d) the residential zone, containing newer and more spacious middle-class housing; (e) the outer commuter-zone typified by good-quality housing in an environment of high amenity with upper-class residents.

However, Burgess's concentric-zone bands do no more than indicate a very broad structure of land use. They are too rigid to conform to actual patterns and are lacking in detail. This is because the theory overlooks the influence of physical features and transport systems on urban structure, fails to recognise the importance of the various aspects of special accessibility, and, apart from the zone of transition which is recognised as being an area of change, ignores the dynamic factors which lead to a continual process of redevelopment (see Chapter 7).

The radial or axial development theory

The radial development theory is an improvement, in that it modifies the concentric zones to allow for topographical features. Thus navigable rivers provided the earliest form of inland transport, whereas later their valleys facilitated rail and road construction. This means that transport costs per unit carried are lower in some directions than in others. For example, a navigable river could distort the concentric zones as in Figure 15.7(a). More realistically, road and rail construction will cause the zones to assume a starfish shape, with their extremities extending along the major transport routes (Figure 15.7(b)). Thus although points *A* and *B* are different distances from the centre, they will portray identical land uses since by *journey time* they are the same distance from the centre. In short, while concentric growth is based upon *proximity* in terms of distance, axial growth is based on *accessibility*, in terms of time, and so on.

Costs of friction hypothesis

This theory, developed by R. M. Haig (1926), is really a development of the Von Thunen model but relating land values to the transport costs saved in different locations.

Any site location involves two costs: (i) the rental (*R*) which has to be paid for the site, and (ii) the transport costs (*T*) incurred by firms (or absorbed by consumers) which are associated with the site. Since the site rent (*R*) would

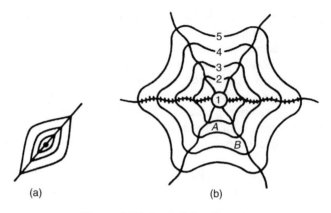

Figure 15.7 Radial development

reflect the transport costs *saved* at a particular site compared with other sites, the total 'frictional costs' of the site will equal $R + T$. The aim of a locational decision will be to minimise this sum in achieving any desired degree of accessibility.

An interesting proposition which follows from this hypothesis is that in any urban area competition will tend to produce the land-use pattern that minimises total site rents and transport costs for the area as a whole. The difficulty here, however, is that the 'minimum cost-of-friction' hypothesis overlooks the revenue-earning capacity of different sites – and revenue considerations also influence the location decision. This can be seen most clearly with residential choice of locality for personal satisfactions are likely to play a dominant role in determining where a household lives.

Yet, in spite of this weakness, the Haig hypothesis was a valuable contribution towards formalising the relationship between site values and transport costs, and later theories have built on its framework while recognising more explicitly the revenue (or benefits) to be derived in alternative locations.

The wedge or radial sector theory

This theory, associated with the work of H. Hoyt (1939), is basically an elaboration of the concentric-zone theory by allowing for the development of a more irregular pattern. It concentrates on the location of housing in urban areas, referring only indirectly to business location.

In order to explain the migration of residential areas as the city grows and the tendency for various socio-economic groups to segregate, it suggests that over time high-quality housing tends to expand outwards from the centre along the fastest travel routes. Once established, the trend continues in the same direction, producing wedges of development which may not conform to the zones through which they pass (Figure 15.8). In contrast, low-income groups are located on the opposite side of the CBD, often in proximity to industrial land uses.

Thus in Hoyt's view the concentric zones become sectors. Residential blocks or sectors radiate outwards from the centre, constraining or segregating manufacturing or wholesaling into other sectors. Thus in Figure 15.8 residential areas are segregated by income and take different directions in different sectors of the city. Moreover, as inner areas become abandoned by high-rent residences they are infilled by lower rental groups (mainly through conversions or multi-occupation).

Although Hoyt's hypothesis is descriptive, it does suggest a pattern of growth and how different rates of growth can occur in different parts of the city. Thus it allows for the development of a more irregular pattern.

On the other hand, the general factors determining urban land use and land values still hold. Indeed sector 5 could be explained by 'special accessibility' factors, people being willing to pay a higher rent to live in proximity with others of similar income, taste and culture. Similarly sectors 3 may remain low-income housing because of the overall run-down appearance, poor schools, and so on, eventually degenerating into a slum sector. Moreover, there are reasons other than transport facilities for sectoring high-quality housing, such as high-lying districts being healthier than badly-drained lowlands, prevailing winds carrying factory smoke away to leeward, and higher land-prices exerting a repelling effect on dissociated activities, such as manufacturing and wholesaling. Above all, in concentrating on the factors influencing high-income housing, it overlooks the factors affecting the location of employment opportunities, which are taken as given. Yet these factors are crucial to the location of low-income housing, the outward expansion of which will depend upon the creation of new employment opportunities.

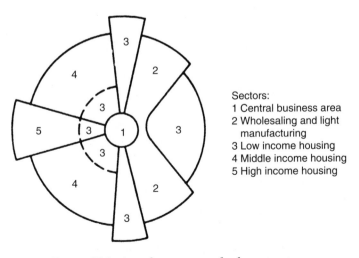

Sectors:
1 Central business area
2 Wholesaling and light manufacturing
3 Low income housing
4 Middle income housing
5 High income housing

Figure 15.8 A wedge pattern of urban structure

Multiple-nuclei theory

In 1945 C. D. Harris and E. L. Ullman departed more decisively from the pattern of concentric zones arranged round a single centre. Their multiple-nuclei theory takes the view that large cities have a structure which is essentially cellular. This results from the tendency to develop a number of nuclei which serve as focal points for agglomerative tendencies, some more important than others. The resulting model is readily discernible in the form of most cities (Figure 15.9).

Such nuclei may have had different origins, existing as minor settlements before city growth began or developing where the growth of population and purchasing power supports a suburban shopping or business centre or a suburban industrial area. Around the separate nuclei, distinctive types of land use have grown up over time, and this existing pattern is strengthened by the general factors determining the allocation of land to specific uses. Thus high rents in the CBD induce firms to migrate or establish themselves in peripheral areas, while the various forms of special accessibility – specialised facilities, external economies or diseconomies (for example, the repellance of detrimental activities) – lead similar firms or households to concentrate in particular locations.

By giving greater weight to such factors as topography, historical influences and, above all, special accessibility resulting from economic and social forces, the multiple-nuclei theory provides a more flexible approach to urban form than the earlier models based on transport costs and accessibility to a single, central core, but the latter notion can be incorporated into the model especially in explaining the CBD and even suburban sub-centres.

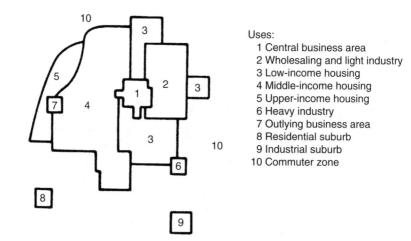

Uses:
1 Central business area
2 Wholesaling and light industry
3 Low-income housing
4 Middle-income housing
5 Upper-income housing
6 Heavy industry
7 Outlying business area
8 Residential suburb
9 Industrial suburb
10 Commuter zone

Figure 15.9 A multi-nuclei urban structure

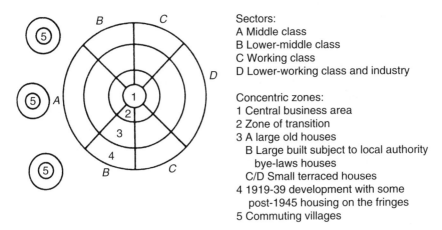

Sectors:
A Middle class
B Lower-middle class
C Working class
D Lower-working class and industry

Concentric zones:
1 Central business area
2 Zone of transition
3 A large old houses
  B Large built subject to local authority
    bye-laws houses
  C/D Small terraced houses
4 1919-39 development with some
  post-1945 housing on the fringes
5 Commuting villages

Figure 15.10 A sector-zone urban structure

Sector-zone theory

The theories considered so far originated in the USA. A presentation by P. H. Mann (*An Approach to Urban Sociology*, 1968) synthesises the previous models for a 'typical' British city.

Essentially his diagrammatic model (Figure 15.10) combines the concentric zone and sector theories, while making some allowance for commuting from 'dormitory' villages. Emphasis is placed on the social structure of the area. The assumption of a prevailing wind from the west results in the location of higher-income housing to the west of the city, and of low-income housing to the east and nearer to the industrial sector.

Conclusion

The various theories described must be regarded as being complementary to one another rather than exclusive, the later ones modifying the earlier to take account of the movement of population and employment to the suburbs. Thus together they explain the patterns apparent in most modern cities: a CBD, older inner industrial area, and newer suburbs with expanding shopping and office sub-centres.

Yet while they suggest *how* cities grow, they fail to explain *why* they grow. This last point is taken up in Chapter 16, which examines the causes and dynamics of urban growth.

Summary

It is possible to explain the optimum/equilibrium location of firms and households in terms of bid rent curves if the assumption is made that the CBD is the point of maximum accessibility. Using simple assumptions it is then possible to explain: the pattern of land use in urban areas, the fall in land values from the centre to the periphery and how the urban area grows. The various theories of urban structure that have developed can explain the pattern of development in most modern cities.

Review questions

1. Why do different types of firm have different bid rent curves?
2. Describe the concentric zones that emerge from Von Thunen's theory of location.
3. How does the 'radial or axial development' theory differ from concentric zone theory?
4. How does the 'wedge or radial sector' theory differ from concentric zone theory?
5. Explain why no single urban structure theory is likely to be adequate in explaining the structure of cities.

Recommended reading

P. N. Balchin, J. L. Kieve and G. H. Bull, *Urban Land Economics and Public Policy*, 5th edn (London: Macmillan, 1995) ch. 2.

A. W. Evans, *Urban Economics* (Oxford: Basil Blackwell, 1985) chs 2, 3, 4 and 7.

P. McCann, *Urban and Regional Economics* (Oxford: Oxford University Press, 2001).

CHAPTER 16

The Growth of Urban Areas

After studying this chapter you will be able to:

- **Explain different theories of urban growth**
- **Evaluate 'urban hierarchy and central place' theory**
- **Describe the advantages and disadvantages of urbanisation**
- **Evaluate 'green belt' policy**
- **Explain policies to deal with 'overspill' and 'urban sprawl'**

Cities begin for many reasons: for example, defence, trade or as political or religious centres. Whatever the reason, economic forces are likely to reinforce the original impetus. Initially growth was associated with industrialisation which induced more intensive use of existing buildings, changes in their use and outward expansion.

More recently, urban growth in developed countries has taken four main forms. First, there has been urban renewal, usually with much higher buildings. Second, there is inter-urban competition resulting in the movement between cities as some grow (for example, Greater London) and others decline (for example, Glasgow). Third, with the rise in income and the development of fast and convenient transport, particularly the car, there has been a movement of population from the inner and older parts of the city to the suburbs and outlying towns and villages so that the sharp distinction which once existed between 'town' and 'country' tends to be diminishing. Fourth, a hierarchy of urban centres has evolved, differing in size and importance – provincial, regional, national and international. We have to explain, therefore, how urban areas grow and how the urban hierarchy comes into being.

16.1   Theories of urban growth

How economic forces generate growth can be shown by examining the following theories, each of which has a somewhat different approach.

The economic base theory

This theory is based on the hypothesis that the size of an urban area depends on the amount of goods and services supplied to outsiders, that is, on 'exports'. Income is derived from exports, which generate purchasing power to sustain demand for the outputs of activities which produce for internal demand and to pay for imports. As demand from outside increases, the urban area grows.

The theory divides urban economic activity into two categories: (i) basic activities, those industries producing goods and services for outside demand; and (ii) non-basic activities, those industries producing goods and services for consumption by the inhabitants of the urban area only. Employment is similarly divided into basic and non-basic categories, and it is assumed that there is a fairly stable relationship between the two. We can further derive the ratio of basic employment to total employment, and of total employment to total population.

The growth of basic activities is seen as the dominant cause of urban growth. Increased demand for basic activities leads to an increased demand for labour. This in turn attracts new labour to the urban area. The resulting rise in the level of income stimulates the growth of non-basic activities, as well as making possible a higher level of import expenditure. Thus total employment increases. The ratio of total employment to total population gives the size of the urban area.

We can illustrate with an arithmetical example. Suppose an urban area has a population of 30 000, of whom 10 000 are employed, with 5000 in basic employment and 5000 in non-basic employment. Thus the ratios are:

basic employment : non-basic employment = 1:1
basic employment : total employment   = 1:2
total employment : total population   = 1:3
basic employment : total population   = 1:6

Assume now that, while the above ratios remain unchanged, the demand for basic activities increases, requiring an extra 2000 basic employees. Given the fixed ratios, equilibrium is restored when the population of the urban area has grown to 42 000 (Table 16.1).

Thus an initial increase in basic employment of 2000 has increased the population of the urban area by 12 000 – the result of a consequential

Table 16.1 The relationship of total population to basic employment

	Equilibrium i		Disequilibrium		Equilibrium ii	
	Initial numbers	Equilibrium ratio to basic employment	New numbers	Disequilibrium ratio to basic employment	New numbers	Equilibrium ratio to basic employment
Basic employees	5 000	1	7 000	1	7 000	1
Non-basic employees	5 000	1	5 000	0.715	7 000	1
Total employees	10 000	2	12 000	1.715	14 000	2
Total population	30 000	6	36 000	5.15	42 000	6

increase in non-basic employment and an overall increase in non-working population. A decrease in basic employment of 2000 would have the same effect in reverse, the population of the urban area falling to 18 000.

Although the theory has been extensively applied in the USA and to a lesser extent in Britain, it has been subjected to a number of criticisms.

First, it does not explain either the existence or the expansion of basic industries.

Second, the theory largely ignores the level of income, which is assumed to be solely dependent on the demand for the area's basic exports. It suggests that if, as an analogy, the UK as a whole is considered, the national economy could only grow by increasing exports; that is, domestic trade is only a 'service' industry and not a 'nation-building' industry. Yet in recent years service industries have been the main source of growth in employment largely because with many, such as insurance, pensions and financial planning, there is a high income-elasticity of demand. Indeed some, such as London's financial operations and insurance, have developed as international export industries. It is unsafe, therefore, to accept that, for a major area of the UK, service industries simply reflect passively changes in basic employment. Instead non-basic industries may themselves stimulate urban change and growth.

Third, in a 'grey' real world, it is impossible to divide industries into 'black' and 'white' categories. Not only do some 'service' industries export part of their output, but 'export' industries may sell some output locally. And how should component suppliers for the basic industries be allocated, since their output ultimately leaves the area? Indeed financial and legal advice to the basic industries could also be regarded as a 'component'.

Fourth, the theory does not take into account the relationship between income and spending on imports. For example, if all export earnings were spent on imports, there would be no extra demand for non-basic goods and services in the area.

Fifth, criticism is directed at the assumptions made about the relationship between basic and non-basic activities, particularly the assumption that increased 'export' demand will produce *predictable* increases in non-basic employment. Too many factors are ignored:

(a) the ratio between basic and non-basic employment probably changes with the growth or decline in the region, since service industries tend to be income-elastic;
(b) there may be unemployed labour within the area to be 'drafted' into basic industries, obviating the need to import labour from outside;
(c) a body of suitable unemployed labour outside the area may not be available to meet increased labour demand in the basic industries;
(d) wage differentials and the distribution of labour skills also influence the distribution of labour between industries and between areas;
(e) there may be spare capacity in basic industries;

(f) output may be increased by substituting capital for labour and by increased productivity;

(g) similarly, (b)–(f) may apply to non-basic industries.

Input-output analysis

This method emphasises the importance of treating an urban area as an open rather than as a closed economy by examining inter-industry and inter-area linkages.

For each industry it is necessary to know the value of its purchases of inputs (labour, raw materials, components, transport, and so on) from all other industries and sectors of the economy (both inside and outside the area). A similar breakdown is made for the distribution of the output of industries. This information can be incorporated in a 'matrix' reflecting the structural dependence of one industry on all other industries in an existing equilibrium position.

The matrix can then be used to trace the chain of adjustments necessary to achieve a new equilibrium position should the conditions of demand and supply in an existing industry change or a new industry be established. From these predictions, the impact on the size of the urban area can be evaluated.

However, the input-output approach has certain weaknesses:

(a) from the point of view of explaining the growth or decline of an area, there may be little indication of why the original changes occur;
(b) calculations are based on the assumption of fixed technical and regional coefficients;
(c) the input-output relationships between industries and sectors may be altered by technological change and the introduction of new products and changes in relative prices, all of which necessitate constant revision of the matrix.

The Keynesian model

The basic Keynesian model of the determination of the income of the national economy can be used to explain the growth (or decline) of the urban economy. Changes in the total *income* of the urban area (not simply 'exports' as with the economic base theory) will result in changes in its level of business activity and employment.

Figure 16.1 shows a simple income-flow model for an urban economy. Households derive income from local firms, external employments and government transfers. A part of this income goes to the government in direct taxation. Remaining income is spent on local output or on goods and services from outside the area (a part going in indirect taxes to the

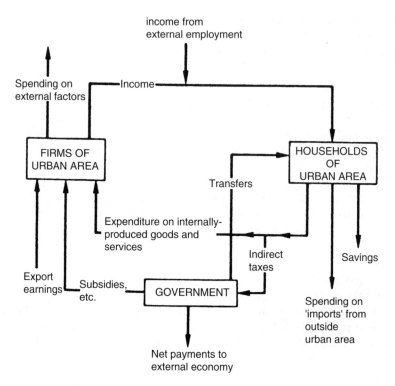

Figure 16.1 Income flow in an urban economy

government) or is saved. Some savings (including undistributed profits) may not be invested within the urban area, thus leading to a fall in income.

Urban growth depends upon the size of net money inflows and the extent to which income is spent within the town. If money inflows ('injections') increase – for example, through increased 'exports' of goods to places outside the area or through external factor employment – the income of the urban area will expand. The extent of the resulting urban growth will depend upon the proportion of the additional income which is spent on internally-produced goods. The greater this marginal propensity to consume on local goods, the greater will be the 'urban multiplier'. Thus if c is the marginal propensity to consume on local goods, the multiplier will be $\frac{1}{1-c}$. For instance, if this marginal propensity to consume were 0.66, the multiplier would be 3; if it were 0.25, the multiplier would be only 1.33.

A principal weakness of the Keynesian approach when applied to urban growth is the lack of statistics available at a local level. Moreover, neither the Keynesian approach nor the economic-base theory can predict when a change in causative activities will occur or explain why any activity serving other than a local market chooses to locate in a particular urban area. Again, both are demand-side theories which do not incorporate the possibility that local bottle-necks may prevent additional supply. Indeed supply-side policies are likely to be particularly important at the urban level.

Finally, both the Keynesian and the economic base theories tend to ignore the dynamic nature of urban growth. For instance, urbanisation itself, by increasing opportunities for specialisation, increases the output of goods and services. This rise in real income leads to an increase in demand, with the enlarged market stimulating still further specialisation. These extensions of economic opportunities attract new firms and labour, and so on.

But why do urban areas grow and decline?

Although the models above throw light on the economic linkages in urban areas, they do not satisfactorily explain *why* cities grow or decline.

Initial growth and decline can both be traced to changes in the conditions of demand or supply. For example, on the demand side we can note a change in tastes, the income-elasticity of demand for the goods produced, the development of substitutes. On the supply side, there may be new competitors from outside, a change in the transport network, the exhaustion of local mineral or oil deposits, automation replacing traditional local skills and such technical change as the substitution of oil and gas for coal in the generation of electricity and in supplying power and domestic heating.

But while growth of an urban area may be adversely affected by a decline in the initial employment base or simply halted as the external costs (such as traffic congestion, air pollution) of further urbanisation exceed its benefits (see pp. 276–9), neither of these may necessarily lead to progressive decline. While the very size of the urban area may have already stimulated diversification through the development of new industries, also influential are the human and political factors. Some cities may have a steady supply of industrial leaders and a dynamic regional authority which responds to the challenge by introducing new industries with the aid of government grants.

Thus the real reasons for growth and decline are probably a complex blend of external economic change and the extent to which firms and local authorities are able and willing to seize opportunities that arise, or to create them if they do not. No theory which ignores the human element, the dynamism of differing institutions, the effect of government policies and other factors on the supply side of the urban economy can be wholly satisfactory.

16.2 The urban hierarchy and central place theory

The 'urban hierarchy' concept

We have examined the pattern of economic activities within cities. Can anything be said about the distribution of cities, towns and villages throughout the country? This is the question that 'central place' theory seeks to answer. (The term 'central place' is a slightly unhappy translation of a German word which means 'town' as well as 'place'.)

The theory was developed by a German geographer, W. Christaller (*Central Places of Southern Germany*, 1933, English translation 1966). Like Von Thunen's theory which strongly influenced it, this theory begins by assuming a featureless plain over which population and resources are uniformly distributed.

Two factors are then likely to determine the location of trading centres: (i) economies of large-scale operation, and (ii) the existence of transport costs, which effectively sets upper limits to the extent of a producer's profitable market. If, for example, we were to assume that economies of large-scale production were insignificant in all lines of production, then competition would produce a pattern of many small producers equidistantly spaced and with each having a market just large enough to allow it to stay in business.

More realistically, different products are likely to have: (i) different minimum demand 'thresholds' to justify setting up in production – for example, compare the market size for a corner shop and an ear, nose and throat specialist; (ii) different economic and technical characteristics as regards economies of large-scale production – for example, compare the minimum scale of operation of a cobbler and a hypermarket; (iii) different transport costs – for example, compare jewellery and furniture manufacturers.

Taking these factors into account means that (i) there will not be as many market networks as there are goods and services, since goods and services which have approximately the same threshold size, transport costs, and so on, will tend to locate in the centre of the same market area; (ii) a system of 'central places' will tend to emerge in which the centres of a number of different market areas coincide, with small central places and their associated market areas being included in those of larger central places.

The smallest central place will cater only for those services of the lowest order – 'convenience' goods, such as groceries, purchased on a daily basis – and will serve only a small 'hinterland'. Larger central places will cater for services of a higher order – 'shopping' goods, clothing, schools, district hospitals, and so on – but will also embrace a hinterland consisting of a number of lower first-order centres. The largest kind of metropolitan centre will tend to supply the whole nation with certain services, such as central government, highly-specialised services, foreign embassies, cultural centres, and so on. A listing of increasingly higher-order centres produces a hierarchy of urban areas, with perhaps only one city falling into the highest category and the numbers in each 'order' increasing as we proceed down through each successive lower order.

Figure 16.2 provides a schematic illustration. Starting with a 'map' of 163 first-order central places equidistant from each other, a hierarchy of central places can be derived by assuming some relationship between a central place and the number of next-lower-order central places which it serves. Thus

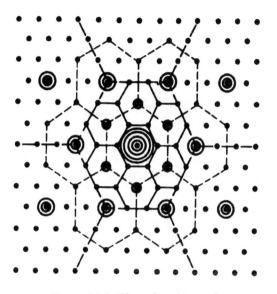

Figure 16.2 The urban hierarchy

Figure 16.2 assumes that each second-order centre serves itself and six first-order places, each third-order place serves itself and six second-order places, and so on.

The different levels of the urban hierarchy form a series of hexagonal figures. Christaller believed that he could discern such hexagons in the distribution of towns and cities in Southern Germany. Others incline to the view that, if there are hexagons, they are distinctly irregular. The useful element in this theory is probably the simple concept of an 'urban hierarchy', with small towns serving small 'catchment areas' and large cities offering a wider range of services for larger areas. In practice, however, distribution of higher-order cities and their respective catchment areas is far from uniform.

Various generalisations have emerged from statistical studies of the relationship between the number, size and rank of urban settlements. One of the best known is the *rank-size rule*, but there are also gravity models such as Reilly's Law of Retail Gravitation (Chapter 6) which apply the general notion of inter-dependence among urban areas.

THE RANK-SIZE RULE

This states that if, in any country, urban areas are ranked by size of population, the size of any area of rank '*r*' will be 'one-*r*th' the size of the largest city. In other words, the product of rank and size will tend to be (approximately) a constant. It is generally expressed as:

$$r \cdot P_x^a = \text{A, where:}$$

r = rank of town X
P_x = population of town X
A = a constant, approximately equal to the population of the largest city
a = a power, approximately equal to 1

Transposing, we have:

$$\frac{\text{population of largest city}}{\text{rank of town } X} = \text{population of town } X$$

The rank-size rule is simply a generalisation indicated by statistical investigations of the size and rank of actual areas. It is not a rigid relationship, but is best regarded as an expression of a regular feature which tends to emerge from the countless locations decisions of individuals. Thus England and Wales do *not* appear to conform to the rank-size rule, largely because of the exceptional dominance of London.

The rank-size rule and similar mathematical models of urban hierarchies have various applications: in regional studies, in planning the location of retail trade and other services industries, and in deciding where to locate new towns and the like (see pp. 283–7).

16.3 Optimum city size

Advantages of urbanisation

A large urban area permits the following.

(1) SPECIALISATION
The transport developments of the Industrial Revolution were vital to the process of urbanisation. First, by bringing food from distant areas they allowed agricultural labour to be released for urban jobs. Second, by improving the mobility of goods and factors of production they extended the market. This allowed greater specialisation both between economic units within the urban area, and between urban areas themselves. For example, where a commodity is demanded by only 5 out of 1000 inhabitants, and a demand for 1000 goods is necessary to employ a specialist, a firm supplying the urban area needs a population of 200 000 if the advantages of specialisation are to be obtained.

(2) LARGE-SCALE PRODUCTION
If the working population is half the total population and only one-fifth have the skills required by a particular firm employing 10 000 workers of whom one in ten has to be skilled, a town of 100 000 people would be necessary. Even so a new firm would probably have to import its own highly-skilled specialist staff.

As the city grows in size, more highly-skilled staff become available, thus attracting other firms and producing further economies of concentration. In this way urban growth feeds itself.

(3) COMPLEMENTARITY BETWEEN ACTIVITIES
Activities may be complementary to one another, either vertically, such as merchanting and financial services, or horizontally, such as specialised repair facilities for office equipment. A large urban area may be necessary to bring such firms together. Vertical complementarity allows greater efficiency: for example, manufacturers can often obtain components from local producers, reducing the size of stocks which have to be carried. Horizontal complementarity means that a more complete range of services is available.

Like specialisation, complementarity is a function of the size of the market. The larger the market, the greater is the possibility for producing specialised goods and services and for interaction between firms.

(4) GENERAL EXTERNAL ECONOMIES OF AGGLOMERATION
As an urban area grows, external economies arise in both production and consumption through the concentration of many types of activity. Even firms in different trades benefit from the larger market, access to large and well-organised labour markets, specialist commercial facilities and improved transport. For people generally a large urban area can allow specialised amenities – such as clubs, churches and cultural societies – to develop, and offers a wide range of job choice, shopping outlets and educational, medical and recreational opportunities.

(5) ECONOMIES IN THE USE OF PUBLIC SERVICES
As cities grow, economies of scale occur in the provision of basic public utilities and services, such as transport, water, gas, sewerage, refuse collection and libraries. Intra-urban transport facilities also become more extensive, thereby facilitating further growth of the urban area.

Disadvantages of urbanisation

Growth in size of the city can eventually give rise to agglomeration diseconomies, as follows.

(1) HIGHER TRANSPORT COSTS
Offices and shops, attracted by the accessibility of central locations, gradually replace residential uses, people being forced to seek housing in the suburbs. Thus while employment increases in the centre, there is an increasing separation of workplace and homes, adding to the cost

and inconvenience of commuting. Eventually the town centre may lose its long-established functions as a 'market place' or as a 'meeting place', that is, it ceases to be the commercial and social heart of the urban area.

(2) TRAFFIC CONGESTION
As the urban area expands and offices in the centre are built higher, traffic congestion increases. Indeed this may eventually result in a fall in central land values, since accessibility diminishes with the saturation of the transport network.

(3) INCREASED POLLUTION
Pollution as urban areas expand takes various forms – noise, smoke and over-crowded housing in the centre, urban decay in the transitional zone as commercial development is anticipated, suburban sprawl along the main road and rail routes, the loss of open space for recreation and the despoilment of the surrounding countryside.

(4) THE DEVELOPMENT OF A 'TOWN V. COUNTRY' DICHOTOMY
People living in rural communities feel that their own way of life and traditions are under threat from the numerically larger urban communities whose interests are largely city-based. For example, demands for the 'right to roam' and the abolition of hunting are seen as the city-dwellers' failure to appreciate fully farmers' difficulties in protecting crops and livestock and in controlling vermin – a view which found a collective 'hands-off' expression in the formation of a pressure group, the 'Countryside Alliance'.

THE OPTIMUM CITY SIZE
The foregoing discussion highlights the fact that cities are built on a complex of 'externalities' associated with locational proximity. Some are 'good', such as defensive strength; others 'bad', for instance increased pollution, noise and congestion, and the cost of eliminating these eventually outweighs the benefit of the 'good' as the city expands.

This suggests that there is a point beyond which an urban area should not expand. It is necessary therefore to consider how the relationship between costs and benefits (internal and external) changes as the total population of the city grows. This is depicted in Figure 16.3.

The average cost per head curve, AC, includes all costs – private (the cost of land and labour), public (the cost of local government services) and social (the cost of congestion, pollution, and so on). It is likely that average cost falls initially as the population increases, but eventually rises as agglomeration diseconomies occur. The minimum average cost point P_m has often been taken to be the optimum city size, but this view fails to allow for the benefits of growth for both households and firms. As the city grows, average benefits per head are likely to increase but at a diminishing rate, giving the curve AB.

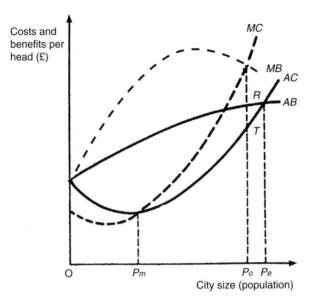

Figure 16.3 Optimum city size

We can derive the marginal cost (*MC*) and marginal benefit (*MB*) curves from the average cost and average benefit curves. Marginal analysis thus gives an optimal city size of P_o. However, this could be maintained only if there were restrictions on further growth since at P_o *AB* exceeds *AC* by *RT*, thereby encouraging migration into the city until size P_e has been reached.

In practice there is no *single* optimum city size. First, each 'central place' within the urban hierarchy performs its own range of functions, and the smaller town would find it difficult to take over the specialised functions of the larger city. Second, average costs per head are a function of the optimum use of land as well as of growth. Third, optimum city size will change with transport costs, the level of income and building technology. In contrast to these dynamic influences, the concept tends to be static in nature.

These weaknesses do not mean that the concept has no practical use. For instance, when planning a new town there must be some notion of its ultimate size, while the idea of a green belt stems from the view that the expansion of the urban area should be halted.

16.4 The problem of 'overspill'

Policies for town expansion

The growth of the town gives rise to two broad types of problem: (i) finding living space for a growing population; (ii) improving the existing urban environment by dealing with inner-city decay, pollution, traffic congestion and poor housing conditions. Although the two problems are interrelated, it is the first which will now be considered. Different aspects of the second will be dealt with in Chapters 17 and 18.

Living space for a growing population can be found by: (i) redeveloping the central area at higher densities; and (ii) developing suburban communities or even new urban communities away from the city. Although there has been some redevelopment of city centres, central sites for housing and new road systems are so costly that the policy is only feasible if large public funds are available. In any case it is often impossible to provide for the growth of population except by outward expansion. It is therefore the latter approach which has been favoured over the past forty years. This approach means that part of the existing population, part of any natural increase and part of any unplanned immigration has to be accommodated outside the existing built area.

Suburbanisation and urban sprawl

Without planning restraints a town may expand by suburban development. As shops and offices take over central sites, people move outwards to the suburbs. In this they have been helped by new road construction and increased car ownership. Moreover, with the rise in real income, they can trade off extra transport costs against more spacious living.

Although most suburban dwellers still travel into town to work, employment opportunities have developed in the suburbs as industry and commerce locate there. Factors stimulating this movement to the suburbs include: (i) transport improvements, such as new road systems; and (ii) improved communications, such as the telephone and, more recently, computer-based information technology for handling and transmitting data. Both have enabled firms to decentralise their paper work.

But although suburban development has advantages from the health point of view, it can have serious defects. Early expansion was uncontrolled and the result was haphazard *urban sprawl* in successive rings of suburbs. Moreover, housing often outstripped the provision of communal buildings and services, which in any case could hardly be all financed by housing alone.

Sometimes, too, the spread took the form of *ribbon development* progressing along each side of a main highway and far into the countryside. Thus rows of low-density semi-detached houses and bungalows were frequently accompanied by new factories, wayside cafés, road-houses, garages, billboards and the like. Ribbon development was dictated by a desire to save on costs of road development, but it only contributed further to the traffic congestion these roads had been built to relieve.

In certain cases, where several towns were expanding, coalescence occurred, thus forming *conurbations*.

Finally, suburban development tends to congregate in the better farming areas where the suburban dweller is more likely to find a well-drained location, good soil, but, most of all, accessibility to all-weather roads, water supplies, electric power, and so on.

Overspill policy

These external costs of suburban sprawl have been recognised. A more planned approach has since been followed, so that a considerable part of an increase in a city's population is now settled outside the urban area. Policy for transferring this 'overspill' population, preferably with supporting employment, has taken three main directions:

(1) *Green belts*, to contain suburban spread;
(2) *New towns*, to settle surplus population and industry outside the urban area and whose size and layout are planned from the outset;
(3) *Expanded towns*, to take the surplus to selected towns which are within reasonable distance and in a position to respond favourably to rapid growth.

16.5 Green belts

Aims of establishing a 'green belt'

Early attempts to limit urban concentration consisted mainly of controlling the density of development. However, this did not prevent urban sprawl through suburbanisation or neighbouring towns merging with one another, and so the notion developed of establishing a girdle of rural land encircling an expanding urban area. Some form of such a 'green belt' would:

(a) check the further growth of the built-up area;
(b) prevent ribbon development;
(c) maintain a town's identity by preventing neighbouring towns from merging;
(d) preserve the character of historic towns, such as Oxford, Cambridge, York, Norwich;
(e) prevent the loss of agricultural land by wasteful urban spread;
(f) provide adequate recreational facilities within the reach of the townsfolk;
(g) reduce air pollution and conserve the environment generally;
(h) assist urban regeneration.

Thus a green belt is not just an attempt to combat the forces making for growth but rather a means of shaping the expansion of a city on a regional scale. This it does by reducing employment in the heart of the conurbation by encouraging the growth of towns which, though partly dependent on the city, enjoy their own independence by providing adequate local employment, shopping facilities and entertainment and recreational opportunities for their own inhabitants.

Weaknesses of 'green belt' policy

The idea of a metropolitan green belt first came to prominence in the 1930s, but not until the Town and Country Planning Act 1947 were county councils given power to designate land for green belts. Today around 12 per cent of England's land surface is covered by green belt land.

Over the past forty years green belts have succeeded in confining urban sprawl. More than that, they have provided a pleasant environmental background for the development of new towns. Indeed they have served to concentrate attention on the need to watch future town expansion.

Nevertheless, criticisms occur (as might be expected when such diverse interests as those of conservationists, developers and planning authorities are directly concerned).

First, implementation of policy has revealed defects of:

(a) adding to the problem of congestion by forcing development in existing urban centres;
(b) failing to ensure that the land is put to recreational use or even made accessible to the public;
(c) not preventing development from bridging the green belt, thereby creating problems for effective village planning.

Second, commuting across the green belt reduces the efficiency of transport systems and adds to the cost, time and strain of getting to work.

Third, green belts have contributed to the spiralling increases in land values in the urban conurbation. However, since the price of land here is mainly determined by the price at which existing houses sell, it would require a massive release of land to lower the price of houses and therefore of land (see Chapter 4).

Fourth, developers claim that, within existing green belts, there are still sites, for example, of redundant hospitals around London, which do not serve the objectives of a green belt, and these should be released for development.

Fifth, present Whitehall policy lacks coherence, with the result that many appeal decisions appear capricious. For instance, past decisions could be used to synthesise the 'very special circumstances', such as job gains and site decontamination, which could override green belt controls.

Sixth, a more flexible strategy is desirable to allow housing and associated functions especially on green belt land which has little environmental merit or recreational potential. Instead of a continuous green belt, there would be a number of wedges serving as 'green lungs' through which the city could 'breathe'.

Nevertheless the 1994 PPG 2 indicates that, in spite of pressure from developers, the government is still committed to restraining building in green belts for purposes other than agriculture, forestry, outdoor sport, cemeteries and other uses appropriate to a rural area.

16.6 New towns

Green belts simply limit the outward expansion of large urban areas; the problem of housing the overspill population still remains.

Early overspill schemes were left to private entrepreneurs – for example, Robert Owen (New Lanark, 1816), George Cadbury (Bournville, 1879), Thomas Neve (Port Sunlight, 1888), Ebenezer Howard (Letchworth, 1903, and Welwyn Garden City, 1920). Public policy dates from the New Towns Act 1946, which provided for the development of new towns. The idea was that such towns should be established as self-contained communities for working and living. The principal aim was that they relieve the 'overspill' housing problem, but some, such as Aycliffe and Peterlee, were developed as growth centres for the area.

Under the Act, the Secretary of State for the Environment designates the appropriate area and appoints a development corporation having powers to acquire by agreement or compulsory purchase the necessary land or property. In reality, a New Town Development Corporation is a statutory speculative builder with the job of building a town, attracting customers, selling and letting real estate and services and showing a return on capital just like any commercial undertaking. Indeed, to encourage the professional and higher-income groups to a new town, the corporation may sell freehold sites on which private enterprise can build individually-designed houses.

The building of a new town means providing houses and all the associated developments, shops, churches, clinics, estate roads, parks, factories, offices and other buildings or services essential for the development of towns. For each 10 000 persons to be housed in a new town it has been estimated that some 525 acres are needed to provide the urban facilities commensurate with modern planning standards. The necessary capital is advanced from central government funds to be repaid over a period of sixty years from the proceeds of the development. The approval of such advances depends on the ODPM and the Treasury being satisfied that the projects are financially sound. Since the Minister's consent is also required for proposed land acquisitions and development, he has strong powers of control. Altogether, 31 new towns have now been established.

The sources of income from which the capital advanced can be recouped are the rents charged on premises erected and the sale of freehold or leasehold sites and properties. The most profitable revenue-earners are the factory sites, shops, public houses, and similar premises. In many cases the corporation will build the factory or shop and lease to a tenant; in others, the site is leased and the buildings are constructed by private enterprise. Though the corporation receives statutory subsidies for overspill housing, no profit is made on rents of the low-cost housing.

When the corporation has substantially achieved its purpose of creating a balanced community – this should normally take about fifteen years – it is wound up and its assets transferred to a central agency, the Commission for New Towns, which is responsible for estate management and any development during the period of consolidation. This has already happened with many of the original new towns, such as Crawley, Hatfield, Hemel Hempstead and Welwyn Garden City.

Problems of new towns

The concept of new towns raises problems as regards both size and planning. We can consider these under three headings.

(1) WHAT SIZE OF NEW TOWN SHOULD BE PLANNED?

New towns must be large enough to become independent, self-contained, self-supporting communities. With this in mind and taking into account such factors as acceptable internal densities and the proximity of homes to places of work, the town centre, schools and open countryside, an upper limit of 50 000 population was accepted by the New Towns Act 1946.

It has since been realised that such a town is too small. Full social provisions, an adequate range of complementary and competitive shops, and a comprehensive choice of employment and of employees could barely be obtained in a town with so small a population. Further, the full economies of scale in development and in the production of goods and services could not be realised. Only if small new towns were sufficiently close to major cities could their populations benefit from services and facilities not found locally or commute to a wider range of job opportunities within the larger urban area. But such a development could be contrary to the principle of self-sufficiency. Hence the latest generation of new towns – Warrington, Milton Keynes, Northampton, Telford and Peterborough – all have ultimate projected populations ranging from 190 000 to 350 000. Unlike many earlier new towns, they have been located close to motorways.

But can we specify an 'optimum size' for new towns as a whole? In practice, the possible size of a new town depends upon its regional setting – the distribution of population, industry, roads, means of transport, public utility services, and so on. Only a very large new town might expect to compete successfully as a shopping centre against the established retail centres of other urban areas in the region. It is important, therefore, to ensure that a new town is located correctly within the urban hierarchy and not within the commercial and social hinterlands of existing towns of a higher order.

Conversely, new town development should not have significant adverse repercussions on lower or similar order towns. It may be difficult to quantify the effects of new development on other towns in the region but an attempt should be made so that steps can be taken to minimise the adverse effects of disturbing the urban hierarchy.

As regards industrial development, planning must again be in the regional context, both in the short and medium term. Initially when the new town is small, it will have to overcome the pulling-power of larger established industrial towns. Thus rapid industrialisation is necessary if development programmes are to run to schedule. It must be recognised that a fully-integrated industrial structure within the new town itself can only be achieved in the long term.

(2) Can the planned size be achieved?

The economic base of a new town will be determined by the amount of basic and non-basic industry that can be attracted to it. As explained earlier the income received from exporting the products of manufacturing and service industries will generate further industry to meet the requirements of the local residential population. It would be useful to know what the ratio between basic and non-basic employment will be when the town is developed. If then the ratio between basic employment and total population could be predicted (see p. 268), a decision could be made on how much basic industry should be encouraged to settle in the town, how much allowance should be made for the growth of the non-basic industries, and what should be the target population.

It should not be assumed that the ratios in towns of similar size are applicable. Other towns may be nearer major cities and so may have a fairly low proportion of non-basic employment, relying on the major city for many local needs. New towns are likely to have a relatively high proportion of young persons and children, so it would not be relevant to accept the ratios of total employment to total population of existing towns. Finally, there are the other difficulties of using basic/non-basic ratios as a guide to growth (see earlier).

Thus the precise population of a new town when it is fully developed cannot be predicted accurately, since it is impossible to know all the factors that might influence the future situation. But it ought to be possible to forecast the order of magnitude – whether, for example, it will be approximately 200 000 or 350 000.

(3) WHY MUST THE LAND USE OF THE NEW TOWN BE PLANNED IN ADVANCE?
In general, a new town's size and land uses should be planned to be as flexible as possible, allowing 'natural' development in response to the interplay of demand and supply. The difficulty, however, is that, as the town grows, changes in land uses for profit-making purposes in response to changing demand conditions tend to be slow, piecemeal and costly, resulting in such problems as urban blight and twilight areas. One object of town planning is to prevent such problems arising. Furthermore, while private land uses change with time in response to market forces, they have to do so within a rigid framework of public land use.

16.7 Expanded towns

The Town Development Act 1952 enables larger cities to negotiate with smaller towns for them to provide housing to take 'overspill' population or to relieve congestion. Although no provision need be made for employment opportunities, the latter would obviously have to be included in a balanced scheme.

Unlike new towns, expanded towns have no development corporation financed by the central government. Administration and finance are almost entirely the concern of the respective local government authorities. Although grants can be made from central funds where appropriate, overspill housing, employment opportunities and public services have generally had to be planned in a climate of financial stringency, the bulk of the finance coming from the exporting authorities and the receiving county councils.

By and large the planning problems of expanded towns are similar to those of new towns. But there are differences.

(a) Before designation, expanded towns are usually 'fully-fledged' urban communities having an established pattern of land use based on the advantages of accessibility. Thus an increase in population and economic activities is likely to have a substantially greater impact than with new towns.

(b) Existing towns will be more fully entrenched in the urban hierarchy than most places scheduled as sites for new towns. Thus, unless overspill activities are on a very large scale, it is likely that there will be less effect upon the urban hinterland and upon urban rank.

(c) If towns are sought which have some excess capacity in the existing urban services, the initial cost of providing for overspill will be less than with building a new town where complete urban services have to be provided. Eventually, however, as population expands, new services and roads have to be provided, and this can create problems – for example, as regards the cost of acquiring land in the town centre.

(d) Whereas a new town's development corporation is dissolved when the development is completed, the expanded town has continuity of administration through the controlling local authority.

(e) Apart from the economy of using the existing services of an old town, the overall cost of an expanded town is likely to be higher than that of a new town. This is because, with a new town, the development takes place on virgin land which the corporation buys *en bloc*. As a result, all the profit resulting from the development (including economic rent accruing to land through the provision of communal services) goes to the development corporation, and the scheme can thus pay for itself. In contrast, with an expanded town, the land on the periphery of an existing town is likely to cost more than the virgin land used in a new town, while in the town centre it is the private owners of shops, houses, and so on who are likely to benefit by the increased economic rent as the larger population brings extra demand.

(f) Whereas new towns can draw overspill population and industry from a wide area, expanded town schemes are negotiated between particular local authorities and can thus be tied to limited exporting areas. This tends to restrict the recruitment of labour and, in consequence, may be a deterrent to the inflow of industry.

The future of overspill arrangements

Because of the fall in the rate of increase in the population of the UK and the increased emphasis on the regeneration of inner city areas, new towns are likely to receive less attention in the future. Recent increases in immigration and in the number of single person households may change this, but recent announcements of new housing development indicate expansion of existing towns in the Thames Gateway, Stansted–Cambridge and Milton Keynes areas. Thus while existing new towns are likely to be built up slowly to their planned size, no further new towns are planned at present.

For the same reasons, there is likely to be less emphasis on formal 'overspill' arrangements. The movement of population out of the central areas of the larger conurbations – especially London – is proceeding much faster than had been expected, and has begun to alarm those local authorities which are losing population. Too rapid a run-down of population may create problems, for example, because it is unbalanced in that the younger, more vigorous and more affluent leave in disproportionate numbers.

Although this does not mean the end of urban planning, the emphasis shifted from sweeping 'greenfield' schemes to the smaller-scale regeneration of old urban areas and to developing districts of 'patchy' development while retaining existing communities. Furthermore, wider car ownership has also meant that people can spread into scattered rural dwellings (see also p. 267).

Summary

Economic forces generate growth in urban areas. Economic base theory is based on the hypothesis that the size of a city is determined by the size of its exports of goods and services. Input–output analysis assesses the value of purchases of inputs relative to the value of output of an urban area in order to construct a matrix that can analyse the impact of demand and supply changes on the size of the urban area. The Keynesian model of national income determination can be adapted to explain the growth of urban areas. It is likely that a combination of economic influences determines the size and growth of urban areas.

Advantages of urbanisation include:

- specialisation of labour
- large-scale production
- complementarity between activities
- external economies
- economies of public services

Disadvantages of urbanisation include:

- higher transport costs
- traffic congestion
- increased pollution
- antipathy between town and country dwellers

Policies to deal with 'overspill' of urban populations include green belts, new towns and expanded towns.

Review questions

1. Why are theories of urban growth based on economics?
2. What factors determine optimum city size?
3. Why is it necessary to regulate suburbanisation or 'urban sprawl'?
4. Explain the rationale for green belts around expanding urban areas.
5. Describe the future of overspill arrangements (or alternatives) in the UK.

Recommended reading

P. N. Balchin, J. L. Kieve and G. H. Bull, *Urban Land Economics and Public Policy*, 5th edn (London: Macmillan, 1995) pp. 27–45.

A. W. Evans, *Urban Economics* (Oxford: Basil Blackwell, 1985) chs 6 and 7.

P. McCann, *Urban and Regional Economics* (Oxford: Oxford University Press, 2001).

M. Newell, *An Introduction to the Economics of Urban Land Use* (London: Estates Gazette, 1977) chs 9 and 19.

H. W. Richardson, *Regional and Urban Economics* (Harmondsworth: Penguin, 1978) ch. 12.

B. Walker, *Welfare Economics and Urban Problems* (London: Hutchinson, 1981) chs 8 and 9.

CHAPTER 17

The Quality of the Urban Environment: Problems of Urban Areas

---

After studying this chapter you will be able to:

- Describe the factors that contribute to the quality of the urban environment
- Explain problems of urban decay in inner cities
- Show how pollution impacts upon the quality of the urban environment
- Explain policies which may be used to reduce pollution problems
- Assess the different methods which have been employed to address the urban traffic problem

In Chapter 16 we saw that, as the city grows, decisions have to be taken on the structural form that overspill should take. But the same economic factors which stimulate outward growth also create problems within the older built-up area – urban decay, economic decline, pollution, inadequate conservation, traffic congestion and neglected housing.

These problems arise because: (i) a built-up area can only adjust slowly to changes in the conditions of demand and supply; and (ii) as the size of the urban area grows, the external costs of more concentration on the centre increase and multiply. Thus though such problems are common to most large towns, they are particularly severe in the conurbations, such as London, Glasgow, Liverpool, and Birmingham.

It must be emphasised that the problems of the *urban* area are really only part of those of the wider environment. A wealthier, car-owning urban-dweller enjoying more leisure requires recreational facilities for playing golf, unspoiled countryside over which to ramble, uncontaminated beaches, theme parks, airports, and so on. But there is often a clash of interests – for example, between ramblers and farmers, urban waste disposal and country dwellers, and national parks imposing restrictions on certain agricultural techniques. How are such clashes of interest to be resolved – through the price system or by government decision or by a combination of both? In this chapter we examine all three methods in the context of the urban area.

All the problems mentioned above are closely interrelated both as regards their causes and their effects on the quality of the urban environment. Nevertheless it is convenient to consider them separately, the first four in this chapter and the fifth, housing, in Chapter 18.

17.1 Urban decay

Urban renewal

As we saw in Chapter 7, over time buildings deteriorate, while changes in the conditions of demand and supply necessitate a change in the use of land resources. The price system responds to such changes.

A building will be demolished and replaced by a new one when the present-use value is less than the value of the cleared site.

But while the price system can perform satisfactorily for comparatively small changes in land use, problems arise with comprehensive urban renewal, whether that be city centre redevelopment or the regeneration of 'twilight' zones and slum areas.

City-centre redevelopment

In the city centre, the limited space available means that the effects of changes in the conditions of demand and supply are accentuated. For example, because any increase in demand for central offices has to be concentrated on a relatively small area, high-rise building soon becomes economically viable and redevelopment proceeds apace.

While much of this city centre redevelopment takes place through the price mechanism, there are disadvantages, most of which stem from the inherent defects of the market economy. First, certain redevelopment may be thwarted by a key site-owner who uses his 'monopoly' power to extort a high price for his interest. Second, renewal may be delayed by the need to wait for leases to expire in order to bring all interests affected within a single ownership. Third, external benefits of conserving aspects of the city centre may be overlooked by developers seeking relatively short-term gains. Fourth, not all possible complementarities may be secured, for example,

linking new shops with such public services as bus termini, libraries, municipal offices, and so on. Fifth, private enterprise has to work within the
existing infrastructure and this may not be efficient, particularly as regards
the road layout.

As a result, some overall control of city centre redevelopment is necessary,
either through planning control (see Chapter 12) or, more directly, by the
city authority undertaking redevelopment itself or in partnership with a
private developer (see Chapter 10). Such redevelopment takes two broad
forms: (i) piecemeal restoration, adaptation and re-building; and (ii)
comprehensive redevelopment.

Piecemeal redevelopment

Piecemeal redevelopment allows the widest possible individual participation,
since the necessary finance is smaller and more readily obtained. Moreover
because it takes place within the existing pattern of land-ownership, it is
cheaper and usually avoids the complex political, social and legal problems
which arise when people and workplaces are forced out. Above all, it
maintains continuity with the past and preserves the distinctive character
of the city centre by retaining buildings of historical, architectural or aesthetic appeal. This gives the citizens themselves a community identity.

The major difficulty, however, lies in reconciling the historical street
system with the needs of modern motor transport. The most usual solution
is for the city authority to convert the old high street into a pedestrian
precinct and to provide off-street car-parks as close as possible. At the
same time one-way traffic flows are introduced to facilitate movement within
the city centre, while new by-pass roads are constructed to take through
traffic (see section 17.4).

Comprehensive redevelopment

Comprehensive redevelopment has been followed where city centres were
devastated by wartime bombing or where resolute city authorities have
decided that urban decay is so extensive that the most satisfactory solution
is to make a clean sweep. Such redevelopment allows complete planning of
the whole area in order to integrate all the activities of the city centre as
regards both accessibility and the environment. Even so, some elasticity
must be incorporated into the overall scheme to allow for future adaptation
in response to changes in the conditions of demand and supply (see also
Chapter 10).

Origins of the 'twilight' zone

Unlike the city centre, where redevelopment proceeds fairly quickly and the
difficulties are mainly those associated with traffic congestion, the twilight

zone, which begins at the edge of the central business district and spreads out to engulf mainly pre-1914 housing, tends to continue to suffer from economic decline, physical decay and social disadvantage. Again these problems are largely associated with the defects of the price system – the immobility of resources, imperfect knowledge, and the existence of external costs which do not enter into private decision-making.

In the twilight zone, renewal responds only slowly to a falling demand for traditional uses of buildings. Middle-income families move to the suburbs or outside the built-up area in order to enjoy more space (see Chapter 14). Old factories and workshops close as production moves to modern factories on the outskirts of towns. Docks become redundant with the decline in sea transport and the growth of containerisation. Warehouses, often on a number of floors, become unsuitable for modern storage methods and are often inaccessible to large lorries.

Whereas factories and warehouses tend to lie derelict, the life of houses may be prolonged by adaptation or transfer to new uses, such as multiple occupation by low-income families or conversion to student hostels. Furthermore, in an effort to maintain net returns from property in the short term, operating expenses (for example, of common services) are pruned and essential maintenance (such as roof repairs, guttering and painting) neglected. The situation is illustrated in Figure 17.1 where the capitalised value of net returns moves from *PV* to *PV'* by such short-term expedients, thereby postponing redevelopment from Year *T* to Year *V*.

Furthermore, even where factories and warehouses are demolished, the sites may be used temporarily as scrap-metal yards, car-breaking premises,

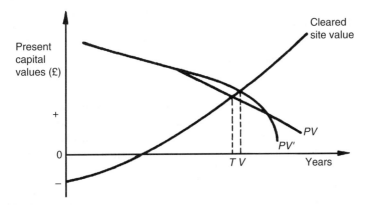

Figure 17.1 Short-term rise in net current-use value by neglecting repairs

off-street car-parks. Worse still, the site may be left derelict while a decision is made on the form of redevelopment or while other sites are acquired.

The problem is aggravated by the fact that existing owners will not risk capital in improving their properties, since the intentions of adjacent landlords are unknown (the 'prisoner's dilemma': p. 192). With shops and houses boarded up, buildings neglected and land lying derelict, the shabby environment contrasts with better conditions elsewhere, making the areas unattractive both to many people who live there and to new investment in housing, industry and commerce. In short, physical decay creates external costs which, by increasing cumulatively, give momentum to the process and result in *slums*, where all the characteristics of degeneration are concentrated in their worst forms in particular neighbourhoods.

Problems of the twilight zones

Thus the problems of the twilight zones (or 'inner cities' as they are now usually called) can be summarised as follows.

(1) ECONOMIC DECLINE

The twilight zone has a higher rate of unemployment than the rest of the city area. The decline in manufacturing industry and the rationalisation of plant has hit the inner-city area particularly severely, especially as new firms prefer peripheral locations where lower rents permit ground-level production and ring roads give better accessibility. Technological changes have also brought about a decline in the old service industries, with the railways being replaced by road transport and the docks moving down river or being changed by containerisation. Warehousing, too, is no longer needed near railway termini or ports. Though the skilled manual workers tend to follow their employment opportunities outwards, the unskilled remain, often augmented by immigrant workers. The new offices and service industries provide few job opportunities for unskilled manual workers.

(2) PHYSICAL DECAY

Although many of the worst slums have been cleared and replaced by modern dwellings, much remaining accommodation consists of old houses in multi-occupation and lacking basic amenities. To some extent rent control was responsible, for it prevented landlords charging a rent sufficient to cover even essential upkeep (see Chapter 18).

Often, too, the inner-city area suffers from an inadequate or neglected infrastructure, especially as regards roads, transport services, school buildings, open spaces and recreational facilities.

(3) SOCIAL DISADVANTAGE

Largely as a result of the high level of unemployment and the lack of job opportunities for married women, inner-city areas tend to have a high concentration of poor people. But the exodus of the skilled worker has added to the relative poverty of the inner-city area. Since he cannot afford to become an owner-occupier, the unskilled worker is reluctant to leave his existing low-rent accommodation. Furthermore, many families have no wage-earner, while those less able to cope in society – the mentally-ill, the alcoholic, the drug addict and the social misfit – tend to find refuge in the twilight area.

Nor is the environmental background conducive to educational achievement. Standards are lowered by poor home conditions, often leading to truancy and drop-out from school, delinquency, vandalism and other behavioural problems. In many cases there are problems of coping with ethnic minority communities – language difficulties, racial discrimination and at times even open hostility from those already living in the area.

Policy for the renewal of the inner-city area

A policy to deal with the problems of the inner city must start from four salient features: (i) the general aspect of physical decay; (ii) the poverty of its inhabitants; (iii) its economic function of providing cheap housing close to employment opportunities; and (iv) an outward movement of both households (particularly those of the skilled, better-off worker) and firms, to newer areas.

As we have seen, all four are interrelated. The degeneration of the area gathers momentum as unemployment and social problems increase and the infrastructure becomes more inadequate and shabby. Government action is essential if the vicious circle in which the inner-city area finds itself is to be broken.

Until the 1960s, policy in Britain concentrated on the physical aspect, with whole areas being bulldozed and completely rebuilt. Precedence was given to providing working-class dwellings to a high density in tower blocks. Commerce and industry were encouraged to go to the suburbs, new towns, and development areas, for example, by the Location of Offices Bureau, or indirectly forced to do so through Office Development Permits and Industrial Development Certificates.

However, the weaknesses of such a policy were eventually appreciated. For one thing, the time taken to rebuild (and at a lower density) created an overspill population which had to be directed to outside dormitory estates, expanded towns and new towns. For another, it failed to recognise that over the centuries the inner city had developed an organic mixture of uses and had become a centre of complex linkages, providing accommodation near the city centre and neighbourhood employment in local industries. Firms, too, were mostly small in size and labour-intensive, employing craft skills to make products where quick alterations in design are necessary in response to frequent changes in demand. Such firms need to be located near their customers, still with low overhead costs. Thus while the bulldozing did provide better housing, firms which were driven out failed to return, so that the problem of physical degeneration was replaced by the new one of a largely unskilled population without employment opportunities, isolated in tower blocks and deprived of its old sense of community.

It became accepted that a purely physical approach to the problem was unsatisfactory and that the correct policy was renovation and gradual rebuilding, accompanied by environmental improvements, the dispersal of the concentration of poverty and ignorance, and economic resuscitation by encouraging rather than hindering the growth of small industry. Thus the White Paper, *Policy for the Inner City* (Cmnd 6845), 1977 set out three major themes for strengthening the economic and social structures of the inner cities while improving their physical environment:

(i) maintaining a sizeable, stable and balanced population in the inner area;

(ii) securing a thriving economic community, particularly of small businesses; and

(iii) carrying out the foregoing aims with an emphasis on rehabilitation and infill rather than by wholesale clearance and redevelopment.

The Conservative government initiated an Urban Programme to tackle the problems of the inner cities. *Enterprise Zones* were introduced in 1981, and funding was increased with *Urban Development Grant*, 1982, and with the *Urban Regeneration Grant*, 1987. The philosophy behind these grants was to make schemes commercially viable for developers by providing grant aid equivalent to the shortfall in the development appraisal. In assessing schemes, an anticipated gearing of 1:4 (£1 of public money to £4 of private money) was the guideline, and this was achieved.

A succession of new schemes and replacement grants followed, usually linked with regional regeneration (see pp. 371–2).

As early as 1949 it was recognised that the quickest way to provide dwellings for families in the lower-income bracket is, where practicable, to carry out essential repairs to the existing stock in order to make it suitable for habitation. Hence much renovation of housing in city centres was supported by *improvement grants*, later termed *house renovation grants*.

These are discretionary grants for repairs and mandatory grants for providing standard amenities (hot water supply, bath and so on) were made available for tenants, private owners, local authorities and housing associations. In addition such a policy, as opposed to wholesale rebuilding, helps to preserve local communities.

In 1980 the conditions of grant were marginally relaxed. The result was that between 1980 and 1984, the take-up of grants by private owners and tenants more than trebled.

Since 1990, however, grants have been means-tested, reflecting the principle that subsidies should be targeted on the person rather than on the property. This has meant that only people on very low income can qualify, although those on state security benefit can obtain the full cost. For landlords the test of resources is the expected increase in income, and possibly in the capital value, which would result from the renovation. This is in keeping with the move towards market rents (see p. 333). But the result of these more rigid financial conditions has been that the number of grants for renovation fell from 320 000 in 1984 to 71 000 in 1987, recovering to around 100 000 in 2001.

17.2 Pollution

Aspects of pollution

Pollution is not a new phenomenon. In the sixteenth century, for instance, the shortage of wood led to coal, mainly from Newcastle, being used for fires in London. The resulting smoke that hung over the capital provoked such a public outcry that eventually the burning of 'sea coles' was prohibited by Act of Parliament. Nor is pollution confined to urban areas of advanced industrialised societies. For example, rural Indian villages have untreated sewage flowing into watercourses and garbage rotting in the streets.

What is new is the recognition of the *problem* of pollution. On the one hand we have the recent rapid industrialisation of the Western world. Economic growth has brought

> the most notorious by-product of industrialisation the world has ever known; the appalling traffic congestion in our towns, cities and suburbs...the pollution of the air and of rivers with chemical wastes...the destruction of wild life by indiscriminate use of pesticides, the change-over from animal farming to animal factories, and visible to all who have eyes to see, a rich heritage of natural beauty being wantonly and systematically destroyed. (E. J. Mishan, *The Costs of Economic Growth*, 1967)

On the other hand, people are now enjoying a standard of living where they can afford to question whether material growth is not being achieved at too high a cost to the environment. Pollution has become a problem because it is now felt that something can and should be done about it. Paradoxically, though economic growth may cause pollution, growth may be an essential prerequisite of environmental improvement. Economic poverty often compels us to accept visual squalor, poor buildings and pollution. It is prosperity which enables us to buy a better environment. Thus the EU's excess production of foodstuffs has made it easier to switch attention to preserving the landscape.

Pollution occurs when, directly or indirectly, man introduces damaging waste matter into the environment. While residual waste is created in consumption (for example, household waste, scrapped consumer durables, litter), it is pollution resulting from production which is more serious (for example, acid rain, smoke, gases, toxic chemicals, pesticide contaminants, liquid effluents, noise, oil spillages) for it affects the whole of the environment – land, sea and the atmosphere. It is harmful to human health, e.g. through carbon monoxide fumes; to agriculture, for example, resulting in lower yields or poorer quality; to buildings, such as in corrosion of stonework; to amenity, such as causing damage to fish, fauna and flora; and to the life of the whole planet through the 'greenhouse' effect produced by carbon dioxide discharged into the atmosphere.

Two aspects of developed economies give particular significance to pollution by waste. First, much waste could be avoided if it were not for the self-indulgent extravagance of modern society. The 'throw-away' mentality simply discards non-degradable waste, for example plastics, car tyres, radio-active material, with little regard for their ultimate disposal. Second, as much waste is derived from non-regenerating basic inputs, for example fossil fuels and minerals, society must show greater willingness to conserve such resources, for example by reducing car-use and by recycling.

Degradation of the environment: definition of pollution

Everybody can recognise evidence of pollution. The economist, however, must have a precise definition. Present-day concern is with the increasing environmental pollution resulting from population and economic growth. Both production and consumption leave unwanted residuals – smoke, poisonous chemicals and gases, noise, household waste etc. Some, such as carbon dioxide gas, can be transformed by the environment into harmless or even beneficial materials (such as oxygen). But this takes time, and *pollution occurs when the flow of residual emissions and waste exceeds the natural environment's capacity to absorb them.* Indeed pollution may even reduce the environment's ability to assimilate waste.

Technology and the control of pollution

Although technological developments stimulate growth, it could be that new technology will allow growth, while containing pollution. Such developments could take the form of: (a) substitute products which are more environmentally friendly, for example, degradable containers; (b) greater efficiency in production to reduce waste; (c) on-site treatment of controlled disposal of waste, for example, desulphurisation of gases by power stations, catalytic converters on cars; (d) the replacement of coal and oil with 'greener' sources of energy, for example, natural gas, wind, tide.

But while such technical developments are likely to occur eventually, what is 'sustainable pollution' must be assessed in the context of the current technology employed. It is here that economic analysis can contribute to a solution of the problem by suggesting and examining a range of broad options.

The economist's approach

As we have seen in previous chapters, the economist emphasises *marginal* decisions. While everybody likes clear air, pure water, a peaceful environment, clean pavements, roads free from congestion, etc., pollution abatement incurs costs. Thus the choice is not the simple one between clean air and polluted air, but between various levels of dirty air. In short, we have to apply the marginal principle and accept that level of pollution where the cost of further abatement exceeds the extra benefit which results.

Why does the market economy fail to control pollution?

In most cases pollution represents external costs. The right to peace and quiet, the right to enjoy a landscape unspoiled by electricity pylons, the right to swim from an oil-free beach are not private legal rights which can be easily enforced. Often, therefore, no *private* cost is incurred for infringing those rights. Thus in Figure 17.2 if there is no cost to a chemical manufacturer of discharging

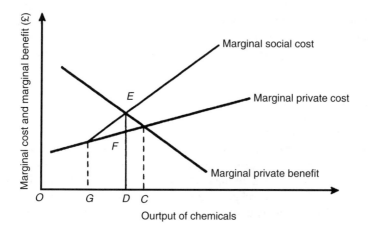

Figure 17.2 Efficient output with external costs

effluent into the river, he will produce chemicals up to the point *OC*. But when we take into account the poisoning of fish, the destruction of vegetation which provides a habitat for insects and birds and the overall loss of visual beauty for ramblers, such spillover costs have to be added to private costs to obtain the aggregate social cost. This means that while *OC* is the efficient level of production for the chemical manufacturer, the *socially* efficient level of production is *OD*, because here marginal social cost equals marginal social benefit (assuming marginal private benefit equals marginal social benefit). In other words, if more than *OD* is produced there is a misallocation of resources.

Policy difficulties

While this analysis of the nature of the problem is fairly straightforward, difficulties occur in devising and applying an appropriate policy.

First, although the costs of pollution control can be measured in money terms, the benefits are 'intangibles', having no price-tag since they are not traded in the market. Take as an example the chemical factory which discharges effluent into a river. While the value of the fishing rights lost can be measured by market information, the value of the loss suffered by bird-watchers and ramblers has no direct market price. This means that the technique of shadow pricing, with all its weaknesses, has to be employed (see pp. 161–8).

Second, most economic assessments of damage are made after the pollution has occurred. But adjustments in response to such pollution may already have been made. For example, the cabbage yield in a market garden may be 20 per cent below that which could have been expected in a clean-air environment. Yet this loss would understate the damage if, in an environment originally free from smoke, more profitable tomatoes would have been grown. In practice, it is extremely difficult to ascertain and measure this 'adjustment factor'.

Third, since pollution occurs in different forms, circumstances and scale, it is necessary to apply different policies to deal with the problem.

Possible policies

(1) 'GREENING' PUBLIC OPINION
Publicity drawing people's attention to the nature of the pollution problem by the government and pressure groups, such as the Green Party and Friends of the Earth, has had a remarkable success in recent years. Households have become waste-recycling conscious and the 'greenhouse' effect has become part of everyday conversation whenever there is a prolonged spell of hot weather.

Firms have responded. Pilkington Glass, for instance, encourage managers to integrate environmental responsibility in all business decision-making, covering such matters as waste and emission reduction, recycling waste and energy saving. Similarly, B&Q, Homebase and MFI have pledged to supply only goods made with timber from sustainable forests, with the sources being monitored.

(2) Setting up an environmental protection agency

Externalities arise because of non-existent, ill-defined or unenforceable private property rights. To overcome this, it may be possible to create an agency in which these property rights are vested, in effect internalising externalities in order to maximise benefits and minimise costs. For example, the Environment Agency co-ordinates drainage, water supply, waste disposal and angling interests.

(3) Market negotiation

If a 'market' in the pollution can be established, the optimum amount of pollution can be arrived at. Suppose a garden owner wishes to burn all his rubbish at the weekend when his neighbours just want to enjoy sitting in their gardens. They could negotiate with the burner to burn at some other time, either by arrangement or at a price. In the latter case, the externality is being 'priced'.

The same principle could apply on the international scale. Brazil could be paid not to clear her equatorial rain forests, and Sweden already assists Poland in reducing acid rain, because the acid rain from Poland damages Sweden.

Usually, however, if the market is to be used to control pollution there must be incentives to avoid pollution by conserving energy or to reduce pollution by the controlled disposal of waste products.

(4) Direct regulation imposing a maximum level of pollution

Here the government decides what each polluter must do to reduce pollution, and enforces it under penalty of law, for example, environmental conditions of planning, no discharge of oil waste by ships within so many miles of the coast. Such a policy, however, provides little incentive to instal anti-pollution devices so that the specified standard becomes the target, involves constant inspection, and tends to impose national (sometimes international) standards instead of allowing for different local circumstances. On the other hand, the policy does allow the polluter to find the cheapest means of achieving the specified maximum.

It should be noted that rigid control is essential where: (a) pollution is a threat to existence, such as blue asbestos dust in workshops; and (b) pollution is cumulative and becomes dangerous at a certain level, such as cadmium absorption by the soil.

(5) Subsidising the reduction of pollution

Where it is impossible or too costly to identify the polluters (for example, litter louts) the government itself takes responsibility for pollution control, the cost being covered from the proceeds of taxation. Alternatively, the government may decide that specific compensation is adequate to deal with the particular pollution, especially where this is localised. Thus in clean-air zones, people are given subsidies to instal smokeless fuel appliances. On the other hand, losers may be compensated, for example, grants to provide double glazing to reduce noise from aircraft. The difficulty is that such public schemes simply mean that polluters are passing on the cost to the taxpayer. Often, therefore, where polluters can be identified, control has to be enforced through individual penalties imposed by the courts, for example, for dropping litter, polluting watercourses.

Alternatively, the government could seek to reduce pollution by directly subsidising: (a) the development of new techniques to reduce pollution or save energy; (b) the production of cleaner substitutes e.g. a reduced tax on unleaded petrol; or (c) the recycling of waste, such as bottles.

(6) Taxing pollution

A charge or tax according to the level of pollution seeks to ensure that the 'polluter pays'. In terms of Figure 17.2 a tax of *EF* would induce the factory-owner to limit his production to *OD*.

Such a policy has the merit of flexibility, and is thus particularly desirable where the benefits can only be ascertained by trial and error or where the aim is to achieve a progressive reduction in pollution since charges can be adjusted accordingly. Moreover, charges have the effect of 'internalising externalities': once the tax is set, the polluter can respond to it as he chooses. Thus a profit-maximising polluter would instal his own pollution control to the point where the marginal cost of doing so was less than the tax saved. Furthermore, the proceeds of a tax can be used to compensate those losing by the residual pollution. Finally, in as much as the charge raises the price of the product, the actual consumer now pays the full opportunity cost of production – a fairer solution than passing on the external costs to society at large.

Even so, a charges policy has its limitations. First, a tax can only be imposed if the individual polluter can be identified. Second, there is the problem of *how* to tax. If it is on units of output, such as tonnes of nitrate fertiliser, the larger producer pays more as his pollution is likely to be greater. But this does nothing to encourage a reduction in the pollution *per unit*. If, however, the degree of pollution can be measured, for example, the quantity of toxic waste being discharged into the river, and taxed accordingly, there would be an incentive to instal an anti-pollution device.

Third, there are distributional implications if the product whose price rises is one which is bought mainly by poor persons, though the proceeds of the tax can be used to compensate.

Fourth, if a country imposes a tax unilaterally, for instance, on the burning of fossil fuels, it may give an unfair advantage to its foreign competitors.

Suppose in Figure 17.2 that output represents the aggregate of all chemical firms on a given river. The government decides to limit pollution to *GD*. Each firm is given a licence to emit a share of *GD*. If the government wishes to raise revenue (equal, say, to *EF*), it can sell or auction the licence. The essence of these pollution permits is that they can be traded on the 'permit' market. Those firms having a high cost of reducing emission will want to buy permits from the efficient firms who sell them for more than it costs them to abate.

This method provides an incentive to those who sell permits to instal equipment which reduces pollution. At the same time, it uses the market to cover much of the regulation required. One difficulty is that as firms become more abatement-efficient, the supply of permits coming on to the market will increase, and their fall in price will allow inefficient firms to buy them. Here the government could itself buy on the market and, by confiscating permits, keep up the cost of pollution.

17.3 Conservation

Conservation is only one aspect of the larger problem of the quality of the human environment in the midst of change. It is not limited to mere preservation but seeks creative continuity by promoting vitality of use of the environment while ensuring that change is sympathetic to the quality of life of both present and future generations. In the use of land resources, conservation has particular significance with regard to green belts, national parks, conservation areas, public bridle-ways and footpaths, common land and parks, nature reserves, National Trust property and buildings of special architectural and historic interest.

Because in essence conservation is synonymous with the optimum use of resources over time, it reflects many of the problems concerned with investment in general. But, largely on account of the distant time-horizon involved and its far-reaching effects on the community at large, there are special aspects of conservation which make it unsuitable to be left entirely to market forces – difficulties of estimating future conditions of demand and supply, choosing an appropriate discount rate, allowing for externalities and the possible irreversibility of wrong decisions. We can illustrate this by analysing the problem of preserving historic buildings, but the approach is applicable to the conservation of 'cherished land', such as national parks, green belts and conservation areas, where development could, in practice, be virtually irreversible.

Possible weaknesses of the market solution

If left to market forces, the demolition of a historic building would take place in Year T (Figure 17.3) where the present values of the current use and of the cleared site are equal. On what grounds may *economics* justify interference with this market solution? The case rests largely on the fact that, with a historic building, assumptions implicit in the model outlined in Chapter 7 have to be qualified:

(1) Forecasting demand often has to start from the position where even *current* demand is not priced, as with, for example, the aesthetic appeal of a historic building. Some 'shadow' pricing with all its weaknesses has therefore to be substituted. Even then, though forecasts can be made regarding future population and income, it is difficult to predict how increased leisure will affect tastes. For instance, there may be a swing from viewing historic buildings to foreign travel. Above all, the estimate of net annual revenues (*NAR*s) from which is derived the present value of the historic building, may ignore 'option demand'. Where decisions are irreversible (as with the destruction of a historic building), many people would pay something just to postpone such a decision. The difficulty lies in quantifying such 'option demand', but its existence is evident in the fact that many people subscribe voluntarily to the National Trust and the World Wide Fund for Nature, for example. The rest enjoy the option as 'free riders', but their demand should also be included. Such higher

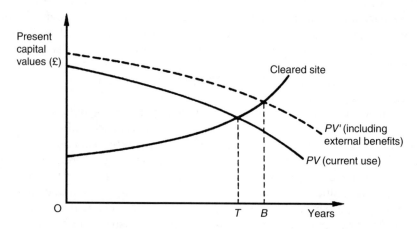

Figure 17.3 Adjustments to the present-value of a historic building for different uses

NARs would give a higher present value curve, for example, *PV'* (Figure 17.3), and postpone demolition to year *B*.

(2) In practice we cannot point to a unique rate for discounting *NARs*. Furthermore, because the rate of social time-preference is lower than that of private time-preference (see Chapter 11), a present value derived from the lower rate of discount appropriate to the social time-preference would be higher than one based on a rate of discount which merely reflected *private* time-preference. Thus the present value curve for a historic building should be higher, for example, *PV'*, Figure 17.3.

(3) *NARs* measure only private assessments of benefits and costs. Thus external benefits, such as the pleasure which the view of a historic building gives to passers-by, are ignored. Again this would produce a higher present-value curve, such as *PV'*.

(4) Knowledge is not perfect, especially when we are dealing with the future. Thus a decision to demolish a building may be based on a defective assessment of the future conditions of demand and supply. This is not serious when we are dealing with *flows*, such as the services provided by offices, since new offices can always be built if demand increases in the future. But demolishing a historic building diminishes a *stock* which cannot be replaced. The situation is illustrated in Figure 17.4.

In period *t*, the historic building has a low value, *OH*. On the other hand, an office block would command price *OP_t*. Over time, however, the value of the historic building increases relatively to that of offices. This is because, with higher incomes and more leisure, people take a greater interest in historic buildings. Increased demand means that in period *t + 2* the price of the historic building has risen to *OH_2*. On the other hand, the demand for offices is not likely to increase so quickly, income-elasticity of demand being lower. Moreover, with technological improvements in construction, the supply curve shifts to the right over time. As a result, in period *t + 2* the price of offices falls to *OP_{t+2}*.

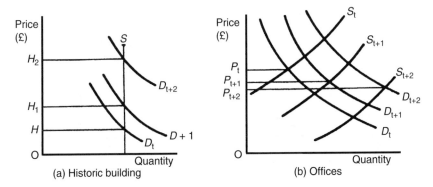

Figure 17.4 Changes in the future relative prices of historic buildings and offices

The situation is transferred to Figure 17.5. We can assume that the price of the office block in period *t* gives a cleared site value of *FD*, so that demolition of the historic building and redevelopment of the site as offices has become a viable economic proposition. Eventually, however, the value of the historic building starts to rise, while the rate of increase in the value of the cleared site declines. Indeed, if demolition in year *D* could be prevented, by year *E* the present value of the historic building once again exceeds the value of the cleared site.

Government policy for preserving historic buildings

The above analysis suggests that the government must intervene in the free operation of the price system in order to preserve historic buildings. Its action can take a variety of forms.

First, the building could be brought under public ownership. Such a policy would usually be followed where the cost of excluding free-riders would be prohibitive, for example, Hadrian's Wall. Equally important, it would allow welfare to be maximised. Finally, public ownership would automatically allow external benefits to be internalised.

Second, the historic building could be left in private ownership but a subsidy given through repair grants or inheritance tax concessions on the grounds of the external benefits conferred. Such a subsidy would increase *NAR*s and so raise the present value (as shown by the dotted line in Figure 17.5). However, there are difficulties. Many external benefits cannot

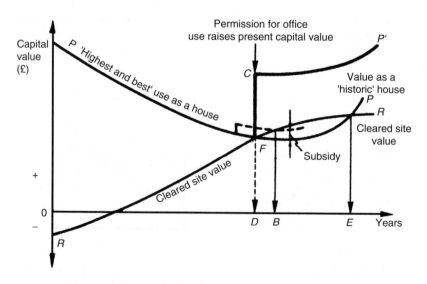

Figure 17.5 Methods of preserving a historic building

be quantified, while shortage of funds could mean that the subsidy was insufficient to raise the present-use value curve permanently above the cleared-site curve, so that demolition is only postponed to Year *B*, unless other action is taken.

Third, any building of special architectural or historic interest may be 'listed'. This means that it cannot be altered or demolished without the consent of the local planning authority. Although this gives protection against positive acts of demolition, it may not cover destruction by the neglect of the owner. Such neglect occurs because high maintenance costs result in negative *NAR*s. Even though in such circumstances the local authority can appropriate the building, there is reluctance to do so since the cost of maintenance now falls on public funds. Thus, in practice, 'listing' in year *D* may be only a 'stop-gap' measure, bridging the years between *D* and *E* (Figure 17.5) until increased *NAR*s raise the value of the historic building above that of the cleared site. More frequently, 'listing' simply imposes a prohibition on demolition until an alternative policy can be formulated.

Fourth, giving permission for the building to be adapted to a more profitable use provides such a policy. Thus stables may be converted into a dwelling, and houses into offices. This has the effect of increasing *NAR*s and thus raising the present value curve so that it is above the cleared-site curve. This change of use is shown as taking place in year *D* and the new present value product is depicted by the line *FCP'* (Figure 17.5).

In consenting to a change of use of a historic building, the objective of the authorities must be to retain as many of the original features as possible. Thus some flexibility of building regulations is necessary, for example, as regards height of rooms, window space and even fire precautions. As in Figure 17.4(a) the distinctive character of the converted building may produce increasing rentals over time, for example, for prestige reasons, so that not only is it preserved but there is no charge on public funds.

17.4 Urban traffic

The benefits and costs of motor transport

In the twentieth century motor transport has increased accessibility for both resources and people through the mobility, flexibility and convenience it affords. It has thus contributed to the improvement of living standards.

Unfortunately as the use of road vehicles has increased, the benefits they afford have been progressively diminished by external costs. The greater mobility afforded by the car has enabled workers to live some distance from their place of employment and has thus been a major cause of urban sprawl. Moreover, people still have to travel from the suburbs to the city centre for work, shopping and leisure activities. Whereas traffic increases as we approach the centre, road capacity decreases. The resulting concentration of traffic imposes environmental costs on non-car users by CO_2 pollution, noise, the danger of accident, visual blight, inconvenience to pedestrians and loss of time to bus travellers. More than that, the expansion of motor transport has led to the demand for road space exceeding supply so that one road-user imposes on other road-users the extra costs of congestion – higher fuel consumption, reduced speed and time spent in traffic jams. Indeed, the problem becomes more acute as income and population increase and the use of cars and commercial vehicles expands.

The urban traffic problem

The major external cost is congestion, for this undermines the chief advantage – accessibility – which motor transport affords. It is necessary, therefore, to analyse the problem and to consider possible ways of dealing with it.

Two salient points should be noted. First, it is basically a peak-hour problem, confined to approximately five hours a day on fewer than 250 working days of the year. Second, it is largely the result of the increased use of the private car for journeys to work. The former tends to restrict the amount of investment which can be profitably undertaken in the transport system. The latter indicates that some effort should be directed towards making the road-user pay the full costs (including external costs) of taking his vehicle on the road.

Bearing these principles in mind, actual policy can follow six main lines:

(1) do nothing;
(2) invest in the construction of more roads;
(3) impose physical controls to improve traffic flows;
(4) restrict parking;
(5) use the price system to allocate existing road space;
(6) use the existing road system more efficiently through a better distribution of the means of travel as between the car and public transport or even cycling.

(1) Do NOTHING

Some people argue that trying to improve movement on the roads is self-defeating: the easier it is to travel, the more people use their cars. As congestion increases, there comes a point where the cost in terms of wasted time and frustration is such that motorists switch to public transport.

But such a policy has snags. First, it provides no *incentive* for motorists to switch to public transport. There should be such an incentive, since those who do switch make travelling easier for those who do not. Second, the high level of congestion envisaged would become a permanent feature, penalising equally the essential car-users and the optional users, those for whom using public transport would impose no severe hardship. Third, the congestion would affect non-car users, such as pedestrians.

(2) INVEST IN MORE ROADS

The long-term solution is increased investment to improve the urban environment and the circulation of traffic. This could take the form of comprehensive redevelopment of existing city centres and improved town planning, such as siting industry away from city centres.

The main thrust, however, would be to build more roads linking the suburbs and city centre. But by-passes also play a part by siphoning off through traffic.

It is doubtful, however, whether this would be a complete solution.

(a) As it is difficult to impose tolls on short-run roads, these have to be financed from taxation and made freely available to all wishing to use them. But as the amount which can be devoted to public investment in general is limited, roads have to compete with defence, health care, social welfare, the modernisation of public transport, and so on. Yet, without direct pricing of road use, there is no precise indication of what people are prepared to pay for more roads and therefore no firm basis for comparing the rate of return with that of alternative capital projects (though CBA may help). Thus there is no answer to the basic question of whether vast investment in new urban road systems is economically viable, bearing in mind that it is largely to provide only for peak-hour travel between the suburbs and the city centre.

(b) Investment in roads, as opposed to extending public transport, involves an income redistribution, since public transport is used mainly by poorer persons. The result is that the decision on whether to invest in more roads is eventually a political one and pressure groups in favour may be successful in spite of the very high cost of urban road construction.

(c) It would take many years for a complete road network to be built. In the meantime, movements in industry and population and transport developments could change needs considerably. This factor largely accounts for the wide discrepancies between forecasts and actual flows, as in the case of the M25 or the M6.

(d) The demand for road space seems to respond to supply, with better roads generating more motor transport. Demand and supply, therefore, are never in equilibrium. This was recognised in 1994 when the government announced a major curtailment of its road-building programme.

This means that we are always faced with a short-term situation of making the best possible use of existing road-space, as follows.

(3) MANAGE TRAFFIC FLOWS

Some immediate improvement in traffic flows can be achieved by clearways, reversible lanes, linked traffic signals, bus lanes, mini-roundabouts, etc. Such adaptation of the existing road layout can often be combined with schemes which improve the environment for example, designating pedestrian-only areas, constructing culs-de-sac in residential districts or simply restricting the movement of heavy vehicles in residential zones.

In the longer term attempts can be made to spread the flow of rush-hour traffic over a longer period (such as by staggering working hours) or to reverse the flow (such as by encouraging offices to locate in the suburbs and the building of out-of-town shopping centres). Nevertheless care must be taken to ensure that the commercial heart of the city is not destroyed as a result. This latter consideration has led to government discouragement of further out-of-town shopping developments.

It must be noted, however, that traffic management can only increase the capacity of the road network when the initial *pattern* of movement is sub-optimal. Even then it only provides a short-term relief from congestion since, unless entry is restrained, improving the traffic flow eventually generates additional traffic.

(4) RESTRICT PARKING

Perhaps the greatest advantage of the motor vehicle is the convenience of door-to-door travel. This needs parking facilities. These contribute to accessibility and – by increasing catchment areas – to the prosperity of shopping and business centres. Yet, paradoxically, too many facilities lead to congestion, and so an appropriate balance between parking and movement has to be sought. Indeed, in order to reduce car dependency, the ODPM is, at present, considering a consultant's recommendation that, for new developments, parking spaces allowed by planning authorities, should be cut by four-fifths for in-town sites and by one-half for out-of-town schemes. It is also proposed to introduce charges on workplace parking spaces in order to discourage car commuters.

Parkers are of two sorts: the 'long-term' parker (the commuter) and the 'short-term' parker (the shopper and the business visitor). The problem is largely one of removing the 'long-term' parker from the streets, so that there will be sufficient accommodation for 'short-term' parkers to pursue their shopping or business activities. The two approaches, 'stick and carrot', are possible – physical control and road pricing. Both involve costs of adequate administration.

Physical controls take various forms, from the restriction of parking to certain days, time, side of street or type of vehicle (such as taxis only) to the complete prohibition of all kinds of waiting, including the loading and unloading of commercial vehicles. Permits may also be issued to give priority to essential users and residents. At one time, planning consents for new buildings stipulated the minimum number of parking spaces to be provided. Present policy for new developments is for planning authorities to exact payment towards their costs of providing car-parks. Furthermore, in order to divert commuters to public transport it is suggested that each private office parking space should be taxed.

While physical controls are unrelated to ability to pay, they lack the subtlety of the price mechanism's rationing function. Where parking is possible, charges can be imposed to bring demand into line with the limited number of spaces available. In order that street parking should be confined to short-term parkers, it is usually linked with the physical control of limiting the time which can be spent at any one bay.

Kerbside parking has to be supplemented by off-street parking, especially for the long-term commuter. Since the cost of this is high, it is more likely to be provided where meter charges are also high. Local-authority car-parks are mostly hardstands and tend to be for short-term parkers only. Multi-storey and underground garages are expensive to build. Since demand drops off at night, they are largely dependent financially on there being sufficient day-time parkers to pay the relatively high charges. If these, however, induce commuters to travel by public transport, there is a net benefit to the community through reduced congestion and less cost of road construction. This would justify any shortfall in revenue being underwritten by the local authority.

The provision of cheaper parking for shoppers and other short-term parkers has also to be considered, especially in the light of current government policy of protecting the vitality of city centres by restricting new out-of-town shopping developments. But without massive local authority subsidy, such parking cannot be provided in the city centre. This suggests that 'park and ride' arrangements will have to be the preferred solution.

(5) USE THE PRICE SYSTEM TO ALLOCATE SCARCE ROAD SPACE

The principle of allocating limited parking space by charges can also be applied to moving vehicles by imposing a tax to reduce the use of vehicles and so relieve congestion.

In addition to his running costs, the private motorist allows for the time his journey will take. The greater the traffic flow, the longer this time. There is thus a rising cost curve, *MPC* (Figure 17.6). The demand curve, *D*, also takes account of this time factor: the greater the congestion, the longer the time journey, so that demand falls as the intensity of traffic-flow increases. Thus, left to the private motorists' decisions, the flow of traffic will be *OP*, where private marginal cost equals marginal benefit (price).

But while the private motorist allows for the time-cost of a heavy traffic-flow, the very fact of his taking his car on the road will add to the time-cost of others. Congestion can be defined as occurring when the private use of his car by a motorist 'impedes' the movement of other road-users, that is, at *OC* (Figure 17.6). There is a marginal social cost which, if added to the marginal private cost, gives the curve *MSC*. Applying the principle that output should take place where marginal social benefit equals marginal social cost the economically efficient flow of traffic would be *OS*.

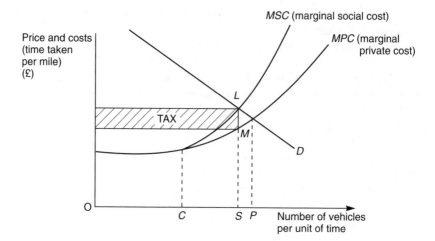

Figure 17.6 Allowing for the external cost of conjection

This could be achieved by imposing a charge equal to *LM*. Ideally such a charge should reflect the time, miles covered on the road, the degree of congestion, the size of car and the location and direction of the journey in relation to the city centre. The difficulty lies in devising a single tax which covers all these requirements and is practical.

Imposing tolls on certain roads discriminates against the poor essential motorist, especially where no suitable alternative route is available. A high motor vehicle licence, by raising fixed costs, simply penalises car-ownership rather than congestion costs. A petrol tax reflects only mileage and size of car, and is thus unfair to the country-dweller.

The most appropriate method of charging is to fit each car with a meter which would electronically register 'units' as certain control points were passed. These control points could be located more closely to each other as the city centre was approached, and the number of units could be varied according to the time of day.

On 17th February 2003 a Congestion Charge was introduced in Central London. It is one of the world's largest and most ambitious plans to tackle urban congestion and involves a £5-per-day charge for vehicles entering the Inner Ring Road charging zone. Even so, a congestion charge does not take account of the degree of congestion or the extent of use within the congestion area.

Some economists consider that an additional advantage of such road-pricing is that it would establish 'road values' and thus rates of return to guide future road investment. But metering faces difficulties.

(a) Though it is economically valid and technically possible, it is only practical if the cost of installation, the periodic reading of the meter and the payment of charges are accepted by the motorist. The costs of administration and enforcement could be high.

(b) Since this meter does not catch the parker, there would have to be additional parking charges.

(c) It raises a distributional problem in that the wealthier motorist would be able to travel on the now uncongested roads, while the poorer *non-motorist* would enjoy better public transport. The relatively-low-income motorist, who would now have to resort to public transport, would lose most. But why should the price mechanism be unacceptable on account of income differences in the road price market and not elsewhere in the economy?

(d) Unless *MC* pricing is imposed in all sectors of the economy and, in particular, on all modes of transport, an optimal allocation of road use will not be achieved.

(e) It has to be decided how the tax yield should be disposed of. Returning it to motorists would simply increase their income so that they could reclaim the road use they have given up.

(6) PRICING POLICIES TO IMPROVE THE SPLIT BETWEEN THE PRIVATE CAR AND PUBLIC TRANSPORT

We have to consider the respective merits of the private car and public transport from both the demand and supply sides.

On the demand side, the car affords a convenient door-to-door means of transport and, in comparison with public transport, is comfortable. It also affords flexibility with traffic jams avoided by the choice of alternative routes and does not involve frequent stops to collect passengers. In contrast, public transport may be irregular, and incur the discomfort of standing. Its great merit is speed, especially with long-distance rail travel. Moreover, the method of charging for car travel as opposed to public transport favours the former. Much of the car's costs are fixed costs – the initial purchase price, the motor vehicle tax, insurance, and so on. The cost of actually using the car – the variable cost – is the cost of fuel and wear and tear (though motorists are inclined to ignore the latter). Thus the private motorist adopts what is virtually a marginal-cost basis of pricing.

In contrast, apart from any subsidies given, fares on public transport have to cover both fixed and variable costs; that is, the fare per mile tends to equal *average* total cost. The price system cannot yield an efficient allocation of resources between private and public transport when different principles are adopted as the basis of pricing.

Moreover, since fixed costs, particularly for the railways, are high, public transport tends to operate under conditions of decreasing cost. This means that the principle of marginal-cost pricing cannot be used if total costs are to be covered (Figure 17.7). Instead public transport seeks to cover total costs by price discrimination, charging higher fares to passengers whose demand is least elastic. Such passengers tend to be commuters and business people –

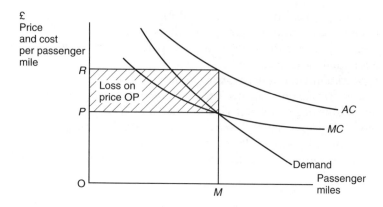

Figure 17.7 The effect of high fixed cost on public transport

and higher fares simply induce them to switch to travelling by car. The alternative is to make good the shortfall by government subsidy.

On the supply side, consideration has to be given to the respective cost patterns of the car and public transport. Figure 17.8 shows that when a relatively small number of passengers have to be coped with, the car has a cost advantage. Since the initial fixed costs to put a car on the road are so small compared with the bus and train, for exposition purposes average cost per passenger can be regarded as constant.

However, as the number of passengers increases, the higher fixed costs of the bus are spread more thinly, so that eventually at *OB* average cost per passenger mile falls below that of the car. Rail transport has to incur even higher fixed costs in maintaining tracks, stations, expensive rolling stock, and so on, and so costs per passenger mile are only below those of the bus at

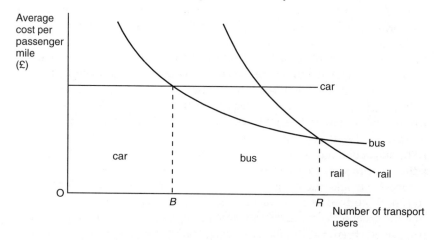

Figure 17.8 Difference in average costs per passenger mile of car, bus and rail transport

a high level of passenger use, *OR*. In addition, development density should be high so that the number travelling from a single station is large. Hence urban rail travel is limited to very large cities.

One further point should be noted: the bus is more flexible in use than the train both in routeing and in dealing with small variations in the number of passengers. In its turn, the car is more flexible than the bus, especially for cross-commuting to employment in suburban offices, and so on.

It must again be emphasised that while the bus and train have a *cost* advantage over the car in dealing with passenger-users above *OB* and *OR* respectively, relative prices for each mode of travel will also depend upon demand. It may be that people's preference for car travel is so high its price would indicate that this mode should prevail even when the number of transport-users is high.

A policy for traffic congestion

The above analysis suggests that on *cost* considerations rush-hour travel is most economically provided by public transport, since this follows the predominantly radial flow to the centre and causes less congestion per passenger carried than the private car.

The logical first step, therefore, would be to tax the private car-user as described earlier. This tax, supplemented by funds from general taxation, could be used to subsidise public transport. The subsidy would:

 (i) enable public transport to cover its fixed costs;
 (ii) recognise the 'fall-back' or 'option' benefit which everybody enjoys simply from there being available public transport facilities;
(iii) reward public transport-users for the external benefits conferred by not increasing road congestion and other environmental costs, and
(iv) redistribute income in favour of the poorer sections of the community who are most dependent on public transport.

In addition, price discrimination could be introduced into the fare structure to allow for differences in the time and direction of travel so that passengers travelling in the direction of the traffic flow during the rush hours pay more.

But there are difficulties. First, the policy is dependent upon the extent to which travellers would respond to the change in relative prices and switch to public transport. People seem wedded to their cars, and public transport is regarded as an inferior good. In other words, there is a low price-elasticity of demand for the private car and a high income-elasticity of demand. Indeed, it can be argued that the decline in the use of public transport is a result more of inconvenience and discomfort (such as draughty bus-stops and over-crowding) than of cost. If this is so, in fairly affluent societies, more convenient and better transport even at *higher* prices would attract more customers than cheaper transport of the traditional type.

Second, the efficiency and equity of public transport subsidies have to be considered. If one aim is to make public transport cheaper for poor persons, then some form of income supplement would be more efficient (see p. 335). Furthermore, a subsidy financed by general taxation is unfair to the person who does not use public transport.

Conclusions

There are many approaches to the traffic problem and considerable controversy as to the most appropriate 'mix' of policies. A system which relies on any *one* mode of transport, or on one single approach, is unlikely to be satisfactory. There is a need for facilities which permit all types of transport: walking, cycling (through the provision of cycle tracks or lanes), car, minibus, bus and rail transport.

The cost of providing new roads to cater for the increasing number of private motorists may be such that some form of congestion tax may have to be imposed. But eventually an integrated city system could be introduced, with some flexibility to allow for individual preferences. The car would be used to get people from places where demand was insufficient to justify the fixed costs of providing public transport. Such people would be taken to collecting points from which they could transfer to public transport, as with 'park and ride.' In the absence of adjustments through the price system, methods of diverting travellers to public transport will have to be effected by physical controls, such as banning cars and goods vehicles from certain areas, extending and enforcing rigorously parking restrictions and creating bus lanes. In the long term, large cities may find that the solution to their traffic problems lies in building new underground railways.

Finally, the traffic problem cannot be solved in isolation from the location of urban activities. In the long run, one of the most effective ways of dealing with it may be to reduce the need for travel by so organising cities that workplaces and residences are nearer each other.

Summary

Inner-city areas or twilight zones arise because the urban area can only adjust slowly to changes in the conditions of demand and supply, and because the larger the city, the greater the external costs of concentration are likely to be. Problems of economic decline, physical decay and social disadvantage are interrelated and need to be addressed using a combination of policies to maintain a balanced population and improve the local economy, and through physical improvement rather than wholesale redevelopment.

Pollution occurs when the flow of residual emissions and wastes exceeds the natural environment's capacity to absorb them. The costs of pollution are often external to the market and therefore require government intervention in a variety of forms in order to deal with them.

One of the major external costs of urban areas is congestion caused by traffic. Various possible solutions to this problem have been tried around the world, including investment in roads, management of traffic flows, restrictions on parking and road pricing. Great interest is currently being taken in the new Central London Congestion Charge, which will almost certainly be adopted by other cities if successful.

Review questions

1. Why is there a 'prisoner's dilemma' type problem in improving a property in an inner-city area?
2. Describe the types of problem that occur in inner-city areas.
3. What policies are available to attempt to reduce pollution problems?
4. Explain, using a diagram, why the market is unlikely to preserve historic buildings.
5. What policies are available to attempt to alleviate traffic congestion in urban areas?

Recommended reading

P. N. Balchin, J. L. Kieve and G. H. Bull, *Urban Land Economics and Public Policy*, 5th edn (London: Macmillan, 1995) chs 6 and 7.

C. Couch, *Urban Renewal: Theory and Practice* (London: Macmillan, 1990) chs 2, 3, 4 and 7.

A. W. Evans, *Urban Economics* (Oxford: Basil Blackwell, 1985) ch. 11.

B. Walker, *Welfare Economics and Urban Problems* (London: Hutchinson, 1981) ch. 5.

K. G. Willis, *The Economics of Town and Country Planning* (London: Granada, 1980) pp. 79–88 and ch. 10.

CHAPTER 18

Housing

After studying this chapter you will be able to:

- **Explain why housing supply is dominated by the stock of existing houses**
- **Describe the main objectives of government housing policy**
- **Explain the short-term and longer-term effects of rent control**
- **Show how housing policies have changed in the last fifty years**
- **Analyse the relationship between housing and inflation**

Much of the analysis previously applied to the real property market in general – for example, its functions, the development process, the relationships of use-demand to investment-demand and the provision of finance – is just as relevant to housing. As a first approach, therefore, we shall outline a model of how the pure market economy would provide housing.

We shall then proceed to describe the defects of the market which give rise to government intervention. The forms and consequences of such intervention will then be examined.

18.1 The provision of housing through the market economy

The dominance of the standing stock

As we saw in Chapter 5, an essential feature of housing is that, except over virtually very long periods, we are dealing with a stock; in 2001, 24.5 m. dwellings in Great Britain increased by only 161 900, the lowest level of completions for 54 years. Even if the construction industry could raise its annual output by a third (which would be a considerable achievement), the yearly rate of increase in the standing stock would only rise from 0.66 per cent to 1 per cent.

The 'stock' nature of housing has important implications as regards housing policy.

(a) In the short period (which may be many years) the only immediate solution to the problem of a housing shortage is to restrict demand to the limits imposed by the fixed stock.

(b) In fully-developed urban areas, the price of old houses determines the price of new houses. Thus the land price is a residual, and high land prices do not restrict the supply of housing.

(c) If 'needs' are not covered by the number of dwellings available, resources must be diverted into house construction. An example of this being done is the plan to build 200 000 new homes in the South East announced by the deputy prime minister in February 2003. This is part of a £22 billion plan to reverse a thirty-year decline in house building and to channel government money into housing and communities.

The process by which the housing stock is increased through the price mechanism will now be examined.

Equilibrium in the distribution of the standing stock

We shall assume that housing is occupied either by tenants or owner-occupiers. This means that there are three parties: tenants, landlords (who can be regarded as investors) and owner-occupiers.

We deal first with the standing stock. This will be allocated as between tenants and owner-occupiers according to preferences expressed through *demand* in the market for renting as opposed to owner-occupation. While the overall demand for housing depends mainly on long-term factors (see p. 331), the choice between renting and owner-occupation will be influenced by the rent charged compared with the cost of mortgage repayments, the desire for independence from a landlord, pride of home-ownership, possible capital gain, and so on.

Let us assume that: (i) initially the stock of dwellings is randomly distributed between renters and owner-occupiers irrespective of preferences; and (ii) there is perfect competition both in the housing and capital markets.

Because, among other reasons, there may be little difference between the rent charged and mortgage repayments on a house, some renters may seek to become owner-occupiers. On the other hand, some owner-occupiers may wish to sell and rent, preferring immediate capital. Since the stock was initially distributed randomly, households will now trade in the market to achieve their preferred positions. Suppose people show a higher preference for renting compared with owner-occupation. Prices of owner-occupied houses would fall, while rents paid by tenants would rise. Landlords would therefore buy owner-occupied houses and rent them out. This increase in rented accommodation would mean that rents would fall until eventually equilibrium between renting and owner-occupation was established, rents being somewhat higher than in the initial situation.

Two further points can be made. First, assuming that a landlord seeks to pay off his interest and capital within forty years, the rent he expects would, other things being equal, be equivalent to mortgage repayments where the term of the mortgage was forty years. Second, since we have assumed perfect competition in the capital market, such a rent produces a long-term equilibrium situation, for the landlord will be obtaining the going rate of return on capital with no alternative investment offering a higher yield.

Suppose now that there is an overall increase in the demand for housing as opposed to other goods. Let us assume, too, that this increased demand occurs in the rented sector. Rents will rise and so will the yield to landlords. In the short term landlords buy owner-occupied houses, renting them to tenants. But the yield on housing as an investment is now higher than the return on alternative investments. In the long term, therefore, landlords would provide the capital for building new rented housing. Eventually, with the additional supply, rents would fall back, and this would continue until equilibrium was restored.

In practice, the model must be varied for real life conditions, as follows:

(a) Mortgages are usually shorter than forty years, so that initial repayments are higher than rents.
(b) On the other hand, rents will be higher because of additions for items often ignored by the owner-occupier: (i) normal profit and administrative costs; (ii) possible adverse changes in government policy, (iii) the costs of repairs (the owner-occupier often doing these himself), and (iv) a sinking fund to recoup capital (the owner-occupier's main concern being that the house will last his lifetime).
(c) A part of the rented market may be 'frozen' by the government, for example, 'social' housing.
(d) Finance may not be available for would-be owner-occupiers, especially the aged and those in the very low-income groups.
(e) Imperfections of the market mechanism and immobilities, such as leases for fixed terms, mean that it takes time to achieve equilibrium.
(f) Legislative provisions, such as rent control, may, on the one hand, force people into owner-occupation, and, on the other, deter landlords from renting out accommodation.
(g) The pattern of taxation and allowances benefits the owner-occupied sector.

It should be noted, however, that the rate of interest will not affect the division of the housing stock between renting and owner-occupation, since capital value adjusts to yields as follows. If we ignore the repayments of capital and the cost of repairs, the monthly rent paid would, as we saw above, equal yearly interest charges on the *capital* value divided by 12. Now if the rate of interest falls, the capital value of an investment in rented houses rises, just as it does with other investments, such as bonds. Thus the total interest charge which has to be paid on the purchase of a house remains the same, so that rents are not changed. Since owner-occupiers will have to pay this higher capital value when purchasing a house, a fall in the rate of interest will similarly leave them in the same position.

The above, however, must be subject to the proviso that, in the long term, a fall in the rate of interest is likely to encourage investment in housing, since it would be particularly beneficial to investments whose yields extend far into the future, and thus increase their profitability as compared with shorter-term investments.

Finally, it is important to remember that: (a) the market allocates housing within the existing distribution of income; and (b) in practice, the short period for housing is so long that for some time it is accommodation within the existing stock which is competed for. Thus for the poorer households only the older, low-quality housing is affordable, indeed often by more intensive occupation. In the long period, however, growth in income and in the housing stock should enable them to spend more on housing and 'filter' upwards as the better-off move into new houses.

The advantages of the free market system in the provision of housing

Until the First World War housing was provided almost entirely through the price mechanism, with 80 per cent of all dwellings rented, 10 per cent tied and 10 per cent owner-occupied. Local authority housing was virtually non-existent.

Such a free market in housing has advantages:

(a) Some accommodation is always immediately available, the quality enjoyed being determined by the rent people are able and willing to pay.
(b) Within their income limitation people can exercise choice in housing according to their preferences. Thus if one landlord will not allow them to keep a dog, they may try to find another who will, though perhaps at a higher rent.
(c) Where the stock of accommodation is small compared with households, rents rise and people are forced to economise in space, possibly by doubling up with other families. In the short term, using available accommodation more intensively is the only possible solution.
(d) High rents stimulate the conversion of large houses into separate flats and new construction, eventually enabling low-income households to filter upwards.
(e) No complex and expensive government machinery is necessary to build and allocate dwellings or to supervise day-to-day maintenance.

18.2 Housing policy

Definitions

The housing market is concerned with the relationship between house-holds and dwellings. A *household* is defined as 'two or more persons living together with common housekeeping, or a person living alone who is responsible for providing his or her own meals'. A *dwelling* is 'a building, or part of a building, which provides structurally separate living accommodation' (*Housing Policy: a Consultative Document*, HMSO, Cmnd 6851, 1977).

Why a 'housing policy'?

The above model indicates how housing can be provided by the market economy, and indeed in the UK today the private sector accounts for 76 per cent of all housing, mostly through owner-occupation. What, therefore, are the economic grounds for government interference?

First, there is the maldistribution of income, some people having insufficient means to secure adequate housing by bidding in the open market.

Second, there are external costs, ignored by both households and land-lords, of bad housing. Some households may not allocate sufficient income to housing, preferring other goods, such as cars, holidays abroad, and so on. Landlords may boost current net income by neglecting repairs; as a result, slums develop, giving rise to ill-health, delinquency, vandalism, and so on.

Third, the government may consider that people generally underestimate the satisfaction they would obtain from extra housing. Thus housing, like education and social insurance, is treated as a 'merit' good, being encouraged by subsidy or provided directly through the public sector (see also p. 392).

Fourth, public intervention is often necessary to accelerate new building, the renovation of dwellings and the elimination of slums. This is the problem of the speed of adjustment to equilibrium.

Unfortunately, much current housing policy has to be directed to rectifying mistakes made by past governments. Worse still, it is dominated by political considerations, which, as we shall see, have thwarted the formulation of a consistent policy and have ignored basic economic principles. In any case, there will always be a 'housing problem' for the same reason that there will always be an economic problem – resources are scarce relative to wants. Can economic analysis help to ensure that the limited resources devoted to housing go as far as possible?

Difficulties of framing a housing policy

In treating housing as a 'social good', governments find little difficulty in stating the ultimate objective of housing policy: that everyone should have a decent home with a reasonable choice of owning it or renting (*Widening the Choice: the Next Step in Housing*, Cmnd 5280).

But while admirable in sentiment, such an aim glosses over the difficulties of framing an actual policy. What, for instance, do we mean by a 'decent home'? The answer involves a subjective judgement, with policy tending to be based on 'needs' rather than on 'demand' (see pp. 330–1). In any case the concept of what is adequate changes over time as people's incomes increase and technical improvements, such as central heating, come about. Policy has, therefore, not only to define what is currently 'decent', but also to decide to what extent *future* minimum requirements should be anticipated. Thus spreading resources thickly on a limited number of houses by councils building to very high standards must be balanced against the fact that it extends the time that many people have to continue living in wretched conditions.

Again, choice in housing means that dwellings should be sufficient in number and variety to enable people to exercise their preferences of tenure as between buying and renting and, within the tenure, of location, space, number of rooms, design, and whether the house or flat is furnished or unfurnished. Such choice promotes people's freedom, eliminating petty rules as to how they use their home and providing increased mobility. Here the price system can play an important role by reflecting such preferences (admittedly within the existing distribution of income) and stimulating production in response to them. What the government has to recognise is that without some form of subsidy, poorer households could not obtain a 'decent home' through the market.

Objectives of a housing policy

As a first approach, we can state the potential role of the government as follows.

(1) To obtain the optimal use of existing housing resources

At any time there is a given stock of housing to meet current needs. Often governments have been so preoccupied with new building programmes that present stock has been neglected by being allowed to remain unoccupied or to fall into disrepair. As we shall see, the policy of rent control contributed largely to both types of neglect.

(2) To ensure adequate housing for all households

Longer-term policy must aim at improving housing conditions. Consideration must be given to individual preferences as regards tenure, type and location of dwellings. Furthermore, policy must allow for a surplus of dwellings over households in order to: (i) provide a 'pool' so that people can change homes, (ii) allow substandard houses to be replaced, and (iii) cover ownership of second homes.

(3) To be responsible for the housing needs of special groups
Certain people, such as the elderly, disabled people and mentally handicapped, must have housing requirements co-ordinated with the welfare
services, for example, through sheltered accommodation or specially-
designed or adapted housing.

(4) To guide the future requirements and location of new housing
New housing should be so located as to take account of current shortages,
employment opportunities, future changes in demand, the existing infrastructure and overall strategic plans.

Because planning permission to build is now necessary, the government
has to estimate likely requirements for at least 15 years ahead, ensure the
capacity of the house-building industry to provide them and to decide where
these new houses shall be located (see 18.10).

(5) To influence the policies of local authorities in allocating
housing
If, as seems likely dwellings for long-term renting will, for the foreseeable
future, have to be provided largely by councils and housing associations,
the government must ensure that certain groups, for example, those who have
just moved into a new area, are not hopelessly handicapped in obtaining a
rented dwelling by the method of allocation, such as the points system.

UK government intervention in the housing market

An active state housing policy really began with the Increase of Rent and
Mortgage (War Restrictions) Act 1915. This controlled the rents of lower-
rated unfurnished dwellings at the August 1914 level, except for rate increases or improvements. Security of tenure, necessary to make rent control
effective, was given to occupiers.

Although originally introduced as a purely temporary expedient, rent
control eventually became the keystone of government housing policy, and
the remnants still linger today.

The reason was that there was no political consensus on phasing it out.
For the provision of housing, Labour governments were biased against the
private landlord and favoured expanding the public sector. In contrast,
Conservative governments promoted increased owner-occupation with its
possible political advantage. Thus instead of a long-term and coherent
housing policy, what emerged was a succession of ad hoc expedients, for
example 'fair' rents and 'reasonable' rents, and frequent changes in subsidies
for public sector building and the owner-occupier.

It follows, therefore, that the starting-point of any explanation of the
current housing situation must be an examination of rent control, the
economic principles it flouts and the consequences which follow.

18.3 The economics of rent control

While rent control may be acceptable as a short-term expedient in an emergency, it has serious weaknesses when employed as the corner-stone of an ongoing policy.

(1) IT DOES NOTHING TO SOLVE THE SHORT-TERM HOUSING PROBLEM
In the short term there is a fixed stock of dwellings, *OM* (Figure 18.1). Let us assume that initially this fixed stock is 'rationed out' by a market rent, *OR*, which equates demand and supply.

Now assume that, through additional household formation, demand increases from *D* to *D*$_1$, but rent is controlled at *OR*. In a free market, rent would rise to *OR*$_1$. This higher 'price' would ration out the existing stock of housing among all households seeking to rent according to the emphasis they place on house space compared with other goods.

Where rent remains controlled at *OR*, however, two results follow. First, landlords cannot secure the extra economic rent, *R*$_1$*RTY*, arising through the increased demand for a fixed supply. Second, persons *who are already occupying a rented dwelling can*, through security of tenure, continue to occupy it at the current rent. The difficulty is that there has been no rise in rent to cause the existing stock to be used more intensively. Some households do double up with relatives, but demand continues to exceed supply, broadly by *MM*$_1$, forcing those who can afford it to become owner-occupiers and those who cannot to fall back on the limited public sector.

(2) IT ALLOCATES HOUSING ARBITRARILY AND OFTEN INEQUITABLY
With a free market mechanism the existing stock of accommodation is allocated by the equilibrium market rent, for this is the 'price' where demand

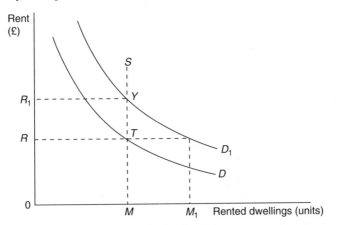

Figure 18.1 The effect of rent control in the short period when the demand for dwellings increases

just equals supply. This rent would be determined by people bidding in the market, reflecting their preferences and income constraint.

Whenever the price system is eschewed, some other means of allocating supply has to be used. Thus the government can divide the limited stock of a good into 'fair' shares which are rationed out. But because of the relatively small flow of new dwellings on to the market, such a method is not suitable for allocating housing. For instance, when petrol was in short supply in 1979, rationing would have been possible, since new flows were constantly coming on to the market. As the size of these flows changed, the ration could be varied. With housing, however, people are occupying the fixed stock; they cannot be turned out in order to implement the principle of 'fair shares'.

Initially, therefore, the housing stock is allocated randomly, simply on the basis of possession. And even where private landlords relet dwellings, many carry out their own 'rationing', preferring to let to companies rather than to private individuals.

(3) It decreases the supply of privately rented dwellings

In the long period the supply of dwellings would extend in response to a higher free market price: rent control obstructs this functioning of the price system. Indeed, supply tends to decrease. First, dwellings may be under-utilised, for example through old people retaining the same accommodation although their children have left home. Second, as rented dwellings become vacant, they are sold in the higher-priced owner-occupier market. Third, as repair costs rise relative to rents, houses deteriorate or remain substandard.

The above can be demonstrated diagrammatically. In Figure 18.2, in the short period (with S_s) when demand increases to D_1, the rent would rise from OR_c to OR_1; but in the long period it would settle at OR_2, with supply extended by MM_2. With rent controlled at OR_c, demand exceeds supply by MM_1. Successive short-period reductions in supply, however, eventually give a new long-period supply curve of SL_1, with excess demand of M_3M_1.

(4) It distorts other prices within the housing market

Households who cannot find dwellings to rent are forced to turn to the uncontrolled owner-occupied sector of the market. This drives up the price of owner-occupied houses. Thus those who are not fortunate enough to obtain rent-controlled dwellings are forced to pay a higher 'rent' than if the whole market were completely free.

(5) It redistributes income arbitrarily

There is no guarantee that households having a rent-controlled dwelling are more deserving than those who are forced to become owner-occupiers at higher house prices. Indeed, some who cannot afford to buy, for example, the poor, newly-weds and those just starting work, are penalised the most. Just as random is the redistribution of income between tenants and landlords especially when prices generally rise over time. In 1961, Cullingworth's

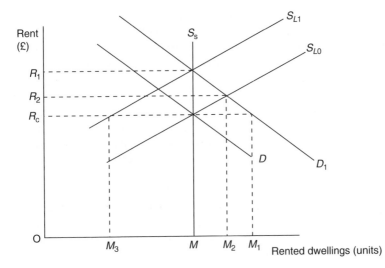

Figure 18.2   The effects of rent control in the long period

survey of Lancaster (*Housing in Transition*, Heinemann, 1963) showed that
one-half of the landlords there were over 60 years of age, owned only one
house and had an average weekly income (including net rents) of less than
£10 a week.

(6) IT CREATES VESTED INTERESTS WHICH MAKE IT MORE DIFFICULT TO
FORMULATE A COHERENT LONG-TERM POLICY
Rent control has given rise to many undesirable 'spin-off' effects. First, by
perpetuating shortages, it fostered demands for further rent control – for
example to furnished dwellings. Second, to match the 'subsidy' which controlled tenants enjoy at the expense of landlords, the government introduced
subsidies for owner-occupiers and council tenants (see pp. 340–4). Third, the
resulting shortages led to a policy which is need-orientated rather than
demand-orientated (see pp. 330–1). Fourth, the artificially low rents
produced by rent control and housing subsidies have influenced the man-
in-the-street's view as to what is a 'reasonable' or 'normal' rent.

Furthermore, once subsidies are in place, beneficiaries resist their removal.
Thus both the Rent Act 1957 (which aimed at some decontrol of rents)
and the Housing Finance Act 1972 (which switched local authority housing
subsidies from tenants generally to only those needing them) met with
such opposition that both policies were dropped by subsequent Labour
governments.

(7) IT DISTORTS THE ALLOCATION OF RESOURCES
One advantage of the price system is that given perfect competition and
the existing distribution of income, it allocates resources so that marginal

private benefits equal marginal private costs. This, unless there are externalities, is an optimum allocation thwarted by rent control.

Moreover, a policy directed to low rents over sixty years influenced
people's views as to the proportion of income it is reasonable to spend on
housing. Thus when rents rise, people looked for government help; in
contrast, when car prices rise, they accept the rise and pay the higher price.
As a result, insufficient resources are attracted into the rented sector.

In the public sector, increased subsidies, necessary if rents are not raised
when costs are rising, add to the PSBR. Thus local authority housing suffers
when cuts to grants have to be made (as in 1993–6).

(8) IT HAMPERS LABOUR MOBILITY

Because the 'subsidy' implicit in rent-controlled housing is attached to the
dwelling, not to the person, it is lost on moving (unless it can be capitalised
by inducing the landlord to pay a money sum for possession). Thus workers
find it difficult to move geographically.

(9) IT INVOLVES ADMINISTRATIVE COSTS

For example, rent officers are required to determine 'fair rents', and rent
assessment committees to hear appeals.

Our next task is to examine how different tenures responded to rent
control.

18.4 Changes in tenure distribution

The private-rented sector

The demand for rented dwellings comes mainly from persons:

(a) too poor to qualify for a mortgage; or
(b) waiting to purchase; or
(c) frequently moving on account of their jobs.

Thus renting is an important alternative to buying.

But whereas in 1914 rented and tied dwellings comprised 90 per cent of
UK housing, by 1951 this had shrunk to 50 per cent, and today (2003) it has
been estimated at only 9 per cent (6 per cent unfurnished, 3 per cent
furnished). This loss of privately-rented dwellings (Table 18.1) was the result
of rent control.

Because rents did not keep pace with inflation, management and maintenance costs left a net return which was uncompetitive compared with alternative investments. Furthermore, in contrast to other forms of tenure, the
private-rented sector received no subsidies. Above all, security of tenure
compounded the landlord's disadvantage, for he was locked into his

Table 18.1   *Changes in Tenure Distribution 1914–2001, GB (percentages)*

	1914	1947	1963	1983	1993	1997	2001
Owner occupied	10	26	45	58.8	66.4	68	69
Rented privately	90	61	27	10.7	9.7	11	10
Rented from:							
Housing Association	–	–	–	2.3	3.7	5	7
Local authority or new town corporation	–	13	28	28.1	20.1	16	14

Source: *Housing Statistics, Office of the Deputy Prime Minister.*

investment until vacant possession was eventually obtained or the property sold on the market at a loss in real terms.

Renting private accommodation through the market enables tenants to exercise their preferences within the income constraint. It is flexible, and facilitates mobility. With one exception, rent control brought this to an end. The exception was furnished accommodation, which was not subject to control. Thus for persons waiting to purchase or moving frequently, such accommodation could be found. Hence the Rent Act 1974 by bringing furnished accommodation within the provisions of rent control was a measure of extreme folly as this small safety-valve ceased to operate almost overnight.

Public sector housing

(1) ITS EARLY DEVELOPMENT

By the end of the nineteenth century concern over the effects on health of bad housing had led to tentative steps towards dwellings being provided by local authorities. But the policy did not gather momentum until after 1919 when, because of the neglect of building during the previous war years, the Town and Country Planning Act required local authorities to prepare plans for providing housing to meet local needs. It was thought that, once the construction industry had fully recovered, public housing would be necessary only for the 'needy' – the poor, old and sick – and for slum clearance.

But the decline of the private-rented sector, meant that the deficiency in low-cost rented dwellings had to be made good by the public sector. However, in implementing policy, rents charged had to be comparable with those of similar dwellings in the *rent-controlled* private sector. This rejection of the market mechanism meant that local authority housing had to be: (a) provided and allocated on the basis of 'need', not demand; and (b) subsidised.

For most authorities, demand exceeded supply and so their housing activities were, with the support of subsidies, extended. Thus waiting lists contained not just those on low incomes but others who simply preferred to rent at a subsidised level rather than buy.

Such by-passing of the market mechanism creates difficulties in allocating the limited supply – as the difference between 'need' and 'demand' indicates.

(2) 'NEED' AND 'DEMAND'

Need measures the extent to which existing accommodation falls short of that required to provide each household with accommodation of a minimum specified standard irrespective of ability to pay. Making such an estimate, however, is not easy. For one thing, projections of households are based on such variables as marriage rates and the size of family, both of which depend upon changes in income and social attitudes. For another, 'need' is more than the difference between aggregate households and aggregate dwellings, since both have to be subdivided and related to size and location. Census returns and statistics from the Registrar-General provide the basic data.

Above all, determining the 'minimum specified standard' presents practical and conceptual difficulties. How do we measure accommodation standards – by the family unit or by area per person? Really we should concentrate on the needs of the different types of family. For instance, a family of six requires less space than three households each consisting of two persons, while two adults and two young children differ in their housing needs from one adult with three grown children. However, since it is impossible to forecast for such refinements, requirements are usually calculated on the basis of so many square feet or rooms *per person*.

Similarly, what standard should be specified? Although this is basically a subjective decision, it has to be related to the overall level of income. Moreover, in formulating building plans, a decision has to be made on whether to aim at a standard to overcome current overcrowding or a future standard which allows for income growth. When there is deficiency of housing, the former tends to be paramount. In the long term, however, when only replacement is called for, it is important to anticipate future standards.

To obtain the number of *households*, the existing population is projected for the target year according to age and sex by applying birth and death rates and allowing for external migration. How many households a given population will form, however, depends upon the marriage rate, the proportion of young people who live separately from their parents, and the number of old people who go to live with their children or are admitted to institutions. In addition, an attempt must be made to classify households according to size by applying statistics relating to the size of the completed family. Finally, since dwellings cannot be moved physically, an estimate should be made of the regional location of households in the target year. Naturally, the more distant the target year, the more inaccurate are forecasts likely to be, since data are influenced by changes in the level and distribution of income, immigration policy, internal migration, and so on.

Ideally, policy should aim at providing housing units of sufficient quantity and quality and in the right location for the households estimated. The stock of *dwellings* has to be estimated for the target year, taking into account new building, demolition, renewals and conversions, all of which are affected by changes in the rate of growth of national income. In addition, the quality of dwellings – in terms of age and standard amenities – and their location are important. Finally, not all the stock will be occupied by a separate household. Some 4 per cent is likely to be vacant to permit mobility, while 1 per cent will be held for second homes, a figure which is likely to rise as real incomes increase.

Demand for housing refers to an economic concept, *effective demand* – what people are willing and able to pay for housing. We are therefore concerned with: (a) preferences at a *price*, and (b) the conditions of demand – the level of income, income distribution, household formation, the rate of interest, the price of substitutes, government policy, changes in tastes, expectations of future price changes, and so on. Demand, therefore, is an expression through the price system of people's preferences for different types of housing. In contrast, where housing is allocated arbitrarily according to 'need', there may be some loss of satisfaction.

In Figure 18.3, for instance, at a market rent of *XY* a household would purchase *OH* housing and *OG* other goods. The local authority charges a subsidised rent of *XY'* but requires that the household occupies *OH'* housing on a 'needs' basis. As a result, the household drops to the lower indifference curve I. In addition the taxpayer suffers loss of welfare through having to cover the subsidy (unless this is compensated for by the knowledge that the poorer family is adequately housed).

However, estimating demand for housing as a guide to *future policy* is far from easy. One method is to apply past statistical relationships between

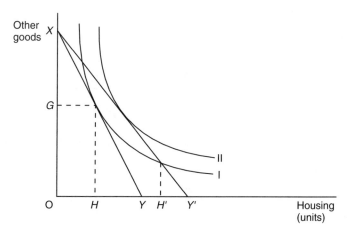

Figure 18.3 Loss of welfare through the inability to allocate income according to preference

demand and house prices, rents, interest rates, and so on. The difficulty here is that the same relationship may not hold in the future, since the conditions of demand change over time. Another method is through direct enquiry, but this has limitations. Not only do people restrict their estimates of demand to two or three years ahead, thereby providing little guide for long-term policy, but such estimates tend to be related to the artificially low rents to which households are accustomed.

The growth in the importance of public sector housing is shown in Table 18.1. From 13 per cent of total housing just after the Second World War it had risen to 31 per cent by 1980, when the UK stock of local authority and new town properties reached a peak of 6.5 m. But, as we shall show later, defective administration led to an accumulation of problems.

(3) THE OWNER-OCCUPIED SECTOR

Table 18.1 shows the relative growth in owner-occupied housing: from 10 per cent in 1914 to 26 per cent in 1947, 56 per cent in 1980, and 69 per cent in 2001.

Although the shortage of houses to rent undoubtedly forced many to buy, it was not the sole cause. With rising incomes among skilled and semi-skilled workers, house-ownership was often a first preference. 'Keeping up with the Joneses' gave it further impetus. Furthermore, schedule A income tax on the imputed income of the house owned was abolished in 1963. But the 'subsidy' of mortgage interest tax relief remained unaffected until 1974, when it was limited to the first £25 000 borrowed. Above all, finance on favourable terms was available through the expanding building societies.

Sources of finance. For most people, a house can be bought only by borrowing for a comparatively long period. This was possible because: (a) the house secures the loan; (b) building societies specialised in this type of finance, and were the main providers (Table 18.2).

Building societies originated in Birmingham in 1775 when a group of working men formed a society to build houses and allocate them on

Table 18.2   Changes in the source of house mortgage finance 1985–2001

	Per cent of total					Gross advances (£m)
	1985	1989	1993	1997	2001	2001
Building societies	79	71	59	38	17.6	25904
Banks	23	28	40	61	81.4	119765
Insurance companies	1	1	0.6	0.4	0.7	1014
Local Authorities	−3	0.2	0.4	0.3	0.3	446
Total	100	100	100	100	100	147129

Source: *Housing Statistics, Office of the Deputy Prime Minister.*

completion. This background may still exert some influence on their policies with recognition of 'social' obligations in lending to first-time buyers at the lower income end and to housing associations.

Their success was based on their ability to compete for small short-term loans from private savers by careful attention to their convenience and preferences and by overcoming the risk inherent in borrowing short and lending long by proven financial stability. Such retail short-term loans meant that they could compete by lending at a lower rate of interest than banks. Nor did they have to compete with each other because they operated a cartel through the Building Societies Association to fix both lending and borrowing rates.

As a result, demand for mortgages usually exceeded supply. This allowed societies to impose conditions which reinforced other policies, chiefly safety of capital. Thus, they showed a preference for certain types of property, in particular brick-built, freehold, three-bedroom houses of traditional design, and on these they were prepared to grant a 90 per cent mortgage. Only when the rise in the price of houses forced first-time buyers to settle for cheaper types of dwelling, particularly flats, did the building societies relax this preference.

This dominant position of the building societies influenced the shape of owner-occupied housing. First, since the purchase of most houses was through building-society mortgages, speculative builders concentrated on the type of house likely to attract a mortgage, particularly the two-bedroom or three-bedroom house of traditional design. Second, their condition of a mortgage that there be no sub-letting without approval reduced a possible source of rented accommodation.

18.5 The 1979 policy watershed

The Thatcher approach

When Mrs Thatcher came to power in 1979, many aspects of the housing situation were bound to conflict with her private enterprise philosophy – rent control, lack of individual freedom of choice in housing and a public sector whose management was not only often inefficient, but whose scale of spending was embarrassing to a government whose macroeconomic policy embodied a reduction in public expenditure.

Mrs Thatcher's strategy, therefore, was to develop a housing system based almost entirely on the private sector. Whatever its weakness, this view did at least give some coherence to policy: efficiency in the allocation of resources devoted to housing could be best achieved by using the market as far as possible. This would allow: (a) consumers to express their choice, and (b) supply to respond accordingly. The first needed a transfer of subsidy from the dwelling to the occupier; the second, the ending of rent control.

Housing subsidies

Subsidies enable certain households to enjoy services below the cost of providing them through the free market. Such a broad definition covers:

(a) the transfer of income from landlords to tenants by rent control;
(b) tax concessions enjoyed by owner-occupiers;
(c) direct subsidies, consisting of:
  (i) central government grants to local authority housing accounts and to the Housing Corporation;
  (ii) housing benefits to tenants on low incomes;
  (iii) renovation grants (see p. 296).

Subsidies have two broad objectives. First, they can be used to redistribute income more equitably, a decision which rests ultimately on a subjective judgement. Second, they can allocate more resources to housing than would be available through the market economy to cover, for example, the external costs of inadequate housing.

However economics can suggest conditions which, as far as practicable, subsidies should observe.

First, subsidy should be given in such a way that consumers can obtain the highest possible satisfaction from a given subsidy expenditure. Where the objective is to enable a consumer to enjoy a minimum standard of housing, a subsidy can either provide more income or reduce the price of housing. The former would appear to be the more efficient method, since it enables the consumer to attain a higher indifference curve for a given subsidy expenditure.

This is illustrated in Figure 18.4. With his initial income the consumer attains indifference curve I, buying at point E other goods OG and housing OH. Because it is now deemed that OH housing is inadequate, a subsidy is given to housing, thereby reducing its price from PR to PV. As a result, the consumer substitutes other goods for housing, buying OG_1 and OH_1 respectively at F. But since the subsidy also represents an increase in income, a higher indifference curve, II, is attained.

Now suppose that, instead of the subsidy to housing (which equals FL in terms of 'other goods'), the consumer is given additional income (for example, by way of Family Credit or a negative income tax) so that he can still purchase OG_1 other goods and OH_1 housing. Since relative prices remain unchanged, this will be shown by moving the original price line further from the origin, TS, to pass through F. Since $TP = FL$ the income subsidy costs the same, being just sufficient to allow the consumer to obtain the same amount of housing in each case.

The big difference, however, is that whereas a housing subsidy distorts relative prices at the same time as income is increased, an income supplement leaves the consumer free to attain his preferred position, J, without any

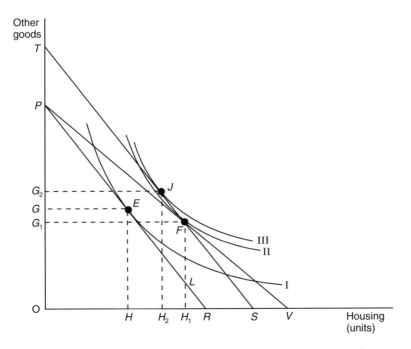

Figure 18.4 The efficiency of a housing subsidy compared with an income supplement

accompanying price distortion. He therefore buys OG_2 other goods and OH_2 housing, achieving a higher indifference curve, III. In other words, there has been a Pareto improvement, for our consumer's welfare has increased and nobody is worse off since the same amount of subsidy is being paid.

But there are two important provisos. (a) Equilibrium at J is based solely on the consumer's private costs and private benefits. In practice, OH_2 housing may still be inadequate in that it gives rise to external social costs, such as ill-health, delinquency and vandalism, which the consumer ignores when spending an income supplement. Society may therefore have to choose a *selective* housing subsidy, such as the housing benefit, rather than a *neutral* income supplement. (b) If the supply of housing is inelastic the extra spending will drive up the price, reducing the amount that can be bought.

Second, if the main reason for a housing subsidy is inadequate income, it should be flexible with respect to changes in income. Again it follows that the subsidy should be attached to the person and not to the dwelling.

Third, the selectivity of any subsidy should be kept under review. The purpose of selectivity is to influence the allocation of resources. Thus housing subsidies are selective as between: (i) housing and other goods;

(ii) housing association and private-rented housing, the former being supported by government grant; and (iii) slum clearance and housing generally, the former attracting higher subsidies. This means that subsidies have to be adjusted to reflect changes in housing needs and for new policy requirements based on experience. For example, a switch from rebuilding to restoring inner-city dwellings can be promoted by reducing general housing subsidies in favour of improvement grants.

Fourth, public expenditure on housing should be related to the financial resources available, particularly as regards the government's other commitments, such as defence, health and education, and the size of the PSNCR.

The switch in housing subsidy

Like housing policy, subsidies evolved piecemeal. Apart from those enjoyed by the owner-occupier, they were applied on the supply side. Exchequer grants to local authorities enabled councils to charge rents at less than the economic cost, and irrespective of tenant's income. In the private sector, landlords provided a virtual subsidy to rent-controlled tenants. In short, the criteria suggested above were not observed.

From 1979, the policy of switching from supply-based to demand-based subsidies, therefore, was on firm ground. In 1982 rent rebates were incorporated in a new *housing benefit*. But the change by which the subsidy would target the person rather than bricks and mortar was really effected by the Social Security Act 1988. Henceforth the housing benefit would be paid to tenants in both the public and private sectors to allow them to afford a rent which matched their needs. This would allow tenants to exercise their preferences as regards housing and could be adjusted with changes in their income.

What was not foreseen, however, was the escalation in the total housing benefit bill from £3.6 bn in 1988 to £8.4 bn in 1993/4. Since public sector housing was occupied predominantly by the old and disabled, single-person households and others on low income, 60 per cent of public sector tenants received housing benefit. Moreover, as it covered the difference between the asking rent and need, there was little incentive for the tenant to negotiate with the landlord or to economise on accommodation. In addition, high rents (especially in the London area) often gave rise to a 'poverty trap' for low-income families who, as a result, refrained from increasing their income in case it triggered a reduction in their housing benefit. Above all the soaring cost was the result of the prolonged recession with 2.5 m. unemployed.

Pressure was put on local authorities to monitor rents to ensure that they do not exceed the local level, and so prompt tenants to negotiate with landlords. But merely imposing a given global limit to government spending on housing benefit would simply undermine the whole strategy of providing housing through the market by regenerating the private-rented sector.

The virtual ending of rent control

Controlled rents coupled with *security of tenure* were highlighted as the main causes of the emasculation of the private-rented sector, and so measures were taken to remove these obstacles.

The Housing Act 1980 introduced: (a) *assured tenancies* for *newly-built* privately-rented property, with rents *market-determined* but tenants having security of tenure, and (b) *shorthold tenancies*, with registered *fair* rents, but security limited to an agreed fixed term. This was merely the first step, with the fair rent condition being finally abolished in 1987 for shortholds.

It was the Housing Act 1988 which finally produced deregulation. For all new lettings within the newly-termed *independent rented sector*, covering both private and housing association lettings, rents can now be freely negotiated between landlord and tenant. Thus in the private-rented sector, rents should tend towards the market clearing rent. Housing associations, however, seek to ensure that low-income households just above the housing benefit eligibility level can afford adequate accommodation, and so set a rent which, while covering their costs, is reduced by the subsidy.

From 15 January 1989 the Act introduced two new types of tenancy: the *assured tenancy* and the *assured shorthold tenancy*.

Under the *assured tenancy* provisions there are no rent controls, while security of tenure provisions are much more favourable to the landlord. At the end of a fixed-term tenancy, a statutory periodic tenancy arises, and the landlord can apply for possession or renew the tenancy at an agreed rent. If the rent is disputed it is determined by a local Rent Assessment Committee (RAC) as being the going *market* rent for that type of accommodation. If the landlord wants possession he must serve the prescribed notices and obtain a court order. Grounds for possession are divided into those over which the court has no discretion (such as substantial arrears of rent) and those where it can make an order only if it considers it reasonable to do so.

With an *assured shorthold tenancy* the rent is negotiated at the market level as with the assured tenancy, but it is easier for the landlord to repossess the premises at the end of the agreed term. This could not be less than six months, and the notice stating that it is a shorthold tenancy had to be served before entry. Here, provided the stipulated conditions, including at least two months' notice, have been fulfilled, the court *must* make an order for repossession at the request of the landlord when the fixed term comes to an end.

The Act also encouraged the letting of rooms by affording no statutory protection for tenants who share living accommodation with their landlord (that is, he must live in the house himself). Thus there is no appeal to a RAC, and no court order is necessary to obtain repossession.

But many long-standing tenants still enjoyed the protection afforded by the Rent Act, 1977 – a 'fair rent' which eliminated the 'scarcity' element as determined by a Rent Officer or RAC, and security of tenure for both the original tenant and a first, or even a second successor, where a wife or child has been living as a member of the family for the previous six months or more.

However, although the Act did not take away any rights which the tenant enjoyed on 14 January 1989, it speeded up the disappearance of regulated tenancies by curtailing rights of succession: (i) the minimum qualification of residence for a member of the tenant's family to succeed was increased from six months to two years, and (ii) where the first successor was not the tenant's spouse, the second succession is abolished.

In practice, because a landlord could obtain repossession under an assured shorthold tenancy, its use predominated, and so the Housing Act 1996 made it the standard form of tenancy. It also gave more freedom to the market by removing the 1988 requirements of pre-tenancy notice and the minimum 6 months' letting term. The tenant can, however, demand a statement of the tenancy conditions.

Thus rent negotiations in the independent rented sector are now little different from those in any other market (see pp. 30–6). Even so rent control still lingers on with some residual protected tenants whose 'fair rent' is determined by a Rent Officer who, by Order, cannot award more than the increase in inflation (RPIX, p. 383) plus 7.5 per cent.

18.6 The impact of the change of policy on tenures

Taken together the above measures represent a radical departure from the housing policy pursued by governments over the past half-century. Even so it will take time to revive the private-rented sector, bring up to standard the 3 m. dwellings deemed to be unfit and provide for the special needs of the aged, disabled, homeless and mentally handicapped.

(1) The private rented sector

The introduction of housing benefit and the ending of rent control were designed to assist the private rented sector.

In the very short-term, the supply is fixed at OM (Figure 18.5) A housing benefit limited to PP_1 (ab) per unit is given to all qualifying tenants. Rent therefore rises to P_1, the market rent for all would-be tenants including those whose income is above the limit to qualify for housing benefit.

In the long term, supply can respond to the higher rent and a new equilibrium is established at a lower OR, but with more accommodation OM_2. The total subsidy now being paid equals $RN.OM_2$ of which $RP.OM_2$ represents the benefit received by landlords.

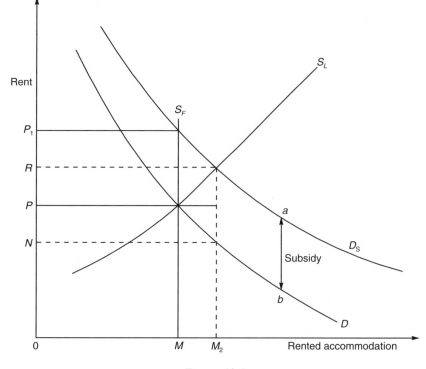

Figure 18.5

Two inducements to increase supply were also introduced by the government on the supply side. First, under the *Business Expansion Scheme (BES)* a taxpayer who bought new shares in a qualifying company could claim income tax relief on the amount invested and pay no capital gains tax on first disposal of the shares provided they had been held for 5 years. The company had to offer assured tenancies for a period of at least four years. Properties had to be unlet at the time of acquisition. With a maximum capital value of each dwelling of £85 000 (£125 000 Greater London) to avoid concentration on the 'yuppie' end of the market. Assured shorthold tenancies were excluded because the purpose was to encourage the long-term provision of rented property.

In its early years the BES scheme was highly successful. It was estimated that by the beginning of 1989 over £100 m. had been raised under BES assured tenancy schemes, often to purchase repossessed properties from building societies. But for the most part, investors were more interested in making a short-term tax-free capital gain rather than renting their properties long-term. Thus the scheme was brought to an end in December 1993.

Second, from 1992 an occupier who lets a furnished room(s) in his main residence can enjoy tax relief of up to £4250 a year.

With the property crash following closely upon the introduction of a market rent policy, such increase in private lettings that did occur was largely in response to special and short-lived circumstances, such as BES lettings, the purchase of 'sale-priced' dispossessions. But with the stabilisation of the housing market the PRS is expanding and has introduced a measure of flexibility in obtaining accommodation – but only for a limited income group (see pp. 351–2).

(2) The provision of affordable 'social housing'

(a) LOCAL AUTHORITY HOUSING

Mrs Thatcher's objective of 'rolling back the state' and subjecting the public sector to the disciplines of the market was evident in her approach to local authority (and new town) housing. And, to do her justice, many local authorities were urgently in need of an overhaul of their housing policies and administration.

Rents, often set by politically motivated councillors, were far below the economic cost of providing the accommodation even though they had had the benefit of a building subsidy. With the *average* weekly rent in 1979 of £6.48 many councils even failed to cover just the management and maintenance costs. As a result of neglect, an early 1980 estimate put the cost of repairing and renovating the public sector stock of housing at £19 bn.

For many authorities, too, efficient management of large property holdings was beyond the capabilities of local councillors. For instance, at any one time, total vacancies could be running at 100 000 units.

Many of these deficiencies stemmed from the fact that the subsidy was attached to the dwelling rather than the consumer. In 1975 the average tenant paid only just over 10 per cent of household income in rent. Many tenants who could afford an increase nearer to the economic cost were not required to do so.

Moreover the overall subsidy bill was proving embarrassing to government macroeconomic policy. The government response was two-pronged: (i) reducing local authority housing expenditure (both capital and revenue), and (ii) privatising public housing.

(i) *Reducing local authority housing expenditure.*   Even before 1979 it had been recognised that allowing local authorities to finance capital expenditure on housing by borrowing, subject only to government loan sanctions, was too lax. Hence in 1978 permissions were related to defined Housing Investment Programmes, and further tightened to reduce government expenditure overall. Thus, whereas prior to 1981–2, 100 per cent of local authority spending on housing was covered by borrowing, by 1989–90 it had been reduced to 22.8 per cent, the balance being found from their own capital receipts. Even spending the proceeds of sales to tenants was limited to 50 per cent in 1980, reduced to 20 per cent in 1985.

On the revenue side the main thrust was towards forcing up public sector rents. Target rent levels were raised progressively, and if these were not achieved, the housing subsidy was reduced. As a result the average weekly rent trebled from £6.48 in 1979 to £20.64 in 1989. When some local authorities sought to avoid increasing rents by transfers from their general rate fund, housing revenue accounts were 'ring-fenced'.

The net result was that gross rents of local authorities in England increased from £1242 m. in 1979 to £3089 m. in 1989, while their housing subsidy fell over the same period from £1323 m. to £240 m. It must be pointed out, however, that an increasing part of these higher rents was supported by housing benefits – a different form of subsidy. However the overall effect was to re-direct subsidised rents from tenants in general to those most in need.

Privatisation policy covers the transfer of financial, management, maintenance and risk responsibilities to the private sector, thereby enhancing the advantage of a right-to-buy sale.

(ii)   *The sale of Council and New Town dwellings.*   Although the Conservative government had in 1970 given a general consent to local authorities to sell their homes at a 20 per cent discount of the market value, there was only a moderate response, and even this dwindled after 1974 when Labour took over.

It was the Housing Act 1980 with its 'Right-to-Buy' (RTB) provision which succeeded in exciting tenants. Depending on the length of tenancy, discounts ranged between 33 and 50 per cent of market value. Sales rose sharply to a peak of 207 050 in 1982. Thereafter they fell back to 145 121 in 1990. Although buyers had the right to obtain a local authority mortgage, 60 per cent of purchasers were financed by building societies.

The 1991 recession and the subsequent slump in house prices caused sales to decline steeply (see pp. 348–9). Even so, by 1998 over 1.6 m of Great Britain's 6.5 m stock of public sector dwellings had been sold at an average price of £22 000, but £33 000 in Greater London.

In favour of the RTB policy it is argued that it:

(1) enabled tenants to fulfil their aspirations of becoming owner-occupiers and liberated them from perpetual dependence on council housing:
(2) resulted in risk and management and maintenance costs being transferred from the local authority to the new owner;
(3) reduced government subsidies by scaling down new council house-building; and
(4) helped in reducing the PSNCR through the privatisation proceeds (which in fact exceeded those of British Telecom).

But opponents argue that it:

(1) decreases the supply of housing available for letting to those most in need:

(2) reduces the range of council housing available since the better houses are those more likely to be sold;

(3) could lead to management and long-term development problems on a housing estate through the diversification of ownership and tenures.

With the object of improving the quality of management, privatisation also took the form of encouraging local authorities to transfer houses to housing associations, while tenants were given the right, providing a majority do not vote against it, to change landlords to a housing association or other approved persons. In fact there has been little take-up of this option.

It is unlikely that a future government would reverse what has proved to be a popular and successful policy. But, with enforced sales at a discount, there would seem little point in councils building further houses to rent, although marginal additions may be obtained at little cost via 'planning gain' (see pp. 412–14).

Nevertheless, with a current stock of nearly 5 m. dwellings local authorities still have an important role to play in providing a residual tenure for those in social need – clearing slums, accommodating the homeless, providing for special groups such as the aged and disabled (for example, through sheltered accommodation). More thought, too, can be given to improving the quality of management.

(b) HOUSING ASSOCIATION DWELLINGS

Now that councils are no longer building new houses, the government has fallen back on housing associations as the main, though still inadequate, source of low-cost rented dwellings – now referred to as 'social housing'.

Housing associations are private sector voluntary bodies set up to provide housing on a non-profit basis. Altogether in GB there are about 2000 registered associations owning over 1.45 m. dwellings (some 5 per cent of the total housing). Most are quite small, nearly one-half managing fewer than 25 houses; but there are some 75 which own over 2500 houses apiece.

The Housing Corporation (established in 1964) provides over half their capital, the government allocating it a yearly Housing Association Grant (HAG). The remaining finance is obtained from local authorities, building societies, banks, institutions (such as the Norwich Union) house-builders (such as Barretts) and even lenders through the euro-bond market. The Housing Corporation also monitors and audits the activities of housing associations registered with it.

Traditionally, the activities of housing associations complemented those of local authorities by providing accommodation in stress areas and for special groups, such as single people, the elderly and disabled people,

Table 18.3 Permanent dwellings started, 1988–2001, GB

| | Private sector | Housing associations | Public sector | | | | All dwellings |
			Local authorities	New towns	Government departments	Total	
1988	221737	14480	15368	553	449	16370	252587
1989	169940	5960	14036	680	456	15172	201072
1990	137000	18428	7778	720	113	8611	164039
1991	136947	22381	3832	134	261	4227	163555
1992	120261	33819	2151	395	131	2677	156757
1993	141188	41261	1663	429	70	2162	184611
1994	147331	36679	1869	113	3	1985	185995
1995	150202	38416	1445	674	5	2124	190742
1996	146676	31531	753	–	–	783	178990
1997	161576	25540	248	–	–	248	187364
1998	156433	21907	224	–	–	224	178564
1999	159668	20971	368	–	–	368	181007
2000	154136	19343	445	–	–	445	173924
2001	165207	16722	201	–	–	201	182130

Source: *Housing Statistics, Office of the Deputy Prime Minister.*

where obtaining mortgages for owner-occupation could prove difficult. For instance, dilapidated houses in the inner cities were acquired, converted into flats or hostel accommodation, and brought up to standard with the help of a renovation grant.

But now that local authorities no longer build new houses, the provision of socially affordable rented dwellings has been largely taken over by housing associations. Indeed some local authorities have handed over the residue of their housing estates to them. The government, considering that they offered more efficient and sensitive management, increased HAG support and relaxed restrictions on their borrowing. As a result they have been able to integrate with the greater lending power of building societies to expand their activities. Thus in addition to rented accommodation, housing associations now provide low-cost owner-occupied dwellings, often on a shared-equity basis, in co-operation with building societies who thereby still retain some of their 'social' tradition.

The original aim of the government was for housing associations to provide an extra 50 000 low-cost units a year at 'affordable' rents made possible through HAG finance. But this has been cut in line with other government spending. As a result rents have had to rise (now being based on the capital value of the dwelling). For the three-quarters of their tenants who qualify for housing benefit, this is not too serious but for others the 'affordable rent' objective has been undermined. Nevertheless, provided they can continue to attract private capital, housing associations are still the most likely providers of long-term (as opposed to shorthold) *rented* accommodation on an assured tenancy basis.

(3) The owner-occupied sector

(a) ITS GROWTH

Owner-occupiers were the main beneficiaries of Thatcher's policy and the sector has expanded from 56 per cent in 1980 to 69 per cent in 2001, with UK numbers rising from 12 m. to 16.7 m. over the same period. The main contributory factors were: (a) the 1.5 m. former local authority and new town tenants who had exercised their right-to-buy; (b) tax concessions; (c) the rapid growth in the economy and in personal income during the mid-1980s; (d) an increase in the availability of mortgages.

The policy of relating subsidies to need was *not* applied to owner-occupation. Indeed in 1983 the ceiling for mortgage interest relief was raised from £25 000 to £30 000, and not until 1991 was it limited to the standard rate of income tax and subsequently reduced in stages until its abolition in 2000. There was no discrimination in favour of the small, first-time buyer even though he was more likely to be on a low income. The freedom from capital gains tax, which also remained, had some justification, since the owner also took the risk of a loss.

(b) SOURCES OF LOANS

The growth of the economy and of personal incomes coincided with the freeing of financial markets which released funds for house purchase. There are two main mortgage sources, (i) banks, (ii) building societies.

(i) *Banks*   Table 18.2 shows the advance of the *banks* since 1985 as lenders for house purchase. Factors contributing to this are:

(a) The greater sophistication shown by depositors in investing their funds encouraged banks to compete by offering savings accounts with a high rate of interest;

(b) The emphasis from 1981 onwards of controlling credit through the rate of interest permitted an upsurge in the banks' deposits. One outlet for funds was loans for house purchase

(c) The building societies were slow in changing their rather rigid financial requirements in granting mortgages. In contrast, the banks competed through the terms offered, especially at the higher end of the market, for example, by a uniform rate irrespective of the size of the loan.

(d) Banks recognise that borrowers through a low-start mortgage may eventually use other customer services.

Today it is not only the commercial banks which have realised that home-buyers are good business. Merchant banks, foreign banks (e.g. America's Citibank), and a new National Home Loans Corporation have all increased competition by entering the market.

(ii) *Building societies*   Such competition forced the *building societies* to realise that they would have to compete by marketing mortgages – for example, by advertising and offering low-start mortgages. They also had to compete more fiercely with the government, banks, insurance companies, unit trusts, and so on for depositors' funds. Moreover, depositors today are more aware of alternative investment opportunities and are more ready to switch their funds even for short periods if this appears to be advantageous. This was noticeable in the privatisation issues when subscribers drew heavily on their deposits. Again, with no capital gains tax on gains of under £7 700 (2002), investments in equities are more attractive for the small investor. In order to compete, societies introduced bonus rates to attract longer-term loans, issued cheque books to substantial depositors, and so on.

But it was the Building Societies Act 1986 which transformed the building societies from a 'movement' pursuing social goals to an 'industry' with sights set on financial targets. Until then their response to the new competition from the banks had been restrained by legal restrictions imposed in recognition of their mutual status and their exclusion from the normal supervision of financial institutions. The Act extended the powers of the building societies, enabling them to: develop an integrated house purchase service covering, for example, estate agency, surveying, insurance and conveyancing; offer new types of loan, such as first-step index-linked, equity-linked and shared-ownership mortgages; own subsidiary companies and land; participate directly in the provision of housing by owning and developing land; provide a full range of personal banking services and, usually through specialist firms, advise on life insurance, pensions, unit trusts, stocks and shares, inheritance tax and school fees; borrow on the wholesale money markets; make unsecured loans up to £10 000 to individuals and, from 1993, acquire assets other than residential mortgages and conduct business other than mortgages up to 25 per cent and 15 per cent respectively of their total assets.

Borrowing on the wholesale markets enabled the societies to obtain additional funds and to even-out fluctuations in the flow of retail savings which now occur more frequently as the popularity of unit trusts and ISAS ebbs and flows.

This wide extension of the functions of building societies has involved considerable capital expenditure in new technology so that only societies which are powerful financially or which have a strong local connection can survive. The Abbey National and Halifax for example, now operate as banks, the Cheltenham & Gloucester has been taken over by Lloyds TSB, and the Nationwide and the Anglia have amalgamated.

One question that has to be asked is: what directions will building societies take once the owner-occupied sector of the housing market becomes saturated? There are a number of possibilities, for example:

(a) forming their own subsidiary companies to provide social housing for first-time purchasers, sheltered housing for the elderly and in conjunction with housing associations, affordable rented accommodation;
(b) extending their traditional skill in obtaining retail funds to provide residential mortgages in the wider EU, where the proportion of owner-occupation is on average less than half that in the UK; and
(c) providing finance to the commercial and industrial property markets.

18.7 The weaknesses of Conservative housing strategy 1979–89

The Conservative government's housing policy was based on the long-term improvements which would be effected by market forces. But it glossed over the immediate problems: homelessness; the 3 m. dwellings unfit or in a state of serious disrepair; the special needs of the aged, and the physically and mentally disabled. Although local authorities were saddled with these responsibilities, and in 1990 were free to specify *housing renewal areas* and given power to acquire land and effect improvements, they were not provided with adequate funds.

Instead the Thatcher government supported the flagship of its housing policy – owner-occupation – with mortgage interest relief at an annual cost to the Exchequer of £6 bn, and this grew with increased owner-occupation and eventual rises in the rate of interest. Phasing out this subsidy would have allowed funds to be switched to the housing needs of the poorer sections of the community and to the provision of affordable rented accommodation through housing associations.

Nor was it appreciated that a housing policy based on housing benefits, the provision of rented accommodation by housing associations, and owner-occupation can only be followed within the framework of overall monetary policy. When this failed, the flagship was blown seriously off course, as follows.

18.8 Housing and inflation

The causes of house-price inflation 1987–9

Price is determined by the interaction of demand and supply. But, as we saw in Chapter 4, because the supply of houses is inelastic, their price is largely demand-determined. We have therefore to examine the factors leading to increased demand in order to explain why, by the end of 1988, the annual rate of house-price inflation was as high as 33 per cent nationally, and in some regions even 50 per cent. The following all played a part.

(1) After the restrictive anti-inflation policies of the early 1980s, the Thatcher government took the reins off the market economy, and the GNP grew at an annual rate of 4 per cent. People, especially young executives, had more spending power, and much of this found its way into the housing market.

(2) The cost of borrowing for a mortgage fell progressively as the Chancellor reduced base rate in stages from 14 per cent in January 1985 to 7 per cent in May 1988.

(3) After 1985 credit control was relaxed, more significantly with 'Big Bang' in 1986. Competition between the main lending institutions – building societies, banks and foreign banks – led to easier mortgage terms, even the building societies throwing aside their traditional caution regarding a safe loan-earnings ratio. Borrowing of 95 per cent, and even 100 per cent, of the price of a property became possible.

(4) The effect of easier credit was reinforced by the 1988 Budget, which reduced the standard rate of income tax from 27 to 25 per cent, and the higher rate from 60 to 40 per cent.

(5) The 1988 Budget announced that, as from 1 August, *multiple* mortgage tax relief (enjoyed by each mortgagee of a joint house purchase) would be abolished. This created a stampede for mortgage funds to beat the deadline, particularly from first-time buyers. House prices rose, initially at the lower end of the market, but eventually having a ripple effect upwards.

(6) Details of the proposed replacement of the rates by the poll tax increased demand for higher-priced houses, since with these the new tax was usually less than the rates, especially where households did not exceed two adults.

(7) Mrs Thatcher's policies of a 'property-owning democracy' and the 'right-to-buy' added thrust to the desire for house ownership as the only alternative to the shrinking rented sector.

(8) A long-term factor – the increasing flow of inherited wealth resulting from the past growth in home ownership by the present 65+ years group – began to make itself felt. This was estimated to have amounted to £8 bn in 1988.

(9) Expectations of a continued rise in house prices often led to spending on a house being regarded as an excellent investment asset which could be obtained by borrowing against a small deposit. That is, houses were demanded by owner-occupiers for 'investing' in addition to 'nesting' (see also p. 381).

18.9 The housing market 1989–99

From boom to bust

In retrospect, the government was too late in recognising the latent inflationary pressures. The easier credit of 1986–8 and the cut in income tax took place just when monetary policy should have been tightened. Aggregate demand was already more than sufficient to sustain the level of growth that could be achieved without causing an uncomfortable pressure on prices. In June 1988 the government had to raise base rate by 1 per cent to 8 per cent. However, as rising prices had gathered their own momentum, further successive increases in base rate brought it up by October 1989 to 15 per cent (see p. 133).

The recession which followed had a traumatic effect on the housing market. By 1991 unemployment had risen to $2\frac{1}{4}$ m. and was continuing to rise. Mortgage rates rose in sympathy with base rate. Not only could potential new owner-occupiers not afford to buy, but recent buyers found that interest payments could not be covered as earnings fell, perhaps through redundancy.

By 1992 over 290 000 households were over six months in arrears with their mortgage payments. Repossessions followed: there were 75 000 in 1991, and though they gradually fell, there were still 34 000 in 1998. The government's 1992 response of making £750 m. available to housing associations to buy 20 000 houses was hardly significant in view of an estimated 200 000 forced vacancies. Repossessions also severely aggravated the problem to local authorities of homelessness, which for Great Britain rose from 70 000 in 1979 to over 178 000 in 1991.

From their peak in the third quarter of 1989, house prices fell by 14 per cent in two years, and continued to fall, averaging 17 per cent by 1994 (Nationwide House Price Index) by as much as 30 per cent in London and the south of England. Thus an estimated 15 m. buyers (70 per cent of whom were first-time), who entered the market in 1987–9 when prices were high, were locked into a situation of *negative equity* (estimated in 1995 at £7.5 bn), where the proceeds of a sale are insufficient to pay off the mortgage debt.

The gloom was prolonged by the shock of the recession on consumer confidence. One incentive to spend was eliminated by the virtual ending of price inflation. But far worse was the uncertainty regarding job security, as competition forced firms to streamline their operations and cut back on production. Potential new buyers were reluctant to take on a mortgage, as is shown by the fact that the house-price/earnings ratio fell from 4.56 in 1988 to 2.81 in 1994.

Post-1995 recovery

The fall in house prices bottomed out in late 1993, but not until 1995 did they start to recover, at first hesitantly, but accelerating between 1996–7, especially in London and the south-east.

The rate of price increase slowed in 1998, reflecting concern of a possible downturn in the economy following the financial crises in S. E. Asia, but by early 1999 prices had improved sufficiently to remove the over-hang of negative equity. Returning confidence, lower mortgage rates following the fall in base rate to 5 per cent, and a shortage of houses coming on to the market brought about an acceleration in price increases so that in the UK as a whole they increased by 25 per cent 1993–9 and in south-east England by over 33 per cent. In 2002 alone house prices rose by more than 22 per cent in England and Wales. The average house price in early 2003 was £145 251 and in Greater London it was £241 838.

It must now be hoped too that future governments will heed the extent to which movements in the housing market are linked to those of the overall economy, and vice versa. Although the housing market cannot be held responsible for the general inflation which forced the government to take disinflationary measures in 1988, it did play a major part. Early on, it had shown itself sensitive to important changes in demand, and the government should have acted sooner once the price signals flashed up.

Nor can the lending institutions, too, be absolved from a large part of the blame, for their lending was imprudent, to say the least. It should not be necessary, for instance, for an individual building society to have to make provision in its annual accounts of over £100 m. against bad debts.

18.10 The future provision of housing

Policy for future housing is concerned with two main issues: (a) expanding the existing stock, and (b) providing the type of dwelling preferred by different households within their income constraint. Each will be examined in turn.

Expanding the existing stock

Projections of future housing requirements are based mainly on underlying demographic factors and trends in household formation. These indicate that between 1996 and 2021 England will need an extra 3.8 m. dwellings.

Allowing for the demolition of old houses, this will require a yearly building rate of 175 000, well within the capacity of the house-building industry, provided planning consents are forthcoming. The main problem is determining where these extra dwellings shall be built – on 'greenfield' or 'brownfield' sites? The decision has to support the current ODPM environmental objectives of preserving the countryside and reducing car journeys in favour of public transport.

The volume house-builders in particular prefer large developments on new greenfield sites, mostly agricultural land, where they can achieve economies of scale and are untroubled by the possibility of contamination, as can occur with brownfield sites. On the other hand, the ODPM wants to preserve the countryside through 'sustainable' development and to replace car journeys by increased use of public transport in order to reduce atmospheric pollution.

However, its National Land Use Database (NLUD) shows that there are insufficient brownfield sites to accommodate all the houses required. Actual policy, therefore, is a compromise of: (a) a target of 60:40 brownfield to greenfield sites; (b) a sequential test introduced by a 1999 draft PPG3 (housing) whereby local planning authorities are required to consider using previously developed land and buildings before releasing greenfield sites.

Since the ODPM has set its face against additional new towns, implementing the above guidelines will involve a staged piecemeal approach in finding the required sites. Suggestions include:

(a) increasing building intensity on urban residential land;
(b) considering a change in use from industrial to residential where possible

(c) developing urban fringes by creating new village communities of around 1000 dwellings, similar to Prince Charles's prototype of Poundbury on the edge of Dorchester;

(d) expanding towns on main transport routes;

(e) infilling, with limited extension, of existing rural villages even in the face of 'not in my backyard' (NIMBY) opposition.

Above all, immediate consideration should be given to the possibility of reducing the 3.8 m. requirement by better management of public sector dwellings – local authority, defence, national health – where there is a running vacancy rate of approximately 2 per cent.

Providing for housing preferences

The 1989–92 crisis in the owner-occupied housing sector diverted attention from the radical change in Mrs Thatcher's approach to solving the persistent housing problem. Her objectives – self-provision of housing through owner-occupation, resuscitation of the private rented sector (PRS) and improved efficiency in the management of social sector housing – were to be secured through the mechanism of the market. With the emergence by 1995 of a more stable market, it is now possible to assess what the policy has achieved and to suggest how it could develop in the future.

Certain new factors would appear likely to put a brake on owner-occupation: a more cautious approach as a result of the early 1990s shake-out; less permanent job security; the ending in 2000 of MIRAS; a low rate of inflation; and the option of now being able to obtain rented accommodation in an expanding PRS.

In the event, the demand of owner-occupiers for housing has proved healthy. Mortgage rates are now lower than at any time during the previous 40 years. For a time in 2002 the market appeared to be overheating (prices rose by 22 per cent), but the general economic slowdown appears to have stabilised the market to some extent. Nevertheless, house prices are expected to rise by 10 per cent in Great Britain in 2003.

There had always been a *PRS* for prime residential properties in London's West End, where their high rateable values freed them from rent control. Indeed research by Savills shows that 37 per cent of such properties are owned and rented as investments on a 8.5–11 per cent yield. Developers such as Regalian and London and Henley have concentrated on building luxury flats – an object lesson of how the market works – and Charterhouse Bank and Schroders have launched residential investment funds to provide capital.

But it is the application of the market mechanism to property in a much lower value bracket which has brought about a transformation in the PRS. Prior to Mrs Thatcher, attempts by Conservative governments to undo the

Rent Acts were repeatedly reversed as the swing of the political pendulum returned Labour to power. But now that New Labour has accepted the legislation which it inherited from the Conservatives, there is added confidence in the letting market.

Although there are no accurate figures for this new PRS, evidence of its expansion abounds. The London *Evening Standard* now has a whole supplement advertising dwellings to let, and this is repeated in other local newspapers. These are mainly short-term of 1+ bedroom houses and flats by people going abroad, but predominantly by individual investors. Rents at £600+ per calender month can yield a retirement income superior to that on an annuity closely related to low-yielding gilt-edged bonds.

Moreover, banks and building societies now flush with funds, provide buy-to-rent mortgages at 6.5 per cent. The snag is that should the mortgage rate rise, the margin available for servicing repayments may be tight, especially if inexperienced renters make an insufficient allowance to cover the costs of management, maintenance, vacancy voids and rent defaults. The position would be similar should an increase in the supply of lettings bring about a fall in rents. Already there is evidence that in this market rents are falling, possibly allowing people on a lower income to filter up.

But there is an important reservation regarding this new PRS – the rents charged mean that it is confined to trainee executives, etc. who by sharing must have a combined yearly income of £40 000 just to conform to the 25 per cent of income norm reckoned to be reasonable for spending on accommodation (rent and council tax). Renting also meets their preference for mobility.

Traditionally, for long-term housing, the low-income families fell back on council and housing association dwellings. But as we saw earlier (p. 314), Mrs Thatcher withdrew building subsidies from councils, leaving only housing associations to provide affordable rented housing. Councils, in order to balance their housing accounts, had to charge appropriate rents. The subsidy was now afforded to tenants by way of housing benefit according to their ability to pay.

The housing benefit subsidy also applied to low-income families who rented in the private sector but, unless their dwellings were 'protected' on 15 January 1989 when the 1988 Housing Act came into force, they had in practice to fall back on assured shortholds with no real long-term security.

But subsidising rents by way of housing benefits has afforded no incentive for poorer tenants to negotiate with landlords. As a result it has exacted a heavy toll in terms of government expenditure, amounting in 2001 to £11.16 bn, (to which must be added £2.57 bn. council tax benefit), and thereby contributing to the burgeoning dependency culture.

Councils still own 5 m. dwellings but have ceased to add to the stock. Their role must therefore be seen as providing for the disadvantaged in the community – the aged, those requiring sheltered accommodation, those with special needs, for example, for physical or mental disability, homeless families and young persons sleeping rough.

Improvement of housing conditions within the urban regeneration programme

The seventy years of rent control has left what remains of the stock of rented dwellings in a poor state of repair, and this in spite of the marginal improvements which have been gradually effected through renovation grants (see p. 296). In 1996 in England, 15 per cent of privately-rented dwellings and 7 per cent of local authority were 'unfit' in that they failed one or more of the nine required conditions. Of these, some 200 000 still lacked one of the basic amenities. In the private-rented sector, the principal exception is the houses and flats at the expensive top end of the market where high rateable values put them outside the Rent Acts.

Council dwellings also reflect unsatisfactory conditions, with the main exception being those of rural authorities. In many urban areas political dogma led to Councils setting low rents, while the high-rise blocks of flats, built to use land more intensively, were generally disliked by tenants. Many dwellings deteriorated, partly through tenants' lack of pride, but mostly through management incompetence which included neglect of maintenance by prompt repairs.

By allowing rents to rise to their market level, Thatcher housing policy made it possible to cover the cost of repairs out of gross income, While this has occurred in the newly-expanded rented sector, there has been little response at the bottom end. The general run-down appearance of a residential district deters a landlord from investing when there is a strong possibility of wholesale demolition in the not too-distant future. In any case there could be uncertainty as to whether other landlords would carry out improvements – the 'prisoner's dilemma' (p. 192). As a result, whole pockets of very poor or even slum housing exist, especially in depressed areas.

Regional policy realised, therefore, that, in order to attract the new type of firm to a region, the offer of a subsidised factory was an insufficient inducement. Physical regeneration had to include the provision of a modern infrastructure, and to be extended to social objectives such as rebuilding communities taking a pride in their environment.

As a result urban regeneration, and thus the standards of housing, became part of regional policy (Chapter 19).

Summary

Housing supply is essentially the stock of existing houses which is added to by less than one per cent per annum. This makes the market very demand determined. Free markets in housing are efficient and lead to availability and choice of accommodation. In addition supply responds in a variety of ways to rises in rents, e.g. conversion of large houses into flats.

Governments have persistently interfered in housing markets since 1900 because:

- inequalities in income mean that some people cannot afford adequate housing
- there are external costs of poor housing
- families may not purchase the amount or quality of housing which society thinks is desirable (housing is a merit good)
- public intervention may be necessary to speed up the response of supply to an increase in demand

Government intervention in the form of rent control has occurred since 1915. It contravenes several economic principles and has led to short-term and long-term problems in housing markets and has contributed to changes in the tenure distribution of UK housing.

The owner-occupied sector of the housing market has expanded from 10 per cent in 1910 to 69 per cent in 2003. There are a number of reasons for this, including the greater availability of finance through building societies and banks, favourable government policy towards home ownership and the general increase in affluence of the population.

Review questions

1. Why is housing supply very inelastic?
2. Is there any economic justification for government interference in housing markets?
3. Explain the economic arguments against rent control.
4. Describe the changes in UK household tenure distribution since 1900 and give reasons for the main changes.
5. Why have house prices in the UK risen strongly in the period 1993–2003?

Recommended reading

J. F. Andrews and D. W. Williams, *Assured Tenancies*, 2nd edn (London: *Estates Gazette*, 1998).

P. N. Balchin, J. L. Kieve and G. H. Bull, *Urban Land Economics and Public Policy*, 5th edn (London: Macmillan, 1995) ch. 9.

K. Gibb and M. Munro, *Housing Finance in the 1990s* (London: Macmillan, 1991).

P. Malpass and A. Murie, *Housing Policy and Practice*, 4th edn (London: Macmillan, 1994).

J. E. Manser, *Economics: A Foundation Course for the Built Environment* (London, E&FN Spon, 1994).

D. Myers, *Economics and Property: A Coursebook for Students of the Built Environment* (London: Estates Gazette, 1994).

White Paper, *Housing: The Government's Proposals*, Cmnd 214 (HMSO, 1987).

C. Whitehead and M. Kleinman, *Private Renting in the 1980s and 1990s* (Cambridge: Granta, 1987).

CHAPTER 19

Regional Policy

After studying this chapter you will be able to:

- **Explain the nature of the UK regional problem**
- **Describe the adverse economic effects of regional depression**
- **Explain the nature of UK government regional policy**
- **Describe European Union regional policy**

19.1 The regional problem

The nature of the regional problem

The regional problem can take many forms but we can distinguish three major types.

(1) A PARTICULAR REGION MAY SIMPLY HAVE POOR NATURAL RESOURCES
An example is the Highlands of Scotland. More generally, with the growth of national income, an agricultural region which does not attract expanding industries – for example, Cornwall and Devon – cannot provide its population with living standards comparable with those of the rest of the country. As a result, either any increased labour productivity is secured solely by emigration, or income per head simply remains below the level achieved in the rest of the country.

With this type of imbalance, the region may be too remote to introduce new industries. Thus any improvement may have to depend largely upon a rise in income elsewhere, provided the region is attractive to tourists – for example, North Wales, the Lake District.

(2) THE RESOURCES OF THE REGION MAY NOT BE FULLY DEVELOPED, USUALLY
THROUGH LACK OF CAPITAL
This applies particularly to the less-developed countries. Here the more
immediate solution is for capital to be provided on favourable terms by
richer regions.

In the long term an improvement in the imbalance may depend mainly on
rising incomes elsewhere. Exploitation of the area's resources may now
become economically viable. For example, prosperity came to Aberdeen
and the Shetlands only when the rise in the price of oil and the development
of modern technology made extraction of North Sea oil an economic proposition.

(3) A REGION'S BASIC INDUSTRY IS EITHER STAGNANT OR IN DECLINE
Such a region is usually characterised by: a rising rate of unemployment;
a level of income which is falling relatively to other regions; a low
activity rate, particularly of female workers; a high rate of outward migration; and an inadequate infrastructure. It is thus this type of regional imbalance which creates the problem for *national* governments; indeed the
depressed regions are normally identified by their unemployment rates
(Table 19.1).

In contrast, other regions may be expanding so rapidly that their further
development results in congestion, inadequate social capital and inflationary
pressures. Yet the problems of both are linked, and policies must take
account of this.

Table 19.1   *Percentage rate of unemployment by Government Office Region*

	April 1993	*April 1996*	*May 1999*	*April 2002*
United Kingdom	10.4	7.6	4.5	5.2
Region:				
North East	12.9	10.9	7.5	6.9
North West	12.7	7.0	4.2	5.5
Yorkshire and Humber	10.4	8.2	5.2	5.4
East Midlands	9.7	7.1	3.9	4.2
West Midlands	11.1	7.5	4.8	5.5
Eastern	9.6	6.2	3.1	3.5
London	11.7	8.9	4.9	6.6
South East	8.9	5.3	2.5	4.0
South West	9.7	6.4	3.3	3.6
Wales	10.3	8.3	5.4	6.1
Scotland	9.8	7.9	5.5	6.8
N. Ireland	13.8	11.2	7.0	5.6

Source: *Labour Force Survey, Office for National Statistics.*

Economic theory and the regional problem

Economic theory can contribute to a solution of the regional problem by dealing with four main questions.

(a) How does the individual firm decide its location?
(b) What factors determine how economic activity is spread over the available geographical space?
(c) What factors cause some regions to flourish while others decline?
(d) What policies are most effective in helping depressed regions?

Of these (a) is concerned with location theory (see Chapter 15); (b) and (c) are examined because the factors determining location lie at the root of regional imbalance; and as regards (d), policies are analysed in the light of our answers to (a), (b) and (c).

19.2 The location of industry in its regional context

Introduction

There is no generally accepted *single* theory of how the location of industry is determined. Much of the existing distribution of industry in the UK reflects a growth from the past, and the influence of historical inertia must never be overlooked. Even so it is possible to treat systematically the major factors influencing location.

At the outset it must be pointed out that the policy objective of a firm may affect its location. The firm can be motivated by the following.

(a) *Minimising costs.* Here the firm trades off distance from raw materials against distance from markets, costs of labour, and so on. Agglomeration economies and diseconomies are also taken into account.
(b) *Maximising revenues.* This objective starts from the assumption that location determines revenue rather than costs. Given the spatial distribution of the market, location will be influenced by the location of competitive firms, in that they may either repel a new firm from a particular district or, because of agglomeration economies, attract it.
(c) *Maximising profit.* The least-cost location only yields maximum profit if the total revenue of the firm does not vary with location. This applies to French firms who, making use of accessibility via the Channel tunnel, rent offices in Ashford, Kent where rates and welfare takes on labour are both lower than in France. Similarly, the maximum revenue location objective is only profit-maximising if costs do not change with location. The profit-maximising motive integrates (a) and (b), and is that upon which the location decision is discussed below.

(d) *Satisficing.* 'Satisficing' behaviour rests on the assumption that firms seek to achieve minimum rather than maximum objectives. Such an objective has more credibility where large firms are run by professional managers who, while seeking to satisfy share-holders with an adequate return, also follow their own objectives, such as power, promotion of their own department, personal preferences. Thus the location of some firms has been determined by the managing director (or even his wife) emphasising recreational facilities (such as sailing) or a congenial social life.

The importance of transport costs

Before the Industrial Revolution, such industry as the country possessed was widely dispersed throughout the country. With the growth of technology and transport, a twofold development occurred: the scale and scope of industry began to expand and a process of selection took place whereby certain industries tended to concentrate in those areas offering them the greatest net advantage.

(1) WEIGHT-LOSING INDUSTRIES
Industries whose raw materials lose weight in the course of production – for example, iron and steel – tend to locate at the source of their raw materials or where those raw materials as a whole are most accessible. Thus with the Industrial Revolution heavy industries in particular were pulled to the coal-fields, but later moved to coastal districts where iron ore (and eventually coal) could be imported.

(2) WEIGHT-GAINING INDUSTRIES
Weight-gaining industries, such as, beer, or those whose finished product is *bulky, fragile* or otherwise *difficult to transport* such as furniture, glass or bread, tend to locate near the market. Such industries, therefore, are fairly dispersed, especially where their raw materials are available in most places (water, gravel, sand and clay).

(3) 'FOOTLOOSE' INDUSTRIES
With many industries, their raw materials lose little weight in production and the cost of distributing the product is only a small proportion of total costs: an example is electrical components. They are thus indifferent as to whether they are located near their factors of production or their markets.

Generally speaking, where there are several markets to be supplied and where there are significant economies to be obtained from large-scale production, firms tend to concentrate production near the largest market and to supply the lesser markets from there. Other things being equal, therefore, the larger the market, the stronger will be the pull of the market on location. Improvements in transport facilities have, in many cases, strengthened such tendencies. Thus road transport has given a greater degree of flexibility to choice of site. Similarly the development of more 'fluid' sources of power (oil and electricity) has freed most producers from direct dependence on coal, enabling them to take full advantage of the market factor.

Other factor-costs affecting location

Manpower may sometimes be a deciding factor in influencing location. This is likely to be so where the firm is cheap-labour intensive or where there is a supply of labour being trained to the firm's requirements.

Indeed, a similar situation may exist with regard to capital, certain firms finding it preferable to locate in London, for instance, because knowledge of possible sources of finance is more perfect there than elsewhere.

Acquired advantages: agglomeration economies

Although the natural advantages may be the initial magnet, once an industry has become established 'man-made' advantages tend to foster further growth in the area, sometimes long after the original advantages have disappeared. Such acquired advantages include: improved transport facilities; the development of subsidiary industries; a pool of skilled labour; the establishment of technical schools geared to local industries; and a worldwide reputation for the area's products.

As an area grows, it also becomes an ever-increasing market for consumer products and thus attracts that type of industry for which market density is important. Consumer services and facilities expand, increasing the area's attractiveness for labour. Moreover, where heavy industry is the main activity, light industries may be attracted by the availability of female labour. Such developments are important for the stability of the area.

Revenue considerations

Location has so far been analysed in terms of minimising costs. But it may also affect earning-capacity, for instance, revenue. This is most notable in the case of shops, but it can apply to other forms of business, such as services. Thus a profit-maximising firm will locate where the difference between total revenue and total costs is a maximum for its anticipated level of output.

Relative advantages and location

Though access to raw materials, labour and markets draws production to certain areas, it is important to realise that the actual selection process takes place in terms of relative, rather than absolute, advantages. Those industries for which an area affords the greatest attraction in terms of profitability will, by offering higher rents, be able to bid sites away from other industries for which the area is not so profitable (see Chapter 18). In other words, selection proceeds on two levels. On the one hand, industries compete with one another for districts; on the other, districts compete with other districts for an industry. The result is that because firms in the same industry are each seeking similar locational advantages, they tend to settle in the same districts, for example, cotton in south-east Lancashire, financial services in the City of London and Canary Wharf (London Docklands).

Location: design or accident?

With many firms, the location chosen has depended mainly on the entrepreneur's individual preferences. Thus cigarettes in Nottingham, chocolates in York, automobiles in Oxford, can all be explained largely by the fact that the founders of these businesses were either born or settled there – coupled perhaps with the adequate local services which existed in those places. Often, however, such firms prospered because the location happened to be quite suitable, added to the fact that over time the man-made advantages may offset any disadvantages of the original location.

Historical background to the regional problem

Up to the First World War, the prosperity of the UK depended largely upon a handful of important industries – coal, cotton, wool, iron and steel, shipbuilding and engineering – which, for the reasons stated, had come to be located predominantly in certain areas. The main areas were, briefly, South Lancashire (coal and cotton), South Wales (coal, steel and heavy engineering), the north-east coast (coal, iron and steel and shipbuilding), the West Riding of Yorkshire (coal, steel and wool), the West Midlands (engineering), and the north-west coast (coal, iron and steel) and south-west Scotland (coal, shipbuilding).

The important feature of this geographical division is that, with the exception of the West Midlands, each of these areas was dependent on a narrow group of basic industries producing either capital goods or providing materials for capital goods industries. Moreover, most of their industries were heavily dependent on overseas demand, and this declined considerably after 1913.

In contrast, the London and Midland regions had industries which were expanding, for example, electrical and light engineering. Even during the depression of the 1930s, therefore, these regions remained relatively prosperous. Such prosperity attracted new firms which in their turn helped to maintain the prosperity of the region.

Why were these expanding industries not attracted to the 'depressed' areas? Some of the reasons have already been indicated: the development of 'fluid' power sources which reduced the pull of the coalfields, and the development of road transport which weakened the pull of the existing railway centres. In addition, many of the newer, expanding industries, being footloose, were pulled to the home consumption market. Thus processed food, radio and electrical equipment and consumer durables of many kinds tended to concentrate in or near the largest home market, London.

Even so, since economic circumstances change, the 'regional problem' is never static. Thus as overseas competition brought about a progressive decline of the UK's manufacturing base, previously prosperous areas producing electrical and light engineering goods, notably the West Midlands, suffered job losses. Nor were these made good by the expanding service industries. Indeed, in the 1989–93 recession, these were the very industries hardest hit, so that, by July 1993, the West Midlands had an unemployment rate of 11.0 per cent.

19.3 Theories and models of regional growth

In order to formulate an effective policy, the causes of the growth and decline of industries and regions must be examined. As with the growth of urban areas (Chapter 16.1), no single theory gives a complete explanation but each contributes to an understanding of the problem.

(1) The classical model

This model considers that industries, like trees in the forest, grow, decline and eventually rot away. But there will always be new industries to which the resources of the decaying industries can transfer. Given full employment, perfect competition in both product and factor markets, perfect knowledge, complete mobility of factors of production, perfectly flexible prices and wage-rates and constant returns to scale, the problem of regional decay can be solved through the market. Should disequilibrium arise in a particular region, for example, through unemployment in some industries resulting from a change in tastes, there will be a fall in wage rates in that region and thus an increase in the return to capital. Hence regional imbalance will be removed automatically by the migration of labour from low-wage to high-wage regions and the migration of firms (that is, capital) in the opposite direction.

The attraction of this model is that the imbalance is corrected by the free play of market forces without government intervention. But it has fundamental weaknesses.

(a) In practice, factor markets adjust much less perfectly than the theory implies. Labour is immobile both geographically and occupationally, and highly resistant to a lowering of wage-rates. Moreover, *national* wage-bargaining weakens the response of the price signals to regional imbalance. Finally, the information available to factor markets is often imperfect. Thus capital markets tend to be centralised in the more prosperous regions of a particular country. If such markets operate with a bias against or with imperfect knowledge of investment opportunities in the peripheral regions, there may well be no injection of investment to cover savings in these regions.
(b) The assumption of constant returns to scale may not hold. Manufacturing in particular is characterised by increasing returns to scale over the relevant output range so that high-wage regions may also generate high returns to capital. Thus firms, like labour, may migrate to the prosperous, high-wage regions. Indeed, as communications improve these regions may gain from the progressive opening up of trade at the expense of the decaying regions. In such circumstances, therefore, market forces do not restore equilibrium. Thus the south-east region of England has benefited from its close connections with the EU.

Eventually external diseconomies – for example, increased congestion and pressure on the infrastructure – halt further growth. Indeed, these may be 'internalised', for example, by firms offering less for sites where congestion increases costs. Even, so firms may not go to depressed areas but simply decentralise activity within the high-growth regions.

Should movement be entirely outwards, the model has additional weaknesses.

(c) It ignores the external costs to society of (i) the loss of social capital and the disintegration of communities in the depressed regions, and (ii) the congestion and inflationary pressures generated in the expanding areas (see below).
(d) Those workers who do move from the depressed regions are mainly the better educated, most highly skilled and more enterprising young adults. As such they are often the leaders of the community. The result is that the region becomes still further depressed and thus unattractive to new industries.
(e) The model follows a purely partial equilibrium approach. It ignores the fact that migration from the depressed regions leads to a loss of income there. The multiplier effect of reduced consumer spending and investment serves to depress the area still further.

It should be noted that even if, as the theory predicts, economic efficiency could be secured through market forces, government action may still be needed on the grounds of equity. The model only predicts that inter-regional differences in factor payments and employment *within a particular industry* will be automatically removed. Per capita *regional incomes* may not be equalised, simply because differences in resource endowments and industrial structure may give some regions high-wage sectors and others low-wage sectors.

(2) The economic base or export base theory

This theory, described in Chapter 16, can be applied similarly to a whole region, though here we are concerned mainly with total employment and only indirectly with total population. Again we distinguish between 'basic' industries (whose outputs are primarily sold outside the region) and 'non-basic' industries (whose outputs are sold within the region). An estimate is made of the number of non-basic jobs supported by each basic job. Demand for the outputs of basic industries will determine non-basic employment, the size of the multiplier depending upon the observed stable relationship which exists between the two types of industry.

But, as explained in Chapter 16, the theory has certain weaknesses. In particular, by concentrating on the growth of basic industries as the dominant cause of regional economic growth, it ignores the magnitude of the flows of goods and services within the region. For example, investment in non-basic industries will affect the regional economy. In the input-output analysis and the Keynesian theory allowance is made for such flows.

(3) Input-output analysis

The input-output approach described in Chapter 16 can be applied to a particular region. It would still, however, face the same practical difficulties as those indicated when the growth of towns was discussed.

(4) The Keynesian model

The Keynesian theory of the determination of the level of income and thus of employment in the national economy can be applied to the regional economy. The approach is similar to that used in Chapter 16 to explain the growth of towns (Figure 16.1, p. 272, being adapted accordingly). Thus 'exports' refer to goods and services 'exported' from the region, while 'imports' refers to goods and services purchased from outside the region.

If, for instance, the region increases its 'export' of goods, there will be an initial expansion of regional income. But the final effect on the level of income will depend upon the proportion of the initial addition to income which is spent on regionally-produced goods as opposed to 'imports'. The greater this marginal propensity to consume regional goods, the greater will be the 'regional multiplier'.

Although this approach is more comprehensive than the previous models, it is limited by the difficulty of obtaining statistics at the regional level, especially for inter-regional flows of goods and services. Furthermore, with the national economy, where a fall in the demand for exports results in an embarrassing balance-of-payments deficit, correction may be possible by devaluation. With a region's economy, however, only deflation is available.

Thus, to stimulate the economy of the region, the government has to increase its spending there. This initial injection of income will produce a further expansion according to the regional multiplier. Moreover, if that spending stimulates 'export' industries to establish in the region, there will be a further increase in income.

19.4 Government policy

Consequences of regional depression

The existence of prolonged depression in certain regions has adverse consequences which can be summarised as follows.

(1) AN UNDER-UTILISATION OF RESOURCES THROUGH UNEMPLOYMENT
Not only does regional unemployment result in lost output for the community as a whole, but it can have serious social and psychological effects on the workers concerned. Moreover, significant differences in people's income between regions has equity implications.

(2) A LOSS OF SOCIAL CAPITAL AS TOWNS AND CITIES DECAY
Where the nation's population is static or falling, outward migration from depressed areas involves social costs in that schools, churches, and so on fall into decay, while certain public services have to be operated below capacity. In contrast, new roads and public buildings, such as hospitals, have to be provided in the expanding areas.

However, the implied assumption that social capital should never be allowed to become obsolete has to be questioned. The stock of social capital in the high unemployment areas tends to be older and of lower quality than in the expanding areas of the south. In other words, it may be due for renewal and can be replaced as easily in another part of the country (subject to the qualification that there are no congestion or inflationary problems there).

(3) EXTERNAL SOCIAL COSTS

Migration from decaying regions results in a loss of welfare through the break-up of communities and the destruction of the 'social character' of an area. It could be, however, that having overcome their reluctance to moving away from friends, people find compensatory benefits, both economic and social, in a more pleasant environment. In any case, it is difficult to assess the loss resulting from this 'destruction of social character'.

Similarly, there may be external costs of excessive urbanisation (such as traffic congestion, noise, pollution and intensive housing) through migration to a prosperous region. Here again, however, the argument needs qualification. In recent years, population movement out of city centres into the surrounding countryside has exceeded other movements of population. Thus Greater London has been losing population at a faster rate than any other area in the country, while the main areas gaining from migration, such as East Anglia and the south-east outside London, are areas of relatively low congestion. Thus present migration may serve to reduce congestion costs as much as to increase them.

(4) DIFFERENCES IN UNEMPLOYMENT BETWEEN REGIONS MAKE IT MORE DIFFICULT TO MANAGE THE ECONOMY

Prosperous regions tend to become 'overheated' through the pressure of demand. This is reflected in higher wage-rates and labour shortages. Higher wage-rates tend to be transmitted even to the depressed regions through national wage agreements, the insistence on traditional wage-differentials, and so on. But anti-inflationary measures, both monetary and fiscal, apply nationally, thus adding to the unemployment problems of the depressed regions. It is argued, therefore, that ironing out unemployment differences between regions would not only reduce inflationary pressure but do so at a lower overall level of unemployment.

(5) ECONOMIC INTEGRATION BETWEEN NATIONS MAY BE UNDERMINED BY THE POLITICAL OPPOSITION OF DEPRESSED REGION PRESSURE GROUPS

The rationale of economic integration between nations, as, for example, in the EU, is to secure greater comparative advantages by the removal of trade barriers and increased factor mobility. However, it may exacerbate the problem of regional imbalance because certain industries, particularly in areas on the periphery, such as Northern Ireland and Scotland, find it more difficult to compete. Political pressure groups in such areas, therefore, may react by opposing economic integration.

The development of government regional policy

Government policy to deal with regional imbalance did not really begin until 1934, when the Special Areas Act was passed to give help to the four special areas of heavy unemployment – South Wales, Cumberland, the north-east coast and south-west Scotland. The measure had only limited success. Hence policy was extended by the Distribution of Industry Act 1945, which initiated many of the current methods of helping depressed regions.

Subsequent experience has led to modifications of policy. Though the decline of an industry is often centred on a particular area – for example, Tyneside, Corby, Clydeside – its effects extend to other towns and the surrounding countryside. Thus the success of specific resources to reverse the decline may depend upon the improvement of the whole region, particularly as regards an adequate infrastructure covering transport, communications, houses, schools, and recreational and cultural facilities. Consequently a *regional* policy has been followed under the Industrial Development Act 1982, whereby selected Assisted Areas are given special assistance. Lately, however, this has been modified to concentrate on smaller areas (see below).

Objectives of regional policy

The objectives of regional policy have widened in the light of experience. In brief, it now seeks to:

(1) reduce the relatively high level of unemployment in certain regions;
(2) achieve a better balance between the population and the environment;
(3) preserve regional cultures and identities;
(4) relieve inflation by reducing the pressure of demand in the expanding regions;
(5) counter possible adverse regional effects of greater international economic integration and of more open economies.

It has to be recognised, however, that these objectives are not always compatible with national economic policy. For instance, diverting firms from their optimum location to a depressed area may hamper growth, while it may be necessary to stimulate exports of goods and services produced in the more prosperous regions in order to improve the national balance of payments. Finally, any regional employment policy has a better chance of success when there is full employment generally in the economy. Not only are unemployed workers encouraged to move to where there are unfilled vacancies, but firms will be more ready to go where labour is available provided it can be trained in the appropriate skills.

The nature of government intervention

The regional problem in the UK has resulted mainly from:

(a) the decline of certain major industries concentrated in specific geographical areas;

(b) the failure of the expanding industries to be attracted to these areas; and

(c) the geographical immobility of labour, so that there has been no large-scale movement of workers from declining areas.

Where an area is depressed, the government can give first aid by placing its contracts there, for example, for defence equipment, and awarding it priority for public-works programmes – schools, new roads, hospitals, the physical regeneration of urban areas, and so on.

In the long term, however, the government must take measures that will, on the one hand, encourage the outward movement of workers, and on the other induce firms to move in to employ those workers who find it difficult to move and also to halt further degeneration of the region. The first is usually referred to as 'workers to the work', the second as 'work to the workers'.

Workers to the work

Taking workers to the work is basically a partial equilibrium approach to overcome market frictions, chiefly the immobility and imperfect knowledge of labour. In pursuing this policy, however, the government must bear in mind the following.

(a) Unemployment arising through immobility is far more difficult to cure when cyclical unemployment also exists, for an unemployed person has little incentive to move if there is unemployment even in the relatively prosperous areas.

(b) Other government interference in the economy may add to the problem of immobility. Thus high rates of income tax whittle away monetary inducements to move and unemployment benefit may reduce the incentive to seek a job elsewhere. Similarly, residential qualifications for local authority housing priorities lead to difficulties in finding accommodation.

(c) Even owner-occupiers in depressed regions may be restricted in mobility by the much higher cost of housing in the prosperous areas.

(d) Many changes of both occupation and area take place in a series of ripples. Thus an agricultural labourer may move to road construction to take the place of the labourer who transfers to the building industry.

The government's first task must be to improve occupational mobility. Entry into certain occupations should be made less difficult, for example, by giving information on opportunities in other industries and occupations and by persuading trade unions to relax their apprenticeship rules. More important, people must be trained in the new skills required by expanding industries, for example, through local Training and Enterprise Councils.

Improving the geographical mobility of workers to the more prosperous regions operates chiefly under the government's Employment Transfer Scheme. This consists of granting financial aid towards moving costs, providing information on prospects in other parts of the country and giving free fares to a place of work away from the home town.

Work to the workers

Although a 'workers-to-the-work' policy has a role to play in correcting regional imbalance, it suffers from: (i) an exclusive concern with unemployment to the neglect of other consequences of regional imbalance; (ii) a failure to recognise the macro effects of the outward movement of workers.

Thus taking work to the workers is now regarded as the policy most likely to effect a long-term solution to the problem, for it reduces regional differences in income and the rate of growth as well as in unemployment. By helping the more immobile workers, such as older people and married women, it stimulates the activity rate. It also avoids forcing workers to leave areas to which they are attached, relieves the growing congestion in south-east England, and prevents the loss of social capital resulting from the depopulation of depressed areas. Above all, it works in harmony with Keynesian macro theory. The 'multiplier' operates for regional economies in much the same way as it does for the national economy. Moving unemployed workers and their families reduces spending in the area (for example, because unemployment benefits are no longer being drawn) and this gives rise to a negative multiplier. In contrast, moving firms into the area generates spending power and produces a positive multiplier, variously calculated at between 1.25 and 1.50.

On the other hand, a policy of locating firms in depressed areas may involve them in higher costs. Their desire to establish plant in the south-east is to secure location advantages, such as a supply of skilled workers, easier and less costly communications, contact with complementary firms and nearness to EU markets.

Assisted Area status now confers eligibility of aid from the EU as part of the EU policy of reducing the level of aid to industry and to prepare for the entry of new states. The Assisted Areas of Great Britain are based upon a map drawn up and agreed with the European Commission in July 2000. The map will run until 31 December 2006. The basis of the map (Figure 19.1) is to provide Tier 1 (Article 87(3)a) and Tier 2 (Article 87(3)c) for Regional Selective Assistance Grants (RSA), and additionally large areas of the UK, where a lower level of grant aid can also be made available to Small and Medium Enterprises (SME). These areas are classified as Tier 3 (additional enterprise grant areas).

In the Assisted Areas *Regional Selective Assistance* is given on a discretionary basis, mainly through *Project Grants* based on the capital cost and the number of jobs created. The budget of over £100 m. is under the control

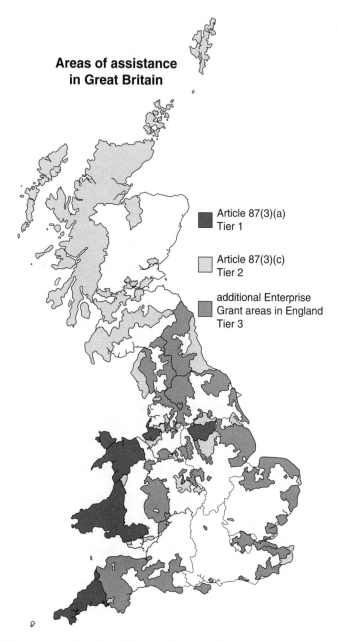

**Areas of assistance
in Great Britain**

Article 87(3)(a)
Tier 1

Article 87(3)(c)
Tier 2

additional Enterprise
Grant areas in England
Tier 3

*Figure 19.1 Assisted Areas, GB as defined by the European Commission
in July 2000. (Note that the whole of Northern Ireland continues to have
special status.)*

of the ODPM's *Invest in Britain Bureau* (IBB) which has had an outstanding success in inducing US, Japanese and South Korean firms to establish overseas centres in Britain, often in the depressed regions.

In the dispersal of industry the government has set an example. Thus the Department of Health and Social Security is based in Newcastle, and the Driving and Vehicle Licensing Centre in Swansea, while much of the work of departments (such as Defence, Inland Revenue) has been re-located to the Assisted Areas.

19.5 Urban regeneration

The development of regional policy

Until the 1980's, regional policy tended to concentrate on attracting firms to the regions where structural change had led to high rates of unemployment. But there were weaknesses. In focusing aid on manufacturing industry it failed to take advantage of the growing service industries. Moreover the objective of actual job creation was lost sight of through the concentration on *investment* grants to attract firms. This simply induced those firms relocating to substitute capital for labour and resulted in a high cost per job created – £26 000 in the case of attracting Samsung to the North-East region. Finally, the emphasis on *regional* differences diverted attention from problems *within* regions where there were pockets of run-down areas. Nor were such areas confined to the industrial North-West and North-East regions. For instance, within London's boundaries there are even today 15 of the 20 most deprived areas in the UK. Often these areas have a predominant ethnic population needing to be taught new skills (and sometimes the English language) in order to find employment.

The shift towards urban regeneration

It was recognised, therefore, that regeneration was not simply tidying up derelict land. It has to rebuild communities by providing them with jobs and decent living conditions, chiefly by attracting investment from the private sector. As a result urban regeneration had to be co-ordinated with regional industrial policy. In fact funds were switched from regional assistance to the urban regeneration programme, though it must be recognised that much of the urban degeneration was in the Assisted Areas. With the object of regenerating these run-down areas the government introduced a variety of Schemes – Enterprise Zones, Urban Development Corporations, City

Grants, City challenge – which were amended in the light of experience or the need to reduce the financial commitment.

Current administration measures

These administrative and spending initiatives have now been replaced by English Partnerships, a Single Regeneration Budget and Regional Development Agencies (RDA), all responsible to the Office of the Deputy Prime Minister (ODPM).

English Partnerships (EP) created in 1997, is a *national* government agency, which has powers to acquire land and decide on planning in a designated area. Furthermore, unlike the previous City Grant where the Treasury required a stipulated rate of public to private funding, EP can itself decide on how it uses its investment fund, amounting in 1998–9 to £435 m., with a budget grant of around £100 m. This means that EP can shoulder risk, providing even 100 per cent of the initial funds as a pump-priming exercise to draw in developers. It was thus able, for instance, to use its investment fund to put together a co-ordinated package which induced Samsung to locate a manufacturing base at Stockton-on-Tees in the North-east region. Its original fund can be augmented by any profits it makes on its initiative and by EU funding where spending occurs in an Assisted Area.

The Single Regeneration Budget (SRB) was set up to achieve overall control of spending on urban regeneration by providing a global sum to cover all the spending of the operating bodies. Its aim is to fund flexible and locally responsive forms of regeneration administered by the Regional Development Agencies.

Much of this funding is competed for on a 'challenge' basis, grants for regeneration schemes and even neighbourhood projects being awarded on an assessment of their relative merit.

For England, nine *Regional Development Agencies* (RDA) have been set up to decide on local regeneration priorities, promote inward investment, help small businesses and co-ordinate regional economic development. Apart from the North-west Region which now includes Merseyside, these have the same boundaries as the Government Office Regions, with which they will work closely.

Scotland, Wales and Northern Ireland have their own agencies for similar functions.

The *New Deal for Communities* aims to tackle multiple deprivation in the poorest areas. To fund this £800 m. has been earmarked for three years in order to improve job prospects, reduce crime, bring together investment in buildings and in people, and to improve the management of the neighbourhood and coordination of its public services, Together, local people, businesses, voluntary organisations and public agencies form a 'pathfinder' partnership in each of the 17 selected local authority districts to formulate proposals for the regeneration of specified neighbourhoods covering about 1000–4000 households. Those partnerships which are successful in the 'challenge' are funded for up to ten years.

Reflections on present progress

Coordinating as far as possible the allocation of land between where and how people live, how they travel and where they work is a logical approach. But implementing the concept involves reconciling diverse interests – for example, the protection of the environment against road transport CO_2 emission, the vitality of town centres in the face of out-of-town supermarket expansion, and a 'one-fits-all' rate of interest which is related to inflationary pressure in the southern regions but which militates against exporters, especially manufacturers, in the northern regions through the strength of sterling.

Apart from the New Deal for Communities concept, however, little of real substance has emerged. In particular there has been no unveiling of an overall strategy. Admittedly the Department has been squeezed out of the legislative programme and could have been better served in the allocation of funds. But the nagging feeling persists that the remit of the ODPM is too large to be dealt with by one man.

This view was endorsed in July 1995 by the House of Commons' all-party Select Committee for the Department. Its criticism included the under-funding of London Underground, poor road maintenance and unsatisfactory air quality standards. In addition, too much was spent on consultants – yet whose advice was often not followed. Its 'could-do-better' report concluded that the department's 'achievements have largely been confined to the publication of documents and policy statements and the establishment of task forces'.

19.6 Regional policy in the context of the EU

A healthy integrated EU – at both economic and political levels – is possible only if progress is made towards reducing disparities in economic opportunity between regions within the Community. Indeed, while the foregoing reasons for regional policy are all relevant at the Community level, additional considerations apply:

(a) Physical controls are more difficult to operate in the EU context. Not only are they at variance with the objective of greater mobility within the EU, but firms have the option of relocating in a prosperous region of another member state.

(b) The depressed peripheral regions of Scotland, Northern Ireland, Southern Italy, etc., are more distant from the expanding centre of the Community – south-east England through to north-east France and Germany – than they are from the centres of their own countries. This EU 'centre' forms a concentrated market to which industries are likely to be increasingly attracted, thereby adding to its dominance.

(c) The EU embraces regions exhibiting wider economic disparities than in any one member state. Moreover, regional problems are more heterogeneous – for example, whereas the UK depressed regions are mainly industrial, Italy has many depressed agricultural areas.

Such considerations mean that the formulation of an effective EU regional policy is a difficult task. Not only must it respond quickly as new regional problems arise, but it has to be linked with, and be complementary to, the individual nation's regional policy. Indeed EU policy should also co-ordinate the regional policies of member states, for example a physical control in one country must not be undermined by a firm being able to locate in another country.

It follows, therefore, that regional policy must be handled to a substantial degree at the EU level and be wide-ranging in the measures employed so that one reinforces the others. Above all, to achieve greater equity, it must envisage substantial transfers of income through incentive funds which are additional to and not a substitute for those provided by the member states (see Chapter 23).

The emphasis of the EU's four Structural Funds is now on regional development programmes rather than on individual projects, and the EU Commission can insist that grants are actually spent in the specified region. These funds are as follows:

(a) The *European Regional Development Fund* (ERDF) funds the development and structural adjustment of less-developed regions (such as Spain, Italy, Portugal and Greece) and declining industrial regions (for example, within the UK, Spain and France). The UK's depressed regions are major beneficiaries of the ERDF:

(b) The *European Social Fund* (ESF) provides funds to organisations running vocational training and job-creation schemes.

(c) The *European Agricultural Guidance and Guarantee Fund* (EAGGF) supports farming in less-favoured or environmentally sensitive areas, and the modernisation of infrastructures.

(d) The Financial Instrument for Fisheries (FIFG) may support projects which modernise the structure of the fisheries sector, and related industries, and encourage diversification of the workforce and fisheries industry into other sectors. It also aims to promote sustainability within the fishing industry by encouraging a balance between fisheries resources and their exploitation.

Loans are available on favourable terms from the European Investment Bank (EIB) and the European Coal and Steel Community (ECSC).

Summary

Regional problems arise for one of three reasons:

- **poor natural resources**
- **poor development of resources**
- **the decline of important basic industries**

Location theory puts forward a number of reasons why industries locate in certain areas, many of them based on transport costs. In an economy increasingly dependent on service industries, however, the attraction of large markets is dominant.

The adverse consequences of regional depression include:

- **under-utilisation of resources**
- **loss or under-utilisation of social capital (e.g. hospitals)**
- **external social costs such as the breakup of communities**
- **problems of economic management if different regions have different growth rates**
- **problems of political unrest**

Current regional policy is determined by the European Union which has regional development programmes through four Structural Funds.

Review questions

1. Why does the UK have a 'regional problem'?
2. Does industrial location theory have relevance in a modern economy where most employment is in service industries?
3. What are the economic consequences of imbalanced regional development?
4. Describe how urban regeneration contributes to UK regional policy.
5. Consider whether European Union regional policy is significantly different from UK government regional policy.

Recommended reading

H. Armstrong and J. Taylor, *Regional Economics and Policy* (Oxford: Philip Allan, 1985).

J. E. Manser, *Economics: A Foundation Course for the Built Environment* (London, E.&F.N. Spon, 1994).

D. Myers, *Economics and Property: A Coursebook for Students of the Built Environment* (London: Estates Gazette, 1994).

PART V

THE GOVERNMENT AND LAND RESOURCES

CHAPTER 20

The Impact of Government Macro Policy on Land and Property Resources

After studying this chapter you will be able to:

- Explain why changes in the level of economic activity occur and how they affect property markets
- Explain how property markets affect the macroeconomy
- Describe the effects of monetary policy on the property sector
- Describe the effects of fiscal policy on the property sector
- Assess how a prolonged period of low inflation is likely to affect the property market

20.1 Cyclical instability

The effect of short-term fluctuations in activity on secular growth

So far we have been mainly concerned with possible weaknesses of the market economy in the allocation of land resources and in examining various ways in which the government can act to improve efficiency, for example, by bringing externalities into the decision-making process, reducing the undesirable use of monopoly power, producing commodity community goods.

379

Yet it still has to be recognised that the market economy looked at as a whole, is basically unstable, with output fluctuating cyclically over time at fairly regular 7–10 year intervals. One major cause is that supply takes time to respond fully to a change in demand so that expectations upon which production decisions were originally based may not be fulfilled. This can occur with both commercial property development (p. 133) and housebuilding (p. 190). Consequently there tends to be a property cycle which can vary with the length of the production timelag, being shorter for industrial property than for offices owing to the considerable time taken to plan, construct and dispose of office property.

The government's main concern is to dampen down short-term fluctuations in the economy generally in order to maintain the full employment of resources (with labour, as the yardstick, having no more than 4 to 5 per cent unemployment). Success in reducing short-term fluctuations would go a long way towards achieving a steady yearly growth rate of 2 to 3 per cent in the national product.

How do changes in the level of activity occur?

An expansion of aggregate demand can be brought about by an increase in aggregate injections – consumption spending, investment, government spending and exports – not matched by an increase in total withdrawals by saving, taxation and spending on imports.

Expansion of aggregate demand may originate on the demand side, for example, by an autonomous increase in consumption spending or, on the supply side, for example, by firms granting demands for wage increases which are not matched by an increase in productivity.

In addition it has to be recognised that today much of the UK production takes place in the context of a global economy. Thus recession can be triggered off by events outside the direct control of the government, such as a rise in the world price of oil (1974) or speculation against sterling holding its value against other currencies (1992).

The influence of the property and construction industries on the level of aggregate demand

While property may not initiate an expansion of aggregate demand, it plays an important role in its subsequent development. In the economy as a whole, any increase in the injections has a multiplier effect which adds still further to the level of aggregate demand. Furthermore, with investment in particular, the upturn gathers momentum through a possible accelerator effect, thereby reinforcing the upswing, but eventually petering out and reversing into a down-turn.

The same process is clearly at work in both commercial development and house-building. Land use and property market decisions are made on the basis of profitability, used in its wider sense to include maximising utility. Cyclical movements in the economy therefore give rise to cycles in the real property and construction industries.

With *commercial property*, a buoyant economy will evoke a parallel response from property developers and investors, with the length of the property cycle generated being shorter for industrial buildings which can be built fairly quickly but depreciate quickly in a depression, and longer for offices which take more time to plan and construct. Thus the macro-economic background affects not only short-term decisions as to how land resources shall be allocated, but also the rate of development over time. A fast-growing economy will require new and better offices, factories and warehouses. And because growth in the economy is reflected in increased spending power, there is an increase in the demand for new shopping facilities and better housing.

Housing similarly contributes to the cumulative increase in aggregate demand. Changes in demand and supply result in changes in relative prices – the micro effect. But the housing industry is so important that any surge in demand is transmitted to the whole economy – the macro effect. This comes about through *dynamic* changes in demand and the interaction of the multiplier and the accelerator which raises income in the economy as a whole, with a possible further feedback on the demand for housing. We shall examine in particular this dynamic housing demand.

Additional demand for housing may be engendered (as in 1988) by observed rises in house prices (which doubled between 1984 and 1988). Here the house is being bought, not solely as a necessary consumer durable affording shelter and so on, but as an *investment asset* which is expected to continue rising in price. More than that when the price of a house rises, a 95 per cent mortgage represents a high gearing ratio showing an excellent rate of return on the original deposit – the equity stake – especially as an owner-occupied house is exempt from capital gains tax.

Since home ownership represents over one-half of personal wealth, rising house prices can have a further impact on consumption spending generally. First, because owner-occupiers feel richer, this can induce them to spend on cars and consumer durables – the 'wealth' effect. Second, existing mortgage-holders are tempted to up-grade their housing by moving to larger and newer houses, often requiring new carpets, furniture and garden equipment. Third, and more serious, this additional spending is financed by a personal loan or a second mortgage granted on the strength of the house price rise. It has been estimated that this 'equity-extraction' amounted to £61 billion in 1988.

Thus house-price inflation has a direct and important effect on the general rate of inflation. Higher house prices encourage the construction of houses. Surplus capacity is soon absorbed, and land prices rise. Eventually bottlenecks appear in labour, materials and components; delivery times lengthen and their prices rise. Thus cost-push inflation may reinforce demand-pull.

More than that, the loan-generated demand for houses, by increasing money GNP, results in increased spending overall. Prices in general rise: the initial house-price inflation has spilled out into the wider economy.

The effect of inflation on the stability of the economy

Since 1960, the root cause of recessions has been the UK's inability to control the rate of inflation. This has meant that from time to time the government has had to cut back on total spending – in the early years, to protect the balance of payments, later, to maintain the sterling exchange rate. Both monetary policy (raising the rate of interest and credit control) and fiscal policy (adjusting the balance between spending and revenue) were used. This 'stop-go' policy resulted in a period of rising unemployment followed, after easing the restrictions, by a gradual expansion of output and employment.

20.2 Monetary policy

The logic of varying the short-term rate of interest

Today the task of holding inflation in check relies on a single weapon – varying the short-term rate of interest. The logic of this is that a change in the short-term rate of interest will affect aggregate demand in a number of ways.

First, a change in the cost of borrowing affects spending decisions in that it alters the relative attraction of spending today as opposed to spending later. Thus a rise in interest rates will make saving more attractive, and borrowing less so. This will, therefore, tend to reduce present spending on both consumption and investment.

Second, a change in short-term interest rates alters the cash flow of both creditors and borrowers having a floating rate for both assets or liabilities. Thus households receive a floating interest rate on deposits in banks and building societies, while floating rate debtors include households with mortgages and companies running an overdraft. Fluctuations in net cash flow may influence spending.

Third, a change in interest rates affects the capitalised value of certain assets, notably property, houses and stocks and shares (see Chapter 6). This 'wealth effect' may influence an owner's willingness to spend.

Fourth, pressure on prices may come about through the influence of a change in the rate of interest on exchange rates. For example, a rise in UK domestic interest rates relative to those overseas tends to result in a net inflow of capital and thus an appreciation of the sterling exchange rate. This will lower the prices of imports, and UK products have to compete by reducing their prices.

Deciding on changes in the short-term rate of interest

Since June 1997 there has been a set of clear rules for keeping inflation in check: (i) the Chancellor of the Exchequer sets a target rate of inflation as measured by an increase in the Retail Price Index excluding mortgage payments (RPIX), now 2.5 per cent; (ii) the Bank of England, through its Monetary Policy Committee (MPC) of nine members is given sole operational responsibility for delivering this target by varying base rate.

The MPC assembles on the Wednesday following the first Monday in each month to consider the latest data covering a wide range of topics which could bear on the future rate of inflation. These include: recent changes in the money supply, the PSNCR, average earnings, wage settlements, house and asset prices, import and export prices and flows, the sterling exchange rate, investment and consumer spending. On the next day (Thursday), following further discussion, the members of the committee decide, on a simple majority basis, whether base rate should be changed, and, if so, by how much.

It must be recorded that over the last five years the MPC has consistently achieved its 2.5 per cent target, no mean feat in view of the fact that there could well be a 2-year time lag between today's base-rate decision and its impact on the future RPIX.

The impact of monetary policy on property and construction activity

The use of the short-term rate of interest as the sole weapon for controlling inflation bears heavily on developers and speculative house-builders, for both are particularly dependent on credit to pay for inputs during the construction period.

A rise in short-term rates, by putting up the cost of advances, is felt immediately as profit margins are squeezed; but most buildings under construction will still be completed. Building society and bank lending are also affected. Monthly mortgage repayments eventually rise and the resulting increase in any repayment–income ratio condition will make mortgages more difficult to obtain. Thus housing activity falls (see Chapter 18).

If the rise eventually extends to the long end of the market, the effects are more fundamental for both new construction and the investment market. Since expected yields on real property stretch far into the future, discounting at a higher rate leads to a greater proportionate reduction in their present values than for other types of investment project where costs have to be recouped within about five years. This would tend to hold back private-sector development, especially by property development companies, thus affecting the construction industry directly.

In the investment market the higher yield on government bonds makes them more attractive compared with assets such as mortgages and real property. Particularly for loans against property, therefore, the lending institutions such as insurance companies and pension funds will require a higher return. But with a steady inflow of funds, they have to take a long-term view as regards inflation and the profitability of property interests. Thus they may continue to invest in freeholds, either by financing new development or by purchasing existing buildings. Eventually, however, when higher relative returns can be obtained elsewhere, they will push up yields on all real property interests. Such lowering of capital values will discourage new construction by developers.

Nor is the public sector, which is responsible for *nearly* one-twelfth of all Gross Fixed Capital Formation, immune from higher interest rates. Local authorities can only afford to raise funds on the same scale by increasing local taxation to cover the higher cost. Reluctance to do this because of its political unpopularity means that, instead, they curtail their housing and other construction programmes. Above all, the central government may be forced to contract its spending (see below).

20.3 Fiscal policy

The influence of the MPC on fiscal policy

The use of monetary policy to maintain a specified 2.5 per cent rate of inflation means that the Chancellor of the Exchequer's fiscal policy must be so structured as to be in harmony with the MPC's objective. If, for instance, the MPC considered that government spending would exceed revenue to such an extent that the PSNCR would breach the 2.5 per cent inflation target, it would simply raise base rate until the inflationary pressure no longer existed.

Fiscal options

Within its broad spending and revenue aggregates, there are alternative ways and means in which the Chancellor can increase spending in chosen directions, for example, on health, education and welfare, and still leave a PSNCR which the MPC would consider as being non-inflationary. Balancing adjustments can be made on either the spending or revenue sides, or both. The following are examples of a few recent adjustments which would affect property or the construction industry directly or indirectly.

On the *spending* side, the opportunities to make cuts are limited since much spending is either contractual or an essential part of the government's commitments in its election manifesto. Only rarely, as with the ending of the Cold War, can there be a substantial cut in regular expenditure; usually the reverse is the case, as with the 1999 Kosovo crisis and the 2003 Gulf crisis.

Even so, improved efficiency may reduce expenditure. Thus a reorganisation of the Valuation Office Agency produced a saving in district offices and personnel which kept it on target for a 30 per cent improvement in efficiency between 1995 and 2000.

Opportunities to increase *revenue* without raising taxation are more available, but mostly only on a one-off or short-term basis. First, in the past the proceeds of the privatisation issues of the nationalised industries have been a major means of reducing the PSNCR, but the scope for this is now limited to minor sales, possibly the Post Office, London Underground and British Nuclear Fuels.

Second, to help fund a hospital and school building programme, improve public transport and regenerate depressed areas at an overall cost of £11 bn, the government, through its Property Advisors to the Civil Estate (PACE), is disposing of a £5.75 bn portfolio of surplus accommodation and land assets. In this way the government is relieved of the necessity to push up long-term interest rates by selling gilt-edged bonds.

Third, following the end of the privatisation programme, the government has embarked on a new approach under the banner of the *Private Finance Initiative (PFI)*. In fact this is in essence only putting a glossy presentation of the motive which underlay the direct selling of Council and New Town dwellings to tenants. This allowed Councils to liquidate their housing assets by introducing private capital in the form of the mortgages provided by building societies and banks.

Today the PFI is closely connected with the government's property requirements. Instead of itself engaging in capital expenditure on redevelopment or refurbishment of the properties it owns, the necessary capital is brought in by a consortium of property companies, probably backed by institutional funds. This sees the scheme through under contract, and then assumes the role of landlord with a lease of up to 125 years and a rent on agreed terms.

Proposals at present in the pipe-line are rebuilding the Treasury behind the existing facade and the redevelopment of Chelsea Barracks. What this means is that the government is spending only on the services which the building provides, foremost of which is working space. But other services can be added, such as maintenance, cleaning, information technology connections, and so on.

20.4 Property in a low-inflation economy

The success of the MPC in restraining the annual rise in the RPIX to 2.5 per cent has led to growing confidence that the UK now has inflation under control. Most important, this has been reflected in a corresponding fall in the rate of wage increases.

During the 1970s and 1980s the property market was to a large extent 'inflation driven'. We, therefore, now have to ask: how is this new situation of low inflation likely to affect the property market? Although the fundamentals of decision-making are virtually the same for both the commercial and residential markets, there are differences which call for separate consideration.

Commercial.   The yield on a property over the year combines two elements, rent and capital appreciation. In the past both have risen with inflation. Rents rise as increases in money income push up prices; capital appreciation occurs through the capitalisation of this higher rent, but also because investors regard property as an excellent hedge against inflation and are prepared to accept a lower rate of return than that obtainable on competing safe assets, in particular, bonds.

Now, with yield mostly stripped of the inflation element, the *investor* in real property has to buy mainly on the basis of the margin of rent over cost, with possible capital appreciation having much less influence. Moreover, these sums must be done with extra care, for no longer will there be inflation to cover up a bad deal. In any case there is now a greater incentive to move into gilt-edged stock as this will be more likely to hold its value, or into shares which offer greater liquidity and depending on the profitability of the company, possible capital appreciation.

To achieve this with property, there could be an extension of securitisation through bonds, and eventually the removal of legal obstacles to the development of the American method of investing in property through Real Estate Investment Trusts (REITS).

This more cautious approach also applies to *lenders* who need to be assured as to the quality of the borrower's covenant and his management skills in recognising development or refurbishment potential.

The *occupier* of property has also to adapt to the new situation. When, as a result of inflation, rents were continually rising, he was willing to accept a 25-year lease, with 5-year upward-only rent reviews and privity of contract. Indeed between rent reviews, he earned an 'economic rent', and found little difficulty in assigning, possibly at a premium, should he wish to move.

Now he has to be more cautious, requiring shorter leases, possibly with a break clause, and is reluctant to agree to privity of contract. To increase his returns he has to work harder to make use of the available space. Office occupiers in particular may require additional services, such as cleaning, maintenance, security and the provision of facilities for full IT services, as part of the rent for the space occupied.

Residential. Apart from the years 1989 to 1993, house prices have been continuously rising and owner-occupation has proved to be an excellent inflation hedge. This demand included an 'investment' element in addition to the occupational benefit. At times this expectation of higher prices was magnified by a 'feel good' factor – the 'wealth effect' – especially when mortgages were easily available from building societies and banks. This induced people to up-grade their present property by withdrawing some of the equity content of their houses or by spending possible windfalls, for example, through building society conversions or inheritance.

In general, with low inflation people are more likely to rent property rather than buy, especially young people who require mobility. Such a change will be reinforced by the government's ending of MIRAS. Renting could also be preferred by multi-national companies in providing residential accommodation for their major travelling managers, especially as mainten-ance, cleaning and other services can be included in the rent.

20.5 The role of the government as regards growth and income distribution

The value of secular growth

So far government macro policy has been examined in the context of the prevention of short-term fluctuations in economic activity, often referred to as the trade cycle. In this context, the main objective is to avoid the un-employment which results from recessions while taking care not to allow an expansion of aggregate demand to bring about inflation. Given this, the UK can reasonably expect her Gross Domestic Product (GDP) to grow cumula-tively each year by two or three per cent.

For the UK, this secular growth has, over the last 50 years, resulted in a threefold increase in real national income – the outcome of investment in capital equipment and technological development, itself the product of research and innovation.

In advanced, market-led economies, such as that of the UK, adequate investment for secular growth can be left to the enterprise of firms responding to market indicators. It is such firms which, over the last fifty years have, by research and its application, provided people with cars, air transport, central heating, dish-washers, theme parks, supermarkets, pension funds. With some products, such as agricultural research and farming techniques, television and video recorders, computers, word processors and mobile phones, the rate of growth has been phenomenal. Even defence, a major function of government, incorporates the innovations of specialist electronic firms.

It is submitted, therefore, that government growth policy can be confined to eliminationg the short-term hiccups which punctuate the upward secular trend. The most serious consequence of such hiccups is unemployment. Even more important than the loss of income through redundancy is the human unhappiness, and even misery, which may follow the loss of a job – especially the feeling of indefinite rejection through old skills no longer being required. It follows, therefore, that the two immediate objectives of government policy must be the provision of income support and training for new skills.

The government and secular growth

Policy must also respond to the consequences of secular growth, some of which are not transparent in the bare statistics of GDP, the measure usually chosen to indicate growth over time.

First GDP may not provide a true measure of, or even reflect, welfare as distinct from wealth (see p. 3). Secular growth often takes the form of increased leisure which is not included in GDP figures. In any case, it is unsafe to assume that everybody views work as onerous. Thus an across-the-board regulation restricting the working week to 48 hours may actually reduce welfare for those workers who prefer work to leisure.

In general, however, leisure-related industries, such as tourism, rambling and hotels, are likely over time to take an increasing proportion of income, and the property and construction industries will respond accordingly.

Second, GDP figures presenting growth of income do not reveal how this increase has been distributed. For instance, retired people relying on state pension for a large part of their income fail to obtain their full share of an increase in growth-related income. Recognising this, the pressure group 'Age Concern' lobbies for the annual uplift in the state retirement pension to be based on the average earnings index instead of the RPIX, for the former reflects the trend in rising productivity as well as that of price-inflation.

Third, as we have seen in previous chapters, there are costs of economic growth – usually 'bad' externalities – which may not be allowed for in GDP calculations. Examples are: the loss of 'cherished' land for the construction of new roads; noise near busy aircraft terminals; CO_2 emission from road transport. On occasions, action to counteract the 'bads' even increases the GDP figure – for example, the cost of noise abatement and of disposal of the waste of the 'throw away' society. These are mostly environmental 'bad' externalities arising through increasing demands on diminishing resources. The elimination or mitigation of such 'bads' must largely be the responsibility of government.

The government and the redistribution of increasing wealth

Most people feel that poverty in the midst of plenty is unacceptable and that all should share in wealth increases. Private giving with this in mind is made to such voluntary bodies as the Salvation Army and the Child Poverty Action Group, and the donors themselves enjoy satisfaction from their generosity.

But only the government can effect the scale of redistribution required. This it may do indirectly in pursuing other objectives. Thus a 'right to roam' policy benefits in particular those who are fit enough to ramble and have the leisure time to do so.

But most redistribution occurs directly by government expenditure and taxation. Redistribution is a specific objective in money and other benefits which are directed towards certain vulnerable groups, such as the unemployed and lowly-paid, the sick and aged. But subsidies, for example to farmers which have other objectives, for example, the preservation of ancient woodland, also effect income redistribution.

How government expenditure and taxation can achieve a wide range of objectives will now be analysed, with the emphasis in particular being directed to their impact on the property market.

Summary

The level of economic activity in the economy as a whole varies cyclically with a trade or business cycle of 7–10 years. Cyclical movements in the economy cause cycles in property and construction which are exacerbated by the time it takes for property supply to respond fully to demand. Property also influences the macroeconomy. Expenditure on property is part of aggregate demand, equity release can stimulate demand and major construction projects can influence the whole economy through the multiplier process.

Governments use monetary and fiscal policy to control the overall economy and each has effects on the property sector. The success of recent UK governments in controlling inflation will have consequences for property markets which in the 1970s and 1980s were 'inflation driven'. Thus far, however, because of the high inflation of capital values in the residential sector (1993–2003) these consequences are not obvious.

Review questions

1. Explain how time-lags in supply might exacerbate property cycles.
2. How does property contribute to aggregate demand in the economy?
3. What is meant by 'equity release'?
4. Explain how monetary policy change can affect property markets.
5. Explain how fiscal policy change can affect property markets.

Recommended reading

J. B. Cullingworth, *Town and Country Planning in Britain*, 8th edn (London: Allen & Unwin, 1982).

A. W. Evans, *Urban Economics* (Oxford: Basil Blackwell, 1985) pp. 146–55.

J. E. Manser, *Economics: A Foundation Course for the Built Environment* (London, E.&F.N. Spon, 1994).

D. Myers, *Economics and Property: A Coursebook for Students of the Built Environment* (London: Estates Gazette, 1994).

CHAPTER 21

Economic Theory and Public Finance

After studying this chapter you will be able to:

- **Explain why there is government intervention in property markets**
- **Describe the different public sector organisations which have an impact on property**
- **Show how public sector property activity is financed**

In our discussion so far we have indicated how the government can intervene to correct the market's allocation of resources by administrative action, for example, through planning control, and by fiscal measures, for example, through subsidies and taxes.

But 'market failure', as explained in Chapter 1, includes a situation where such goods and services as defence would not be provided through the price system because 'free-riders' cannot be excluded. Provision of such goods, therefore has to be the responsibility of the government. As shown below, this government provision is extended in practice to somewhat similar goods.

Our task in this chapter is to demonstrate how economic theory can assist in reaching decisions on: (a) what goods and services should be provided by the government; (b) the extent of such provision in the context of maximising welfare; and, (c) the most appropriate means of financing this provision. We follow this by showing how different taxes may, apart from the initial purpose of raising revenue, send ripples through the economy, and how these may affect both the availability and the ultimate allocation of resources in general and of real property in particular.

21.1 The provision of goods and services by the public sector

Public-sector goods and services

We can explain the reasons why the government directly provides goods and services by classifying them as follows:

(1) COMMUNITY GOODS
Community goods, such as defence, police, street lighting, pavements and flood control, cannot be supplied through the price system because of *indivisibility* (there must be a complete supply or none at all) and *non-excludability* ('free-riders' cannot be excluded). Thus individuals cannot be charged a price on the basis of use.

(2) COLLECTIVE GOODS
Collective goods, which satisfy people's collective needs (for example, parks, motorways, bridges, water supply, refuse collection and drainage), entail such high fixed-capital investment that production takes place under conditions of decreasing cost. Some monopoly element is therefore inevitable, but 'free-riders' can be excluded by charging entrance fees, tolls and so on. Given these two conditions, a public body may be able to achieve a more optimal output than a private monopolist (see pp. 396–9).

(3) MERIT GOODS
Merit goods, such as education, health care and housing, are provided by the state because it is felt that they would be inadequately consumed (either, through lack of income or simply spending preferences) if left entirely to market forces. Undesirable external costs, such as an untrained or physically poor labour-force, could result. In subsidising the consumption of such goods, the government redistributes income and so makes a subjective judgement.

Forms of public-sector organisation

The provision of goods and services through the public sector may be undertaken by a government department, state-owned industries, quasi-governmental bodies (variously termed agencies, authorities, boards, commissions, councils or committees) or local authorities. The actual form adopted depends upon both constitutional and economic considerations.

Constitutionally, the *government department* form of organisation achieves a high degree of public accountability because the minister in charge is directly responsible to Parliament for all aspects of the department's work. Moreover, the department's finances come under the close scrutiny of the Treasury.

Generally speaking, the central government provides those goods and services which are of national importance (such as defence, trunk roads, health care) where most of the cost has to be covered by taxation and where local differences in the standard of provision would be unacceptable. Moreover, the expenditure involved enables the government to consider its effects on stabilising the economy and, through taxation, on the distribution of income, two objectives which by and large should be left to the central government.

Because the strict accountability of the government department form of organisation may conflict with economic efficiency, the *State-owned industries*, for example, the Post Office and Civil Aviation Authority are subjected to less direct accountability. With these the minister concerned exercises control over their broad policies, but not their day-to-day operations. They are fairly free to choose their own pricing policies but have to submit an annual report to Parliament. Thus some accountability is sacrificed in the interests of economic efficiency.

Quasi-governmental bodies have usually been formed to operate particular services where only minimum accountability is required, for example, the National Parks Commission, the Countryside Agency. In practice the degree of accountability varies. Thus, in their composition, certain official representatives may have to be included; or there may be the simple requirement that an annual report be laid before Parliament. These bodies are usually set up to administer services which have social overtones and where spillover effects are extensive or economies of scale can be secured. A good example is the Environment Agency which administers the whole complex of river basins as regards water supply, sewerage disposal, angling and so on.

However, the *urban* public sector is mainly concerned with the operations of *local authorities* to whom Parliament delegates functions, chiefly those where economies of scale and spillover effects are relatively weak. Services are divided between the counties and districts on the basis of the optimum scale of operation, the county being responsible for education, police, the fire services, and so on, and the district for personal and environmental services where economies of scale are of less importance. The new unitary authorities cover all functions.

Delegating such services to local authorities has certain advantages:

(a) those who run local services are local people responsible to local needs and attitudes;
(b) it allows close contact between the governed and those who govern;
(c) it provides for division of power between Whitehall and town hall, reminding the central government that its decisions must respect local feelings and loyalties;
(d) local authorities reduce the burden of central government administration.

If these advantages are to be secured, however, there must be real local *government*, not simply local administration on lines largely dictated by Westminister. This has important implications as regards the way that local authorities raise revenue to finance their activities (see pp. 416–18).

21.2 Public-sector expenditure

Two problems can be distinguished with regard to public expenditure: (i) its overall size relative to revenue; and (ii) its distribution between individual items.

The overall level of government expenditure

As successive governments have discovered, it is very difficult to reduce expenditure, for the more the government provides by way of welfare services and economic assistance, the greater are the demands of pressure groups for such aid, for example, the Child Poverty Action Group advocating increased child benefits, the National Farmers' Union wanting higher guaranteed prices, and Age Concern demanding higher retirement pensions.

The distribution of public expenditure

Public expenditure has obvious allocative effects, e.g. through direct subsidies. But it also influences the *distribution of income*, either indirectly through the services chosen for support or directly through the incidence of subsidies granted. Thus relative expenditure on the different items depends largely on political decisions.

Spending by local authorities

As regards the urban economy it is the spending by local authorities with which we are primarily concerned. In spite of recent government efforts to reduce local authority spending, for Great Britain it is expected to increase from £44 bn in 1995 to £53 bn in 2001, largely the result of an extension of services (public services generally tend to have a high income-elasticity of demand), a higher proportion of aged people in the community and the impact of wage-inflation on what are mainly labour-intensive services.

Increases in local government expenditure affect the government's function of stabilising the economy, since it entails increased borrowing from the central government and more dependence on government grants which now cover 85 per cent of total local authority spending. Both add to the PSNCR. Thus when the government has to take restrictive measures to stabilise the economy, local authorities, too, feel the squeeze.

21.3 Financing public-sector services

Government-provided goods and services can be financed by: (a) borrowing, (b) user-charges, and (c) taxation.

Borrowing

In practice, the *central government's* current expenditure is so vast that what would normally be regarded as capital items, for example, the cost of new warships, are covered by the yearly estimates of expenditure as approved by the House of Commons. The same applies to other one-off payments, for example, a grant towards the regeneration of London's dockland or a subsidy to keep British Nuclear Fuels in production despite heavy losses.

However, schemes for which a large amount of up-front capital is required and which can be repaid from future earnings, for example, Network Rail, can be financed by government borrowing (see Chapter 7). This is particularly true of extensive land development schemes where the government has to take account of a complexity of externalities. An example of such government borrowing is the finance provided through the New Towns Commission to acquire land to build a new town. Largely through the enhanced value of the land when developed, the loan can be repaid by the sale of houses, offices and industrial premises. Even so, the amount which the government can borrow is subject to the demands of the current monetary situation, as revealed by the size of the PSNCR (see Chapter 20).

Local authorities borrow both short-term and long-term, the former mainly to cover shortfalls between revenue and current expenditure, the latter to meet the cost of capital projects, such as school and housing construction, and even extensive urban and city centre re-development. However, because the central government must retain overall control of public sector spending, the amount which local authorities can borrow is subject to government approval, and usually in accordance with a projected programme for long-term capital expenditure. Short-term funds are obtained through the money markets, but long-term projects are financed mainly through the Public Works Loans Board, supplemented by issues on the open market.

21.4 User-charges

Merits of user-charges

Where they can be levied, charges promote economy in use and achieve equity in that the beneficiary pays. The recent shift towards them aims to avoid increasing taxation to pay for services. Water, currently in short supply, is an example. Where a household pays for it through a charge based solely on rateable value, the marginal cost of water consumed is zero. In contrast, metered water charges means that payment is related to each litre consumed.

One other advantage of charges is that they can throw up a valuable guideline for investment. For example, metered water charges reveal demand at the current price, and from this some estimate can be made of future demand.

User-charges or tax-financing?

With *community goods*, where free-riders cannot be excluded, no price can be charged, since nobody will pay when private rights to them cannot be granted. Here the cost has to be covered entirely from taxation.

But with other goods, there is a choice between charges, taxation or a combination of both. Here the decision is governed by economic, technical and political considerations.

In the case of *collective goods*, economic theory can justify public owner-ship on the grounds of efficiency in the allocation of resources. In addition, when deciding how they shall be financed, the concept of a Pareto improve-ment is relevant where marginal cost is zero.

We can illustrate this with reference to a public garden in the centre of a town. To simplify, let us assume that: (i) people derive pleasure from the flower gardens and would be willing to pay for this benefit; (ii) the garden can be fenced round so that, by excluding 'free-riders', a price can be charged; and (iii) the only cost is the initial price, which includes a capitalised sum for future maintenance, giving marginal cost of zero up to the capacity of the gardens to take visitors. The situation is depicted in Figure 21.1, where the ATC curve is a rectangular hyperbola and the capacity of the gardens is OZ after which more visitors involve serious overcrowding.

If the gardens were provided privately by a monopolist, he would charge OP, limiting visitors to OM, where marginal cost (OZ), equals marginal revenue, and where total revenue is at a maximum because elasticity of demand equals unity.

Suppose now that the gardens were taken over by the local authority By lowering the price to OP', a larger number of people OM' could enjoy the gardens at no extra cost, and total costs would be covered by a user-charge of OP' where there are OM' visitors.

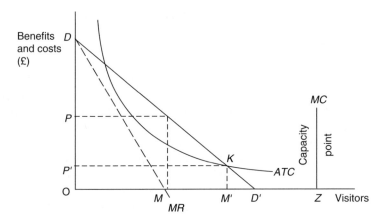

Figure 21.1 Public provision of collective and public goods

Nevertheless it is still possible to effect a Pareto improvement. Where, as in our model, marginal cost is zero (for example, with parks, bridges, motor ways and art galleries), enjoyment by an extra person imposes no sacrifice on others. Such 'non-rivalry' means that maximum benefits can be obtained only if such goods are provided by the State at no charge. Thus, in our example of the garden, if no charge is made, benefits could be increased by *KM'D'* at no extra cost (since marginal cost to *OZ* is nil). But, because total cost is no longer covered, the garden would have to be entirely tax-financed as with community goods. Likewise, an income re-distribution may be involved – from an old lady who rarely goes to the park towards the large family making much use of it.

Technical difficulties may outweigh economic considerations in the method of financing a service. Thus while motorways could be financed by toll charges, the effect on the traffic flow, especially during rush hours, has led the UK to pay for them from general taxation.

Where demand at zero price for a collective service is not likely to be too high and the cost of collecting fees is not disproportionate to the revenue raised, the choice between tax financing and user-charging could reasonably rest on the question: who benefits from the service? Where the community as a whole benefits – for example, street lighting and by-pass roads – tax-financing is appropriate. In contrast, if only certain individuals benefit, the cost is best, and more fairly, covered by individual fees (for example, for public tennis courts and swimming pools), or if a particular group benefits, a special levy can be imposed, for example, street-making charges.

With *merit* goods in particular, it may be desirable to recognise the uneven distribution of income when considering charges. For instance, charges for essential education would be highly regressive on low-income families with children of school-age. Alternatively, the regressive impact of charges can be modified by price discrimination. Thus low-income families are given housing benefits, while persons over retirement age do not pay prescription charges.

Generally, therefore, the choice between charges and taxation is, in practice, likely to be decided politically, especially where income redistribution figures prominently. But the economic constraints on charging less than the free market price must be emphasised, for an extended demand may impose a heavy burden on taxation generally. The result is that some form of administrative rationing according to need may have to be imposed, for example, the 'points' system for allocating council dwellings. More seriously, hidden rationing may prevail through depreciation of the quality of service provided, for example, state medical services and education. Indeed, this could apply to BBC television, where a possible 'community good' is converted to a 'collective good' by a compulsory legal licence. Through this creation of excludability, the cost falls on TV owners.

In addition, charging for a service at less than its full economic cost leads to pressure for an extension of the service – for example, subsidised public transport and housing – by consumers who benefit most. The minimum necessary condition for this to occur is that benefits are significantly more concentrated or localised than the costs which have to be met.

It should be noted that practical considerations may mean that over time methods of covering expenditure may be changed, as the history of road-financing illustrates. Tolls were satisfactory when there were few roads, but they had to give way to special levies (for example, Road Fund revenues) as the government assumed responsibility for a rapidly-growing road network. Eventually the Chancellor of the Exchequer realised that expenditure on motor vehicles could be a source of tax revenue, and the idea of Road Fund gave way to covering the full cost of roads out of general taxation. However, the attributes of user-charges outlined above suggest that a return to toll-financing for motorways and, if technical difficulties can be overcome, the introduction of some form of pricing for the use of urban roads (see Chapter 17) may now be appropriate.

User-charges and price discrimination

Even when it has been decided to cover the cost of a service by charges, difficulties may arise where there are relatively very high fixed costs, as with public transport, electricity, and natural gas, since supply by competing firms would simply mean that none could be financially viable. In any case, for technical reasons, a monopoly may be necessary. For instance, only one firm can be given the right to acquire land for laying a gas main or for running a water pipe under the roads, while, for public transport, competing firms cannot be allowed to 'skim' the profitable commuter traffic with none providing a service at other times or on other routes.

This necessity of having to create a monopoly because of decreasing costs or of special technical conditions of supply strengthens the case for the provision or supervision of certain services (for example, passenger transport) by the government or local authorities. More than that, it also allows a policy of price discrimination to operate whereby the service can be financially viable without subsidy. Figure 21.2 illustrates this. If average total cost and demand are as depicted by curves *ATC* and *PD* respectively, it is impossible to cover total cost at a single price, since at all outputs *ATC* will always exceed average revenue.

In practice the problem has been overcome in three ways.

(i) The difference has been covered by a *subsidy*, either directly, for example, for city transport, or indirectly, through writing off accumulated deficits from time to time, for example, for coal and railways.

(ii) A *standing charge* is levied irrespective of units consumed, for example for electricity and metered water. The standing charge goes to meet fixed costs; the price per unit consumed covers variable costs.

(iii) The industry is allowed to exploit its monopoly position by *price discrimination*. This is possible where different customers, having a different elasticity of demand for the product, can be kept separate, each being charged the price he is willing to pay. By 'charging what the traffic will bear', total revenue is increased. Such price discrimination by consumer category is used, for example, by the railway operators, where cheap-day trippers, senior citizens and students are charged lower fares than commuters.

The highest degree of charging 'what the traffic will bear' is where the undertaking could discriminate perfectly between every consumer and charge different prices to each. Thus in Figure 21.2, provided $\triangle PLS$ is larger than $\triangledown SRC$, the service would be profitable. Although this is impractical, a modified form, 'block pricing', separates additional amounts of the product and charges them at decreasing prices.

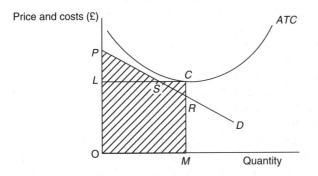

Figure 21.2 The possibility of supply through price discrimination

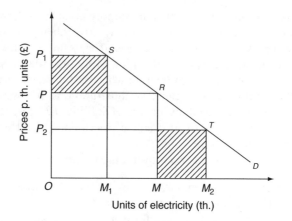

Figure 21.3 Increasing revenue by 'block pricing'

Thus in Figure 21.3 total revenue from a single electricity price *OP* would be *POMR*. But if a consumer is charged OP_1 for the first OM_1 units, *OP* for the second block of M_1M units, and OP_2 for the third block of MM_2 units, the extra revenue realised is shown by the two shaded areas.

21.5 Taxation

The classification of taxes

Traditionally, classification of taxes rests on the administrative distinction between direct and indirect taxation. A direct tax is one which is paid direct to the revenue authorities by the person taxed – examples include income tax, corporation tax, inheritance tax, local rates, motor-vehicle licence duties. An indirect tax is one which is collected via importers, manufactures, distributors or other intermediaries – for example, customs and excise duties, VAT.

Such a classification, however, is not very helpful in analysing the effects of taxation. Analytically we need to distinguish between: (a) *neutral taxes*, which do not directly affect the relative cost of and the demand for different goods and services, and (b) *selective taxes*, which have effect on demand or supply and thus on relative prices of different goods. To a large extent such a distinction does match up with the administration classification for most direct taxes have only general effects on the economy as whole. On the other hand, local rates are akin to a selective tax in that they affect the prices of particular properties as regards both type and location, and the price of real property as compared with other goods.

It should be noted, however, that a tax does not have to be 'direct' to be neutral. Thus a general sales tax (such as a VAT system which taxed *all* goods and services at the same rate) would be neutral because it would simply lower private expenditure (that is, reduce disposable income) by the amount raised by the tax. Since the consumer cannot switch to a cheaper untaxed substitute, relative prices would remain unchanged.

Neutral taxes

(1) Taxes on income

(a) *Income tax.*   In the UK tax is levied on the net income of persons and partnerships (companies are subject to corporation tax).

A high rate of tax on income can be expected to affect 'incentives', but this is by no means clear-cut. Attention is usually focused on its effect on how hard or long people work but it can also penalise risk-raking. Assuming that taxpayers are able to work more in order to earn more income, we can examine how various types of tax may affect their decision.

A *poll tax* (that is, a tax which does not vary with income) would reduce net income but leave the rate of reward for additional effort unchanged. Such a tax would, if anything, increase the supply of effort, since people might be expected to work harder to make up the income forgone. Any tax based on income, since it reduces total net income, has this 'total income' effect. But an *income tax*, unlike a poll tax, also alters the 'price' of income in terms of leisure by reducing the financial reward for sacrificing desirable leisure. This 'substitution' effect would thus work to reduce the supply of effort. Since the two effects work in opposite directions, the net effect will depend on which is stronger. Where the marginal rate of tax is substantially higher than the average, the substitution effect may outweigh the 'total income' effect and so justify the conclusion that a highly-progressive income-tax inhibits effort more than a proportional or less progressive one. Of course in the short run much depends on the extend to which institutional factors (such as terms of employment, insurance and mortgage commitments) allow income to be adjusted to avoid tax.

Even more important for high-income earners is that a high marginal tax rate may reduce the attractiveness of risk-taking. The essence of risk – whether accepting a new job or developing a new product – is that things can go well or badly. A high marginal-tax-rate tilts the balance against risk. If the gain from a successful outcome is taxed at a high rate, the risk differential is reduced, so that risk-takers choose the safer option.

The disincentive disadvantages of a markedly progressive income tax may be off-set by its 'built-in' stabilising effect on the economy. Assuming constant government expenditure and tax rates, tax receipts tend to fall in periods of deflation and to rise in periods of inflation, thereby stabilising budget deficits and surpluses.

(b) *Corporation tax.*   In 1965 the profits tax was replaced by a corporation tax. Under the 'imputation' system adopted in 1973, all profits, whether distributed or not, are taxed at the same rate (30 per cent in 2000, but 20 per cent for small companies up to £300 000 profit a year).

In the short run a tax on the net income of an enterprise falls on economic surplus or rent, and will not affect price and output decisions. This is true, but not particularly interesting since most of the important problems occur in the long period. Even in the short run, however, problems arise. For example, accounting profits as measured for tax assessment may be greater than the true economic net surplus. If they are (for example, through inflation), the tax will fall in part on production costs with consequent contraction in the long period.

(2) Taxes on capital
Taxes on capital can take three main forms:

(a) a tax on capital passing at death (inheritance tax);
(b) an annual charge on a person's capital (wealth tax);
(c) a tax on increases in the value of capital, usually levied when the asset is sold (capital gains tax).

The effects of different taxes depend more on what they are paid out of, rather than what they are levied on. If a capital tax is defined as one which is paid out of capital, no difficulty arises. More usually, however, a capital tax is one which is levied on capital. This gives rise to the analytical difficulty that the tax may be paid out of income – for example, a person may pay out of current income the premium on an insurance policy to cover possible inheritance tax when he dies. Conversely, some taxes assessed on income or on current outlay may be paid out of capital (for example, the car tax and VAT on a new car). A rough-and-ready line of division can be drawn: all taxes tend to be paid out of income except where the size of the tax makes this impossible. When a tax is large and/or abnormal it tends to be paid out of capital irrespective of whether the Inland Revenue regards it as an income tax or a capital tax.

Developing this argument, an annual tax based on the capital values of income-bearing assets may be regarded as an alternative to an income tax on investment income. If, for example, a perpetual investment yielded a rate of return of 5 per cent, the revenue from a capital tax of $2\frac{1}{2}$p in the £ levied on capital values would be the same as that from an income tax of 50p levied on income. Given a uniform capitalisation factor (number of year's purchase) for all types of investment income, there would be no difference between the two taxes. But obviously a riskier income will be capitalised at a lower number of years' purchase than a well-secured income. For instance, a capital tax of 6p in the £ of capital value levied regardless of the use to which the capital is put, would bear least heavily on riskier types of investment. Thus the deterrent effect of high rates of income taxation on production would be reduced by the substitution of a tax on capital.

(a) *Inheritance tax.*   In 1986, a capital transfer tax was replaced by the inheritance tax on lifetime gifts. After the first three years, tax is paid at reducing rates and no tax is paid if death occurs after seven years from gifting. There are concessions for small businesses and farms.

(b) *Wealth tax.*   A wealth tax, not currently used in the UK, is an annual charge on a person's capital assets. As an alternative to a tax on capital gains, its great economic advantage is that it does not deter the most efficient use of capital.

Although theoretically plausible, however, a general wealth tax could be difficult to administer because of the need to keep valuations up to date. Also, in the absence of well-defined markets in all types of asset, including property, valuation itself might involve inequity between holders of assets.

(c) *Capital gains tax*   In strict economic terms, personal 'income' refers to a person's command over economic resources over a given period. So defined, it is the amount a taxpayer could spend during a given period so as to leave himself no worse off at the end of the period than he was at the beginning. Thus it includes any growth in the value of wealth over the period as well as of income in its more usual sense.

Interpreting income in this sense of spending-power, therefore, argues for a general tax on expenditure (reflecting a command over resources). However, since a tax on *all* spending would require a massive readjustment of the tax system. Britain has preferred the alternative of adding a separate capital gains tax to the existing income-tax structure.

Selective taxes: as part of the overall tax structure

'Indirect' taxes have to be related to the overall tax structure as regards their *equity* and *economic efficiency*.

Since they cannot easily be related to taxpayers' income (even where the commodities to be taxed and the rates of tax are carefully chosen), they tend to be a *regressive* form of tax (that is, the effective incidence is heaviest on poorer households). Ideally, therefore, indirect taxes should be confined to goods which are not necessities but which are consumed on a broad enough scale to provide the revenue required. The difficulty is that the higher the general standard of living, the wider is the definition of 'necessities'! In any case, other considerations may be dominant when applying indirect taxes.

Thus if the disincentive effect of income tax is greater than that of expenditure taxes, some substitution of expenditure taxes for income tax may be desirable.

From the standpoint of *economic efficiency*, any expenditure tax imposed *selectively* on some goods and services alters relative prices, brings about a reallocation of consumers' expenditure and distorts the pattern of consumption and production. If that pattern were already ideal, this distortion would result in a less than optimal distribution of resources. This suggests that if economic efficiency is to be combined with equity, expenditure taxes should be levied on goods which have a low price-elasticity of demand (minimising any reallocation effect) but which also have a high income-elasticity of demand (for these are also likely to be 'non-necessities').

Selective taxes: allocative effects

Since selective expenditure taxes distort relative prices, we have to consider their effects in specific sectors of the economy. We do so by examining the *shifting* and *incidence* of such taxes. *Shifting* refers to the possibility that a tax can be 'shifted' on to others by the person who originally pays the tax, while *incidence* refers to its final resting-place. But the analysis, although helpful in formulating tax policy, cannot predict precise effects. Rather it is limited to indicating tendencies in terms of 'more' or 'less' relative to the particular time period.

Selective taxes affect owners of productive resources, firms and consumers. We consider their impact on each in turn.

(1) OWNERS OF PRODUCTIVE RESOURCES
With land resources the significant feature is that supply is often only variable after a considerable lapse of time. This applies when analysing the effects of taxes on unimproved land, land bearing specific resources (such as minerals, timber, coal, iron) and improvements to land (for example by buildings, race-courses, and so on).

Fixity of supply is the feature of non-reproducible resources, such as minerals. Here, since earnings consist wholly of economic rent, the owner must bear all the tax. If he tries to sell the resource, the purchaser will simply capitalise the tax and deduct it from his offer price. This is the basis for the taxation of 'betterment' (see Chapter 20).

(2) FIRMS
'Firms' are situated midway between factors of production and final consumers. The effect of taxes levied on firms will therefore alter economic relationships both in factor markets and in the final product market. As firms respond by changing the extent and direction of their activities, they shift the tax burden – backwards on to factors of production and forward on

to final consumers. Which of these two groups will finally bear most of the burden depends on the relative elasticities of consumer-demand and factor-supply. If the elasticity of product-demand is greater than the elasticity of factor-supply, the tax shifting will be mainly backwards, and vice versa. For instance, if a tax is levied on carpets the demand for which is very sensitive to price changes and which are made by firms employing specialists in carpet-making who have no alternative occupation, then, unless the firm is willing to accept lower profits, the wages of carpet-makers are likely to suffer. Conversely, if the demand for carpets is very inelastic and if the factors employed in carpet-manufacture are in highly elastic supply (that is, have alternative occupations to which they can readily turn), the tax is likely to be borne largely by the buyers of carpets.

Taxes levied on firms fall into two groups:

(i) *Taxes fixed independently of output.* Local rates, for example, the Uniform Business Rate (UBR), are, analytically, an addition to the fixed costs of the firm and so reduce profits. In the short run, however, this is unlikely to have any effect on supply since marginal revenue and marginal cost are unchanged by the tax. There is thus little possibility of shifting the tax in the short run.

But in the long run, if the tax reduces returns in this line of production relative to other lines, supply will tend to decrease and price to rise depending on the elasticity of demand. Thus part of the tax originally borne by the firm will tend to be passed on to consumers as firms leave this line of production.

Furthermore, decreased production reduces the demand for factors of production whose prices therefore fall. Thus part of the burden of the tax will be borne by factors of production according to their elasticity of supply in that line of production.

(ii) *Taxes levied on output.* These taxes can be divided into two types: (a) those levied proportionally to *output*, such as specific taxes on tobacco and beer, and which analytically constitute a *fixed* addition to variable cost per unit; and (b) those which vary more than proportionately with output, for example, an *ad valorem* tax such as VAT, and which by varying with the cost of production, represents a *varying* addition to variable cost per unit of output.

Both types can be analysed in the same way. A rise in variable cost per unit of output means one-off rise in marginal cost. Thus output will be reduced and the price of the product is likely to increase even in the short period. But in the long period productive capacity can be varied, and producers who do not cover total costs will leave the industry, thereby reducing supply. There will thus be an increased tendency towards a higher product-price (net of tax) and a shifting forward of the tax to consumers. Furthermore, reduction of supply will reduce demand for factors, resulting in lower factor-prices and a shifting backwards of the tax if factor-supply is less than perfectly elastic.

(3) CONSUMERS

As explained above, the burden of taxation may be shifted forward from the firm to consumers. But, consumers themselves, as sellers of labour, can try to shift the burden backwards by claiming higher wages. Similarly, when the burden of tax is shifted backwards on to labour, workers, as consumers of final products, reduce their demand and so tend to shift the burden back again to sellers of final products. The final incidence of the tax as between consumers and producers will depend upon the relative elasticities of supply and demand. The greater the producer's elasticity of supply compared with the consumer's elasticity of demand, the more will the tax be borne by the consumer, and vice versa.

Have we argued ourselves into a circle as regards the final incidence? Not quite. The circle may be broken in a number of places, and it is one of the functions of 'shifting' analysis to indicate where it is likely to occur in a particular situation, for example, by legislative price control, by lags in the adjustment of wages to changes in the cost of living, or by the fact that those whose income is not derived from work cannot shift the burden forward to consumers. While shifting analysis cannot determine exactly who 'pays', it is useful in throwing light on processes.

Summary

Governments intervene in markets for the provision of community goods, collective goods and merit goods. Public sector provision of land and property resources takes place through:
- government departments
- state-owned industies
- quasi-governmental bodies
- local authorities

The finance for the activities of these public sector organisations comes from:
- borrowing
- user-charges
- taxation

Taxes on income and capital and local authority charges have different effects on the property sector and the impact of specific property taxes, such as stamp duty, can be considerable.

Review questions

1. How are local authority services financed?
2. Compare the financing of collective goods by user-charges or by taxation.
3. Assess the economic efficiency of local authority taxation.
4. How can revenue be increased by 'price discrimination'?
5. What is meant by 'tax shifting'?

Recommended reading

C. V. Brown and P. J. Jackson, *Public Sector Economics*, 2nd edn (London: Martin Robertson, 1982) chs 1–5.

N. P. Hepworth, *The Finance of Local Government*, 7th edn (London: Heinemann, 1984) chs 1–4.

B. Walker, *Welfare Economics and Urban Problems* (London: Hutchinson, 1981) ch. 7.

CHAPTER 22

The Incidence of Taxation on Land Resources

After studying this chapter you will be able to:

- **Assess the impact of various taxes on property**
- **Explain what is meant by 'planning gain'**
- **Explain the impact of VAT on property**
- **Describe the advantages and disadvantages of local property taxes**

In previous chapters there have been frequent references to where *government expenditure* is, for various reasons, specifically related to real property. These include housing subsidies, housing benefits, farm improvement grants, compensation for Sites of Special Scientific Interest (SSSIs), and listed building repair grants.

As regards *taxation*, however, only local rates and the petroleum revenue tax are specific to real property, although sales of land and buildings are singled out for a high rate of stamp duty compared with other asset transfers.

In this chapter we examine the ways in which taxation affects real property. We begin by considering certain aspects of the main direct taxes. But, as explained in Chapter 21, with all selective indirect taxes there is over time the possibility of shifting the tax backwards to factors of production or forward to consumers. Most of our discussion, therefore, will concentrate on the main taxes directed to property – local taxes – in order to suggest their eventual incidence on the efficiency and allocation of land resources, and their distributive effects.

22.1 Direct taxation and land resources

As explained in Chapter 21, while direct taxes may affect incentives to effort and risk-bearing investment, they are basically *neutral* in their effects on individual items of expenditure. Nevertheless, special provisions within the broad tax arrangements may have marginal economic effects, as follows.

(1) Income Tax

Interest relief on income tax for home-owners started in 1803. Until 1950, when only 10 per cent of households were home-owners, the cost to the Exchequer was small. But the subsequent increase in ownership led to the qualifying loan being limited to £25 000 in 1974. This was raised to £30 000 in 1983 with the introduction of 'mortage interest relief at source' (MIRAS), under which the borrower paid the tender interest less the tax relief.

This home-ownership subsidy peaked at £8 bn in 1991, but concern for the PSNCR meant that the rate was subsequently reduced in steps to 10 per cent. On 6 April 2000, when MIRAS was abolished, the Exchequer saved only 1.4bn a year. Over the previous years, however, this subsidy, by favouring owner-occupiers, effectively moved housing tenure from the rented to the owner-occupied sector (see Table 18.4).

(2) Corporation tax

In the computation of corporation tax (income tax in the case of an unincorporated business) agricultural and industrial buildings enjoy capital depreciation allowances. Commercial and residential buildings, however, can only offset *actual* repair and maintenance costs against tax. As a result agricultural and industrial buildings tend to have a shorter life irrespective of technical considerations, while landlords of residential properties are deterred from making *improvements* to buildings with a limited life.

(3) Inheritance tax

To avoid the break-up of agricultural estates which occurred in the past in order to pay inheritance tax upon the death of a major owner, there is now no tax payable on agricultural land, while businesses have a reduced rate of 50 per cent.

But the tax advantage of leaving farm land rather than other assets influences demand. A person who wishes to pass on his wealth to an heir may purchase and enjoy the amenity of owning a rural estate for at least two years can, if he so wishes, carry on the actual farming through a contractor or similar device. Moreover, since there is inheritance tax relief for requests to the National Trusts, it tends to decrease the land available for holding in private hands.

(4) Capital gains tax (CGT)

Since owner-occupied houses are exempt from CGT, the owner receives a further 'subsidy' compared with other asset-holders, thereby increasing demand for houses as compared with other assets such as equities, unit trusts and expensive antiques, which are subject to CGT.

Moreover, where the gains made on the sale of business assets are fully reinvested in similar business assets within three years, the tax may be deferred. This 'roll-over' concession tends to maintain demand for such assets; or, as the holders often put it, they are 'locked in' to such assets.

(5) Stamp duty

Stamp duty is levied on the value of transactions in land and buildings:

£	per cent
60001 – 250000	1
250001 – 500000	3
Over 500000	4

As regards property:

(a) it discriminates against investment in property as opposed to shares which pay only 0.5 per cent;
(b) it depresses overall property values;
(c) by increasing purchase costs, it reduces market liquidity;
(d) where more accommodation is required, it can make it cheaper to build on one's current house rather than move to a higher-priced house;
(e) it has a disproportionate effect on south of England properties, where property prices are highest.

(6) Development land tax (DLT) and 'planning gain'

Under the Community Land Act 1975, all development land was to be brought under public ownership over a period of about ten years. In the meantime, 'betterment' was to be collected through a DLT. In theory, as explained below, the tax was sound; in practice, it was a flop, and eventually dropped. But it did provide the background for the concept of 'planning gain'.

From the point of view of economic analysis a high rate of DLT should have no effect on the supply of land for development since the tax falls on economic rent. This is the return over and above the 'transfer price' which accrues to a factor through fixity of supply. Transfer price covers what the factor can earn in its best alternative use plus any return (often termed 'normal profit') required by the owner to overcome his inertia or inconvenience in effecting such a transfer. This can be illustrated both arithmetically and diagrammatically.

Suppose undeveloped farmland surrounding a town is required for housing. The current-use price is, say £2000 per acre; this is the transfer price, that is, what another farmer would be prepared to pay for the land for agricultural use. Planning permission is now given for a housing development on 12 acres of a particular farm. As a result the price of these 12 acres rises to £80 000 an acre. Their enhanced development value would equal current market price *minus* current-use value, that is, £936 000. If the rate of *development tax* on this *gain* were, say, 60 per cent, the farmer would still be left with £398 400 (£960 000 tax minus £561 600 tax). Thus he can obtain 199 acres to replace the 12 sold.

The above argument is shown diagrammatically in Figure 22.1. If no planning permission were required and all the agricultural land surrounding the town were suitable for housing, we can assume that any price above the agricultural price will secure the land for housing. In other words, the supply (S_a) of land is perfectly elastic at OY, that is, at £2000 an acre. Demand for agricultural land is given by the demand curve D. Any increase in demand for land for housing, XX_1 can be supplied without any rise in price. In other words, because supply is perfectly elastic, the increase in demand to D_1 has no effect on price.

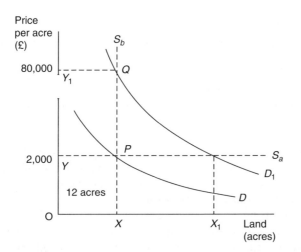

Figure 22.1 Economic rent arising from restricted planning permission

In practice, however, planning permission is restricted to twelve acres, OX and supply curve S_b. Thus the price of these soars above their agricultural-use value to £80 000 an acre, OY_1. There is a windfall gain, or betterment, to the farmer of $Y_1 YPQ$. The whole of this windfall gain can be taxed away without making any difference to the farmer's willingness to supply the land for housing, assuming that his inertia costs were included in the price OY. DLT could thus rise to almost 100 per cent.

In theory, the argument is neat; in practice, it runs up against snags. The first is that we do not know for certain how much the farmer will actually require to cover his inertia and upheaval costs. Subjective valuations cannot be ignored. He may feel, for instance, that the after-tax £398 400 left to him is insufficient compensation for land which has been in the possession of his family for generations.

A second snag is that the theory is essentially static, making no allowance for expectations. The farmer may speculate against a future rate of DLT, refusing to sell if he thinks it might be reduced in the near future, or being more ready to sell if he fears an increase. If there is a lack of voluntary sales, the price of development land will rise (other things being equal), while if compulsory purchase has to be invoked, development will be delayed by the time-consuming procedures of a local public enquiry.

In practice the DLT had high costs of collection relative to yield and a restrictive effect on the supply of land. It was therefore abolished so that betterment is now collected through capital gains tax and 'planning gain'.

PLANNING GAIN

Unlike a tax, planning gain has no legal backing and lacks a precise defin-ition. Thus we have to fall back on the generally accepted meaning: a benefit, either in cash or kind, accruing to the local authority from the grant of planning consent. The absence of any precise official definition has the advantage of permitting flexibility. But the result is that interpretation of what planning gain should actually cover has widened over the past twenty years.

The early view was that planning gain should relate solely to the external costs of the *actual* development and so should be limited to a contribution to such costs as road access, water supply, and sewage disposal, necessary for the development to proceed.

Subsequently planning gain was widened to cover payments on items which may be divorced, both functionally and geographically, but could be considered material to achieving an acceptable balance of uses in mixed developments. For example, this would cover the cost of the developer providing 'social' housing and a library.

Section 106 of the Town and Country Planning Act 1990 allows a devel-oper to put forward in his application for planning permission a package of what he proposes to build *plus* details of what he is prepared to offer by way of planning gain to cover works which he considers will commend his development to the local authority. But without any precise definition or examples of what planning gain should be limited to, the procedure regarding planning consents often followed a course which was highly suspect.

On the one hand, the developer offers a level of inducement, which on occasions might be little short of a bribe, to cajole the local planning authority, to give consent. There seemed to be no limit to the nature of such offers. For instance, in 1992 Sainsbury, in its application for a super-store at Plymouth, offered benefits costed at £3.66 m. for items which included a tourist information centre, an art gallery display, a bird-watching hide and access to a nature reserve!

On the other hand, many local authorities saw their role of ruling on planning applications as a means of collecting betterment – a unilateral imposition of what was virtually its own DLT in order to fund functions, such as social housing, normally financed from general taxation. To this, the Conservative government which had cut grants to local authorities in order to reduce the PSNCR, seemed to turn a blind eye.

In practice, 'betterment' would be split between the developer and the local authority by a process of bilateral bargaining (more simply, 'horse-trading') depending on the assessment of the strengths of the opposite side. If agreement is reached, the developer gets his planning consent without going through a lengthy and costly appeal procedure, and the local authority obtains its social affordable housing, etc. At times, however, the local authority may over-play its hand, and the developer withdraws. This happened in 1998 when Berkeley Homes pulled out of a scheme to convert an office building into 24 flats because Camden Council would not com-promise on its demand for £420 000 by way of commuted compensation for not including 6 affordable flats, that is 25 per cent of the scheme.

The above arrangement has given cause for serious concern. Meetings may be held in secret, thereby eliminating the transparency essential for democratic control. More than that it can undermine confidence in the planning system. There is only a thin line between planning gain and selling planning permission. The planning gain may become a bribe by the devel-oper to induce the council to ignore or over-rule technical considerations, as when, for example, affordable social housing is accepted irrespective of the excess traffic it might generate on already congested local roads.

There are two methods by which what has been described as 'the only lawful form of corruption left in the United Kingdom' can be brought under control. First, an aggrieved third party may appeal to the courts, though in practice the courts have been liberal in their interpretation of what is acceptable. Secondly, the Minister may decide that 'enough is enough'. This happened in what is known as the Tesco-Witley case.

Tesco had applied to the local planning authority, Oxfordshire District Council, to redevelop land in Witney as a foodstore. The local authority had previously decided to build a link road, but at a considerable distance from the Tesco site, in order to relieve traffic congestion. In spite of the fact that the foodstore was unlikely to generate more traffic than other permitted users of the site, Tesco offered to fund this road.

The Secretary of State refused planning permission, thereby over-ruling the view of his planning inspector at the local public inquiry. Tesco appealed, and eventually the House of Lords had to decide: (a) whether Tesco's offer comprised a 'material consideration'; (b) if so, did the Secretary of State fail to have regard to it? Its 1995 ruling was that, while there was some element of material consideration in Tesco's offer, the Secretary of State had, after due consideration, given little weight to it in arriving at his decision.

This decision can be regarded as a milestone in defining the section 106 conditions which a local planning authority may impose when deciding on a planning application and the obligations which may be accepted by the developer. Even though there will be further legal challenges, the Tesco case is a step in restoring the integrity of the planning system and in reversing the planning gain bonanza which had come into being.

22.2 The impact of VAT on real property

The nature of VAT

All goods and services are classified by Customs & Excise as 'standard-rated', 'zero-rated' or 'exempt' supplies. The standard rate is 17.5 per cent of the value of the supply; zero-rated and exempt supplies do not attract any VAT.

VAT is intended to be a tax on final consumers, and not on economic intermediary producers. Thus suppliers of standard-rated and zero-rated goods and services can reclaim all the VAT they pay on their inputs (for example, raw materials, components, office supplies).

'Exempt' indicates a liability to VAT, not an exclusion. The essential point is that with 'exempt' goods the supplier cannot reclaim VAT paid on inputs.

If VAT were levied at the standard rate on all goods and services, it would be a neutral tax. But the different categories described above mean that its incidence is different between certain goods. Indeed, as regards property, it may apply or may not, as explained below.

VAT and real property

Until 1989 the construction and sale of new buildings was zero-rated, while rents were exempt. In 1988 the European Court of Justice ruled that only residential construction could be zero-rated, though all other rents could continue to be exempt.

Accordingly the government enacted that from 1 April 1989 VAT must be paid at the standard rate on all *new* non-domestic buildings and civil engineering works, and on the sale of freehold or leasehold non-domestic building land as soon as construction begins.

Rents would remain 'exempt'. But this posed the major problem of how the developer, if he retained the building as an investment or the purchaser of the new construction (the landlord/investor), could recoup the VAT paid on the construction. Here the government made a concession which has important implications for real property. The developer or landlord could become a taxable supplier by charging VAT at the standard rate on rent. This is known as the 'option to tax' (OTT) and is exercisable unilaterally by the landlord (with a lease or licence) or by the vendor (in the disposal of land or buildings).

It should be noted that exercising the OTT is irrevocable by the opting owner for both current and future leases. Any subsequent sale is automatically standard-rated, although a new owner would be entitled to decide afresh whether to exercise the option. Nor can the option be exercised piecemeal – it has to apply to the whole building. Consequently where a building is multi-let the owner cannot vary the OTT according to the particular VAT liability of different tenants.

The effects of exercising the OTT

It is likely that developers retaining properties and other landlord-investors will exercise their OTT when the new building is bought (the developer who retains his construction has to pay VAT by 'self-billing'), but VAT can be recovered on a building so extensively refurbished or subsequently refurbished that it is considered to be a 'new' building, and thus subject to tax. Nor, with one possible exception, will the OTT affect the rent obtainable. With industrial and retail property, the occupiers can reclaim the VAT on rent as an input. The same applies to offices let to accountants, lawyers, surveyors and similar services whose supplies are standard-rated.

The one major exception is services whose supplies are mainly 'exempt' – chiefly banks, insurance companies, pension funds, building societies and finance companies. Here the owner of the property would have to look at the likely future tenant of the building and ask what effect the OTT might have on the rent at which it could be let, and thus on its capitalised value.

In most localities such 'exempt services' will still have to compete for premises (for example, in the high street) with 'reclaimable-VAT' tenants. Furthermore, as rent usually forms only a very small fraction of total costs, demand for space is fairly inelastic. Thus such exempt services will continue to pay the *same* going rent *plus* the VAT. But there are localities where 'exempt-service' tenants predominate, notably the City of London, but also such office-concentrated centres as Reading, Swindon, Bristol and

Edinburgh. Here, because of the external economy, of 'special accessibility', rents obtained include an element of economic rent over and above that which would be paid by other users. In this case the incidence of the VAT would be on the economic rent element and thus on the landlord since his premises can now be let only at a lower rent. This means that the owner now has to compare his saving by not paying VAT on the initial capital cost with a possible loss of rent, resulting from the imposition of VAT on rents, both now and at subsequent rent reviews. These losses could be capitalised in the usual way using DCF in order to show the loss in capital value. Eventually this could be reflected in a fall in demand for land (and thus its price) in such specialised locations.

One other effect of VAT is that in those areas, such as the City of London, where occupiers predominate in providing financial and other exempt services, a two-tier market can result. Offices constructed since 1989 are likely to have had the OTT exercised and thus achievable net rents could be lower. In comparison, for older buildings there would be little advantage, apart from recovering VAT on service charges and professional fees, of exercising the OTT as this would destroy their higher net rent differential. This two-tier market will only diminish as the older buildings are replaced.

Charities may be put at a disadvantage by the OTT. Buildings which are actually used for charitable or community purposes continue to be zero-rated. Again, a charity shop would be able to reclaim VAT on its rent, provided it was registered for VAT. But if the new building is to be used for business purposes other than making taxable supplies (for example, a fee-paying school or private hospital, where such services are exempt), the VAT charged by a building contractor (for instance, on a new classroom block or a new ward) would not be reclaimable, and would thus represent an additional cost.

22.3 Local taxes based on property

Merits of a local property tax

It is against the overall objectives of local government (see p. 393) that local property taxes have to be examined. If it is judged that in providing certain services local *government*, as opposed to mere local *administration*, has advantages, then local people must be allowed to make their own decisions as to the type of service they prefer and be responsible for raising the necessary revenue. In this respect, taxes on property have many advantages.

First, they promote local autonomy and accountability. By having a clear base and giving local authorities their own source of revenue, property taxes afford a degree of financial independence from the central government.

Moreover, by being raised on a local basis with the rate determined annually, they make local authorities responsible to local people. However, such accountability is limited, in that only residential property is directly linked to the electoral process: no local voting powers are enjoyed by commercial and industrial property, though political influence may be exercised through pressure groups, such as the local Chamber of Commerce.

Second, local property taxes are generally accepted. Having been levied for nearly 400 years, they conform to the view that 'an old tax is no tax'. Moreover in form they are simple, easily understood and appear equitable in that property benefits from local services, and those occupying the largest properties tend to be the richer members of the community.

Third, there is certainty of yield. Not only are property taxes difficult to evade, but being based on fixed property any increase in the rate of tax cannot easily be shifted geographically (unlike a sales tax where people can shop in a cheaper area). Only in the long term can occupiers respond to high rates by moving to another area.

Fourth, property taxes have administrative advantages in that, once rateable or capital values have been assessed, the rate is easily calculated and can be adjusted when additional revenue is required. Furthermore costs of collection are relatively economic, being less than 2 per cent of yield.

Fifth, since a property tax is a lump-sum tax on housing, it penalises under-occupation and thereby provides an incentive to let rooms or move to a smaller property.

Disadvantages of a local property tax

In spite of these advantages, however, local property taxes are not without criticism.

First, because domestic rates are a selective tax on a particular good, there is a loss of welfare compared with a direct tax which raises the same amount of revenue (see pp. 334–6). Furthermore, a tax on housing services is illogical in the light of the government's policy of subsidising housing as a merit good.

Second, local property taxes, like all selective outlay taxes, distort market prices and thus, at least in the long period, have allocative effects. In order to show this we will assume:

(a) there is a competitive free market in housing;
(b) houses are homogeneous;
(c) all houses are rented on a weekly tenancy;
(d) no rates are being levied initially;
(e) the demand for rented housing is depicted by the *D* curves (Figure 22.2 (a) and (b)).

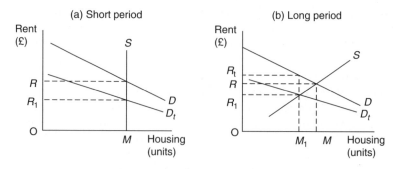

Figure 22.2 The effect of the imposition of rates on rents and the supply of housing

Initially the rent paid is OR (Figure 22.2(a)). If rates are now imposed on the tenant on an *ad valorem* basis, the demand curve shifts to D_t. In the short period, the stock of rented houses is fixed, and the new rates will be borne by landlords for net rent will fall from OR to OR_1 unless the tenant is under a long-term contract to pay exclusive of rates. In the long period, however, the supply of houses is more elastic since, assuming no planning consent is required, owners will adapt them to other uses or simply not replace them as they wear out, switching to lower-taxed and more profitable forms of investment. This means that some of the rate burden is now passed on to the tenant, the extent depending upon the relative elasticities of supply and demand. Thus in Figure 22.2(b) RR_t of the rate of burden is shifted forward to the tenant, and RR_1 backwards to landlords, the total rates paid being $R_t R_1 \times OM_1$. Furthermore, rented housing decreases by MM_1.

It should be noted, however, that if the new rates result in improved local services, especially education, roads and transport facilities, there could be an increase in the demand for property in the area, the demand curve shifting to the right. As a result the impact of the rates on the landlord is partly offset by a rise in rents so that rented housing will not decrease by as much as MM_1.

Furthermore, when the rate system itself is made selective by varying the poundage between different types of property (as, for instance, when agricultural land pays no rates and domestic buildings pay at a lower rate than businesses) there are additional allocative effects.

Third, the yield from property taxes lacks buoyancy – the result of the narrowness of the tax-base together with its rigidity in the face of inflation. Concentrating on a single form of wealth – property – allows other types, such as works of art, jewellery and antiques, to escape tax. Consequently, a rise in local government expenditure results in a considerable increase in the rate poundage. Though, as we have seen, this promotes accountability, it hampers progressive authorities who wish to extend their services. Again, though the yield from such taxes as income tax and VAT automatically increases with inflation, the rise in property prices takes time to be reflected in higher taxable values because revaluations may through administration difficulties, be continually postponed. Worse still, local government services tend to be labour-intensive so that the yearly rate-poundage increase tends to be proportionately higher than the rate of inflation, which in the past has led to periodic outbursts of discontent.

Fourth, local property taxes tend to be regressive and inequitable. Not only do poor people tend to spend a higher proportion of their income on housing, but the tax levied may be unrelated to ability to pay. Nor is there any direct link between the property tax and local services used. A pensioner, for example, has little call on education or refuse collection. However, rate (or Council Tax) rebates do help to offset the burden for poorer persons. In any case, the rating system must be viewed in relation to the overall national fiscal structure where more progressive taxes and free social benefits can compensate.

Similar considerations of equity apply to business undertakings. No rates are levied on agricultural land and buildings. On the other hand, small firms probably find what is virtually a lump-sum tax more onerous than large firms which have a higher turnover, while a rate increase imposes a heavier burden on those forms of production which are building-intensive, such as retailing, compared with those which are labour-intensive and machinery-intensive, such as light industry.

Fifth, groups bearing the lowest rate burden, such as householders, especially those on housing benefit or with children at school, tend to press for more goods and services to be provided by local authorities, since others bear a larger proportion of the costs.

Sixth, local property taxes accentuate relative differences in local authorities' resources. Often the authority with a low rateable value has more to spend on new infrastructure, housing and education, and is thus forced to levy a high rate-poundage. This means that the rates paid on similar properties can vary from one part of the country to another, and even between different parts of the same urban concentration. Such 'fiscal zoning' has allocative consequences, households and firms tending to move to those areas where the rate-poundage is lowest. Although inequalities between districts may be corrected by central government equalisation grants, this may be only at the expense of undermining local autonomy.

Different bases of local property tax

It is usual for local property taxes to be levied *ad valorem*; but the tax base chosen may be net annual value, capital value or site-value.

(1) NET ANNUAL VALUE
When the basis of assessment is Net Annual Value (NAV), it is likely to be determined as follows. First a Gross Annual Value – the yearly rent that the

property might reasonably be expected to be let for on a determined date – is given to the property, and then statutory deductions are made for maintenance and insurance to give the NAV.

Compared with a site-value base, NAV has certain advantages. First, because the base includes buildings as well as land, the yield is higher, especially for properties whose building cost is a high proportion of the total cost. Second, it is easier to assess, since in a free market rentals can be calculated by comparison with similar properties.

On the other hand, NAV has significant defects. First, because the tax falls on buildings as well as on land, it tends to be more regressive as regards houses, which are occupied by poor persons as well as rich. Second, NAV is not neutral as regards building improvements, for these are taxed. In the long period, therefore, capital tends to move to untaxed uses, an owner-occupier, for example, preferring to buy antique furniture rather than build a garage. Third, apart from the above problems of principle, NAV may, as the experience of the UK has shown, involve practical difficulties. Thus rent control and the loss of the private sector has meant that, in assessing rentals, evidence of free market rentals was confined to about 2 per cent of a sector which accounts for only 15 per cent of total dwellings. Moreover, anomalies occur. Not only is agricultural land de-rated with a severe loss of possible revenue to rural authorities, but relieving charities of rates penalises those authorities (such as Westmister, Oxford and Cambridge) which contain a high proportion of charities within their boundaries, especially as the NAVs are included in the valuation list which the central government uses in assessing its 'needs' grant.

(2) CAPITAL VALUE

Here the tax is the value of the premises if sold freehold in an open market, given a willing seller. Provided the capital value is equal to the NAV capitalised at the relevant rate of interest, it will produce an equivalent base for taxation as NAV.

In practice, however, marginal divergencies between the two methods may have allocative effects. If potential-use value is included in capital value, vacant and underdeveloped sites pay more tax than under NAV, thus accelerating redevelopment, discouraging non-occupation of buildings and stimulating greater use of existing property.

Other variations in assessing capital values may affect the rate of renewal of property, particularly dwellings. Capital-value assessments in the USA, for example, allow for the state of repair and length of life of the property and for risk of rental default. Such factors lower the capital value of such property as slum housing even though net returns relative to gross yields are high since little is spent on upkeep. Thus the tax base is smaller than it would be if net returns were capitalised to obtain the capital value, and it is suggested that the resulting tax advantage tends to retard urban renewal.

(3) SITE-VALUE RATING

The idea behind SVR as the basis of assessment is that the tax falls only on the land element of real property, that is, the open market value of the site on the assumption that it is currently available for its most profitable use. Thus, compared with an NAV or capital value base, the buildings are not taxed, but potential value is taxed (Figure 22.3).

As the basis of a property tax, SVR has certain advantages. First, it has strong moral backing in that it is closely associated with taxing 'betterment'. The argument is founded on Ricardo's theory of economic rent: since land is fixed in supply, its value is determined solely by demand, SVR is a tax on this demand-determined value and is thus a means by which 'betterment' can be returned to the community. Moreover, because sites are, for spatial reasons, fixed in supply, the tax falls entirely on economic rent with no effect on supply.

Second, SVR should improve the efficiency of land use. Because site-value is the sole tax-base, it is in effect a lump-sum tax which is levied irrespective of how the site is used, the value of the building on it, or whether the buildings are improved. That is, SVR is neutral as regards the type of use, intensity of use and improvements. There is thus an incentive to develop sites to their most profitable use, since the burden of the given tax would then be spread over higher gross receipts. Even if speculators continued to hoard land – vacant central sites and agricultural fringe land – SVR would ensure that they had to pay towards the cost of public services provided. Furthermore, the improvement of existing buildings would be encouraged. Thus SVR should speed up the renewal of inner-city areas.

Third, SVR could have benefits for housing. In the short period, the rate burden would tend to shift to central sites and away from suburban houses.

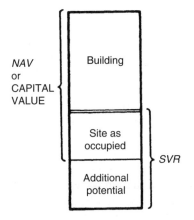

Figure 22.3 Comparison of the incidence of NAV, capital value and SVR on buildings and land

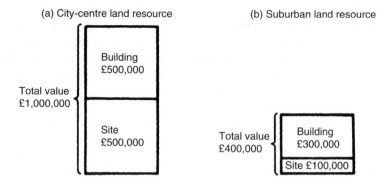

Figure 22.4 The incidence of site-value rating

Figure 22.4 shows that under SVR, (a) will pay rates on one-half of the original base, whereas (b) will pay on only one-quarter. In the long period, the more intensive use of central sites should, given no change in the demand for land resources, reduce the demand for and thus the price of peripheral land, the main source for new housing.

Fourth, SVR should produce external benefits. Given no change in the demand for land resources, its impetus towards the redevelopment of central sites would reduce city sprawl. On the other hand, this could be accompanied by external costs – increased city-centre traffic-congestion and the loss of open space, such as large private gardens and centrally-situated recreational facilities, which could be taxed out of existence. Planning controls, however, could partly deal with such costs.

Fifth, SVR would reduce 'fiscal zoning' since, in the long run, the movement of business and people to 'low-rate' areas would be self-defeating in that it would simply raise site-values there.

Sixth, SVR should promote objectivity in making planning decisions. Because the NAV-system rates both buildings and land, the local authority has a built-in reason for approving a proposed development through the higher rateable value which would result. With the building element removed by SVR, planning decisions can follow a consistent policy based solely on environmental considerations.

Nevertheless though SVR has advantages, it faces objections on principle and difficulties in implementation. First, the true site value can only be ascertained when there is *competition* for a *vacant* site, because only then will the most profitable use under present conditions be indicated. At other times indirect methods of valuation have to be used, and these give rise to difficulties in ensuring accuracy and uniformity. Comparability is the safest method, but even so the personal judgement of the valuer cannot be eliminated when allowing for differences in the size and position of sites. Moreover, the difficulty of isolating the site element from any value resulting from improvements or the enterprise of the owner could provide scope for challenge, appeals and litigation. But if the residual method is used, the valuer has to assess the most profitable use and ultimately the cost of the building which will secure this. In short, the specialised expertise of all types of developer has to be embodied in the official valuer. Moreover, unless there were detailed local plans for the site, he would also have to make assumptions about the most profitable use likely to be allowed!

Second, precise identification by the planning authority of permitted development covering the use and type of building for every site would be a departure from the current practice of broad structure plans. Not only would it lead to rigidity, but it would increase centralised decision-making.

Third, policy would have to stipulate whether site-value should be assessed on short-run or long-run potential. If the latter, 'hope' value would be relevant. But this is a 'floating' value in that it cannot settle on all possible properties when development actually takes place. Thus to attribute a long-term potential value to all properties would involve double-counting. Furthermore, it would in effect be a tax on income since the owner could do nothing to recoup that part of the tax based on potential. The site-value assessment would be greater than the capitalised current net return from the site. This means that the incidence of the tax no longer falls entirely on betterment, and, by impinging on current resources, exaggerates a failure of the NAV system, in that it may be unrelated to the taxpayer's present capacity to pay.

Moreover, by assessing potential site values, SVR would not only tax increased value before it was realised, but would tax an increase in value which might *never* be realised. For one thing, there could be several interests in the land resource with no individual owner being able to redevelop because he could not acquire the other interests. For another, even though the land resource was taxed for a number of years on potential development value, that potential might be lost before it could be realised because of a change in planning policy or development elsewhere (for instance, a new hypermarket).

In the above ways, therefore, SVR could penalise the owner who has to postpone development in order to acquire adjoining land or complementary interests for a comprehensive scheme. In so doing, it could encourage piecemeal development detrimental to satisfactory town planning.

Fourth, apart from planning restrictions, such encumbrances as long leases and private covenants would have to be taken into consideration in estimating site value.

Fifth, assessment of site value can only be provisional when the environment is constantly changing. For instance, a new motorway would improve accessibility, but site values may not rise if the motorway increases the supply of sites. In any case, the betterment may be thinly spread and accompanied by 'worsement' in the areas from which people move. Thus a period of at least five years may have to elapse following the completion of the motorway before there is reliable evidence of the resulting change in site values. However, once site values have been determined they will not be subject to the many assessment changes which under NAV follow structural alterations and additions.

Sixth, while the inclusion of the potential value of vacant and under-developed sites may provide an initial tax base equal to NAV, SVR could prove less onerous if building costs increased relatively to site values, for example, through a shift in shopping from city-centres, where sites are fixed in supply, to out-of-town hypermarkets, where alternative sites are available.

Seventh, though the tax would be paid by owners instead of by occupiers, in the long period its incidence as regards particular uses can be passed on to occupiers according to the relative elasticities of demand of occupiers and the elasticity of supply by owners. Inasmuch as the tax would be paid by owners but hidden in rents, SVR tends to weaken the link between local taxation, and representation and accountability. Against these difficulties must be set the fact that owners are fewer in number than occupiers, making the tax easier to collect.

Finally, in weighing up the pros and cons of introducing SVR into the UK, we have to remember that because the uncertainties in assessing site-values would give rise to considerable challenge by owners, a transition period of several years might have to elapse before it could become fully operative. In the meantime it might not provide a predictable basis for financing local services.

The strength of SVR (already operative in such countries as Denmark and New Zealand) lies in the incentive it provides towards development and improvement. It has particular merit, therefore, for underdeveloped countries. On the other hand, in the UK the main need is to *direct* development into the best channels, an aim which is probably more effectively achieved by planning requirements. Moreover, the other objective of appropriating betterment for the public purse can, as an alternative, be achieved by a capital gains tax and planning gain.

22.4 Present finance of local government

UK local government finance now has four elements:

(1) The Uniform Business Rate (UBR)
(2) Government grant
(3) Charges
(4) The Council Tax

(1) The UBR: a national non-domestic rate

Prior to 1 April 1990, businesses were subject to the same rate poundages as domestic hereditaments. As such, business rates had four main defects. First, they bore no direct relationship to ability to pay, for they were harder on building-intensive users and afforded no rebates for firms suffering a serious fall in profits. Second, being fixed arbitrarily by the local authority, they changed considerably over time through a change in the political party in power. Third, they could vary markedly between different authorities. Fourth, they carried no accountability restraint on the local authority since businesses, although paying some 60 per cent of the local rate revenue, enjoyed no local vote. This allowed high-spending local authorities to off-load a large proportion of the necessary financing on to businesses located in their areas.

On the other hand, business rates are easy and cheap to collect and do ensure that firms contribute to local expenditure on collective services, such as police, roads, street lighting and open spaces. In addition, it is probable that rates form only a small percentage of total costs. In any case they are tax-deductible (from profits).

In 1990 the response of the government to the weaknesses of the business rate was to take away the power of the local authority to levy it. A new rating list was compiled by the valuation officer appointed for each charging authority (the district borough or city council), using an unchanged formula of a notional rental value – what the premises could be let for *less* rates and taxes, insurance and maintenance expenses.

A rate (now known as 'the multiplier') is set for England and Wales by the ODPM. During the year 1994–5 this was 42.3 per cent and adjusted in subsequent years only in line with a change in the Retail Price Index. Revaluations of the rating list take place every five years, the next being in 2005.

The product of the new rate is paid into a national pool and then distributed to local authorities in proportion to their adult populations. There are separate pools for England and Wales.

The incidence of the UBR is complex, as the revaluation of 1990 was the first since 1973. Compared with the old rate payments, the manufacturing Midlands and the north of England have benefited by a reduction of 2 per cent. But businesses in south-east England, particularly retailing and services where rentals had increased considerably, had a large jump in their rate payments, 39 per cent for Inner London, for instance. Subsequent falls in office rents were only partially allowed for in the 1995 revaluation.

It is doubtful whether businesses, while still relying on local authorities for services, will find their needs treated with more respect now that they are paying a national rather than a local tax. Indeed, when businesses paid the *local* tax, their Chambers of Commerce were listened to and could exert influence. Thus 'accountability' could be less under the UBR.

What is likely to be the effect of increased rates on rents? In the short period, only if the demand for a firm's product is completely inelastic can the whole of a rate increase be passed on to the consumer through higher prices. Since the firm has to sell in competition with other firms, it is likely that it will have to bear most of the increase.

In the long term when a rent review is due, a firm may be able to pass some of the higher cost on to the landlord by a rent reduction, depending on the relative elasticities of demand and supply. To some extent this appears to have happened, for it has been estimated that, for example, rents in Brompton Road (where Harrods is located) have fallen by 10 per cent (though some of this may have been the result of stagnation in retail sales). However, any such fall would reduce capital values and so apply a brake on future development. Moreover, where rateable values for out-of-town superstores have undergone a more than proportionate increase than town-centre shopping, there could be a shift back to the latter, thus reinforcing the PPG 6 policy.

(2) Government grants

Government grants, together with the UBR distribution, now (2000) provide 75 per cent of local authorities revenue. They:

(a) offset the defects of the rating system by transferring more of the burden to general taxation;
(b) assist local authorities with services of national concern, for example, roads, police, education;
(c) ensure a minimum standard in the provision of such services;
(d) encourage local authorities to provide services above the minimum required; and
(e) assist in special emergencies, such as floods.

The basis upon which grants are made must achieve their objective without destroying local control or initiative, or committing the government to excessive expenditure. Thus though grants based on a *percentage* of cost or of so much per *unit* encourage local authorities to spend more than the bare minimum, they make it difficult for the government to control its own spending. A *block* grant – a single, annual lump sum to be used at the local authority's discretion – avoids this, but only at the risk of discouraging those authorities who are keen to improve and develop services since extra expenditure has to be covered locally. The result is that today there are two main types of grant.

(I) Grants in aid of specific services
Calculating the grant on a percentage basis, for example, police (50 per cent), highways (50–75 per cent according to the class of road), encourages high

standards but necessitates careful central audit to ensure that spending is not wasteful. Thus a grant of so much per unit, irrespective of whether standards above the minimum are provided, is easier to administer.

(II) THE REVENUE SUPPORT GRANT

This is a 'needs-related' block grant (revised in 1980) designed to compensate authorities for differences in the cost of providing other services at a standard level. The government fixes the aggregate level of grant, based on its own estimates for each category of service. It is paid to local authorities on a per capita basis according to the government's estimate of their needs with reference to its Standard Spending Assessments. 'Needs' are calculated on a formula covering a number of factors, such as the rate resources of the authority, the density of population and the number of young and old people in the area.

However, providing a high proportion of local authority revenue through grants can give rise to problems. First, local councils tend to lose their autonomy, for 'he who pays the piper calls the tune'. Second, it lessens the accountability of councils to those paying local taxes. Third, it may create difficulties for the government in its stabilisation policy, for any reduction can bring it into conflict with the local authorities.

(3) User-charges and fees

Charges have the advantage that those who benefit from the service pay at least a part of its cost, as with rents for housing, admission fees to swimming-baths, and planning applications. But while some trading services (especially lotteries) make a profit, most local government activity is concerned with providing community, collective and merit goods whose cost has to be covered mainly from taxation, either central or local (see pp. 391–4).

Raising revenue by increased charges is limited to a few services, such as swimming-baths, allotments, planning applications, building control, libraries. At times it has been suggested that education, the major spender, could be treated in a special way. Vouchers to a certain value would be issued by the central government to parents who would then 'spend' them at the school of their choice, perhaps supplementing them from their own resources if they so wished. This would relieve the local authorities of the cost of education (so that the rate yield was adequate for remaining services) and achieve accountability to parents through the price system.

(4) The council tax

The amount by which the area authorities' spending exceeds revenue from the previous three sources has to be covered by levying a council tax on households.

In essence it is a reversion to the old rating system, but instead of a notional annual letting value, for which market evidence was deficient, it is based on the 1 April 1991 capital value of the property – what it would have sold for on that date. To allow for the difficulties involved in making a *precise* valuation of each individual dwelling, values are divided into eight bands, A to H, with all households in the same band paying the same amount of tax, but increasing upwards to H, whose payment band is treble that of band A and double that of D. There is a 50 per cent discount for unoccupied dwellings and second homes. There is no provision for a general revaluation, but a future sale or a change in the locality, such as a new nearby motorway, may afford grounds for a revaluation.

For single residents there is a 25 per cent discount, but people exempt from the council tax are ignored for the purpose of determining the single-person discount. Exempt people include: students, student nurses, apprentices, youth trainees, those on income support, the severely mentally handicapped and elderly dependent relatives.

22.5 The future of local finance

Many attempts have been made to find a tax which is fair, reserved for local revenue, practicable and cheap to collect, ensures the authority's account-ability to local voters and harmonises local autonomy with the central government's macroeconomic policy requirements. Suggested new sources all lack one or more of these attributes.

Not only would *revenues assigned from national taxation* (such as motor-vehicle duties) be inadequate for the poorest authorities, but their transfer could force the government to increase its other taxes to make good lost revenue. A *local sales tax* would be difficult to superimpose on VAT and in such a small country as Britain could be undermined by people shopping in areas where tax rates were low. A *pay-roll tax* would similarly induce firms to locate in low-rate areas, apart from leading to the replacement of labour by capital and being inflationary.

The Layfield Committee (Cmnd 6453, 1976) favoured a local income tax. But this faces the technical problem of running a local income tax in con-juction with Britain's accumulative PAYE system. Not only would revenue have to be split between national and local government on each pay day rather than yearly as under other systems, but the tax could be levied where a person works, rather than where he lives. In view of these difficulties and the necessity to avoid capricious differences in local income tax rates, a local income tax system might simply result in assigning some of the national income tax revenue to local authorities. This could clash with a govern-ment's aim of reducing the basic rate of tax.

An alternative proposal, that the central government could accept full *financial responsibility for services of national importance*, such as education, police and social services, would simply further weaken provision of services according to local preferences and circumstances.

After the convulsions in local finance in 1990, a period of consolidation is now required. Thus at present it would be inappropriate to graft on new sources of revenue in order to restore to local authorities the autonomy which they have lost through the loss of revenue as a result of rate-capping, capital spending controls, the switch to housing benefits, and the transfer of the non-domestic rate to the central government.

Summary

Direct taxes are mainly neutral in their effects on property, but they can have marginal economic effects e.g. mortgage interest relief via income tax and exemption from CGT have encouraged home ownership; and capital allowances against corporation tax for agricultural and industrial buildings shorten their life. The impact of indirect taxes and in particular VAT on property is complex and the OTT may affect exempt and non-exempt occupiers in different ways. Planning gain is a benefit accruing to a local authority from the granting of planning consent. Developers may offer inducements to local authorities in the form of provision of amenities such as roads or parks in return for planning permission for their scheme.

Local property taxes promote local autonomy and accountability. They are equitable in the sense that larger properties (which tend to be occupied by the richer members of the community) pay larger local taxes. They are difficult to evade and easy to collect and calculate.

Review questions

1. What are the economic effects of stamp duties levied on property transactions?
2. Give three examples of 'planning gain' agreements.
3. Analyse the impact of local property taxes on market rents and housing supply.
4. Why did the Community Charge or 'Poll Tax' fail as a reform of the system of local taxation?
5. Describe the key features of the Uniform Business Rate.

Recommended reading

C. V. Brown and P. M. Jackson, *Public Sector Economics*, 2nd edn (London: Martin Robertson, 1982) ch. 9.

A. W. Evans, *Urban Economics* (Oxford: Basil Blackwell, 1985) ch. 10.

Green Paper, *Paying for Local Government*, Cmd. 9714 (London: HMSO, 1986).

N. P. Hepworth, *The Finance of Local Government*, 6th edn (London: Allen & Unwin, 1984) chs 4 and 14.

G. Keogh, 'The Economics of Planning Gain', in S. Barrett and P. Healey (eds), *Land Policy: Problems and Alternatives* (Gower, 1985).

D. Myers, *Economics and Property: A Coursebook for Students of the Built Environment* (London: Estates Gazette, 1994).

G. Stoker, *The Politics of Local Government* (London: Macmillan, 1985).

A. Wenban-Smith and B. Pearce, *Planning Gains: Negotiating with Planning Authorities*, 2nd edn (London: Estates Gazette, 1998).

CHAPTER 23

UK Property and the European Union (EU)

After studying this chapter you will be able to:

- Explain the benefits of the single European market to the UK property industry
- Analyse the case for and against UK membership of European Monetary Union
- Evaluate the possible effects of membership of European Monetary Union on the UK property market

There are two aspects of the relationship of the UK property industry to the EU each of which raises different issues and which will therefore be considered separately: (i) the access of UK property to the Single European Market (SEM) irrespective of whether the UK accepts the conditions of Economic and Monetary Union (EMU), signified by adopting the euro as the common currency; and (ii) the UK's position as regards membership of the EMU and its relationship to her property industry.

23.1 The EU's single market

The EU consists of 15 member states: France, Germany, Italy, Belgium, the Netherlands, Luxembourg, Denmark, the Irish Republic, Greece, Spain, Portugal, the UK, Austria, Finland, and Sweden.

The 15 states provide a common market of some 370 m. people, protected from outsiders by common external tariffs. However, the object of the SEM is, by removing barriers, to allow goods and factors of production to move freely within the EU through the operation of the price system. Only then can the full benefits of the larger market be realised.

But it was recognised that this would take time to accomplish, for member countries had already developed their own monopoly policies, individual taxes, welfare benefits, full employment policies, methods of removing balance-of-payments imbalances, and so on. 'Harmonisation' measures, therefore, began to be introduced prior to the SEM coming into effect in 1993. Examples of these are: a common agriculture policy (CAP), uniform rules on competition, a common transport policy, harmonisation of tax systems, a common regional policy, a social policy, and stable exchange rates between member countries. 'Harmonisation' is still proceding, but it is exchange rate stability which for the UK is at present causing the most difficulty, and this will be examined later.

23.2 SEM and the property industry

The benefits which the SEM can confer on the property industry

Not only does the SEM provide a market equivalent in size to that of the USA, but it should generate a high rate of growth through the economies of scale it offers in finance, production, management ability, research, etc. These advantages can be secured by the UK development and property companies and investors in property.

Since the demand for property is derived from the services it provides to other industries – manufacturing, retailing and financial services – the large SEM is likely to increase demand for factories, distribution warehouses, shops and offices. And UK developers and property companies should be well-placed for responding to this demand. Not only have they acquired expertise through their operations in the UK, but these have been carried out in the context of the similar high level of income which exists in most European cities.

Consideration must also be given to the likely effect of the SEM on dealing in property as an investment asset.

Developers and property companies in the larger market

It has to be admitted that, for the most part, the UK property industry has stayed aloof from the Continent, mainly because the opportunities existing there can only be exploited by the largest UK companies whose current strategy is to hold large, modern buildings (particularly offices and shops) in prime positions but focused in a limited geographical area.

Even so, among these companies, views differ as to the advantages of positioning operations on the Continent. All are interested in yield and prospective growth in the properties held and stress the demands on management time which the dispersal of operations give rise to. But here the weight which the individual managing directors place on conflicting objectives, and their ability to handle them, are the decisive issues.

Hammerson, the UK flagship in northern Europe, sold properties and development land held in Australia, the USA and Canada and in 1995 replaced them by purchasing prime retail outlets and offices in France and Germany which, by active management, could add value by development or refurbishment. A similar approach by Slough Estates has meant that its industrial property and developments abroad are largely confined to Belgium, and in particular, to Brussels. Moreover, although its continental holding accounts for only 4 per cent of its total holdings, it intends to increase its interest in Europe.

In contrast, MEPC has sold its European portfolio to reinvest in the USA and Australia. Similarly Brixton Estates expects to sell its holdings in Belgium and France 'when the time is right' to focus its activities in the western Home Counties of which it has detailed local knowledge and is considered to offer better opportunities than northern Europe for fulfilling its objective of good initial yields. And Land Securities, the UK's largest property company, remains 100 per cent committed to the home market.

The reluctance or hesitancy of even the large property developer companies to expand into Europe has a variety of explanations. First, the initial presentation of the general advantages of the new SEM coincided with the 1990 crash in property and only a slow return of confidence in the attributes of property as an investment asset. Second, there has been little harmonisation of national differences relating to property. Thus purchasers of property to let, for example, insurance companies, prefer the 15-year institutional lease with its 5-yearly, upward-only rent reviews to the European 9-year term with a break-option every 3 years and an annual rent review in line with construction costs (France) or the cost of living (Germany). Moreover transaction costs still favour the UK (4.5 per cent) compared with France (18 per cent) and Germany (6 per cent).

The harmonisation of tax structures

EU countries are given considerable flexibility in deciding their own forms and rates of taxation.

Mostly UK rates are the lowest in the EU and it has to be admitted that the UK has shown little enthusiasm for harmonisation. Thus the 1989 levying of *VAT* on new non-residential construction was really forced upon the UK by a decision of the European Court of Justice. Similarly, raising the VAT rate in 1991 to 17.5 per cent (and thus closer to that of all the major EU countries except Germany) was really to fund government expenditure rather than the pursuit of a harmonisation objective. Indeed the Commission would like VAT rates for each member country to fall within two bands – a standard rate between 14 per cent and 20 per cent (which would include construction and new buildings), and a reduced rate between 4 per cent and 9 per cent for certain essential necessities. It would also like to abolish the zero rate, so that eventually VAT could be applied even to the construction of new dwellings.

As regards *direct taxes*, the UK has the lowest rate of *corporation tax* on profits (30 per cent), compared, for instance, with France's 50 per cent and Germany's 56 per cent, and of *capital gains tax*. Only the UK's *local tax* – the Uniform Business Rate – tends to be higher than the local taxes on income levied by Germany, Italy, Luxembourg and Portugal.

The significance of institutional differences in the continental and UK property markets

At present property developers have to adopt to countries' different planning requirements and market operations. For transactions in real property and property assets, markets on the Continent are less active (and thus more imperfect) than in the UK. Reasons for this are: (a) a greater preference by occupiers for owning their own property; (b) the source of long-term finance is bank loans rather than equity capital as in the UK; (c) an adherence to historic values in the accounts, thus masking the returns which are really being earned on capital values; (d) lease terms tend to limit the investor's share of rental growth; (e) portfolio management is impeded by the tax structure and transaction costs which, for example, could in France add 18 per cent to the purchase price. Such factors tend to inhibit property trading and active portfolio management.

Thus, in spite of the globalisation of finance, we cannot expect a unified European property market to develop until institutional frictions have been removed. Nevertheless, provided London maintains its preeminence in expertise, inventiveness and adaptability it should hold and even increase its share of business. For example, there could be scope for the building societies, by drawing on their unique experience, to extend their mortgage business on the Continent (see p. 346).

It must also be noted that the high equity content of UK property companies leaves them vulnerable to acquisition by continental property companies seeking a higher flow of investment income and economies of scale. Although expansion can be achieved by organic growth, taking over the whole of a company's assets is quicker and economically more efficient, when the net asset value per property share stands at a substantial discount to the market price of the share and the costs of purchasing property direct are high.

The preference of firms on the Continent for owning their own freehold premises reduces the supply of suitable properties in which to invest. There is thus a strong incentive to look elsewhere, merging with or bidding for entire property companies. Offering an attractive price for shares may induce a majority share-holding to accept. Thus, Rodamco (the Netherlands) attempted unsuccessfully to take over Hammerson in 1990.

Any depreciation of sterling on the foreign exchange market would increase the possibility of such a take-over, since it would be less costly to an overseas bidder.

23.3 The position of the UK in the global market for top-grade property

In addition to (i) firms owning property they occupy, (ii) dealers who acquire development land and properties for trading on, (iii) property companies which develop, refurbish or hold properties to provide a regular cash flow, there is an increasing demand from (iv) institutions, such as insurance companies and pension funds, who wish to hold property long-term as a given proportion of their investment portfolio. Standard Life, for instance, owns properties worth £300 m. in Paris, and is now developing offices in Paris, Brussels and Madrid.

The positive income-elasticity of demand for such services ensures, through the regular premium payments and pension contributions, an increasing flow of funds for investment in order to cover future contractual commitments. Since the top-grade commercial and agricultural properties preferred by these institutions are found in the wealthier countries throughout the world, the EU market for these properties is merely an important part of this highly competitive global market.

In contrast to the limited response of UK property developers to EU opportunities, the international agents who make this market have been dynamic in adapting to its requirements. As a result they have either amalgamated or been taken over, thereby achieving economies of scale. For example, FPD Savills has teamed up with the Far Eastern group, First Pacific Davies, and is now seeking a North American link up; Jones Lang Wootton has merged with the US property management group, La Salle Partners; and Richard Ellis UK has been taken over by the US Insignia Group. Such integration has enabled these companies to offer a full range of services worldwide as estate agents, consultants, advisers, valuers, and possibly in-house accountants and lawyers.

23.4 The impact of the SEM on the UK

While it would seem that the SEM has not galvanised UK developers and property companies into major activity on the Continent, it has made an impact on the UK itself in a number of ways.

First, the EU now accounts for 55 per cent of Britain's overseas trade. Parallel with this has come an increased two-way, cross-channel movement of people, the Channel Tunnel and a faster direct rail link between London and Paris/Brussels. Major complementary developments, such as hotels, have followed near the chief east-Kent towns of Dover and Ashford.

Second, it has shifted the regional income balance of the UK still further in favour of London and south-east England to which the newer hi-tech production, linked-services and research have gravitated. This highlights the necessity of improving the motorway and road connections to the industrial north of England.

Third, warehouse development has taken place at strategically-based distribution centres, both national and regional. Such distribution centres originated in the 1980s when the retail sector moved its stock-holding operations away from valuable prime High Street sites. These national distribution centres now focus on the Midland triangle, bounded by Birmingham, Northampton and Leicester from which it is possible to serve 75 per cent of the population of England within four hours. Distribution centres for components of manufactured goods are situated further north, having largely resulted through other industries adopting where possible the Japanese 'just-in-time' method of bringing in car components.

In siting both types of distribution centre, the emphasis has been on the convenience and flexibility of road transport. But the environmental costs, such as CO_2 emission, are in future likely to be increasingly targeted by the government which would like to see more traffic being diverted to the rail network. The solution may be the development of swap-body technology enabling trailers to be used on both road and rail. The alternative may be to simply fall back on the restriction of lorry use, as in Austria and Switzerland.

23.5 Economic and Monetary Union (EMU): the single currency

The advantages of a single currency

To achieve open competition within the single market, it is essential to eliminate the possibility of one member being able to secure an advantage for its exports by lowering the exchange rate of its currency. An exchange rate union which goes no further than agreed irrevocably-locked exchange rates between member countries would cover the basic harmonisation requirement. But it has three weaknesses:

(i) a member could renege on the arrangement, realigning its exchange rate unilaterally;
(ii) a risk premium to cover such a possible devaluation would mean having a higher rate of interest set by the EU central bank; and
(iii) costs would still be incurred in exchanging currencies.

A single currency eliminates all three weaknesses. It removes any uncertainty as to possible exchange rate realignment, thereby encouraging trade and investment. More important, it eliminates the costs of currency exchange for firms engaged in intra-EU trade and for individuals travelling within the EU, such as tourists.

Moreover, by being managed by an independent European Central Bank (ECB), committed to a low rate of inflation, it would prevent monetary policy being slanted by a state-controlled central bank for electoral advantage. The resulting lower 'uncertainty premium' should produce a ECB rate of interest which would be lower than that required by an individual state to achieve the same low level of inflation.

Finally, a single currency and a common ECB responsible for overall monetary policy would help to unify the single market.

The present (2003) situation

To ensure that a single currency would not lead later to excessive adjustment costs (for example, through enforced deflation), the Treaty of Maastricht 1991 laid down the fulfilment of four criteria as a condition of joining, but it was only by a 'flexible' interpretation that 11 countries were able to proceed. Greece failed; and the UK, Denmark and Sweden declined, partly for political reasons and partly because they felt that they were not yet economically ready.

The single currency began on 1 January 1999, with a 3-year transitional period as follows:
1 January 1999

(i) exchange rates of member countries' currencies locked irrevocably with the Euro;
(ii) responsibility for the formulation and implementation of monetary policy passed to the ECB, which also decides on exchange rates with outside currencies, manages the reserves and intervenes in the market. It will be the sole issuing authority of the single currency;
(iii) ECB monetary and foreign exchange operations conducted in euros.

1 January 2002 – euro notes and coins issued with legal tender became the medium of exchange rather than simply a unit of account. These at first circulated alongside national currencies in participating member countries.

1 July 2002 – national currencies were no longer legal tender in participating member countries and the euro became the currency throughout most of the EU.

Possible difficulties to be faced by all members of the EU

The EMU with its single currency represents the most important change in the international monetary system since Bretton Woods in 1944. Yet while the advantage of increased trade through the SEM has been proved, members of the EU must appreciate that the final step of a single currency is a leap into the unknown and fraught with difficulties.

First, there were heavy initial costs of its introduction. Businesses had to alter all their money machines (such as cash dispensers, tills, vending machines). In addition, computer programmes had to be re-calculated to cover the change from the old currency to the euro.

Individuals, too, have had to adapt, with wages, salaries, state benefits, mortgages, monetary assets, etc., being expressed in euros. Since this would be less easy for older persons there is here a psychological cost.

Second, member countries may not be equally sensitive to ECB changes in its 'one-fits-all' rate of interest because they have reached different stages in the trade cycle (see p. 439)

Third, with the impossibility of exchange rate depreciation to lower a country's costs, the alternative – deflation – is only acceptable if labour costs are flexible downwards. If not, prolonged unemployment can result (see p. 440).

Fourth, certain regions which are poor in natural resources or whose basic industry is in terminal decline will have to be given assistance from the EU's Structure and Social Funds. But the danger is that such subsidies, by relieving the pressure to accept lower wages or to move to more prosperous regions, may persist indefinitely.

23.6 An outline of the main pros and cons of UK membership of the EMU

At present UK politicians, businessmen and academic economists are divided as to whether the UK should join the EMU.

Those in favour claim that membership would:

(a) allow trade to flow more freely according to the law of comparative costs by *eliminating* the *costs* of exchanging national currencies and of exchange rate fluctuations;

(b) *increase trade* through the keener competition resulting from the transparency provided by showing all prices in euros;

(c) lead to a *lower rate of interest* through the commitment of an independent ECB to controlling inflation;

(d) proclaim the UK's commitment to Europe, and so ensure that continuation of *inward investment* by countries outside, e.g. Japan, USA;

(e) fulfil an essential condition for the *City of London* to maintain its preeminence as a financial market in the face of a challenge by Frankfurt;

(f) enable the UK to help *shape policies* from within rather than, by delaying entry, having to converge on policies already decided.

Those who *oppose* membership do so because:

(a) the UK would be unable to adjust the sterling *exchange rate* and shortterm rate of interest according to the needs of her own economy:

(b) the raising of the UK's relative low *labour cost* through the adoption of the social chapter could undermine her major comparative cost advantage;

(c) through its newly-granted independence in determining base rate, the Bank of England is equally effective as the ECB in *controlling inflation*;

(d) *inward investment* to the UK is not dependent on her being within the EMU, but is mainly determined by her prospective economic growth, relative labour costs, professional expertise, subsidy support, political stability and the use of English as the common language of trade;

(e) while for itself the *City of London* would prefer to be in the EMU, it feels that even outside it would, through its proven adaptability and expertise, still retain its leading position in what is now a global market.

(f) in place of exchange rate flexibility and interest rate adjustment, macro policy has to rely on *deflation* to stem rising costs even in the face of wage-rigidity and labour immobility (and the resulting unemployment).

The key difficulties facing the UK will now be examined in more detail.

The UK's reservations on EMU participation

The UK co-operated fully in establishing the single market, recognising that some diminution of sovereignty and majority voting had to be conceded. But as regards the EMU she has reservations concerning:

(1) THE SPEED OF TRANSITION
The Maastricht Treaty 1991 envisaged a 4-year transitional period prior to 1 January 1999 to enable members to stabilise exchange rates, converge on a low inflation rate and achieve financial and fiscal integrity.

The UK felt that this period, truncated by the 1 January deadline, was too short and in particular, since her economy was in the boom phase of the trade cycle, she required a higher rate of interest than Eurozone members in order to hold her 2.5 per cent rate of inflation.

(2) The ECB's 'one-fits-all' rate of interest is insensitive to the needs of individual countries

The impact of a change in the ECB's interest rate may differ as between member countries. As explained above the UK required a higher rate because her economy was expanding. Similarly, because her borrowing is mostly on variable interest rates, the UK might bear a disproportionately larger share of the burden of adjustment following a rise in the ECB's rate than Germany, whose borrowing is mostly on fixed rates.

(3) The inability to use exchange rate depreciation as a means of cushioning unforeseen economic shocks

While the reverberations of economic shocks are usually felt by most countries, on occasions a shock may be more specific to a particular country. For the UK this might be the case if there were a considerable fall in the price of oil, or if a major trading partner, such as the USA, ran into serious recession.

With a single currency, where no one member can alone depreciate, realignment has to come about by the deflation of prices, including wages, and then only after a prolonged period of unemployment. Such a policy has in the past proved unacceptable. The UK's attempt in 1992 to maintain a fixed ERM exchange rate against heavy speculation illustrates the point. Raising her interest to support sterling merely added to her ongoing recession and unemployment.

(4) The extent and nature of the sovereignty conceded

With the single currency every element of money creation is controlled as to timing, form and amount by the ECB. The central banks of member countries retain only an advisory role through membership of the European System of Central Banks (ESCB), which simply oversees monetary and foreign exchange markets. Yet they would still be responsible for implementing the ECB's policy decisions.

(5) The possible political and constitutional consequences which could evolve

As the overall income of the EU increases over time, it is likely to be accompanied by a need to enlarge its structural fund from which its poorer members are supported (see p. 374). While the UK considers that more money could be found by reducing CAP expenditure and dealing with corruption, she accepts that some will have to come from additional taxation. However, she is concerned that this is not in a form which discriminates unfairly against her interests, which include maintaining her high level of inward investment.

Although countries each retain the right to veto EU proposals concerning taxation, it has been suggested that UK objections could be side-tracked by pushing tax changes through as a SEM harmonisation proposal, where majority decisions apply. This it is held would really entail her surrender of fiscal control to bureaucratic institutions, the European Commission and ECB, unaccountable to national parliaments. In doing so it goes directly to the heart of British parliamentary sovereignty – the safeguard of democracy – which was founded on the House of Commons sanction of only supplying funds subject to 'the redress of grievances'.

Some critics are even more apprehensive fearing that the Structural Fund required would be so large that raising this revenue and distributing the proceeds would be through a federal body, as in the USA and, on a much smaller scale, with the UBR in the UK. If this should happen, the UK would lose much of her independence by eventually being drawn into a Federal Europe.

23.7 The EMU and the UK property market

The possible benefits of membership

The raison d'etre for the EMU is that it will generate increased output from which all members will benefit, either directly in increased income, or indirectly through a re-distribution from a structural fund. Such an increase in income should be reflected in additional demand for property by occupiers of shops, offices, factories and houses. For instance, at a minimum it should stimulate cross-border retail trade, similar to that embarked upon by Tesco, and lead to the erection of warehouses at strategically-placed distribution centres.

Failure to join the EMU, however, will not preclude UK property developers, property companies and investors from trading freely in the Eurozone for all EU members are within the SEM to which the UK is committed. But, in addition to her peripheral cross-Channel location, she would be exposed to possible fluctuations in the £:euro exchange rate, the cost of exchanging currencies and probably a higher rate of interest when borrowing.

We can accept that by generating growth the EMU should open up new development and investment opportunities in Europe, but the insular attitude of UK companies revealed earlier in this chapter raises the question of whether they want to compete and operate there. Or are there, at least for the time being, more attractive propositions in the home market? As noted previously, in the early 1990s only a few of the larger property-development companies, such as Hammerson, Slough Estates and Standard Life showed any enthusiasm although at that time competition with Europe was on a level playing field since each country had to exchange currencies. It would appear from a random examination of recent issues of the *Estate Gazette*, that overseas agents have formed a similar impression for only very rarely does one carry an advertisement of a continental development proposition which might possibly be of interest to a UK company.

Thus while British industry and commerce in general can perceive advantages in UK membership, as far as property development is concerned there is mostly indifference. It should also be noted that, for the present participants, such as Hammerson, currency exchange costs or exchange rate movements are hardly likely to be important since the spread of their operations between the UK and the Eurozone would provide an adequate cash flow in the appropriate currency to cover maintenance costs, ground rents, local taxes, dividend distributions, etc. Even for further borrowing in euros, properties already held and the company's financial standing would support a direct capital loan in euros.

As we saw earlier, the institutions with funds to invest and their agents would operate very actively and competitively in Europe which they would probably regard as the most important part of the international market in which they operate.

The City of London and EMU

Financial services is now the UK's largest industry with most business being concentrated on the City of London and her financial markets. Through the worldwide abolition of exchange controls and revolutionary changes in all forms of communications technology, financial dealings have been transferred from small-scale domestic markets to the large euro-markets centred in London. Thus during the 1990s the City expanded its financial business rapidly and in addition acted as a magnet for the head offices of the European operations of multi-national companies. As a result 300 000 persons are now employed within the Square Mile.

The City of London would like the UK to be within the Eurozone for this would make it easier for it to ward off the threat to its business from Frankfurt, already the location of the ECB. But in or out, it feels the worldwide confidence in its markets, expertise and adaptability will enable it to resist the challenge. To this end, therefore, the City Corporation has relaxed its planning restrictions on the height of office buildings and granted permission for the construction of seven skyscrapers.

It is evident that the fortunes of the City's property market and its financial services industry are directly related. Moreover City of London office development is tied to a rapidly-expanding industry, unlike commercial property generally which is linked to the slower-growing economy as a whole.

But, paradoxically, UK membership of EMU could, through the application of its proposals to member countries universally, cut off the City of London's lifeblood and threaten her unique position. Thus the proposed 20 per cent 'withholding tax' on bond interest passing through London could cause dealing to be transferred to countries, such as Switzerland, where no such tax is deducted.

UK housebuilders and EMU membership

UK housebuilders and landowners could both derive an indirect benefit from EMU membership. Inasmuch as it would enable house-purchasers to obtain mortgages at a lower rate of interest, demand for houses would increase as more households could afford to become owner-occupiers. Landowners selling the necessary building land would also have a windfall gain (economic rent).

But this conclusion must be qualified because of the 'one-fits-all' interest rate which is fixed by the ECB. First, whereas 80 per cent of total UK mortgages are borrowed at variable rates, 90 per cent of German and French debt is held on fixed long-term rates. Any change in the ECB rate will, therefore, have a greater impact on UK borrowers. Second, because an across-the-board ECB interest change may not be appropriate to a particular country's current trade cycle phase, it could accentuate fluctuations in its rate of housing construction and in house prices. In 1999, for instance, Ireland's 6 per cent rate of growth was accompanied by a 20 per cent rise in house prices – yet the rate of interest set by the ECB was not increased.

The initial effects on exports and asset prices of UK joining EMU

In joining EMU the UK would be required to merge irrevocably the £ sterling with the euro at a given rate of exchange. Since any further devaluation of the £ would be impossible, the UK would be likely to seek as low a rate as possible in the interest of maintaining exports. If this represented an initial, though small, devaluation, there would be a boost to exports, especially of manufactures, which have suffered through the recent strength of the £.

The UK would also have to accept the current ECB short-term rate of interest, which could be lower than the UK base rate. This fall in the short-term rate would eventually follow through to the long-term gilt rate; that is, the price of gilt-edged bonds would rise.

As a result the price of close substitute assets would rise in sympathy. In particular, the price of prime properties is closely related to the gilt value, usually to yield a slightly higher return to reflect their illiquidity and risk as against possible future growth.

Operational adjustments

Increased competition resulting from the single currency is likely to accelerate *mergers* between property companies seeking economies of scale. It is possible that the larger companies thus formed may be more motivated towards engaging in property development on the continent.

Insurance companies and pension funds could find that within EMU it is easier to extend their business, especially as many members, such as Germany and France, have an increasing proportion of people who are *investing in private pensions* to augment their inadequate basic state retirement pensions. At least part of this additional inflow of funds is likely to be invested in prime properties within the EU.

From 1 January 1999 property can be purchased and rents paid in either national currencies or euros. While euros are not legal tender in the UK new *leases* are likely to specify the landlord's preferred currency. The decision will rest on where payments for maintenance, etc. have to be made.

Possible adverse pressures on the UK property market

There is a difference in the underlying philosophy between the UK and the present twelve euro-members which influences their respective policies for solving current problems. This has become evident in arriving at decisions on how to harmonise welfare benefits and increase taxation to augment the Structual Fund.

Germany considers that her 4m. unemployed is the result of a restrictive macroeconomic policy with tight budgets. On the other hand, the UK (alongside the OECD and IMF) blames high labour costs, a rigid labour market and the impotence of the German government in the face of the need to cut back on the add-on welfare costs of employing labour. Thus the UK rejects the view that harmonisation should follow the German welfare pattern which makes the cost of labour 50 per cent higher than Britain's. For the UK such a policy could lose export markets outside the EU and deter inward investment. Only in laying down a minimum wage and putting restrictions on working hours during the week has the UK implemented the 'social chapter'. Even in this it has run into difficulties, having itself to obtain a special dispensation to cover long hours worked by junior hospital doctors!

At present the EU's Structure Fund supports those members having poor natural resources or basic industries in terminal decline. But the Fund's already stretched resources will have to be increased as future growth in EU prosperity is likely to be confined mainly to those countries producing manufactures and services where income-elasticity of demand is high, and leaving behind those countries dependent mainly on agriculture, whose income-elasticity of demand is low. In addition, ten comparatively poor states from central and eastern Europe are to be admitted in May 2004, with Bulgaria and Romania to follow in 2007.

As a first step the EU is reassessing the needs of current recipients. The UK has been required to reduce the size of its Assisted Areas, to which EU grants are tied. This could influence the level of spending on the regeneration of certain depressed regions in the UK.

But the bulk of extra revenue will have to come from additional taxation; and the UK, while considering that some money could be found by reducing CAP expenditure and preventing fraud, accepts this. It will, however, be necessary for her to ensure that any new taxes, such as the proposed withholding tax, or any increases in the rate of tax are not detrimental to her own vital interests. A rise in her comparatively low rate of corporation tax, for instance, could deter inward investment, and both of the UK's major parties now agree that, in the interests of growth and equity, income tax should be reduced rather than increased.

Some forms of additional taxation could affect property in particular, Stamp duty already 4 per cent on transfers above £500 000 could be raised still further to bring it into line with Euro countries' rates. Similarly, VAT might be levied on new building and not just on repairs as at present. Moreover any extension of inheritance tax to rural estates and agricultural land could lead to a division into smaller, perhaps uneconomic, units.

Although each EU member has a veto on taxation matters, proposals may be made acceptable by offering concessions elsewhere, such as on Assisted Area regions. But what is more serious is the hint from other members of the EU that certain proposals could be pushed through by majority voting under SEM 'harmonisation' measures which the UK has agreed to. Indeed, as suggested earlier, the possibility is that ultimate decisions on taxation could be taken by a Federal body.

A summary of the UK's present position as regards the euro

The real advantage for the UK of joining the euro would be the elimination of the cost of exchanging currencies, thereby facilitating trade and travel with the EU. It should also enhance the City of London as the world leader in providing financial services.

On the other hand, the UK would face pressure for her economy to conform more closely to the economies of other members, with their more rigid labour markets, higher taxation and under-funded State retirement pensions. Any resulting increase in UK costs could adversely affect her export trade and inward investment with countries outside the EU. A further weakness is that the particular interests of individual members may intervene in formulating long-term policies. An example is the obstruction by France of proposals to reform the CAP without which the terms for the entry to the EU of the twelve central and eastern European nations are complex and difficult.

It must also be observed that the advantages claimed refer only to *economic* gains, and against these must be set not only the cost of implementing regulations and filling in forms, but the possible undermining of democratic control of macroeconomic policy through the House of Commons. It is essential that politicians balance the wide interests of the UK against prospective economic growth.

The earlier assertion that the euro could be accepted as a reserve currency appears over-optimistic in that it lost over 12 per cent of its exchange value against the dollar during the first twelve months of its existence. This lack of confidence could stem from a recognition of the absence of decisive leadership. On the other hand it might reflect an insufficient convergence of economies during the run-up period.

Sterling has weakened in 2003 against both the euro and the dollar. As the June 2003 deadline for the government to pronounce on the 5 Tests for euro entry approaches, uncertainty persists; but it is highly likely that a referendum will be delayed, at least until after the next General Election. It is extremely difficult to make a conclusive case for early entry, and a referendum appears unwinnable in the near future.

Summary

The single European market is equivalent in size to that of the USA and the economic benefits of membership should be reflected in greater derived demand for commercial property. UK property investment companies have not yet made significant investments in continental Europe for a number of reasons, one of which is the differences that exist in treatment of property in other countries. Membership of EMU would remove the uncertainty associated with the £:euro exchange rate, but the prospects of a successful referendum on this seem remote.

Review questions

1. Why might the single European market have benefits for the property sector?
2. What institutional differences are there in the continental and UK property markets?
3. With reference to the current market situation, assess the position of the UK in the global market for top-grade property.
4. Analyse the possible effects of EMU membership on the City of London.
5. Describe the likely effects of membership of EMU on the UK property market

Recommended reading

J. Harvey, *Mastering Economics*, 5th edn (London: Macmillan, 1999) ch. 29.

Index